Evan M. Spangler

Swiss Supervisory Laws and Regulations for the Business of Insurance

Evan M. Spangler

Swiss Supervisory Laws and Regulations for the Business of Insurance

Stämpfli Publishers Ltd. Berne · 2011

eleven
international publishing

Bibliographic information published by the Deutsche Nationalbibliothek
The Deutsche Nationalbibliothek lists this publication in the Deutsche Nationalbibliografie; detailed bibliographic data are available on the Internet at http://dnb.d-nb.de.

Produced by
Stämpfli Publications Ltd., Berne
Printed in Switzerland

ISBN 978-3-7272-1473-8 (Stämpfli)
ISBN 978-94-90947-08-8 (Eleven)

FSC
Mix
Produktgruppe aus vorbildlich bewirtschafteten Wäldern und anderen kontrollierten Herkünften
Zert.-Nr. SGS-COC-005773
www.fsc.org
© 1996 Forest Stewardship Council

for

Käthe Santagata

my German teacher

and to the memory of

G. Kent Frandsen

my professor of insurance law

Acknowledgement

Valuable comments were provided by Marc D. Nagel on the translations of the Financial Market Supervision Law, the Insurance Supervision Law and the Regulation on the Supervision of Insurance Businesses and by Sarah Anna Meyer on the translations of the circular letters and the introduction. Their contributions are acknowledged with gratitude.

Sumary

Abbreviations

CO	Code of Obligations
CR	Regulation on Capital and Risk Distribution for Banks and Securities Dealers
EEA	European Economic Area
FINMAG	Federal Law on the Federal Financial Market Supervision
FOPI	Federal Office for Private Insurance
ICL	Insurance Contract Law
ISL	Insurance Supervision Law
ISR-FINMA	Insurance Supervision Regulation-FINMA
RBC	Risk-bearing capital
SAV	German abbreviation of the 'Swiss Actuaries Association'
SR	Supervisory Regulation
TC	Target capital

Glossary of Selected Terms

German – English

Abfindungswert	settlement value
Abschlusskosten	acquisition costs
Abwicklung	completion or performance of a transaction; settlement; run-off
Abwicklungsdauer	loss development period
Abwicklungsplan	run-off plan
Aktiengesellschaft	corporation
andere Schuldanerkenungen	other unconditional debt obligations
anteilgebundene Lebensversicherung	unit-linked life insurance
Anteilscheine	share certificates
Antiselektion	adverse selection
Anwartschaftliche Risikoversicherung	deferred life insurance
Aufsicht	supervision
berufliche Vorsorge	occupational pension plan
Beteiligung	ownership interest
Beteiligungspapiere	participating securities
Betriebsrechnung	operating account
bewegliches Vermögen	moveable assets
Bilanz	balance sheet
Bundesanwaltschaft	Federal Prosecutor's Office
Deckungskapital	actuarial reserves
Depot	custody account
Direktversicherung	primary insurance
eidgenössische	federal
Eigenkapital	equity capital
Eigenmittel	capital resources

Eintrittsverluste	initial losses
Erlebensfallgarantie	guaranteed benefits upon maturity
Erfolgsrechnung	income statement; profit and loss account
ergänzendes Kapital	supplementary capital
Ertragswertberechnung	income capitalization calculation
Ertragsvermehrung	increasing income
Erwerbsvorbereitungsgeschäft	transaction in preparation for an acquisition
Forderungen	payment obligations, accounts receivable
Gebäudeversicherung	Building insurance required by law to be purchased from a cantonal building insurance institution.
gebundenes Vermögen	restricted assets
Generalbevollmächtigte	general agent
Genossenschaft	mutual corporation
Geschäftsleitung	executive board
Hypothekardarlehen	secured loan
Hypotheken	mortgage loans
interne Revision	internal audit function
immaterielle Vermögenswerte	intangible assets
Inventardeckungskapital	actuarial reserve
Jahresbericht	annual report
kapitalbildende Versicherung	capital-accruing insurance
Kapitalisationsgeschäft	capital redemption insurance
Kataster	plat book
Kernkapital	core capital
Konfidenzniveau	confidence level
Konzern	corporate group
Konzernrechnung	group financial statement
Langlebigkeitsrisiko	longevity risk

latente Steuerverbindlichkeiten	accrued tax liabilities
Lebensversicherung mit Sparteil	life insurance with a savings component
Leibrentenversicherung	annuities
Leitlinien	guidelines
mathematische Rückstellungen	actuarial reserves. mathematical reserves
Mindestquotenpflichtiges Geschäft	Business subject to a minimum surplus distribution obligation
Mittelflussrechnung	Cash flow statement
nicht verbrauchte Prämien	unearned premiums
Niederlassung	office, branch or subsidiary; an establishment
Organe	governing bodies; directors and officers
Organigramm	structure chart used to show a group or conglomerate structure or a management structure
Organisationsreglement	by-laws
Partizipationen	ownership interests
Partizipationsscheinkapital	non-voting share capital
passive Rückversicherung	ceded reinsurance
Pensionsgeschäft	securities repurchase transactions (repo transactions)
Persönlichkeitsrechten	personal privacy rights
Praktikermethode	practitioner method
Prämienübertrage	unearned premiums
Privatverwertung	private sale
Prüfgesellschaft	audit firm
Restschuldversicherung	credit life insurance
Revisionsstelle	external auditors
Risikokomponenten-Method	A method of setting the discount rate used in a discounted cash flow valuation based on a rate assumed to represent the risk-free interest rate for the relevant period, plus increases to this base rate based on the riskiness of an investment.

Richtlinien	guidelines
Risikoversicherungen	risk insurance
Rundschreiben	circular letter
Schadenquote	loss ratio
Schadenrückstellungen	case reserves
Schadenversicherer	nonlife insurer
Schadenversicherung	nonlife insurance
Schuldschein	debt certificate
Schuldscheindarlehen	debt certificate loan
schwebende Schäden	pending claims
SICAV (Société d'Investissement À Capital Variable)	investment company with variable capital
sichernde Massnahmen	protective measures
Sollbetrag	required amount
Solvabilitätsspanne	solvency margin
stille Reserven	undisclosed reserves
Tagessätze	Day-fines. Fines determined on the basis of the offender's income per day.
Tarif	premium rate; rate
Tarifierung	rating; pricing
Teilbestand	sub-portfolio
Titel	security (financial instrument: stock, bond, etc.)
Tochtergesellschaft	subsidiary
Todesfallversicherung	whole life insurance
Überschussanteile	shares of surplus
Überschussfonds	surplus funds
Umwandlungen	changes in legal form
verbrauchte Prämien	earned premiums
Verbrechen	crime; felony

vergehen	crime; misdemeanor (a less serious offense than *Verbrechen*)
Verkehrswert	market value
Verordnung	regulation
versicherungsmathematisch	actuarial
Versicherungsvermittler	insurance intermediary
Versicherungsunternehmen	insurance business
Zweigniederlassung	branch

Introduction to Switzerland's Laws for the Supervision of the Business of Insurance

I.
Laws, Regulations and the FINMA

Switzerland's supervisory laws and regulations for the business of insurance are structured in three layers comprising federal laws; regulations prescribed by the Federal Council (*Bundesrat*), Switzerland's federal executive body; and regulations and circular letters (*Rundschreiben*) issued by the Eidgenössische Finanzmarktaufsicht [hereinafter Federal Financial Market Supervisory Authority or FINMA].

The FINMA was established as a self-financing, independent public law institution by the Bundesgesetz über die Eidgenössische Finanzmarktaufsicht vom 22. Juni 2007 (SR 956.1) [Federal Law on the Federal Financial Market Supervision, hereinafter Financial Market Supervision Law or FINMAG[1]]. The FINMA acquired legal personality on 1 February 2008 and became fully operational on 1 January 2009. The FINMA is a consolidation of three former departments of the Swiss federal government: the Federal Office for Private Insurance (FOPI), the Federal Banking Commission and the Control Office for the Prevention of Money Laundering. This consolidation gave responsibility to a single regulator for the enforcement of seven federal laws central to the supervision of the financial services industry (Financial Market Laws):

- Pfandbriefgesetz vom 25. Juni 1930 [Pfandbrief Law];
- Bundesgesetz über den Versicherungsvertrag vom 2. April 1908 [Federal Law on the Insurance Contract];
- Bundesgesetz über die kollektiven Kapitalanlagen vom 23. Juni 2006 [Federal Law on the Collective Capital Investments, hereinafter Collective Investments Law];
- Bundesgesetz über die Banken und Sparkassen vom 8. November 1934 [Federal Law on the Banks and Savings Institutions, hereinafter the Banking Law];
- Bundesgesetz über die Börsen und den Effektenhandel vom 24. März 1995 [Federal Law on the Securities Exchanges and Securities Trading, hereinafter the Securities Exchanges Law];
- Bundesgesetz über die Bekämpfung der Geldwäscherei und der Terrorismusfinanzierung im Finanzsektor vom 10. Oktober 1997 [Federal Law

1 This is the widely used short-hand reference to this law, reduced from Finanzmarktaufsichtsgesetz.

on the Prevention of Money Laundering and the Financing of Terrorism in the Financial Sector]; and

- Bundesgesetz betreffend die Aufsicht über Versicherungsunternehmen vom 17. Dezember 2004 (SR 961.01) [Federal Law concerning the Supervision of Insurance Businesses, hereinafter Insurance Supervision Law or ISL].

With the Financial Market Supervision Law and the creation of the FINMA, Switzerland followed a trend toward the integrated supervision of financial services industry institutions and their intermediaries, as exemplified by the Financial Services Authority (FSA) in the United Kingdom, the Federal Institution for the Supervision of Financial Services (BaFin) in Germany and similar institutions in other countries. The FINMAG did not bring with it radical changes in the Financial Market Laws; on the contrary, it specifies that the provisions of the Financial Market Laws take precedence over the provisions of the FINMAG.[2]

The FINMA's charter under the FINMAG is "the protection of creditors, investors, insureds,[3] as well as the protection of the ability of the financial market to function. [Financial market supervision] serves thereby to strengthen the reputation and competiveness of the Swiss financial marketplace."[4] The FINMA is required to "exercise its supervisory authority in accordance with the Financial Market Laws and in accordance with" the FINMAG.[5] It is to regulate "only to the extent needed in view of the regulatory objective" and it is required to take into account "the costs to those subject to supervision and resulting from the regulation," "how the regulation affects competition, the ability to innovate and the international competitiveness of the Swiss financial marketplace" and "the varying business activities and risks of those subject to supervision. . . . "[6]

The statutory framework for the supervision of insurance businesses is provided by the Insurance Supervision Law, which delegates the specification of many of the details of insurance regulation to the Federal Council.

---

2 FINMAG Art. 2.

3 "The main goal . . . is not to prevent insolvencies at any cost. The responsibility of supervision is rather to protect policyholders from the consequences of insolvency." Herbert Lüthy, The New Supervision Philosophy, 23 May 2006. <*www.finma.ch/archiv/bpv/download/e/doc.pdf*>. *Cf.*, Financial Services Authority, Reasonable expectations: Regulation in a non-zero failure world, September 2003 ("[W]e do not aim to prevent all failures of firms or all lapses of conduct. We commonly refer to this as a 'non-zero failure' regime. *Id.* p. 3).

4 FINMAG Art. 5.

5 FINMAG Art. 6, para. 1.

6 FINMAG Art. 7, para. 2.

The Federal Council's Verordnung über die Beaufsichtigung von privaten Versicherungsunternehmen vom 9. November 2005 (SR 961.011) [Regulation on the Supervision of Private Insurance Businesses of 9 November 2005 hereinafter the Supervision Regulation or SR], which reiterates provisions of the ISL and elaborates on the matters delegated to it, entered into force on 1 January 2006, the effective date of most of the provisions of the ISL. This regulation also delegates rule-making authority to the FINMA.

The Verordnung der Eidgenössischen Finanzmarktaufsicht über die Beaufsichtigung von privaten Versicherungsunternehmen vom 9. November 2005 [Regulation of the FINMA on the Supervision of Private Insurance Businesses of 9 November 2005] (with effect from 1 January 2006) contains only seven articles. Most of the FINMA's regulations for insurance businesses are found in its circular letters (*Rundschreiben*) that prescribe rules on the required organization and structure of an insurance business, its internal processes and corporate governance, the position of the responsible actuary, the internal audit function and the external auditors, reporting to the FINMA, solvency and reserves and the investment of free and restricted assets.

Systems for the supervision of insurance businesses generally deploy an array of regulatory instruments to reach their goals, such as guarding against abusive market practices, limiting losses to insureds caused by the insolvency of an insurance business and shielding society from the harms of a systemic failure in an important segment of the financial services industry. These systems of supervision typically require that an insurance business be licensed or authorized in each jurisdiction where it intends to offer insurance products or services. The license will be issued only to insurers deemed to have adequate capital resources, 'fit and proper' management and an effective system of risk management. Following the grant of a license, the insurer will be subject to ongoing reporting obligations, audit requirements and regulatory examinations. The failure to comply with the requirements of a system of supervision may result in the loss of the license to transact business, civil fines and other penalties, and criminal prosecution resulting in fines or imprisonment. Swiss supervision of the business of insurance follows this pattern of regulation. The primary instruments of supervision are described in the next section.

II.
Primary Instruments for the Supervision of Insurance Businesses

A. The License Requirement; Application and Business Plan

A license to engage in the business of insurance is required for Swiss insurance businesses which write primary insurance or reinsurance and for insurance businesses domiciled in a foreign country in respect of their insurance activities conducted in Switzerland or conducted from Switzerland, subject to any contrary provisions of an international treaty.[7] An insurance activity in Switzerland exists, regardless of the type of contract and where it is concluded, if a natural person or legal entity domiciled in Switzerland is among the policy holders or insured persons or if property located in Switzerland is insured.[8]

Insurance businesses domiciled in a foreign country which only engage in reinsurance in Switzerland (including the Swiss branch of a foreign insurance business) may transact reinsurance business in Switzerland without a license.[9] In addition, foreign insurance businesses domiciled abroad and which do not have a branch in Switzerland are not subject to supervision in Switzerland if they only provide coverage for risks in connection with marine transport, air transport and cross-border transportation; risks located outside Switzerland; or war risks.[10]

An insurance business which engages in insurance activities in Switzerland which are of slight economic importance or which affect only a small group of insureds may, if special circumstances justify it, be exempted from supervision by the FINMA.[11]

A license is required for each line of business[12] the insurance business intends to write. A license to write a line of insurance includes a license to write rein-

---

7 ISL Art. 2, para. 1, a. and b. In addition, insurance intermediaries are subject to supervision under the ISL and, under some circumstances, are required to register with the FINMA. *See infra Regulation of Insurance Intermediaries*. Insurance groups and insurance conglomerates may also be subject to supervision by the FINMA. *See infra* II. J. *Supervision of Insurance Groups and Conglomerates.*

8 SR Art. 1, para. 1. This provision prohibits a Swiss resident from obtaining a policy from an unlicensed insurer outside Switzerland, a practice that is sometimes referred to as 'self-procurement'.

9 ISL Art. 2, para. 2 a.

10 SR Art. 1, para. 2.

11 ISL Art. 2, para. 3.

12 The lines of business are defined in SR Annex 1.

surance for the same line.[13] Life insurers may not write nonlife business and nonlife insurers may not write life insurance. A Swiss insurer or reinsurer may only engage in businesses which are directly related to insurance business, but FINMA can approve the conduct of other businesses if these do not endanger the interests of the insureds.[14]

An application for a license must be submitted to the FINMA, together with the applicant's business plan.[15] The business plan is the focal point of the licensing process and under ISL Art. 4, para 2 normally must include:

- a copy of the applicant's articles of incorporation;[16]
- a description of the geographic scope of the applicant's business and, if the applicant is the member of an insurance group or conglomerate, of such group or conglomerate;
- a copy of each license from each foreign supervisory authority if the applicant transacts insurance or reinsurance business outside Switzerland;
- information about the applicant's financial resources and a statement of its reserves;[17]
- the applicant's financial statements for the past three years, or if none, its initial balance sheet;
- the identity of each person or entity that owns 10% or more of the applicant's capital or voting rights or which in any other way can significantly influence its management;
- the identity of the persons responsible for the ultimate management, supervision and control of the applicant, or if the applicant is a foreign business establishing a branch in Switzerland, the identity of its general agent in Switzerland;
- the identity of the responsible actuary;[18]

---

13 SR Art. 3, para. 5.

14 ISL Art. 11.

15 ISL Art. 4, para. 1.

16 The applicant for a license to engage in the business of insurance or reinsurance domiciled in Switzerland must be organized as either a corporation (*Aktiengesellschaft*) or a mutual company (*Genossenschaft*). ISL Art. 7.

17 ISL Art. 16, para 1 requires an insurance business to establish sufficient insurance technical reserves for all of its business activities. Reserve requirements are discussed under II. E. "*Reserves*", below.

18 The responsible actuary is required under ISL Art. 23 ff.

- the identity of the external auditors (including the identity of the persons responsible for the audit assignment) and, if the applicant is a member of an insurance group or conglomerate, the identity of the external auditors for the group or conglomerate;
- copies of contracts or other agreements for the outsourcing[19] of significant business functions;
- the lines of insurance the applicant intends to write and the nature of the risks it will insure or reinsure;
- the reinsurance plan, or if the applicant is a reinsurer, its retrocession plan;
- the expected cost of establishing the company or branch in Switzerland;
- *pro forma* income statements and balance sheets for the first three financial years; and
- a description of how risks are recognized, monitored and limited.

An insurance business is required to specify the conditions for the establishment and release of insurance technical reserves in its business plan and to document the reserving method used and the valuation of the insurance technical liabilities.[20]

An insurance business that writes life insurance is required to use risk-based, biometric and capital markets-based underlying materials and calculation methods for the rating of its contracts. Binding validity periods are to be given in the business plan for the underlying materials and calculation methods used.[21] If an insurance business grants insureds the right to increase the insurance coverage during the term of the contract without a new medical examination, then the prerequisites for an increased coverage guarantee must be included in the business plan.[22]

Amendments of the business plan relating to ISL Art 4, paragraph 2, letters a, h, i, k and r, as well as those resulting from mergers, divestitures and restruc-

---

19 For the general requirements for outsourcing, see Federal Office for Private Insurance, Explanations of the Business Plan, Issue 08/2007, Form J Contracts or other agreements by which principal functions are to be outsourced. This document is available in the archive section for the Federal Office for Private Insurance at <*www.finma.ch*>.

20 SR Art. 54, para. 3.

21 SR Art. 120, para. 1.

22 SR Art. 126, paras. 1 and 3.

turings of insurance businesses must be notified before they take effect;[23], those relating to ISL Art. 4, paragraph 2, letters b, c, d, f, g, j, l, m, n and q are to be notified to the FINMA within 14 days from the occurrence of the relevant circumstances[24] and are deemed approved if the FINMA does not initiate a review of the submission within four weeks.[25]

The licensing requirements are essentially the same for foreign and Swiss insurers. Subject to provisions in international treaties to the contrary, a foreign insurer intending to transact insurance business in or from Switzerland must, in addition:[26]

- be licensed as such in its jurisdiction of incorporation;
- establish a branch in Switzerland and appoint a general agent to manage the branch who is authorized to legally bind the insurer;
- have in its home jurisdiction a solvency margin that complies with the requirements of the ISL;
- establish an organizational fund in Switzerland (to cover the costs of establishing the business in Switzerland); and
- provide a security deposit in Switzerland in an amount equal to the share of the solvency margin attributable to the business written in or from Switzerland.

B. Minimum Capital Requirements

1. Minimum capitalization

If the applicant for an insurance license is incorporated in Switzerland, then under the ISL it must have a minimum capitalization in a range from 3 million to 20 million francs, depending on the lines of business it writes.[27] The SR specifies additional minimum limits for insurance lines in life insurance ranging from 5 to 12 million francs,[28] in nonlife insurance ranging from 3 to 8 million francs[29] and in reinsurance ranging from 3 to 10 million francs.[30] The amount

23 ISL Art. 5, para. 1.
24 SR Art. 5.
25 ISL Art. 5, para. 2.
26 ISL Art. 15, para. 1.
27 ISL Art. 8, para. 1.
28 SR Art. 7.
29 SR Art. 8.
30 SR Art. 9.

is to be determined on a case-by-case basis by the FINMA[31] and deviations from the limits set by the SR for specific lines of insurance are permitted, within the ranges set by the ISL, "if the risk exposure of the insurance business and the planned scope of business justify it."[32]

Foreign insurers applying for a license must deposit funds with the Swiss National Bank in an amount equal to 10% of the required solvency margin, subject to minimum amounts ranging from 450,000 to 600,000 francs for insurance lines in life insurance[33] and 40,000 to 280,000 francs for nonlife lines of insurance.[34]

2. Organizational fund

An insurance business also must have an organizational fund to meet the costs of establishing and developing its business or a significant expansion of its business.[35] The SR states that the organizational fund is generally required to be an amount equal to 20% of the required minimum capital,[36] but the amount is to be determined on a case-by-case basis by the FINMA.[37] The organizational fund may be used for other purposes "no earlier than three years after its establishment and only with the approval of the FINMA."[38]

3. Solvency margin

Beyond the minimum capital and organizational fund requirements, each supervised insurer and reinsurer is required to have "sufficient free and unencumbered capital in relation to all of its activities (solvency margin)", which specifically takes into account the risks it is exposed to, the lines of business it writes, the geographic scope of its activities and internationally recognized principles.[39] The solvency margin is determined with two tests, Solvency I and the Swiss Solvency Test (SST). Both methods are used independently of each other.[40]

---

31 ISL Art. 8, para. 3.

32 SR Art. 10.

33 SR Art. 15, paras. 2 a. and 2 b.

34 SR Art. 15, paras. 2 c., 2 d., 2 e. and 2 f.

35 ISL Art. 10.

36 SR Art. 11, para. 1. "For insurance businesses that are authorized to write insurance line C3, the organizational fund amounts to at least 300,000 francs." SR Art. 11, para. 2.

37 SR Art. 11, para. 3.

38 SR Art. 11, para. 1.

39 ISL Art. 9, paras. 1 and 2.

40 SR Art. 22.

a. *Solvency I*

Solvency I measures the solvency of an insurer or reinsurer on the basis of its required capital resources in relation to the volume of its business (required solvency margin) and its creditable capital resources (available solvency margin).[41] The SR specifies the calculations required for the determination of the required solvency margin for life insurance in Arts. 23-26, nonlife insurance in Arts. 27-32 and reinsurance in Arts. 33-36. The calculations for the available solvency margins are specified in Arts. 37-40.

b. *Swiss Solvency Test - SST*

The SST is both detailed and technical, characteristics that preclude a satisfactory summary here. Briefly, the SST is a risk-based solvency standard. It seeks to "relate the actual risk taken on by an insurance business to its capital requirement."[42] The capital requirement is met if an insurance business has sufficient capital available so that "even in an unlikely situation (e.g., one with a probability of 1%), there is (on average) enough capital to allow the assets and liabilities of the company to be transferred to a third party," which means there must be sufficient assets to cover the insurance liabilities and the future capital costs of the assuming insurer.[43]

Accordingly, the SST requires an insurance business to calculate its target capital, which is the amount of "risk-bearing capital that must be available at the beginning of the year in order for the average of the possible valuations of the risk-bearing capital at the end of the year which are below a certain threshold[44] (value at risk) (expected shortfall in accordance with Annex 2 [to the SR]) to be greater than or equal to the minimum amount" specified in SR Art. 41, para. 4.[45] "The minimum amount is the cost of capital for the risk-bearing capital to be provided during the pendency of the development of the insurance technical liabilities."[46] "Risk-bearing capital is the difference between the market value of the investments and the discounted, best-possible estimated

---

41 SR Art. 22, para. 1, a.

42 Federal Office for Private Insurance, *White Paper of the Swiss Solvency Test*, November 2004, p. 6 (hereinafter the SST White Paper). "[I]t is an aim of the SST to be compatible with the future European Solvency II framework." *Id.*

43 *See* SST White Paper, p. 5.

44 "The threshold of the risk-bearing capital is the value it will sink below only with a certain occurrence probability. The FINMA shall define the probability. . . . ." SR Art. 41, para. 3.

45 SR Art. 41, para. 1. *Cf.* SST White Paper p. 5. "target capital is the amount [of risk-bearing capital] needed to be sure at the chosen confidence level that the assets at the end of the year are sufficient to cover the liabilities."

46 *Cf.* SST White Paper at p. 17. ("[T]he discounted value of the future costs of maintaining the SST target capital level if the insurance portfolio was being run off by a third party. For the field test 2004, cost of capital was set at 6%.")

value of the insurance technical liabilities."[47] The determination of target capital is based on "a model for the quantification of the relevant risks," "an evaluation of a series of scenarios" and "an aggregation procedure which brings together the results of the model and the scenario evaluation."[48]

The requirements for the risk model are specified by the FINMA in Circular Letter 2008/44 SST. The starting point is "whether the FINMA's prescribed standard model is used or an internal model. An internal model is to be used if the standard model is not able to appropriately capture all relevant risks of the insurance business."[49] The model must "take into account the relevant risks from all positions which are components of the near market balance sheet[50] for the determination of the [target capital],"[51] including insurance technical risks, market risks, credit risks" and "other types of risk," such as operational risks, liquidity risks, risk concentrations and model risk.[52] In addition to the scenarios specified in the FINMA's standard model, an insurance business must develop and apply "its own scenarios which take into account its own individual risk situation."[53] The results of the models and the evaluation of the scenarios are aggregated to determine the target capital.[54] According to the SST White Paper:

> Calculating the 1-year risk capital . . . using the standard models, a probability distribution [results] which describes the situation of the company given none of the scenario events occurred.
>
> In most cases, scenarios will cause an extra loss for the company so that risk-bearing capital is correspondingly reduced.
>
> * * *
>
> Therefore the economic state of the company is again described by the probability distribution obtained using the standard models, however shifted using the extra loss under the scenarios.

---

47 SR Art. 41, para. 2.

48 SR Art. 42, para. 1.

49 Circular Letter 2008/44, margin para. 67.

50 All assets and liabilities are to be valued consistently at near market value, i.e. mark-to-market value and only if market prices are unavailable, mark-to-model. See Circular Letter 2008/44, margin paras. 30-47.

51 Circular Letter 2008/44, margin para. 78.

52 Circular Letter 2008/44, margin paras. 93-96.

53 Circular Letter 2008/44, margin para. 97. The scenarios are to be documented appropriately and reviewed annually. *Id.* Examples of these scenarios are given in the SST White Paper, pp. 23-27.

54 *See* SST White Paper, p. 10; SR Art. 45.

* * *

> These probability distributions are then aggregated with the distribution from the standard models using a weighted average, where weights are given by the probabilities of the scenarios.[55]

An insurance business must "deliver to the FINMA documentation of the various modules of the internal model, as well as the relationships between these modules. The documentation must be self-contained. It should permit a knowledgeable third party to understand, within a reasonable period of time, whether the regulatory requirements for the approval of the internal model have been fulfilled. The documentation shall explain the method (theories and assumptions) which are the basis for the internal model, as well as their use within the insurance business. It shall describe the limitations and weaknesses of the internal model."[56]

Target capital and risk-bearing capital are to be determined annually[57] as of the "beginning of the year"[58] and an insurance business must prepare a report on their calculation which is to be signed by the members of its executive board and delivered to the FINMA.[59] "As from the business year 2011, the result of the SST must be delivered to the FINMA not later than 30 April of each year."[60] "Under Art. 202 SR, groups issue an SST Report each semester. The FINMA shall align the submission date with the submission dates for the legal entities belonging to the group . . . ."[61]

If the ratio of risk-bearing capital to target capital falls below 100%, the FINMA will impose protective measures. *See infra* III. D. *Solvency-Related Protective Measures.*

C. Responsible Actuary

ISL Art. 23 requires an insurance business to appoint a responsible actuary who must ensure that "the solvency margin is calculated correctly and the re-

55 SST White Paper, p. 27-28.

56 Circular Letter 2008/44, margin paras. 130-131.

57 "If the risk situation of an insurance business changes significantly, then target capital is to be determined during the year by approximation and notified to the FINMA." SR Art. 51, para. 2.

58 Circular Letter 2008/44, margin para. 71. As a practical matter, for valuation and risk measurement, "the positions as of 31.12. may be used, corrected for any changes, such as, for example, portfolio transfers." Circular Letter 2008/44, margin para. 75.

59 SR Art. 53, para. 1.

60 Circular Letter 2008/44, margin para. 157. The FINMA is required to adopt a transition plan for the due date for the SST Report before 2011. *Id.*

61 Circular Letter 2008/44, margin para. 159.

stricted assets meet the requirements of the supervisory regulations," "factually accurate accounting information is used" and "sufficient technical reserves are established."[62] If the responsible actuary finds deficiencies, these must be notified to the executive management of the insurance business without delay.[63] The responsible actuary "is to deliver a report at regular intervals to the executive management, or in the case of a foreign insurance business, its general agent" in Switzerland.[64]

The responsible actuary "must enjoy a good reputation, be professionally qualified[65] and able to correctly assess the financial consequences of the activities of the insurance business."[66] The responsible actuary also "must be knowledgeable about the Swiss situation (legislation, supervisory regulations, insurance market)."[67] In order to avoid conflicts of interest, the notice to the FINMA of the appointment of the responsible actuary must state "the relationship he or she has to the insurance business"; if the responsible actuary is also "a member of the management board or the board of directors, the FINMA reserves the right to impose conditions on the appointment."[68]

Circular Letter 2008/16 prescribes a "Statement of Professional Ability" that the responsible actuary is required to sign upon accepting his or her appointment. If the responsible actuary resigns or his or her appointment is terminated, this must be notified to the FINMA "without delay."[69]

---

62 ISL Art. 24, para. 1.

63 ISL Art. 24, para. 2.

64 ISL Art. 24, para. 3.

65 The responsible actuary must have attained the qualification "Actuary SAV [Swiss Association of Actuaries]" or an equivalent qualification, but the FINMA may, upon request, "recognize relevant education, coupled with at least five years' professional experience as an actuary, as evidence of professional ability." SR Art. 99. The FINMA recognizes a fully qualified actuary ("fully qualified member, "full member") of a foreign association of actuaries which has standards equivalent to the SAV as equivalent to "Actuary SAV". Circular Letter 2008/16 Responsible Actuary, margin para. 2. The FINMA provides references to websites listing recognized foreign associations of actuaries. *Id.* margin para. 3. An academic degree in mathematics or physics is considered "relevant education." *Id.* margin para. 4.

66 ISL Art. 23, para. 2.

67 SR Art. 99, para. 3. "Knowledge of the Swiss situation . . . is considered to exist if a person has, during at least the last three years, engaged in a wide range of actuarial activities in Switzerland in the lines of business engaged in by the insurance business. Persons who do not fulfill these conditions must prove that they possess equivalent knowledge commensurate with the scope of their duties." Circular Letter 2008/16, margin para. 6.

68 Circular Letter 2008/16, margin para. 9.

69 ISL Art. 23, para. 3.

D. 'Fit and Proper' Standard

Article 14, para. 1 of the ISL requires, as a condition for the grant of a license to engage in the business of insurance, that those who have ultimate responsibility for ultimate management, supervision and control, as well as the conduct of an insurer's business "enjoy a good reputation and be able to provide assurance that business will be conducted in an irreproachable manner" -- literally, in a manner that is 'free from any objection'. Nearly identical requirements are to be found in the Banking Law[70] and the Securities Exchanges Law.[71]

Considering that the business of insurance relies for its success on probabilities and estimates and that all flesh, even the most conscientious and honorable, is fallible,[72] who could honestly say that he or she would, or could, manage an insurance business in a manner that is beyond reproach?

The meaning of this requirement is perhaps better understood with the assistance of a historical perspective. The idea that a financial services business must be conducted by people who can offer the assurance that business will be conducted in an irreproachable manner became a part of Swiss federal law with the entry into force of a revision of the Banking Law on 1 July 1971. This provision was adopted in response to a 1968 decision of the Federal Court (*Bundesgericht*) which held that the law in force at the time authorized the Federal Banking Commission (*Eidgenössische Bankenkommission*) to withhold a banking license from an applicant with an inadequate governance structure based on a review of its articles of incorporation, by-laws and organizational structure, but not because the primary business manager had previously served as a director of a bank and in that position had demonstrated that he had "an unreliable character and was professionally incompetent."[73] The "assurance" (*Gewähr*) requirement filled that regulatory gap.

---

70 Banking Law Art. 3, para. 2, c., which requires that "those persons who are entrusted with the administration and management of the bank enjoy a good reputation and offer the assurance of irreproachable business activities."

71 Securities Exchanges Law Art. 3, para. 2, b., which requires that "the securities exchange and its responsible employees can demonstrate the necessary professional knowledge and offer the assurance of irreproachable business activities."

72 Warren Buffett, perhaps the most celebrated insurance manager of our time, has made a ritual of confessing his mistaken business decisions in his Chairman's Letters in the annual reports to shareholders of Berkshire Hathaway Inc. These letters are available at <*www.berkshirehathaway.com*>.

73 For a detailed account of the origins of 'the assurance of irreproachable business activities', *see* Marcel Livio Aellen, Die Gewähr für eine einwandfreie Geschäftstätigkeit gemäss Art. 3 Abs. 2, lit. c. des Bankengesetzes (1990) [The Assurance of an Irreproachable Business Activity under Art. 3, para. 2 lit. c of the Banking Law].

E. Reserves

1. Life insurance

Article 16 of the ISL states that "[a]n insurance business is required to establish sufficient insurance technical reserves for all of its business activities" and delegates the detailed regulations on reserving to the Federal Council. The SR requires an insurance business writing life insurance to establish technical reserves contract-by-contract[74] on a gross basis (excluding reinsurance).[75] A life insurance business is required "to use the same or more conservative biometric data than those it used for the rating"[76] and to "increase the insurance technical reserves as soon as these are shown to be insufficient on the basis of rating materials which are considered appropriate."[77] Technical reserves must at all times cover redemption values, less capitalized acquisition costs.[78] The SR requires the establishment of volatility reserves in order "to offset the volatility of the business, while taking into account the diversification, size and structure of the insurance portfolio."[79] SR Art. 54, para. 4 states that "[t]he FINMA shall regulate the details concerning the type and scope of insurance technical reserves."

Consistent with ISL Art. 24, para. 1, c., FINMA Circular Letter 2008/43 Life Insurance Reserves places responsibility for the establishment of sufficient insurance technical reserves on the responsible actuary.[80] Reserving assumptions must be made in accordance with "conservative principles" and a "margin of safety.[81] The adequacy of the insurance technical reserves must be reviewed at least once each year.[82] In performing the review, the insurer must divide its portfolio into at least the sub-portfolios specified in the annex to this circular letter and the reserves must be sufficient for each sub-portfolio.[83] If not, then they must be increased and the business plan is to be amended accordingly.[84] The increase in reserves may be determined at the sub-portfolio

74 SR Art. 58, para. 1. The categories of reserves taken into account in determining the required amount of restricted assets are listed in SR Art. 55.

75 SR Art. 59.

76 SR Art. 61.

77 SR Art. 62.

78 SR Art. 63.

79 SR Art. 54, para. 1, b.

80 Circular Letter 2008/43, margin para. 4.

81 Circular Letter 2008/43, margin para. 12.

82 Circular Letter 2008/43, margin para. 25.

83 Circular Letter 2008/43, margin para. 26.

84 Circular Letter 2008/43, margin para. 28.

level.[85] Releases of volatility reserves and increases in reserves that are no longer required are to be notified to the FINMA in advance.[86]

If an insurance business or one of its large portfolios is in run-off, any increasing cost factors and decreasing risk diversification must be taken into account. The FINMA may specify the parameters for the required reserves.[87]

The FINMA may require an interim review of the adequacy of reserves and may require that it is performed by an external actuary at the expense of the insurance business. The FINMA may also specify the "assumptions and methods" to be used for the determination of the reserves.[88]

The report that the responsible actuary is required to deliver to the insurer's executive board pursuant to ISL Art. 24, para. 3 and ISR-FINMA Art. 2, para. 2, as well as the supervisory report pursuant to ISL Art. 25, para. 2 are required, among other things, to include:

a. an assessment of whether business plan provisions for insurance technical reserves have been observed and whether the insurance technical reserves are sufficient;

b. the most important assumptions and methods for the determination of the insurance technical reserves and any relevant changes in the assumptions and methods in comparison to the previous year;

c. an assessment of the chosen assumptions and methods, noting "any possible risks."[89]

2. *Nonlife insurance*

Insurance technical reserves for nonlife insurers comprise reserves for unearned premiums, case reserves, security and volatility reserves, age reserves, reserves for contractually agreed participations in surplus, reserves for pension coverage capital and "additional technical reserves, the description and purpose of which is to be identified and described precisely."[90] Circular Letter 2008/42 Reserves in Nonlife Insurance addresses these categories of reserves under unearned premiums,[91] case reserves,[92] security and volatility

85 *Id.*

86 Circular Letter 2008/43, margin para. 44.

87 Circular Letter 2008/43, margin para. 33

88 Circular Letter 2008/43, margin para. 34.

89 Circular Letter 2008/43, margin paras. 39-43.

90 SR Art. 69.

91 Circular Letter 2008/42, margin para. 11.

92 Circular Letter 2008/42, margin paras. 12-13.

reserves,[93] reserves for contractual policyholder surplus,[94] actuarial reserves for pensions[95] and other technical reserves.[96]

Under Circular Letter 2008/42, reserves for unearned premiums "comprise the portion of the premiums which is to be allocated to the period after the reporting date" and not be set off against capitalized acquisition costs.[97] "Case reserves, as of the reporting date, comprise all of the payments and costs that will be paid after the reporting date for all loss events that occurred before the reporting date," including reserves for incurred-but-not-yet-reported claims (IBNR) and reopened closed claims as of the reporting date.[98] Security and volatility reserves offset unfavorable loss development.[99] "Reserves for contractual policyholder surplus as of the reporting date comprise the share of the policyholder surplus that is owed after the reporting date which is to be allocated to the period before the reporting date."[100] Special rules are prescribed for actuarial reserves for pensions, depending on whether the insurer shares in the fund securing future pensions,[101] and for pensions other than those covered by the Federal Law on Accident Insurance.[102] "Other technical reserves are to be established as needed in accordance with the [general] principles for sufficient insurance technical reserves described in paragraph III [of the circular letter]. Their designation and purpose are to be described in the business plan."[103]

The general principles for the establishment of sufficient insurance technical reserves are:

a. "Insurance technical case reserves, as of the reporting date, are an estimate of the payments that will become due after the reporting date and the costs for all insurance claims under insurance agreements in existence as of the reporting date. The payments may not, with the exception of the actuarial reserves for annuities, be discounted."[104]

---

93 Circular Letter 2008/42, margin paras. 14-19.
94 Circular Letter 2008/42, margin para. 20.
95 Circular Letter 2008/42, margin paras. 21-25.
96 Circular Letter 2008/42, margin para. 26.
97 *See* Circular Letter 2008/42, margin para. 11.
98 *See* Circular Letter 2008/42, margin para. 12.
99 *See* Circular Letter 2008/42, margin paras. 14-19.
100 Circular Letter 2008/42, margin para. 20.
101 *See* Circular Letter 2008/42, margin paras. 23-24.
102 *See* Circular Letter 2008/42, margin para. 25.
103 *See* Circular Letter 2008/42, margin para. 26.
104 Circular Letter 2008/42, margin para. 6.

b. "Expressed mathematically, the insurance technical case reserves are a provisional, unbiased estimate of the provisionally expected value of future cash flows on the basis of the information available at the time of the estimate. They are therefore considered a best estimate and are therefore neither on the cautious nor on the incautious side and specifically do not include any conscious reinforcement."[105]

c. "Volatility reserves are needed because of uncertainties in setting the case reserves (security or parameter risk), such as the probability volatility inherent in a loss event (volatility risk in the narrow sense). They serve to completely or partially offset unfavorable developments in the insurance technical case reserves."[106]

"Sufficient insurance technical reserves must nevertheless be at least as large as the near market value of the obligations. This value comprises the best-possible estimate of the value of the obligations pursuant to Annex 3 SR and the minimum amount[107] under Art. 41, para. 4 SR."[108]

An insurance business is required to have a system for reserving losses at the individual loss level. This process must "specify rules for the recording, adjustment, release and monitoring of the individual case reserves which take into account the special characteristics of the various types of losses and reserving methods (individual case reserve, general reserve)." The process must ensure the quality of loss estimates and compliance with the guidelines on estimates, and shall verify them. [109] The data used in setting loss reserves are required to be current and reserves must be promptly adjusted on the basis of loss developments. Case reserves must be set on the basis of "recognized actuarial principles."[110]

F. Restricted Assets; Investment Restrictions

ISL Art. 17 requires each insurance business to provide security for its claim payment obligations by designating investments as restricted assets. If an insurance business becomes insolvent and goes into liquidation, policyholders and insureds have a priority claim against these restricted assets.[111] Under ISL

---

105 Circular Letter 2008/42, margin para. 7.

106 Circular Letter 2008/42, margin para. 8.

107 SR Art. 41, para. 4 states that "[t]he minimum amount is the cost of capital for the risk-bearing capital to be provided during the pendency of the development of the insurance technical liabilities."

108 Circular Letter 2008/42, margin para. 9.

109 Circular Letter 2008/42, margin para. 27.

110 Circular Letter 2008/42, margin para. 29.

111 ISL Arts. 19, para. 1 and 54, para. 4; Circular Letter 2008/18 Investment Guidelines for Insurers, margin para. 19.

Art. 18, the required amount of restricted assets "is equal to the insurance technical reserves under [ISL] Article 16[112] and an appropriate surcharge" set by the FINMA.[113] The required amount is determined at the conclusion of each financial year.[114] Within three months thereafter, an insurance business is required to report the required amount and an inventory of restricted assets to the FINMA.[115] The required amount must be covered by investments designated as restricted assets at all times[116] which have been made in the eligible investments specified in SR Art. 79 and which are unencumbered (SR Art. 84, para. 2). If an insurance business determines that there is a coverage shortfall, restricted assets must be increased immediately. The FINMA can in special cases grant a cure period for effecting the increase.[117] Assets designated as restricted assets, subject to SR Art. 91, para. 3 on derivative financial instruments, may not be offset against obligations that have been allocated to restricted assets.[118]

The ISL delegates to the Federal Council the promulgation of "regulations concerning the provision, location, coverage, alteration and control of restricted assets" and authorizes the Federal Council to "delegate the specification of the technical details to the FINMA."[119] "Moveable investments allocated to restricted assets may be held at the headquarters of the insurance business in Switzerland or at the office for all Swiss business, as applicable, (own custody) or be held by a third-party custodian."[120] Foreign custodians, other than those in Belgium or Luxembourg, are generally prohibited.[121]

The FINMA has issued Circular Letter 2008/18 Investment Guidelines for Insurers which sets forth detailed restrictions on the investments that may be allocated to restricted assets. Overall, the FINMA requires that restricted assets be chosen by taking into account safety, return, diversification and liquid-

112 When first established, the value of restricted assets must equal at least 750,000 francs for life insurers and 100,000 francs for nonlife insurers. SR Art. 70.

113 The surcharge has been set in Art. 1 of the Regulation of the Financial Market Supervisory Authority on the Supervision of Private Insurance Businesses: for life insurers, 1% of the insurance technical reserves used as the basis for the determination of the required amount and for nonlife insurers, 4% of the reserves under SR Article 68, para. 1, a. - c., but at least 100,000 francs.

114 SR Art. 71, para. 1.

115 SR Art. 72, para. 1. "An insurance business domiciled in Switzerland must in addition produce a report about each foreign insurance portfolio for which it is required to provide security in a foreign country." *Id.*, para. 2.

116 SR Art. 74, para. 1; Circular Letter 2008/18 margin paras. 23-26.

117 SR Art. 74, para. 2.

118 SR Art. 84, para. 2; Circular Letter 2008/18 margin paras. 21-22.

119 ISL Art. 20.

120 SR Art. 86, para. 1.

121 Circular Letter 2008/18, margin para. 133.

ity.[122] The FINMA defines safety as comprising two concepts: economic security, which it defines as the stability of the principal amount of the investment; and legal security, which means the ability to dispose of the investment without difficulty.[123] The 'return' criteria emphasizes the stability of an investment's returns.[124] Diversification is defined as diversification among obligors, geographic regions and industries,[125] but emphasis is placed on counterparty risk. The "exposure to a counterparty may not be greater than 5% of the required amount of restricted assets."[126] Investments denominated in a currency not matched with an insurance obligation are limited to 20% of the required amount of restricted assets.[127] Finally, liquidity is considered a function of the term of an investment or the ability to sell it quickly. An insurer must be able to meet its expected liquidity needs at all times.[128]

Acting on its authority under the SR to set limits for individual categories of investments,[129] the FINMA has prescribed limits within restricted assets on the type and amount of investments in the asset categories permitted under SR Art. 79: cash and cash-equivalents, bonds and other debt obligations, structured products and securitized payment obligations (asset-backed securities), equities, real estate and loans secured by real estate in Switzerland, alternative investments, and collective capital investments (investment funds). Circular Letter 2008/18 also regulates securities repurchase and reverse repurchase transactions (repos and reverse repos).[130] Apart from observing general sound investment principles, there are no restrictions on the investment of assets not allocated to restricted assets[131] or on the investments of reinsurers because reinsurers are not required to designate restricted assets.[132] The use of derivatives, however, is restricted by the circular letter for all insurance businesses, both for transactions involving restricted assets and free assets.[133]

---

122 Circular Letter 2008/18, margin para. 42.

123 Circular Letter 2008/18, margin paras. 48-50.

124 Circular Letter 2008/18, margin para. 52.

125 Circular Letter 2008/18, margin para. 53-59.

126 Circular Letter 2008/18, margin para. 55.

127 Circular Letter 2008/18, margin para. 56.

128 Circular Letter 2008/18, margin paras. 60-62.

129 SR Art. 83.

130 Circular Letter 2008/18, margin paras. 590-595.

131 Circular Letter 2008/18, margin para. 5. "As part of its solvency supervision, the FINMA requires, however, that the unrestricted assets (free assets) are invested and managed in accordance with generally accepted investment principles. This also applies to the assets of Swiss reinsurance businesses which are not required to establish restricted assets." *Id.*, margin para. 6.

132 Circular Letter 2008/18, margin para. 6.

133 Circular Letter 2008/18, margin para. 15.

1. Cash investments

Cash investments include bank deposits and money market investments with a term of up to 12 months.[134] The deposit agreement must exclude any security interest, retention of title, offset or similar right.[135] Instruments that are mere payment obligations of an obligor domiciled abroad and not a security (*Wertpapier*) may not be included in restricted assets because the Swiss bankruptcy preference for insurance payment obligations secured by restricted assets may not be enforceable and there is a risk that a Swiss insurer's payment obligations to the obligor would be offset against the obligor's obligation to pay on the debt instrument if the obligor becomes subject to bankruptcy proceedings.[136]

"Money market book-entry obligations and securities with a variable interest rate without a fixed maturity date will be credited, at most, at market value. If they are not listed on a securities exchange, then a customary market valuation method will be used. All other investments, including . . . time deposits will be valued, at most, at par value, taking into account the security and the distribution rate."[137]

2. Bonds and convertible bonds

Bonds and convertible bonds include bonds issued by corporations, governments and supranational organizations, public law institutions and synthetic bonds.[138] "Investments cannot be allocated to this category which are, in fact, issued as bonds, but because of their characteristics they are governed under another investment category in the investment guidelines."[139] Mandatory convertible bonds, for example, must be allocated to the equities category, as well as a bond with a market value greater than 130% of its par value.[140] The convertible bonds of foreign issuers are subject to the restrictions referenced in note 136 and the accompanying text.

Fixed income securities with a fixed maturity date and specified currency are to be valued in accordance with either the scientific or linear cost method.[141] Convertible bonds are to be valued at not more than market value.[142] "Under

---

134 SR Art. 79, para. 1, a.; Circular Letter 2008/18, margin para. 142.

135 Circular Letter 2008/18, margin para. 144.

136 Circular Letter 2008/18, margin para. 143, referencing margin paras. 134-136.

137 Circular Letter 2008/18, margin para. 145, quoting SR Art. 93, paras. 1 and 2.

138 SR Art. 79; Circular Letter 2008/18, margin para. 147.

139 SR Art. 79; Circular Letter 2008/18, margin para. 148.

140 SR Art. 79; Circular Letter 2008/18, margin para. 150.

141 Circular Letter 2008/18, margin para. 152, quoting SR Art. 88, para. 1.

142 Circular Letter 2008/18, margin para. 152, quoting SR Art. 88, para. 2.

the scientific amortized cost method, the difference between cost and redemption value during the remaining term of the security, on each financial statement reporting date, is to be increased or reduced to the extent necessary that the original internal interest rate (return to maturity) can be maintained."[143] "Under the linear amortized cost method, the difference between cost and redemption value during the remaining term of the security, on each financial statement reporting date, is to be distributed in equal amounts over the remaining term as depreciation or appreciation, as applicable."[144]

3. Structured products and securitized obligations

a. Structured products

Circular Letter 2008/18 defines structured products as "investments in the form of a bond or debt instrument through which a cash market instrument (e.g., a fixed interest security) is linked to one or more derivative financial instruments to make a single legal and economic instrument. Derivative instruments are linked to one or more underlying assets (e.g., shares, bonds, interest rates, exchange rates, alternative investments)."[145] Structured products are permitted in restricted assets if (1) the individual components (e.g., cash market instrument and derivative) meet the requirements of the relevant category of restricted assets, (2) the structured product does not have physical delivery or acceptance obligations and (3) the structure product does not impose any additional payment obligations or have a negative interest feature which requires the investor to make interest payments.[146]

Structured products are valued and credited to restricted assets by one of three methods: (1) valuing the structured product as a whole at market value under the rules for the investment category applicable to it,[147] (2) dividing the structured product into its constituent components and valuing and crediting each component under the rules for the investment category applicable to it[148] or (3) valuing the structured product as a whole at amortized cost.[149]

A structured product may be valued at amortized cost only if (1) the embedded derivative is linked solely to an interest rate or inflation, (2) the economic char-

---

143 Circular Letter 2008/18, margin para. 153, quoting SR Art. 89, para. 1.

144 Circular Letter 2008/18, margin para. 153, quoting SR Art. 89, para. 2.

145 Circular Letter 2008/18, margin para. 157.

146 Circular Letter 2008/18, margin paras. 158-161.

147 Circular Letter 2008/18, margin paras. 163-167. "If the structured product has various embedded risks, then under this valuation method it must be allocated as a whole to the most restrictive category (i.e., the category which on the basis of the greatest risk results in the strictest requirements for allocation / credit)." *Id.*, margin para. 166.

148 Circular Letter 2008/18, margin paras. 168-169.

149 Circular Letter 2008/18, margin paras. 170-179.

acteristics and risks of the derivative are closely connected with those of the cash market instrument, (3) at least 90% of the purchase price is capital protected by a protection seller rated at least single A, (4) all cash flows are in the same currency and are not affected by fluctuations in currency exchange rates, (5) the structured product does not incorporate a significant leverage effect (i.e., more than double the market return on a fixed interest rate bond denominated in the same currency, with the same term and an issuer of the same creditworthiness) and (6) the term of the structured product does not exceed 12 years.[150]

"Structured products linked solely to interest rates or inflation may be included at the value determined by the scientific amortized cost method (in the category "debt obligations in a fixed amount"). The cost amortization is to be determined on the basis of the interest rate which is the internal rate of return resulting from the purchase price and the minimum cash flows (capital protection and any minimum coupons)."[151]

A structured product or the individual elements of a structured product (in the case of division) fall under the relevant limits of the category to which they are allocated under para. III.C.a.cc[152] of the circular letter.[153]

Structured products are also subject to the restrictions referenced in note 136 and the accompanying text.

b. Securitized obligations

SR Art. 79, para. 1, c. authorizes the inclusion of "securitized payment claims" in restricted assets, but Circular Letter 2008/18 excludes group internal transactions,[154] investments in insurance-linked securities,[155] "the high risk tranches" of asset-backed securities ("ABS"),[156] ABS backed by actively managed asset pools (such as managed pools of collateralized debt obligations ("CDO"s) if this hinders the insurance business in assessing "the risk and stability of value" of the investment[157] and layered structures, such as CDOs of CDOs.[158] An insurance business that invests in ABS is required to have a

150 Circular Letter 2008/18, margin paras. 170-176.

151 Circular Letter 2008/18, margin para. 177.

152 Circular Letter 2008/18, margin paras. 162-177.

153 Circular Letter 2008/18, margin para. 179.

154 Circular Letter 2008/18, margin para. 184.

155 Circular Letter 2008/18, margin para. 185.

156 Circular Letter 2008/18, margin para. 186. "Investments in higher tranches (senior tranches, super-senior tranches) are also excluded if they, after considering all relevant aspects, do not comport with an investment-grade (BBB)-quality investment." *Id.*

157 Circular Letter 2008/18, margin para. 187.

158 Circular Letter 2008/18, margin para. 188.

qualified staff "that is able to assess the stability of value and the risk content of the investment,"[159] a "a well-documented investment process which is tailored to the special characteristics of this investment category"[160] and "a due diligence process which guarantees a comprehensive and in-depth analysis of the structure, underlying risks and conditions of the securitized obligations."[161] The employees responsible for investments in ABS and the scope of their authority must be specifically identified.[162] Circular Letter 2008/18 cautions against reliance on the ratings assigned by credit rating businesses. "The evaluation of the inherent risks of securitized obligations generally should be based on the [insurance business's] own analysis . . . ."[163] Investments in this category are also to be monitored by the insurer's risk management staff.[164]

Investments in ABS are limited to 10% of the required amount and the credited value for an investment in an individual issue of ABS may not exceed 1% of the required amount.[165] "Securitized obligations will be credited at not more than market value."[166]

4. Other unconditional debt obligations

The category "other unconditional debt obligations" recognized by SR Art. 79, para. 1, d. is narrowed by Circular Letter 2008/18 to "debt certificate loans to public law bodies, banks and other debtors domiciled in Switzerland to the extent that the latter are assigned a minimum rating of A . . . ."[167] The circular letter specifically excludes (a) debt certificate loans made to foreign borrowers if the obligation has not been issued as a security (*Wertpapier*)[168],[169] (b) loans to private equity businesses,[170] (c) policy loans because these were already deducted in determining the required amount,[171] (d) loans to debtors whose cred-

159 Circular Letter 2008/18, margin para. 191.

160 Circular Letter 2008/18, margin para. 196.

161 Circular Letter 2008/18, margin para. 203.

162 Circular Letter 2008/18, margin para. 191.

163 Circular Letter 2008/18, margin para. 192. *See also* margin para. 203 ("The availability of external ratings does not excuse an insurance business from the duty to investigate the risks in the investments.")

164 Circular Letter 2008/18, margin para. 200.

165 Circular Letter 2008/18, margin para. 204.

166 Circular Letter 2008/18, margin para. 207.

167 Circular Letter 2008/18, margin para. 209.

168 *See* the text accompanying note 136 and Circular Letter 2008/18, margin paras. 134-136 for the FINMA's explanation of the need for a security.

169 Circular Letter 2008/18, margin para. 212.

170 Circular Letter 2008/18, margin para. 213. These loans are covered by the alternative investments category.

171 Circular Letter 2008/18, margin para. 214.

itworthiness cannot be verified[172] and (e) intra-company loans within the insurer's corporate group.[173]

Investments in this category are valued at the nominal value of the loan, subject to an assessment of the stability of its value.[174]

5. Equities and other listed ownership interests

The investment category for equities includes shares, participation certificates (*Genusscheine* and *Beteiligungsscheine*), convertible bonds with equity character, share certificates (*Anteilscheine*) of mutual companies (*Genossenschaften*) and similar securities "if the issues are traded on a regulated market and can be sold on short notice."[175] Equity investments in related companies are not permitted.[176] Circular Letter 2008/18 also allocates the shares of listed real estate companies to this category, but the limits applicable to real estate investments must be observed.[177]

A maximum of 30% of the required amount of restricted assets may be invested in this category, including investments in the equity component of collective capital investments, single-investor funds and instruments which increase the exposure to equities.[178] Equity investments are to be valued, at most, at market value.[179]

6. Real estate

Real estate is an authorized category of investment for restricted assets,[180] but investments may be made only in the form of improved land[181] and, unless the FINMA grants an exception, only in real properties located in Switzerland.[182] Circular Letter 2008/18 excludes numerous other categories of real properties from restricted assets: (1) construction starts, (2) production facilities, (3) warehouses, (4) factories, (5) distribution centers, (6) sport facilities, (7) shopping centers, unless they are "municipal center areas or distinguishable by a peripheral use," (8) hotels, (9) properties acquired by the insurance

172 Circular Letter 2008/18, margin para. 215.

173 Circular Letter 2008/18, margin para. 216.

174 Circular Letter 2008/18, margin para. 219.

175 SR Art. 79, para. 1, e.

176 Circular Letter 2008/18, margin para. 224.

177 Circular Letter 2008/18, margin para. 223

178 Circular Letter 2008/18, margin para. 225

179 SR Arts. 79, para. 1, e. and 93, para. 1; Circular Letter 2008/18, margin para. 227.

180 SR Art. 79, para. 1, f.

181 *See* Circular Letter 2008/18, margin para. 237.

182 *See* Circular Letter 2008/18, margin paras. 239 and 242.

business upon the enforcement of a mortgage held by it, (10) restaurants, (11) residences for the elderly or nursing homes, (12) luxury properties and properties that will not draw a large number of potential buyers, (13) vacation properties, (14) properties held in joint ownership and (15) properties subject to environmental impairments.[183] An investment in a real estate company is also ineligible for restricted assets if it is not listed on a securities exchange and its share of its ownership interests is 50% or less.[184] Consistent with the requirement in SR Art. 84, para. 2 that restricted assets may not be encumbered, properties owned by an insurer which secure the repayment of a debt owed by it may not be credited to restricted assets.[185]

The FINMA may grant an exception to the exclusion of a real property investment from restricted assets if a plausible justification exists.[186]

Investments in real properties may not be credited to restricted assets for more than 25% of the required amount[187] and the value of an individual property may not exceed 5% of the required amount.[188] Under SR Art. 90, para. 1, real properties may not be credited to restricted assets at more than market value. A valuation at 100% of market value is permitted if the insurer's audit firm does not state in its report on restricted assets that the insurer did not comply with the rules on the plausibility of real property valuations in the investment guidelines in Circular 2008/18.[189] The valuation of owner-occupied real properties is to be made in accordance with US GAAP, IFRS[190] or Swiss GAAP FER[191];[192] for properties held as an investment, US GAAP or IFRS are to be used.[193]

If market values determined under the relevant accounting standard are not available for real properties held as an investment, the insurer is to value the properties under either the income capitalization method or the discounted

183 Circular Letter 2008/18, margin para. 237.

184 Circular Letter 2008/18, margin para. 240.

185 Circular Letter 2008/18, margin para. 241.

186 Circular Letter 2008/18, margin para. 242.

187 Circular Letter 2008/18, margin para. 250.

188 Circular Letter 2008/18, margin para. 251.

189 Circular Letter 2008/18, margin para. 257.

190 International Financial Reporting Standards.

191 Fachempfehlungen zur Rechnungslegung [Professional Recommendations on Accounting Standards]. See <*www.fer.ch*>.

192 Circular Letter 2008/18, margin para. 259.

193 Circular Letter 2008/18, margin para. 258.

cash flow method.[194] The same method must be used for all properties and for all succeeding valuations.[195]

If an insurance business owns more than a 50% ownership interest in a real estate company that is not listed on a securities exchange, the interest is credited at per share net asset value (NAV). The real properties held therein, to the extent that they can be credited pursuant to para. III.F.a.aa.[196] [of the circular letter], are to be valued like a direct investment, taking into account any liabilities.[197]

The plausibility of the valuations of all properties is to be tested individually by a professional real estate appraiser, on a staggered basis, during a cycle of 10 years in order to verify the near market value of the properties reported in the insurer's financial statements. The testing concept is to be included in the insurer's investment regulation.[198] Circular Letter 2008/18 also specifies the documentation an insurer is required to maintain in its file for each property in its portfolio.[199]

7. Mortgage loans

A insurer is allowed under SR Art. 79, para. g. to invest in loans secured by real property located in Switzerland, but loans secured by real properties of the types ineligible for real estate investments in restricted assets are also not eligible as security for loans in this category.[200] An insurer may not credit mortgage loans to restricted assets in an aggregate amount greater than 25% of the required amount[201] and an individual loan may not exceed 5% of the required amount.[202] The creditable amount is further limited by the ratio of a loan's principal amount to the market value of the property securing the loan – the loan-to-value ratio (LTVR). The LTVR limit for residential or commercial buildings is 66⅔%,[203] but 80% for residential buildings if the debtor is making payments or providing additional collateral to reduce the loan exposure below

194 Circular Letter 2008/18, margin para. 260. The FINMA explains the two valuation methods in detail in Annex 1 to Circular Letter 2008/18.

195 Circular Letter 2008/18, margin para. 261.

196 Circular Letter 2008/18, margin paras. 230-232.

197 Circular Letter 2008/18, margin para. 263.

198 Circular Letter 2008/18, margin para. 266.

199 *See* Circular Letter 2008/18, margin paras. 270-280.

200 Circular Letter 2008/18, margin para. 284. *See also* the excluded categories of real property in the text accompanying notes 183, 184 and 185. Loans secured by property with joint owners are, as an exception, permitted in this investment category.

201 Circular Letter 2008/18, margin para. 286.

202 Circular Letter 2008/18, margin para. 287.

203 Circular Letter 2008/18, margin para. 291.

66⅔%.[204] Other limits apply for properties with partially permitted uses.[205] An LTVR of 100% is possible for loans additionally secured by policies with a redemption value "that cannot suffer negative fluctuations in value."[206] The insurance business may not be subordinated to any other creditor of the borrower. Credit may be given if other creditors rank equally with the lending insurer only if the LTVR calculated on the basis of all of the secured obligations does not exceed the relevant LTVR limit.[207]

The market value of the encumbered property is to be estimated by the income capitalization method, the discounted cash flow method, hedonistic methods or 'practitioner' methods,[208] in each case by an internal or external, professionally qualified real estate appraiser.[209] If the borrower is in payment default for more than seven months, an "appropriate adjustment" in the value of the loan is to be made.[210] If the borrower is in default for more than 12 months, then the loan may not be credited to restricted assets.[211]

An insurance business is required to verify the valuation of the encumbered real properties using one of the appraisal methods specified in III.G.d.cc. of Circular Letter 2008/18.[212] The circular letter also specifies documentation requirements for the file an insurer is required to maintain in respect of each loan and the property securing it.[213]

204 Circular Letter 2008/18, margin para. 292.

205 Circular Letter 2008/18, margin para. 293.

206 Circular Letter 2008/18, margin para. 294.

207 Circular Letter 2008/18, margin para. 295.

208 Circular Letter 2008/18, margin para. 297.

209 Circular Letter 2008/18, margin para. 298.

210 Circular Letter 2008/18, margin para. 300.

211 Circular Letter 2008/18, margin para. 301.

212 Circular Letter 2008/18, margin para. 302. *See* note 208 and the accompanying text for a description of the generally applicable appraisal methods.

213 Circular Letter 2008/18, margin para. 304.

8. Alternative investments

Investments in alternative investments[214] are authorized by SR Art. 79, para. 1, h. The FINMA acknowledges the potential benefits of investing in this asset category: it "should give insurance businesses the opportunity to diversify the investment portfolio more broadly through alternative investments and to achieve an optimization of stable returns,"[215] but it also imposes numerous prerequisites on an insurer wanting to invest in the category. Briefly summarized:

- an insurance business must fulfill organizational, know-how and investment process requirements, i.e., it must have specially qualified staff,[216] "have a well-documented investment process tailored to investments in alternative investments," anchor alternative investments in the investment strategy of the entire business and properly incorporate them in its asset allocation, have a quantitative analysis system and a due diligence procedure "so that the selection as well as the ongoing monitoring of the investments is performed in accordance with high quality standards" and have a separation of staff between the investment process and risk management. (Circular Letter 2008/18, para. III.H.c.aa.);

- risk management must continuously monitor alternative investments (Circular Letter 2008/18, para. III.H.c.bb.);

- an insurance business must have "a due diligence process that guarantees a comprehensive and in-depth analysis of the management, strategy, structure, performance and terms and conditions of the fund." (Circular Letter 2008/18, para. III.H.c.cc.);

- an insurance business must "investigate legal risks in depth." (Circular Letter 2008/18, para. III.H.c.dd.).

---

214 "Based on current knowledge, the following investments are allocated to this category:
   a. Hedge funds;
   b. Private equity funds;
   c. Currency-overlays;
   d. Commodity indexes and baskets;
   e. Structured products, which are linked to an alternative investment and, under the provisions of para. III.C.a., must be classified as alternative investments.
   f. Collective capital investments which invest in traditional investments with increased risk or in alternative investments (e.g., Arts. 68 ff. of the Collective Investments Law "other funds for traditional investments" and "other funds for alternative investments.")

   Circular Letter 2008/18, margin para. 309.

215 Circular Letter 2008/18, margin para. 323.

216 Circular Letter 2008/18, margin para. 328.

"If an insurance business cannot fulfill all of the special requirements that are mentioned in this section,[217] then it may only invest in funds-of-funds. An insurance business will, however, not be excused from the obligation to implement the processes mentioned in paras. III.H.c.aa. through III.H.c.dd, but individual steps may be omitted if these are already performed in sufficient detail by the fund-of-funds manager. The due diligence relates to the fund-of-funds and must be carried out in full."[218]

In addition, alternative investments may be credited to restricted assets only if the portfolio of alternative investments "as a whole is appropriately diversified",[219] an exit from the investment (excluding private equity investments) is possible within a period of not more than 24 months,[220] the highest possible loss is limited to the amount invested and investment commitments are limited to a specific amount[221] and payments-in-kind received upon the termination of an investment are made only in assets that may be credited to restricted assets.[222] "Investments based on indexes and baskets are permitted to the extent the investment is broadly diversified and has high liquidity."[223] Indeed, such investments and investments in commodity funds "are only permitted for the purpose of further diversifying the entire portfolio of alternative investments."[224] "Currency-overlays may not include any short sales."[225] Direct investments in alternative investments, such as a private equity investment in a business "generally may not be included."[226]

Alternative investments may not comprise more than 10% of the required amount of restricted assets. The credited value for a single fund may not exceed 1% and for a fund-of-fund may not exceed 5% of the required amount. Nevertheless, an insurance business must set internal limits "so that a risk diversification through sufficient funds / managers will be achieved." Alternative investments may be credited to restricted assets at not more than market value.[227] The quality of valuations received for private equity investments must be verified[228] and the value of hedge fund investments is based on the market

217 The "Special requirements" section, Circular Letter 2008/18 section III.H.c., margin paras. 323-341.

218 Circular Letter 2008/18, margin para. 342.

219 Circular Letter 2008/18, margin para. 316.

220 Circular Letter 2008/18, margin para. 318.

221 Circular Letter 2008/18, margin para. 319.

222 Circular Letter 2008/18, margin para. 320.

223 Circular Letter 2008/18, margin para. 321.

224 Circular Letter 2008/18, margin para. 317.

225 Circular Letter 2008/18, margin para. 322.

226 Circular Letter 2008/18, margin para. 312.

227 SR Art. 93, para. 1; Circular Letter 2008/18, margin para. 360.

228 Circular Letter 2008/18, margin para. 362.

value of the fund's assets. An insurance business must receive NAV reports at least monthly.[229]

9. Derivative financial instruments

a. Generally

The SR recognizes three permitted uses for derivatives by an insurance business: reducing risks related to capital investments or liabilities to insureds and the efficient management of capital investments[230] and it requires that all liabilities resulting from the use of derivatives be "covered,"[231] i.e., with cash or cash equivalents equal to the amount of the potential liability for derivatives with purchase or payment obligations or by holding the underlying asset for derivatives with delivery obligations.[232]

Insurance businesses which use derivative financial instruments are required to adopt an investment strategy for their use.[233] The investment strategy is to set the parameters for the use of derivatives by the insurance business, including the methodology for risk analysis and risk exposure limits.[234] The risk analysis must be performed as often as necessary, but at least once each week for market risks and once each month for credit risks.[235] The results of this risk analysis are to be reported to the executive board "as often as the situation requires," but at least once each month for market risks and once every three months for credit risks.[236]

As with investments in alternative investments, insurers that use derivatives must have a suitable organizational structure[237] and system of management (including detailed instructions to the persons managing transactions in derivatives) and control (with the control function performed by independent persons independent from transaction management).[238] The persons performing transaction management and the control function must "have the special knowledge

229 Circular Letter 2008/18, margin para. 361.

230 SR Art. 100, para. 1.

231 SR Art. 100, para. 2.

232 Circular Letter 2008/18, margin para. 369.

233 SR Art. 101. The investment strategy is to be prepared by the executive board and approved by the board of directors. It must also "comply with the usual principles for capital investments, in particular those in respect of security, liquidity, return, diversification and allocation." SR Art. 102, para. 2.

234 SR Art. 102, para. 1. "Risk exposure limits are to be set in a manner commensurate with the financial and organizational capabilities of the insurance business." SR Art. 103.

235 SR Art. 104, para. 2.

236 SR Art. 104, para. 4.

237 SR Art. 105.

238 SR Art. 106.

required and qualifications necessary for the task."[239] The executive board is responsible for ensuring that the investment strategy and derivative instruments used are in conformity with the FINMA's principles in Circular Letter 2008/18.[240] An activity report on the use of derivative financial instruments must be submitted to the board of directors of the insurance business every six months[241] and a report on transactions in derivative financial instruments is to be submitted to the FINMA once each year.[242]

b. Derivatives for the hedging of asset portfolios within restricted assets

The Supervisory Regulation permits the use of derivatives within restricted assets which serve hedging purposes, have no leverage effect[243] on restricted assets, for which the underlying is in restricted assets[244] and for which credit for them is adjusted in response to market fluctuations.[245] Instruments which serve to finance a hedge, but which do not actually provide a hedge, may not be allocated to the derivatives category in restricted assets.[246] Derivatives based on indexes may be allocated to restricted assets if the index closely conforms to the portfolio being hedged.[247] There are no limits on the hedging of asset portfolios.[248]

c. Derivatives within restricted assets in preparation for an acquisition, for increasing revenue, and for hedging cash flows from insurance technical obligations

The SR provides that under "certain conditions and to a certain degree [specified by the FINMA], derivative instruments can also be allocated to restricted assets for purposes of preparing for an acquisition, increasing revenue and hedging cash flows from insurance technical obligations."[249]

Acquisition preparation. The FINMA specifically permits two forms of transactions in preparation for an acquisition:

239 SR Art. 107. Circular Letter 2008/18, margin para. 391.

240 Circular Letter 2008/18, margin para. 384.

241 SR Art. 108.

242 SR Art. 109.

243 *See also* Circular Letter 2008/18, margin para. 399.

244 The underlying assets must be permitted assets in restricted assets. Circular Letter 2008/18, margin para. 398.

245 SR Art. 79, para. 1, i; Circular Letter 2008/18, margin paras. 397-399. The requirements for hedging transactions are reiterated and elaborated in margin paras. 404-416.

246 Circular Letter 2008/18, margin para. 412.

247 Circular Letter 2008/18, margin para. 413.

248 Circular Letter 2008/18, margin para. 473.

249 SR Art. 79, para. 2.

- the use of long call options or short put options to potentially acquire assets, provided that the liability for the payment of the purchase price upon the exercise of the option is covered by liquidity or cash equivalents;[250] and

- a synthetic strategy using long futures, long forwards and swaps,[251] provided that the derivative is acquired to replicate the underlying assets,[252] the "combination between the derivative and liquidity has a similar market risk profile and at least the same liquidity as the replicated investment,"[253] the liquidity coverage obligation is met[254] and the transaction does cost more than the acquisition of the direct investment.[255]

Increasing income. "The strategy of increasing income aims to generate additional income from existing assets, whether through tactical implementation of the investment strategy on the basis of market opportunities or market risk or through premium income from writing options."[256] Here, the FINMA allows the use of call and put options[257] and credit default swaps on both individual securities and securities indexes if the insurer is the protection buyer and the credit default swap does not qualify as hedging,[258] provided that the "incurred contract volume is covered at all times" by the underlying asset or liquidity, as applicable.[259]

"The open derivative financial instruments for purposes of preparing for acquisitions and for purposes of increasing income are limited to 10% of the required amount of restricted assets.[260] The limit is to be met at all times."[261] "The limit of 10% refers to the open contract volumes or the nominal values of the underlyings. The amount of the contract volumes results from the multiplication of the market value of the underlying asset, the number of contracts and

250 Circular Letter 2008/18, margin paras. 447-448.

251 Circular Letter 2008/18, margin para. 454.

252 Circular Letter 2008/18, margin para. 451.

253 Circular Letter 2008/18, margin para. 450.

254 Circular Letter 2008/18, margin para. 452.

255 Circular Letter 2008/18, margin para. 453.

256 Circular Letter 2008/18, margin para. 459.

257 Circular Letter 2008/18, margin para. 460.

258 Circular Letter 2008/18, margin paras. 461 and 462.

259 Circular Letter 2008/18, margin para. 459. *See also, id.*, margin paras. 368-380.

260 Circular Letter 2008/18, margin para. 475. "Excluded from this limit are derivatives used for the replication of a strategy (para. III.I.b.ee.bbb.), synthetic bonds (para. III.I.b.dd.aaa.) and the sale of call options (para. III.I.b.ff.) if all of the conditions in the relevant paragraph have been fulfilled." *Id.*

261 *Id.*

the multiplier. In taking into account the value of options, a delta adjustment can be performed."[262]

Hedging cash flows from insurance technical obligations. The FINMA permits the hedging of long-term cash flows from insurance technical obligations through synthetic bonds[263] and options or swaptions,[264] provided that a hedge of insurance technical liabilities is achieved,[265] it is probable that the instruments can be held to maturity,[266] the FINMA is informed about the transaction by submitting the documentation to it[267] and the use of these instruments is focused on stable returns and not for the purpose of terminating them in order to realize a gain.[268]

"The premiums of the open derivative instruments for the hedging of cash flows from insurance technical obligations . . . are limited to 5% of the required amount of restricted assets. The limit is to be met at all times. The open positions in swaption and similar options are to be valued at amortized cost . . . ."[269]

d. Valuation

"Derivative financial instruments generally may be included in restricted assets at not more than market value or securities exchange value. Specifically, this means that the replacement value is considered market value. The replacement value is the price at which an open derivative position could be closed (terminated). Restricted assets must, therefore, be credited with the positive or negative replacement value . . . ."[270] In the absence of market prices, valuation models are to be used. "The FINMA accepts generally recognized methods of financial mathematics for the valuation of unlisted instruments."[271] "Swaptions and similar instruments for the hedging of insurance technical liabilities are included under the cost amortization method . . . ."[272] Derivatives used for the replication strategy described in the text accompanying notes 251-255 (Circu-

262 Circular Letter 2008/18, margin para. 476.
263 Circular Letter 2008/18, margin para. 438.
264 Circular Letter 2008/18, margin para. 440.
265 Circular Letter 2008/18, margin para. 442.
266 Circular Letter 2008/18, margin para. 443.
267 Circular Letter 2008/18, margin para. 444.
268 Circular Letter 2008/18, margin para. 445.
269 Circular Letter 2008/18, margin para. 474.
270 Circular Letter 2008/18, margin para. 481. *See also* SR Art. 91, para. 1.
271 Circular Letter 2008/18, margin para. 482.
272 Circular Letter 2008/18, margin para. 485.

lar Letter 2008/18, margin paras. 449-458) are "valued according to the categories to which they have been allocated."[273]

d. Netting

Consistent with the prohibition on offsetting payment obligations against restricted assets, close-out netting under a master agreement for derivatives transactions is permitted only if the master agreement applies to an individual restricted asset. In all master agreements relating to a restricted asset, "it must be expressly provided that the counterparty waives the right to offset payment claims which are outside the scope of the [master agreement]. This waiver is to be expressly declared binding in the event of the insolvency of the insurance business."[274] Master agreements may only be entered into if a legal opinion has confirmed that the netting provision is enforceable under the law applicable to the transaction and the netting agreement and only with a counterparty domiciled in a jurisdiction for which there is a legal opinion confirming the enforceability of the netting agreement in the counterparty's country (including Switzerland).[275] Obligations to deliver collateral must be mutual and included in the netting process, including in bankruptcy proceedings for either party.[276] The foregoing requirements do not apply if the insurance business trades derivatives only on a regulated securities exchange.[277]

If the 1992 Master Agreement of the International Swaps and Derivatives Association is used, the 'second method' must be used[278] and automatic termination is to be elected in respect of a Swiss party.[279]

10. Collective capital investments and single-investor funds

a. Collective capital investments

An insurance business may credit a collective capital investment to restricted assets if the fund is subject to effective supervision for the protection of investors and ownership interests in the fund are either traded on a regulated, liquid market or they can be sold at any time.[280] The fund's investment strategy must

---

273 Circular Letter 2008/18, margin para. 486.

274 Circular Letter 2008/18, margin para. 495.

275 Circular Letter 2008/18, margin para. 500. *See* margin paras. 501-505 for the requirements for the netting opinion.

276 Circular Letter 2008/18, margin para. 506. *See* margin paras. 508-513 for additional requirements in respect of the provision of collateral.

277 Circular Letter 2008/18, margin para. 514.

278 Circular Letter 2008/18, margin para. 496.

279 Circular Letter 2008/18, margin para. 497.

280 SR Art. 82, para. 1.

be consistent with the FINMA's requirements for safety, return, diversification and liquidity.[281] If the fund is domiciled outside Switzerland, its share or ownership certificate "must have the character of a security [(*Wertpapier)*]."[282]

b. Single-investor funds

The FINMA views an investment by an insurance business in a single-investor fund as a partial outsourcing[283] of the insurer's investment operation. Ownership interests in a single-investor fund may be credited to restricted assets if the FINMA's general requirements on outsourcing are fulfilled,[284] all of the ownership interests of the fund will be held by the insurance business, the fund is subject to effective supervision, the fund's investments are eligible investments for restricted assets, the insurance business has the right to take possession of the fund's individual investments at any time and any third-party custodian of the fund's assets is liable to the insurance business in Switzerland for the fulfillment of its obligations as custodian.[285] The fund's constitutive documents, i.e., "articles of incorporation of the fund management company, the investment regulation, the collective investment agreement," must be notified to the FINMA before the fund is formed and any amendments to these documents must be notified to the FINMA before they become effective.[286] The collective investment agreement governing the single-investor fund must be terminable at any time.[287]

c. Valuation and allocation

Investments in collective capital investments are valued at not more than market value (or if the fund's shares are not listed on a securities exchange, net asset value). The fund's investments must be allocated to the various categories of restricted assets on an aggregate basis in accordance with the invest-

281 Circular Letter 2008/18, margin para. 527.

282 Circular Letter 2008/18, margin para. 528. *See* the text accompanying note 136 and Circular Letter 2008/18, margin paras. 134-136 for the FINMA's explanation of the need for a security.

283 "The outsourcing of portions of restricted assets in single-investor funds is, under Art. 4, para. 2, provision j ISL, an outsourcing of a significant function of an insurance business and therefore an amendment of the business plan which must be notified to the FINMA." Circular Letter 2008/18, margin para. 539. The requirements for the notice to the FINMA are specified in margin paras. 540-549.

284 Circular Letter 2008/18, margin para. 531. *See also supra* note 19.

285 Circular Letter 2008/18, margin paras. 529-530. The custodian must be located in Switzerland, Belgium or Luxembourg. *See* margin paras. 538 and 133. The custody arrangements must be made on the basis of a prescribed form of agreement. *See* margin para. 538 and Annex No. 4 to the circular letter.

286 Circular Letter 2008/18, margin para. 535.

287 Circular Letter 2008/18, margin para. 533.

ment classes identified in SR Art. 79 (e.g., cash, debt instruments, equities, etc.).[288] An investment in a single-investor fund is allocated to the categories of restricted assets on a security-by-security basis and each security is to be valued in accordance for the rules for that category.[289]

11. Securities lending

Securities lending is permitted pursuant to a master agreement that meets specified criteria[290] with a counterparty with "recognized and first-class credit worthiness."[291] An insurance business "must remain the economic beneficiary" of the securities it loans and retain the right to receive interest or dividend payments paid on the securities during the term of the loan.[292] An insurance business must be able to require the redelivery of the loaned securities at all times and the redelivery obligation must be secured by a pledge of securities or a cash deposit with an intermediary.[293] This collateral must be held in a separate custody account maintained in the name of the insurer or pledged to it.[294] The value of the collateral must equal at least 105% of the market value of the loaned securities (102% if the securities loaned are denominated in Swiss francs and have a credit rating of at least 'A', but the collateral must be either a cash deposit of Swiss francs or bonds denominated in Swiss francs with a 'AAA' credit rating).[295] The collateral must be eligible for inclusion in restricted assets, be capable of daily valuation or trading and be rated at least 'BBB'. Securities issued by a counterparty to a securities lending transaction may not be used as collateral.[296]

"A maximum of 30% of the coverage value of the required amount of a restricted asset may be loaned. Loaned underlyings also must be taken into account in complying with the prescribed investment limits and be credited accordingly."[297]

The notice period for the termination of the securities lending agreement may not exceed 10 banking days.[298] Borrowed securities may not be credited to

---

288 Circular Letter 2008/18, margin paras. 560-561.

289 Circular Letter 2008/18, margin paras. 562-563.

290 These criteria are specified in Circular Letter 2008/18, margin paras. 574-578.

291 Circular Letter 2008/18, margin paras. 565-567.

292 Circular Letter 2008/18, margin para. 568.

293 Circular Letter 2008/18, margin para. 569.

294 Circular Letter 2008/18, margin para. 580.

295 Circular Letter 2008/18, margin para. 582.

296 Circular Letter 2008/18, margin para. 583.

297 Circular Letter 2008/18, margin para. 587.

298 Circular Letter 2008/18, margin para. 568 and 571.

restricted assets or used in derivatives transactions.[299] Collateral provided in favor of an insurance business lending securities is to be credited to restricted assets, but not counted in determining the coverage of the required amount because the securities are allocated to securities lending and the loaned securities are credited toward coverage of the required amount.[300]

12. Securities repurchase transactions

Assets allocated to restricted assets may not be used for securities repurchase transactions nor may securities received through such transactions be credited to restricted assets.[301]

13. Intra-group investments and loans

Investments in, and loans to, other member entities of a supervised insurance business's corporate group are generally considered unsuitable for inclusion in restricted assets, but an investment in an investment company or real estate company may be included in restricted assets, as well as a loan to such companies if the borrower has not made any loans to other group companies.[302]

G. The Internal Audit Function and the External Auditors

The ISL requires an insurance business to "appoint an internal audit function (Inspektorat) which is independent from management."[303] The internal audit function must "issue a report of its activities at least once each year and deliver it to the external auditors."[304] The FINMA describes the internal audit function as "an instrument of control of the board of directors. It conducts independent and risk-oriented examinations of the processes and structures of an insurance business, an insurance group or conglomerate. It supports the organization in achieving its goals by analyzing and evaluating the effectiveness of risk management, the internal control system, as well as the management

299 Circular Letter 2008/18, margin para. 573.

300 Circular Letter 2008/18, margin paras. 586, 588-589.

301 Circular Letter 2008/18, margin paras. 593-595.

302 Circular Letter 2008/18, margin paras. 601-613.

303 ISL Art. 27, para. 1. "The FINMA can exempt an insurance business from the requirement to appoint an internal audit function in individual cases when good cause is shown." ISL Art. 27, para. 2. The internal audit function is to be "organizationally independent from operational business activities. It shall operate independently from daily business activities. It shall have unlimited inspection and audit rights within the insurance business. All information is to be provided to it that is necessary for the performance of its audit duties." Circular Letter 2008/35 Internal Audit of Insurers, margin para. 15.

304 ISL Art. 27, para. 3. "The internal audit function shall promptly issue a proper written report on all of the important findings of an audit to the board of directors or, if applicable, the audit committee." Circular Letter 2008/35, margin para. 18.

and monitoring processes with systematic and goal-oriented methods and by issuing a report thereon."[305] "The performance of the internal audit function cannot be combined with that of the responsible actuary."[306] The FINMA may excuse an insurance business from the obligation to establish an internal audit function if the insurance business does not have a complex risk structure, for example, it has no significant operational risks, market and credit risks (including group internal transactions), and no significant insurance risks.[307]

The head of the internal audit function is to be appointed by the board of directors and is to report directly to it.[308] The FINMA recommends that an insurance business adopt an audit regulation or charter defining the scope, responsibility and authority of the internal audit function.[309] "The internal audit function shall be knowledgeable[310] and staffed with sufficient personnel. The audits are to be performed with the necessary professional care."[311]

The FINMA recommends that the members of the board or directors or, if applicable, the audit committee discuss the reports from the internal audit function. "Processes should be established that ensure that the recommendations made in a report are addressed and any necessary measures are adopted within a reasonable period of time."[312] It also recommends that a "quality review" of the internal audit function be performed "by an independent, professionally qualified organization at regular intervals, but at least once every five years. This reviewing audit firm can be, for example, an audit firm authorized for insurance audits, the internal audit function of another insurance business or an organization to be designated by the Swiss Institute of Internal Auditing."[313]

"The responsibilities of the internal audit function or parts thereof may, subject to the approval of the FINMA, be outsourced" to the internal audit function of the highest group company, to the extent that the supervised insurance business is included in the group-wide control and management processes or ei-

---

305 Circular Letter 2008/35, margin para. 7.

306 Circular Letter 2008/35, margin para. 16.

307 Circular Letter 2008/35, margin para. 23.

308 Circular Letter 2008/35, margin para. 10.

309 Circular Letter 2008/35, margin para. 14.

310 Among other things, the members of the internal audit function must, as a group, "possess fundamental knowledge, in particular about the business of insurance, insurance audits, corporate governance, risk management and internal control systems" and have "comprehensive knowledge of auditing principles, procedures and techniques, as well as accounting principles and procedures in the area of insurance." Circular Letter 2008/35, margin para. 17.

311 *Id.*

312 Circular Letter 2008/35, margin para. 13.

313 Circular Letter 2008/35, margin para. 21.

ther an audit firm recognized by the FINMA or an external service provider which is independent from the insurance business's audit firm.[314]

An insurance business also "must appoint a licensed audit firm to review its conduct of its business,"[315] to determine "whether the annual financial statements conform, in respect of form and content, to statutory requirements, the articles of incorporation and by-laws,"[316] and to "examine annually whether the insurance group has complied with the obligations [under the Supervisory Regulation] and has implemented the risk management procedures" it is required to adopt under SR Art. 196. The audit firm also must prepare and deliver a report to the FINMA.[317] If the audit firm notes any criminal acts, serious irregularities, "violations of the principle of irreproachable conduct of business" or circumstances that may endanger the solvency of the insurance business or the interests its insureds, it must report these to the FINMA "without delay."[318]

"The internal audit function shall issue at least once each year a complete report on its audit activities for delivery to the board of directors (or, if applicable, the audit committee). The report is thereafter to be delivered to the audit firm; vice versa, the audit firm shall deliver its audit report to internal audit."[319] The audit firm and the internal audit function are required to coordinate their activities.[320]

H. Corporate Governance; Risk Management and Internal Control

1. Corporate governance

The FINMA, in reliance on the ISL's 'fit and proper persons' provision and its requirement that an insurance business be "organized in a manner that, in particular, permits it to recognize, limit and monitor all significant risk," has specified minimum standards for corporate governance in Circular Letter 2008/32 Corporate Governance of Insurers. The corporate governance system for a supervised insurance business generally must (1) clearly document "existing corporate governance structures and reporting processes, e.g., in the articles of incorporation, organizational regulation (*Organizationsreglement*[321])" and rules governing board and management committees, (2) ensure regulatory compliance, (3) provide guidelines and instructions which require ethical be-

314 Circular Letter 2008/35, margin para. 22.

315 ISL Art. 28, para. 1.

316 ISL Art. 29, para. 1.

317 SR 203, para. 1.

318 ISL Art. 30.

319 Circular Letter 2008/35, margin para. 20.

320 *Id.*

321 The functional equivalent of corporate by-laws.

havior by its employees, (4) establish appropriate compensation and incentive systems which serve the long-term interests and the long-term fulfillment of the goals of the business and promote ethical behavior, (5) comply with principles for the avoidance of conflicts of interest and misconduct, (6) create a compliance function, to the extent this is appropriate to the size and scale of the businesses, (7) provide for the training of employees in corporate governance matters, (8) ensure the independence of the internal audit function and (9) create "an appropriate environment" in which the responsible actuary can perform his or her duties.[322]

a *Board of directors*

The board of directors is "responsible for the ultimate management, organization and supervision of the Business (Art. 716a, para. 1 CO,[323] *see also* Arts. 894 ff. CO[324]) and must be constituted so that, as a whole, it can fulfill these obligations." The board of directors must:

- collectively have the necessary strategic insurance knowledge, in addition to general professional knowledge, needed to fulfill its responsibility for the supervision and ultimate management of the business; and
- "be able to provide assurance that business will be conducted in an irreproachable manner, in that they possess appropriate professional knowledge . . . and appropriate experience (fitness) and a good reputation (properness) (Art. 14 and 67 ISL)."

Members of the board of directors must avoid conflicts of interest to the fullest extent possible. The president of the of the board of directors may not also be the president of the executive board. Depending on the size and complexity of the insurance business, the board of directors shall appoint committees of the board of directors for the purpose of improved management and monitoring (e.g., an audit committee, a nominating committee, or compensation commit-

---

322 Circular Letter 2008/32 Corporate Governance of Insurers, margin para. 9.

323 This article of the Code Of Obligations lists the "non-delegable and non-removable" responsibilities of the board of directors: (1) the ultimate management of the corporation, (2) establishing the organization, (3) establishing accounting and financial control functions and financial planning "to the extent necessary for the management of the corporation," (4) the appointment and removal of management and persons entrusted with the representation of the corporation, (5) the ultimate supervision of management, specifically in respect of compliance with laws, the articles of incorporation and by-laws and instructions from the board of directors, (6) preparation of the annual report, the meetings of shareholders and the implementation of the resolutions of the shareholders, (7) the notification of the judge if the corporation becomes over-indebted.

324 The administration (*Verwaltung*) of a mutual company consists of at least three persons, a majority of whom must be members (*Genossenschafter*) of the mutual company.

tee). Finally, the board of directors is required to "adopt measures so that the principles of [Circular Letter 2008/32] are implemented."[325]

b. *Executive Board*

Like the members of the board of directors, the members of the executive board of an insurance business "must be able to provide assurance that business will be conducted in an irreproachable manner, in that they possess appropriate professional knowledge and appropriate experience (fitness) and a good reputation (properness)." They also must "have the necessary knowledge and appropriate experience for the management of the areas under their control" and "arrange their personal and business relationships so that conflicts of interest" are avoided to the fullest extent possible. The executive board must notify the FINMA without delay "about all developments that are relevant for supervision."[326]

2. *Risk management and internal control*

An insurance business is required to ensure through "risk management appropriate to the characteristics of its business and through internal control mechanisms" that it is able to promptly recognize potential risks and implement measures to guard against significant risks and aggregations of risk.[327] In the SR, the Federal Council listed five necessary elements of a risk management system: (1) "the selection and regular review by management of strategies and measures for all assumed risks," (2) a hedging policy which addresses "the consequences of the business strategy," (3) appropriate procedures for risk monitoring throughout the business, (4) identifying all significant risks and monitoring and measuring them and (5) an "internal reporting system for the determination, evaluation and control of risks and risk concentrations."[328] The required risk management system is to be documented and updated continuously.[329]

---

325 Circular Letter 2008/32, margin para. 10.

326 Circular Letter 2008/32, margin para. 11, relying on FINMAG Art. 29, para. 2. *In respect of notifications, see also* Circular Letter 2008/25 Reporting Obligations of Insurers.

327 SR Art. 96, margin para. 1; *see also* Circular Letter 2008/32, margin para. 12.

328 SR Art. 96, margin para. 2. The FINMA requires that the internal risk reporting "reflect the actual risk situation and risk concentration, including a statement of the methods, instruments and procedures that have led to these assessments," be provided in a timely manner to the relevant decision makers and "include statements on the effectiveness and the weaknesses of risk management and the internal control system." Circular Letter 2008/32, margin para. 37.

329 SR Art. 97, margin para. 1; *see also* Circular Letter 2008/32, margin paras. 13 and 15. The FINMA requires that the documentation specifies the (1) "organization, including tasks, authorities and responsibilities," (2) requirements for risk management and the internal control system. (3) risk strategy, including risk tolerance, (4) procedures for the identification of

The FINMA further requires that an insurance business "define the scope and suitability of [its] internal structures and processes, as well as the business-internal organization, responsibility and allocation of responsibilities between risk management and the internal control system."[330] Among the appropriate risk management and control measures, the FINMA identifies "guidelines and controls for underwriting, investments, reinsurance, insurance technical reserving, claims management, among others,"[331] which "should take into account the current state of the art, in particular in respect of economic and actuarial methods."[332] Operating and control activities are to be separated appropriately to prevent conflicts of interest.[333] "The goals of risk management and the internal control system are to be communicated business-internally on a timely basis to the proper recipients" and "information is to be given to the relevant decision-makers. Information and escalation procedures are to be defined."[334] Finally, the FINMA requires an insurance business to evaluate "the existence and functioning of the elements of the risk management and the internal control system and . . . improvements in quality over time."[335]

3. Swiss Quality Assessment

In December 2007, the FOPI announced two new "Swiss Quality Assessment" (SQA) instruments or "tools" which are intended to further the implementation of the obligation to establish a risk management function and system of internal control and the requirement that "those who are responsible for the ultimate management, supervision and control as well as those responsible for the conduct of business under Art. 14 ISL must be able to offer the assurance of irreproachable business activities."[336]

The SQA instruments, issued in the form of questionnaires, seek information about an insurer's corporate governance policies and risk management and internal control system in order to determine whether:

---

significant risks, as well as a statement of the methods, instruments and processes for their identification, measurement and monitoring, (5) the applicable system of limits for risk exposures, as well as the control mechanism and (6) business-internal guidelines for risk management, the internal control system and the related procedures. Circular Letter 2008/32, margin para. 36.

330 Circular Letter 2008/32, margin para. 14.

331 Circular Letter 2008/32, margin para. 26.

332 Circular Letter 2008/32, margin para. 31.

333 Circular Letter 2008/32, margin para. 32.

334 Circular Letter 2008/32, margin paras. 31 and 32.

335 Circular Letter 2008/32, margin para. 39.

336 Swiss Quality Assessment (SQA) - Informationen zu den Tools betreffend Corporate Governance (CG) und Risikomanagement/Internes Kontrollsystem (RM/IKS) [Swiss Quality Assessment (SQA) - Information about the Tools concerning Corporate Governance (CG) and Risk Management/Internal Control System (RM/ICS) [hereinafter SQA Information Notice], pp. 1-2.

(1) the insurer has documentation in each of these areas and what documentation is available;

(2) whether the documented procedures in each of these areas are actually practiced; and

(3) whether the documentation and practices are, from the point of view of the insurer, appropriate to achieve the relevant objectives.

Insurers were required to complete and submit the two SQA tools for the first time by 31 March 2008. The FOPI stated that it would review the responses provided in the tools to determine whether they evidence an appropriately designed and implemented system of corporate governance and risk management and internal control. It also stated that it may follow up with conversations with the chairman of the board of directors, the CEO and chief risk officer, as well as any "other person in the company who, on the basis of his or her function or knowledge, can provide useful information." If this review reveals that additional measures need to be adopted, then the FOPI will engage in a "risk dialogue" with the company, before recommendations are made or other measures are required. FOPI's stated goal is to "cause the affected company to propose appropriate measures for improvement on its own initiative and to implement them under the supervision of the FOPI."[337]

The SQA instrument "Corporate Governance" must be completed by the parent company of an insurance group, as well as each insurance company in the group which is subject to supervision in Switzerland. The SQA instrument "Risk Management / Internal Control System," however, must be completed only at the group level, unless subsidiaries subject to supervision in Switzerland have different policies or practices.

Each of the SQA instruments concludes with a series of self-assessment questions about the quality and effectiveness of the insurer's corporate governance procedures and its risk management and internal control systems. Both the chairman of the board of directors and the head of the executive management must sign the SQA questionnaires.

In its 2008 Annual Report issued in March 2009, the FOPI stated that although it was:

> still too early to make any detailed statements about the results of the analysis of the submitted reports, what is already apparent is that two of the objectives of qualitative supervision have been achieved:

337 SQA Information Notice, p. 3.

- Firstly, the information obtained from the SQA lends itself to being integrated into the normal supervisory processes. This provides the supervisory officer with useful information for tailoring supervision to an individual company even more intensively.
- Secondly, it can be said in general that there has been a tangible increase in the significance attached to corporate governance, risk management and ICS by most companies, both big and small.

See, Federal Office for Private Insurance, Annual Report 2008, p. 5.

I. Reporting Requirements

Switzerland's laws and regulations for the supervision of the business of insurance require numerous notices and reports to be submitted to the FINMA. These notice and reporting requirements can be divided into three broad groups: reports required at regular intervals, such as annual financial and regulatory reports, reports and notices required following the occurrence of an event, such as an amendment of an insurer's business plan or a large insured loss and reporting by third parties, such as the insurer's audit firm or firms providing services to an insurer under outsourcing agreements. Prominent examples of these notice and reporting obligations are given below.

1. Event reporting to the FINMA

FINMAG Art. 29, para. 2 imposes a general obligation on "the supervised . . . to [report] to the FINMA any circumstances which have material importance for the supervision" and Circular Letter 2008/25 elaborates on this "self-reporting" obligation.[338] Many specific events, however, trigger reporting obligations and some of the significant ones are listed below.[339]

- "An insurance business with its domicile in Switzerland which intends to acquire an ownership interest in another business must report this to the FINMA when the ownership interest equals or exceeds 10, 20, 33 or 50

---

338 Circular Letter 2008/25 Reporting Obligations of Insurers, margin para. 7.This circular letter addresses, in particular, reporting on five categories of events: (1) events jeopardizing solvency, (2) the "[r]eduction of the ownership interest in another business below the thresholds of 10, 20, 33 or 50 percent of the capital or voting rights or a change in the ownership interest to such an extent that the business is no longer a subsidiary," (3) Criminal proceedings, as well as administrative law proceedings of a supervisory authority against an insurance business or members of its board of directors or its executive board, (4) closing a portfolio in the supplementary health insurance segment and (5) "[m]edia-relevant events." *Id.* Margin paras. 1-5.

339 Life insurance businesses have specific notice and reporting requirements. *See, e.g.*, SR Art. 147, paras. 3 and 4; Circular Letter 2008/40 Life Insurance, margin paras. 135 and 194.

percent of the capital or voting rights of the other business." ISL Art. 21, para. 1. *See also* Circular Letter 2008/25 Reporting Obligations of Insurers.

- Mergers, divestitures and changes in the legal form of insurance businesses require the FINMA's approval. ISL Art. 3, para. 2. These fundamental corporate changes can be recorded in the commercial register only after the FINMA's approval has been given. SR Art. 4, para. 3.

- The acquisition or the sale (including merger or liquidation) or the creation of a significant ownership interest, as defined in Circular Letter 2008/28, by a member company of an insurance group or conglomerate must be notified to the FINMA not later than the conclusion of the agreement governing the transaction ISL Art. 192, para. 2; Circular Letter 2008/28, margin para. 3; and a change in the composition of such a company's shareholders that meets certain thresholds must be notified to the FINMA without delay, but in any case these events must be notified to the FINMA before notice of the transaction is given to news media. Circular Letter 2008/28, margin paras. 14 and 24 and Circular Letter 2008/25, margin para. 16.

- Amendments to the business plan which relate to the elements of the business plan under ISL Article 4, paragraph 2, letters:

    - a, h, i, k and r are to be submitted to the FINMA for its approval before they are implemented. In addition, amendments of the business plan which result from mergers, divestitures and restructurings of insurance businesses are to be submitted for approval. ISL Art. 5, para. 1.

    - b, c, d, f, g, j, l, m, n and q "are to be notified to the FINMA within fourteen days from the occurrence of the relevant circumstances"[340] and they are deemed approved if the FINMA does not initiate a review of the submission within four weeks. ISL Art. 5, para. 2.

- The termination of the appointment of the responsible actuary or his or her resignation. ISL Art. 23, para. 3.

- Important group internal transactions must be reported to the FINMA within 14 days. SR Art. 194; Circular Letter 2008/29, margin para, 2 and 13. Transactions that are important are defined in Circular Letter 2008/29, *see* margin paras. 16-19.

- Changes in an insurer's risk management documentation must be reported to the FINMA within one month. SR Art. 196, para. 1.

---

340 SR Art. 5.

- A significant change in an insurer's risk situation triggers an obligation for the insurer to recalculate its target capital by approximation and to report it to the FINMA. SR Art. 51, para. 2.

- An insurance business shall report to the FINMA aggregated losses exceeding thresholds defined in Circular Letter 2008/44, margin paras. 184-188. Further, if an event occurs which could lead to "relevant losses," then an estimate of these losses is to be notified without delay. A new estimate of the risk-bearing capital is to be notified not later than two weeks after such losses become known. *Id.* Margin para. 183. In addition, "[t]he FINMA is to be notified pursuant to Art. 51, para. 2 SR without delay of significant changes in the risk situation of an insurance business. Significant changes in the risk situation exist at least if the [target capital] changes by 20% or more since the last calculation." *Id.* Margin para. 189.

- The "location of custody, the custodian and the manner of custody" of restricted assets and any change in respect thereof must be notified. SR Art. 87 and Circular Letter 2008/18 margin para. 129. Copies of the prescribed form of custody agreement also must be submitted. Circular Letter 2008/18 margin para. 129.

- If an insurance business exceeds the 5% counterparty limit imposed by Circular Letter 2008/18, this must be notified to the FINMA immediately for approval. Circular Letter 2008/18, margin para. 55.

- If an insurance business intends to invest in alternative investments, it must submit a concept to the FINMA in advance that shows how the special requirements for investing in alternative investments will be or have been met. Circular Letter 2008/18, margin para. 363.[341]

2. *Scheduled reporting to the FINMA*

Many reporting requirements must be met on a set schedule. Among these are the requirement to submit to the FINMA:

- an annual financial report as of 31 December of each year (ISL Art. 25, para. 1) and an annual regulatory report. ISL Art. 25, para. 2. Both of these reports must be delivered by 30 April of the following year, except that insurance businesses engaged only in reinsurance are required to submit their reports by 30 June of the following year. ISL Art. 25, para. 3. "Foreign insurance businesses shall deliver . . . a separate annual financial report in respect of their business in Switzerland, as well as a sepa-

---

341 For examples of other investment-related notification requirements see Circular Letter 2008/18, margin paras. 440, 444, 535 and 539.

rate regulatory report concerning the financial year then just ended." *Id*, para. 4.

- an annual report from the internal office that an insurance business is required to appoint "to control the available solvency margin." The report is prepared as of the end of the year and must be submitted within three months after the report date. SR Art. 40, para. 1. The solvency report for insurance groups and conglomerates must be submitted semi-annually within three months after the close of the relevant financial half-year. SR Arts. 202 and 204.

- an annual SST report on "the calculation of target capital and risk-bearing capital." SR Art. 53, para. 1. As from 2011, this report must be submitted by 30 April of each year. Circular Letter 2008/44, margin para. 157. The SST reports for insurance groups and conglomerates must be submitted semi-annually within three months after the close of the relevant financial half-year. SR Arts. 202 and 204.

- an annual restricted assets report showing "the required amount for each restricted asset, together with an inventory of the assets covering them." SR Art. 72, para. 1. This report must be submitted within three months after the close of the financial year. *Id.*

- an annual report on "transactions in derivative financial instruments." SR Art. 109. The report is due on 30 April of each year.[342]

- "a complete group [or conglomerate] structure chart in which all entities of the insurance group are shown," annually, within three months after the close of the financial year. SR Art. 192, para. 1; Art. 204.

- an annual report on all group or conglomerate internal transactions. SR Art. 194, para. 1; Art. 203, para. 2; Circular Letter 2008/29, margin para. 2. Circular Letter 2008/29 specifies the requirements for this report.

- the risk management documentation of an insurance group or conglomerate, annually, within three months after the close of the financial year. SR Art. 196, para. 1.

3. Reports to the FINMA by an insurer's audit firm

An insurer's audit firm is required to deliver a report:

342 See, *e.g.*, Wegleitung derivative Finanzinstrumente Berichtsjahr 2007 [Instructions Derivative Financial Instruments Reporting Year 2007] at <*www.finma.ch*>.

- "concerning its examinations[343] to the ultimate management body of the one . . . who is examined and to the FINMA" FINMAG Art. 27, para. 1. In addition, it is required to "notify the FINMA without delay in the event of serious violations of provisions of supervisory law or serious irregularities." FINMAG Art. 27, para. 3.
- to the FINMA on whether the insurance group has complied with its obligations under the SR and has implemented the risk management procedures it is required to document pursuant to SR Art. 196.

4. Other reporting obligations

Whoever intends to:

- "directly or indirectly acquire an ownership interest in an insurance business domiciled in Switzerland must report this to the FINMA when the ownership interest equals or exceeds 10, 20, 33 or 50 percent of the capital or voting rights of the insurance business." ISL 21, para.1.
- "reduce an ownership interest in an insurance business domiciled in Switzerland below the thresholds of 10, 20, 33 or 50 percent of the capital or to reduce the voting rights or to so alter the ownership interest that the insurance business is no longer a subsidiary must report this to the FINMA." ISL 21, para. 2.

J. Supervision of Insurance Groups and Conglomerates

1. When group or conglomerate supervision applies

The ISL authorizes the FINMA to supervise insurance groups[344] and insurance conglomerates[345] if the group or conglomerate either is actually managed

343 "The audit firm shall review whether the annual financial statements conform, in respect of form and content, to statutory requirements, the articles of incorporation and by-laws. In addition, it reviews, in accordance with the instructions of the FINMA, compliance with this law and its implementing regulations." ISL, Art. 29, para. 1. "The explanatory report of the audit firm is to be submitted once each year with the group [conglomerate] financial statements. The explanatory report of the audit firm consists of the detailed report on the audit results and the activity report of the internal auditors. Circular Letter 2008/31 Insurance Group Report, margin para. 11.

344 Two or more businesses constitute an insurance group if (a) at least one is an insurance business, (b) they are, as a whole, primarily engaged in the field of insurance and (c) they constitute an economic unit or otherwise, through influence or control, are connected to each other. ISL Art. 64.

345 Two or more businesses constitute an insurance conglomerate if (a) at least one is an insurance business, (b) at least one is a bank or a securities dealer of economic significance, (c) they are, as a whole, primarily engaged in the field of insurance and (d) they constitute an economic unit or otherwise, through influence or control, are connected to each other. ISL Art. 72.

(a) from Switzerland or (b) outside Switzerland, but is not subject to an equivalent group supervision.[346] Group or conglomerate supervision is supplementary to the supervision of individual insurance businesses in Switzerland.[347] If foreign supervisory authorities also exercise complete or partial supervision over an insurance group or insurance conglomerate, the ISL requires the FINMA to "consult with the foreign authorities concerning the responsibilities, methods and subject of the supervision, while preserving its own authority and taking into account any [group or conglomerate] supervision" and to consult with the businesses in the insurance group or conglomerate that have their domicile in Switzerland before rendering a decision on whether to assert group or conglomerate supervision.[348]

The ISL authorizes the FINMA to issue regulations on group or conglomerate internal transactions and group or conglomerate-wide risk concentrations[349] and it applies several of the supervisory instruments applicable to insurance businesses licensed and supervised in Switzerland to insurance groups and conglomerates. The persons who are responsible for the ultimate supervision, control and conduct of the business of the insurance group or conglomerate must:

- be able to provide the assurance that the business of the group or conglomerate will be conducted in an irreproachable manner;[350]
- have an audit firm;[351] and
- comply with the reporting obligations imposed by ISL Art. 47 for all of the businesses of the group or conglomerate.[352]

2. Group and conglomerate organizational structure

The SR requires insurance groups and conglomerates to have an "organizational structure[353] that is consistent with the business activities of the insurance

---

346 ISL Art. 65 in respect of an insurance group; ISL Art. 73 in respect of an insurance conglomerate. *See also* ISL Art. 2, para. 1 d.

347 ISL Art. 66 in respect of an insurance group; ISL Art. 74 in respect of an insurance conglomerate.

348 ISL Art. 65, para. 2 in respect of an insurance group; ISL Art. 73, para. 2 in respect of an insurance conglomerate.

349 For groups, ISL Art. 68.; for conglomerates, ISL Art. 76.

350 For groups, ISL Art. 67; for conglomerates, ISL Art. 75.

351 For groups, ISL Art. 70; for conglomerates, ISL Art. 78.

352 For groups, ISL Art. 71; for conglomerates, ISL Art. 79.

353 An insurance group or conglomerate is required to "submit an illustration of the organizational, control and management structure to the FINMA and any changes thereto within 14 days after they become effective." SR Art. 191, para. 2 and SR Art. 204. A complete group

group and appropriate to the risks;"[354] and, like an individually supervised insurance business, a properly designed and documented system of "risk management appropriate to the characteristics of its business."[355] An insurance group or conglomerate must submit its risk management documentation[356] and a report on risk concentrations[357] to the FINMA within three months after the close of its financial year. Significant amendments of the risk management documentation must be reported to the FINMA within one month.[358]

SR Art. 191, para. 2 and Art. 204 require insurance groups and conglomerates to submit descriptions of their organizational, control and management structure to the FINMA and any changes thereto within 14 days after they become effective. The group or conglomerate organization chart should depict the business segments or other separate business areas or the group or conglomerate and describe them.[359] The control structure chart is to show "the designated members of the board of directors who are responsible for the supervision of the internal control system as well as the audit activities of the internal audit function and the audit firm."[360] The management structure chart identifies the members of the board of directors and the "persons entrusted with management at the group management or conglomerate management level." Further, the "assigned areas, tasks and responsibilities [of these persons] are to be documented in the articles of incorporation, by-laws, regulations on the delegation of authority and code of conduct."[361]

In addition, the FINMA requires insurance groups or conglomerates to describe "the organization of the management structure [and] the tasks and the responsibilities of management in the form of an organizational regulation." This document is to be structured in a manner similar to a corporation's bylaws and is to include:

---

or conglomerate structure chart must be submitted each year within three months after the close of the financial year. SR Art. 192, para. 1 and SR Art. 204.

354 SR Art. 191, para. 1 and SR Art. 204.

355 SR Art. 96, applied by analogy through SR Arts. 195 and 204. *See also* notes 327-329 and the text accompanying them on the risk management requirement for an individually supervised insurance business.

356 SR Art. 196, para. 1.

357 SR Art. 197.

358 SR Art. 196, para. 1.

359 Circular Letter 2008/27 Organization of Insurance Groups, margin para. 5.

360 Circular Letter 2008/27, margin para. 6.

361 Circular Letter 2008/27, margin para. 7. The chart is to include "the management structure and the subordinate level of management, including functional title, name and responsibilities if possible" and "the date of appointment or the assumption of the role at that level of management." Each person's curriculum vitae and a description of each person's management duties within the group or conglomerate also are to be submitted *Id.* Margin paras. 8-10.

- Its basis and scope of application
- Its goals
- The function and procedures of the board of directors
  - Composition
  - Meetings and their frequency
  - Authority to adopt resolutions and the manner of their adoption
  - Minutes
  - Tasks and responsibilities
  - Compensation
  - Conflicts of interest
- The committees of the board of directors
  - Composition
  - Meetings and their frequency
  - Reporting to the board of directors
- The management
  - Appointment and organization
  - Tasks and responsibilities
- The internal audit function
  - Appointment and organization
  - Tasks and responsibilities
- Common provisions
  - Signing authority
  - Recusal
  - Entry into force[362]

Finally, a table of the most important directives of the group or conglomerate is to be submitted (e.g., underwriting guidelines, claims management guidelines, etc.).[363]

All of these submissions are to be made for the first time in accordance with the order of the FINMA subjecting the group or conglomerate to supervision.[364]

---

362 Circular Letter 2008/27, margin para. 11.

363 Circular Letter 2008/27, margin para. 12.

364 Circular Letter 2008/27, margin para. 13.

3. Group and conglomerate solvency requirements

ISL Art. 69 (groups) and Art. 77 (conglomerates) direct the Federal Council to "specify what will be credited as capital resources" and directs the FINMA to set capital requirements.

Under the SR, the solvency of an insurance group or conglomerate, like that of an individual insurance business, is determined by the Solvency I standard and the SST.[365] *See* II.B.3(a) *Solvency 1* and II.B.3(b). *Swiss Solvency Test, supra.*

a. Required solvency margin

The required solvency margin for an insurance group is "the sum of the required solvency margins for life insurance operations, nonlife insurance operations and reinsurance operations [calculated in accordance with SR Arts. 23 ff.], as well as for entities without supervisory law capital resources requirements."[366] The FINMA is to set the solvency requirement for businesses without supervisory law capital requirements.[367] The FINMA may permit alternate calculation methods "under exceptional circumstances" or exclude businesses from the calculation if "inclusion would be unsuitable or misleading."[368]

The required solvency margin for an insurance conglomerate "equals the sum of the required solvency margins in the insurance segment and the financial segment, as well as those for entities without supervisory law capital resources requirements in the financial segment."[369] In the financial segment, the required solvency margin it is calculated on the basis of international or, with the consent of the FINMA, nationally recognized principles in the banking segment. For entities without supervisory law capital resources requirements in the financial segment, the FINMA is to determine the calculation of the required solvency margin.[370]

b. Available solvency margin

If an insurance group or conglomerate prepares its financial statements in accordance with internationally recognized accounting principles,[371] then its cred-

365 SR Arts. 198 and 204.

366 SR Art. 199, paras. 2 and 3.

367 SR Art. 199, para. 3.

368 SR Art. 199, para. 4.

369 SR Art. 206, para. 2. *See also* Circular Letter 2008/30 Solvency 1 Insurance Groups, margin paras. 28 and 30 ("The required solvency margin in the finance segment is equal to the capital resources requirements for this segment").

370 SR Art. 206, para. 3.

371 Internationally recognized accounting principles are the International Financial Reporting Standards (IFRS) and the United States Generally Accepted Accounting Principles (US

itable assets are its consolidated assets, increased by the value of the minority interests it holds[372] and reduced by the value of its intangible assets, planned dividends and returns of capital, and capitalized acquisition costs in its nonlife business.[373] The FINMA may allow credit for subordinated loans and "other items with the same character as capital resources."[374] If the financial statements of the group or conglomerate have not been prepared in accordance with internationally recognized accounting principles, "the FINMA shall specify the creditable resources."[375]

4. *Group internal business transactions*

An insurance group or conglomerate is required to submit a report about each important intra-group transaction to the FINMA within 14 days after the transaction's legal effective date. In addition, the FINMA is to be informed annually, within three months after the close of the financial year, about all group-internal transactions.[376] "Important group internal transactions are those which significantly change the financial condition of an individual entity or which significantly change, or will change, the insurance group as a whole [and which exceed a threshold to be set be the FINMA] . . . ."[377] Those thresholds are:

- if the value of the transaction exceeds "1% of the available solvency margin at the Group/Conglomerate level . . . at the end of the preceding financial reporting year;"[378] or
- if "the sum of the nominal values (in the case of reinsurance, the premium) of [the transactions in] all categories [i.e., loans, guarantees and off-balance sheet transactions, transactions relating to creditable capital resources, capital investments, reinsurance transactions, cost-sharing

GAAP). Circular Letter 2008/31, margin para. 13 and Circular Letter 2008/30, margin para. 17.

372 Circular Letter 2008/30, margin para. 25, also allows an increase for the "acquired present value of future profits (PVFP): the present value of future profits from acquired insurance contracts (PVFP in the purchase price of newly acquired portfolios) is creditable analogously to the limits prescribed by the EU."

373 SR Art. 200, para. 1. More detailed descriptions of the required reductions are provided in Circular Letter 2008/30, margin para. 26.

374 SR Art. 200, para. 2.

375 SR Art. 200, para. 3.

376 SR Art. 194, para. 1. In Circular Letter 2008/29 Internal Business Transactions at margin paras. 14 and 31, the FINMA states groups and conglomerates are required to submit an annual overview of existing important group internal transactions.

377 SR Art. 193, para. 2.

378 Circular Letter 2008/29 Internal Business Transactions, margin para. 19.

> agreements and other risk transfer transactions[379]] equals or exceeds 100% of the net assets[380] of one of the involved companies. . . . If this threshold is exceeded, all group/conglomerate internal transactions of this individual company which exceed 20% of net assets are to be reported."[381]

The FINMA has specified minimum content requirements for reports on intra-group transactions. *See* Circular Letter 2008/29, margin paras. 20-27.

The FINMA is authorized to require additional reporting about intra-group transactions[382] which it has stated is particularly justified if:

- the group is in a period of accelerated change and the portfolio of group internal transactions is therefore subject to rapid change;
- the change in important group internal transactions has an effect on the solvency situation of an individual business in the group or conglomerate or the group or conglomerate as a whole;
- the FINMA needs the current status of the structure in order to be able to evaluate the financial situation of the group or conglomerate at a specific point in time.[383]

5. Group and conglomerate reporting

All supervised insurance businesses are required to prepare (a) an annual financial report as of the end of each calendar year consisting of financial statements and an annual report and (b) a regulatory report. If the insurance business is part of an insurance group or conglomerate, group financial statements are required.[384] The detailed requirements for this reporting by insurance groups and conglomerates are specified in the FINMA Circular Letter 2008/31 Insurance Group Report.

The calculation of the required and available solvency margin for groups and conglomerates is performed semi-annually and the results are to be submitted

---

379 These categories are found in SR Art. 193, para. 1. The FINMA provides examples of transactions in each of these categories in Circular Letter 2008/29 in a chart at margin para. 11.

380 "Net assets are to be understood as the total of the assets, minus the short- and long-term liabilities, including minority interests." Circular Letter 2008/29, margin para. 19.

381 *Id.*

382 ISL Art. 68.

383 Circular Letter 2008/29, margin para. 15.

384 ISL Art. 25, para. 1. Circular Letter 2008/31, margin para. 6, describes the contents of the group report as comprising the financial statements and the explanatory report of the audit firm.

to the FINMA within three months after the close of the relevant reporting period using prescribed electronic spreadsheets.[385]

Circular Letter 2008/31 states that the reporting should, on one hand, present in detail the various elements of the required and available solvency margin and, on the other hand, show the figures for at least three half-year periods, i.e., the current period, the period six months earlier and the period 12 months earlier.[386] Changes in the applied method of calculation, as well as the required and the available solvency margin are to be presented comparatively and explained. Changes in the basis of the calculation, such as the valuation method, changes in assets and liability positions, etc. are to be listed and presented comparatively.[387] The solvency calculation is to be submitted for the first time in accordance with the administrative order imposing supervision.[388] The FINMA will state its views in writing on the comparative presentation before the method of calculation is officially accepted.[389]

6. Role of the external auditors in group and conglomerate supervision

The external auditors of an insurance group or conglomerate are responsible for verifying whether the group or conglomerate has complied with its obligations under the SR and the procedures in its risk management documentation.[390]

K. Regulation of Insurance Intermediaries

1. Registration

The ISL, for the first time, places insurance intermediaries - persons who, without regard for their title or description, "offer or conclude insurance contracts on behalf of insurance businesses or other persons"[391] - under regulatory supervision and requires the FINMA to maintain a public register of insurance intermediaries.[392] Intermediaries that are not affiliated in any way with an insurance business must be registered, but intermediaries with affiliations to insurers nevertheless have the right to be registered.[393] An applicant for regis-

385 Circular Letter 2008/30, margin paras. 19 and 39.
386 Circular Letter 2008/30, margin para. 33.
387 Circular Letter 2008/30, margin para. 34.
388 Circular Letter 2008/30, margin para. 36.
389 Circular Letter 2008/30, margin para. 38.
390 SR Art. 203.
391 ISL Art. 40.
392 ISL Art. 42.
393 ISL Art. 43.

tration must demonstrate sufficient professional qualifications[394] and have professional liability insurance[395] or have provided similar financial security.[396] Insurance intermediaries also must not be under any legal disability, have any penal judgments against them on account of actions which are incompatible with the business of an insurance intermediary and which have not been expunged from the penal register or any outstanding certificates of debt against them.[397]

The ISL excludes from mandatory registration insurance intermediaries with "a dependent relationship to a policyholder, to the extent that they act in the interest of this policyholder and the companies controlled by it."[398] The SR also excludes an insurance intermediary from the registration obligation if:

- the majority of the commissions the intermediary receives during a calendar year are predominantly from one or two insurance businesses;
- the intermediary receives compensation or other financial advantages from insurance businesses that do not conform to customary compensation for insurance intermediation and therefore could affect the intermediary's independence;
- the intermediary has entered into a cooperation agreement or other agreement with insurance businesses which affect the intermediary's freedom to act on behalf of other insurance businesses;
- the intermediary directly or indirectly owns more than 10% of the equity capital of an insurance business; or
- the intermediary has a management function in an insurance business or otherwise exercises influence on the business processes of an insurance business;

394 ISL Art. 44, para. 1, a. Sufficient professional qualifications are demonstrated by successfully completing an examination prescribed by the FINMA or through other equivalent evidence. The FINMA determines the equivalence of other professional certifications. SR Art. 184. An intermediary that is a legal entity must show that it has sufficient employees who possess these qualifications. ISL Art. 44, para. 1, a.

395 ISL 44, para. 1, b. The annual policy limit for all claims must amount to at least 2 million francs, but the insurance requirement does not apply to an intermediary if a third party has obtained a professional indemnity insurance which includes the intermediary in its coverage. SR Art. 186.

396 ISL Art. 44, para. 1.

397 SR Art. 185.

398 ISL Art. 2, para. 2, c. SR Art. 182 also excludes "intermediary activities abroad by an insurance intermediary with its headquarters or domicile in Switzerland."

- an insurance business directly or indirectly owns more than 10% of the equity capital of the insurance intermediary;
- an insurance business has a management function with the insurance intermediary or otherwise can exercise influence on the business of the insurance intermediary.[399]

The FINMA is authorized to establish additional exemptions from the registration requirement if "special circumstances" justify it.[400]

An insurance intermediary's registration must include the intermediary's name and address, legal form, the names of the insurance businesses an affiliated insurance intermediary represents, the lines of insurance for which the intermediary transacts business and the intermediary's relationship to the insurance businesses, if applicable, the name of the intermediary's employer, the date of the initial registration and the intermediary's registration number.[401]

A registered insurance intermediary is required to notify the FINMA, within 14 days after becoming aware of the relevant event, of name changes, the loss of the financial security or failure to meet the minimum guarantee requirement, the replacement of professional liability insurance with equivalent financial security, or vice versa, the termination of its activities as an insurance intermediary, a change from insurance intermediary business not affiliated with an insurance business to one affiliated with an insurance business, or vice versa, a change of the affiliated insurance business for which insurance is intermediated by the insurance intermediary, a change of the insurance intermediary's employer or the insurance intermediary's address.[402]

An insurance business from which an insurance intermediary has obtained professional liability insurance must notify the FINMA without delay of the suspension or lapse of this insurance or if the coverage no longer meets the prescribed minimum amount. Similarly, a person who has provided equivalent security in respect of an insurance intermediary must notify the FINMA if this security is no longer provided or it is less than the minimum amount.[403]

2. Market conduct

Upon contacting an insured, an intermediary must disclose, in a "durable and accessible form,"[404] the intermediary's identity and address, "whether the in-

399 SR Art. 183, paras. 1 and 2.
400 SR Art. 183, para. 3.
401 SR Art. 187, para. 1.
402 SR Art. 189, para. 1.
403 SR Art. 189, paras. 2 and 3.
404 ISL Art. 45, para. 2.

surance coverage offered by the intermediary in a particular line of insurance is provided by only one or several insurance businesses and which insurance businesses are involved," the names of the insurance businesses for which the intermediary acts and the contractual relationships it has with them, the identity of the "person who can be held liable for negligence, mistakes or incorrect information" in connection with the intermediary's professional activities, what personal information about the insured will be processed and, in particular, "the purpose, scope and recipients of the data, as well as the storage of it."[405] If there is a change in this information, the insurance intermediary "must inform customers about it at the time of the next contact with the customer."[406]

405 ISL Art. 45, para. 1.

406 SR Art. 190.

III.
Instruments of Supervisory Intervention

A. Examinations

The FINMAG authorizes the FINMA to conduct supervisory examinations, directly, through third parties appointed by it or through audit firms appointed by the supervised.[407] The supervised are required to provide any appointed audit firms or third parties with "all information and deliver to them all documentation which they require for the fulfillment of their responsibilities."[408]

B. Cross-Border Examinations

The FINMA is authorized to "conduct direct examinations of foreign establishments of those supervised for which it is responsible for consolidated supervision as part of home-country supervision, either on its own, through audit firms or designated third parties."[409] Conversely, the FINMA is authorized to permit foreign financial market supervisory authorities to conduct direct examinations of Swiss establishments of foreign institutions to the extent that these authorities (a) are responsible for the consolidated supervision of the examined institution as part of home-country supervision and (b) the prerequisites for official assistance[410] are satisfied.[411] Only information which is necessary for the consolidated supervision of a foreign institution may be collected through a cross-border direct examination, including, in particular, information about whether an institution, group-wide, is appropriately organized; appropriately recognizes, limits and monitors the risks of its business activities; is managed by persons who offer the assurance that business is conducted in an irreproachable manner; fulfills capital resources and risk-distribution regulations on a consolidated

407 FINMAG Art. 24, para. 1.

408 FINMAG Art. 25.

409 FINMAG Art. 43, para. 1.

410 Under FINMAG Art. 42, the FINMA "may only provide nonpublic information and documentation to foreign financial market supervisory authorities to the extent that they are required to observe governmental or professional confidentiality obligations" and they (a) "use the information exclusively for the direct supervision of foreign institutions" and (b) "forward the information to responsible authorities and bodies which are entrusted with the supervisory responsibilities in the public interest only on the basis of a general authorization in an international treaty or with the FINMA's consent." The FINMA is required to refuse its consent if "the information will be forwarded to law enforcement authorities and legal assistance in criminal matters would be unavailable." This decision is to be made in consultation with the Federal Office of Justice.

411 FINMAG Art. 43, para. 2. "The FINMA may accompany foreign financial market supervisory authorities in their direct examinations in Switzerland or allow them to be accompanied by an audit firm or designated third parties. The affected subjects of supervision may request that they are accompanied." FINMAG Art. 43, para. 4.

basis; and properly fulfills its reporting obligations to supervisory authorities.[412] Subsidiary corporations, branches and representative offices incorporated or established under Swiss law by "those subject to supervision or foreign institutions" and "other businesses to the extent that their activities are subject to consolidated supervision by a financial market supervisory authority" must "provide foreign financial market supervisory authorities and the FINMA with the information that is necessary for the performance of direct examinations or for official assistance by the FINMA and give them access to their records."[413]

C. Enforcement Proceedings

"If one subject to supervision violates a provision of [the FINMAG] or a Financial Market Law, or if other irregularities exist," then the FINMA is required to restore compliance.[414] According to the FINMA, the question is usually whether licensing requirements, organizational guidelines, due diligence requirements or other legal rules or standards have been breached in some way.[415] The responsibility of an insurance business's corporate governing bodies, management, employees and owners may also be the subject of an administrative proceeding.[416] "If there are indications of violations of provisions of supervisory law and the FINMA commences a proceeding, it shall give notice thereof to the parties."[417]

If an insurance business or an insurance intermediary does not comply with the requirements of the ISL, a regulation or order of the FINMA, or if it appears that the interests of the insureds are otherwise endangered, then the FINMA is required to adopt protective measures for the protection of the interests of the insureds. These measures may include (1) a prohibition on the unrestricted disposition of the assets of the insurance business, (2) an order requiring the deposit or restriction of assets, (3) the assignment, in whole or in part, of the responsibilities and authorities of the officers and directors of an insurance business to a third person, (4) the assignment of the portfolio of insurance policies and the related restricted assets to another insurance business with the consent of the insurance business accepting them, (5) an order for the liquidation of the restricted assets, (6) requiring the dismissal of the persons entrusted with the ultimate management, supervision, control or conduct of the

---

412 FINMAG Art. 43, para. 3.

413 FINMAG Art. 43, paras. 5 and 6.

414 FINMAG Art. 31.

415 *www.finma.ch*: Types of proceedings - Enforcement in the regulation of institutions. <www.finma.ch/e/finma/taetigkeiten/gb-maerkte/enforcement-marktaufsicht/pages/verfahrenstypen.aspx>.

416 *Id.*

417 FINMAG Art. 30.

business, the general agent or the responsible actuary and (7) the removal of an insurance intermediary from the register.[418]

In addition, the FINMA is responsible for taking action against businesses and persons engaging in a regulated financial market activity without the required license. The FINMA may appoint an independent, professionally qualified person to investigate the facts and the FINMA will take enforcement action based on this investigation. This may include the liquidation of the business involved.[419]

1. Negative list

If, for example, the business or persons involved conduct their business outside Switzerland or cannot be found in Switzerland and the FINMA therefore cannot take enforcement action against the business or such persons, the FINMA can place the business or persons on its "negative list."[420]

2. Findings of fact

"If the proceedings establish that one subject to supervision has committed a serious violation of provisions of supervisory law [but] it is no longer necessary to order measures for the restoration of compliance, the FINMA may issue a decision setting forth its findings of fact."[421] If a serious violation of provisions of supervisory law occurs, the FINMA may disclose its final order including personal information therein, after it has become legally binding, in electronic or printed form.[422]

3. Revocation of license

"The FINMA shall withdraw the license, the recognition, the admission or the registration of one subject to supervision if it no longer fulfills the prerequisites for the relevant activity or it seriously violates provisions of supervisory law."[423]

4. Bar on employment

If the FINMA finds that a serious violation of supervisory law has occurred, it can bar the responsible person from holding a management position in a supervised insurance business for a period of up to five years.[424]

---

418 ISL Art. 51.

419 *www.finma.ch*: Types of Proceedings - Subordination.

420 *Id.*

421 FINMAG Art. 32.

422 FINMAG Art. 34, para. 1.

423 FINMAG Art. 37, para. 1.

424 FINMAG Art. 33.

5. *Asset seizure*

The FINMA is also authorized to seize the profit (or the amount of an avoided loss) that a supervised insurance business or one of its managers obtained through a serious violation of provisions of supervisory law.[425] "If the amount of the assets to be seized cannot be determined, or cannot be determined without disproportionate effort, the FINMA can estimate it."[426]

D. Solvency-Related Protective Measures

The FINMA has issued non-binding guidelines, as the fourth annex to Circular Letter 2008/44 SST, which describe the measures it may impose if an insurance business does not meet the SST's solvency requirements. This annex specifies three thresholds, based on the ratio of risk-bearing capital to target capital, for a progressive intensification of regulatory measures based on the solvency of the insurance business.

An insurance business is required to "report to the FINMA any circumstances which have material importance for the supervision,"[427] including events that jeopardize solvency.[428]

1. *The green zone*

If risk-bearing capital exceeds the required target capital, an insurance business meets the SST and the SST quotient therefore will be more than 100%. So long as an insurance business has an SST quotient greater than 100%, it is above the first threshold and in the "green zone."[429] "To the extent an insurance business is in the green zone, the FINMA does not impose measures on the basis of the SST solvency situation."[430]

2. *The yellow zone*

If the ratio of risk-bearing capital to the required target capital is between 80% and 100%, an insurance business is in the "yellow zone".[431] "If an insurance business is in the yellow zone, an increased risk exists for the interests of the insureds as a result of the solvency situation. In this situation, the FINMA will

---

425 FINMAG Art. 35, paras. 1 and 2. A seizure under the Swiss Penal Code takes precedence over the FINMA's authority to seize assets. FINMAG Art. 35, para. 5.

426 FINMAG Art. 35, para. 3.

427 FINMAG Art. 29, para. 2.

428 Circular Letter 2008/25, margin para. 1.

429 Circular Letter 2008/44, Annex 4, margin paras. 4, 5 and 8.

430 Circular Letter 2008/44, Annex 4, margin para. 13.

431 Circular Letter 2008/44, Annex 4, margin paras. 4, 6 and 8.

intensify the risk dialogue with the insurance business with the goal of reducing the risk for the insureds."[432] The insurance business will be required to prepare a report analyzing the causes of its failure to meet the SST and an action plan, which requires the FINMA's approval, specifying binding measures for the improvement of its solvency.[433] The action plan must include:

- immediate measures for the improvement of the SST quotient (for example, an increase in capital, risk reduction, obtaining reinsurance). These are, as appropriate, to be implemented before the action plan is submitted;[434]
- a strategy for the improvement of the SST quotient in the medium term;[435]
- a list of important, long-term individual measures as components of this strategy;[436]
- a time plan for the implementation of the measures;[437]
- a projected income statement, a projected balance sheet with a projected time line of at least four quarters from the completion of the rehabilitation plan.[438]

"The action plan is to be designed so that the green zone will be reached, as a rule, one year after the notice to the FINMA."[439] The FINMA may order additional measures if the insurance business fails to comply with the action plan[440] or following an evaluation of the insurance business's business situation.[441] Following the evaluation of the business situation, the FINMA, in particular, may:

- have examinations performed by independent experts which verify the valuations used in the near market balance sheet or the appropriateness of the procedures for the determination of target capital;[442]

---

432 Circular Letter 2008/44, Annex 4, margin para. 14.
433 Circular Letter 2008/44, Annex 4, margin para. 15.
434 Circular Letter 2008/44, Annex 4, margin para. 16.
435 Circular Letter 2008/44, Annex 4, margin para. 17.
436 Circular Letter 2008/44, Annex 4, margin para. 18.
437 Circular Letter 2008/44, Annex 4, margin para. 19.
438 Circular Letter 2008/44, Annex 4, margin para. 20.
439 Circular Letter 2008/44, Annex 4, margin para. 15.
440 Circular Letter 2008/44, Annex 4, margin para. 21.
441 Circular Letter 2008/44, Annex 4, margin para. 23.
442 Circular Letter 2008/44, Annex 4, margin para. 24.

- require that important ratios are measured during the year and reported to the FINMA;[443] or
- order supplementary scenario analyses which permit the review of the effectiveness of the rehabilitation measures in the prescribed time period with various assumptions about the development of the risk factors.[444]

3. The orange zone

If the ratio of risk-bearing capital to the required target capital is at least 33% but less than 80%, an insurance business is in the "orange zone". In this zone, the FINMA may apply any of the measures contemplated for the yellow zone or make them more strict.[445] In addition, the insurance business is required to prepare a rehabilitation plan "that will return the insurance business to the yellow zone as a rule within two years and to the green zone as a rule within three years after the notice to the FINMA" that the insurance business has entered the orange zone.[446] The rehabilitation plan must address the same issues as the action plan, but "the projected time line for the projected income statement and the projected balance sheet must amount to at least six semesters from the completion of the rehabilitation plan. The rehabilitation plan must, in addition, show which risks the insurance business is able to immediately reduce" and how. "The influence of various - including negative - scenarios on the effectiveness of the rehabilitation measures is to be determined."[447] If necessary, the FINMA may:

- order special liquidity planning;[448]
- order an approval obligation for especially risky new business and renewals;[449]
- prohibit new business and renewal business;[450]
- prohibit risky and complex transactions to the extent it is not assured that these serve the improvement of the SST quotient;[451] and

---

443 Circular Letter 2008/44, Annex 4, margin para. 25.
444 Circular Letter 2008/44, Annex 4, margin para. 26.
445 Circular Letter 2008/44, Annex 4, margin para. 28.
446 Circular Letter 2008/44, Annex 4, margin para. 29.
447 Circular Letter 2008/44, Annex 4, margin para. 30.
448 Circular Letter 2008/44, Annex 4, margin para. 32.
449 Circular Letter 2008/44, Annex 4, margin para. 33.
450 Circular Letter 2008/44, Annex 4, margin para. 34.
451 Circular Letter 2008/44, Annex 4, margin para. 35.

- require the insurance business to make organizational changes, such as more intensive controlling, monitoring, reporting and auditing by the internal audit function.[452]

4. The red zone

If the ratio of risk-bearing capital to the required target capital is below 33%, an insurance business is in the "red zone" and it must "take immediate measures for the protection of insureds." The FINMA must be able to see, within a short period of time, whether the measures adopted by the insurance business will be successful.[453] "A continuation of the business with the objective of writing profitable business and thereby to improve the solvency situation incrementally through retained profits is not an acceptable alternative in the red zone."[454]

In the red zone, the FINMA may require an immediate increase in risk-bearing capital or a reduction of the target capital,[455] a voluntary transfer of the insurance portfolio[456] or a partial transfer of the insurance portfolio in order to bring the insurance business out of the red zone.[457] "If it is not possible for the insurance business to adopt appropriate measures and the measures ordered by the FINMA also do not lead to short-term success, the FINMA shall withdraw the insurance business's license."

"If the directors and officers do not carry out the measures imposed by the FINMA in the yellow, orange or red zones in a manner that avoids a further jeopardization of the interests of the insureds, the FINMA" will require the termination of their employment[458] and if "the responsible directors and officers do not comply, then the FINMA shall exercise its authority under ISL Art. 51, para. 2, c." to assign in whole or in part the responsibilities and authorities of the officers and directors of an insurance business to a third person.[459]

E. Liquidation

The commencement of bankruptcy proceedings in respect of an insurance business requires FINMA's approval, which is to be given if rehabilitation is not

452 Circular Letter 2008/44, Annex 4, margin para. 36.

453 Circular Letter 2008/44, Annex 4, margin para. 37.

454 Circular Letter 2008/44, Annex 4, margin para. 42.

455 Circular Letter 2008/44, Annex 4, margin para. 38.

456 Circular Letter 2008/44, Annex 4, margin para. 39.

457 Circular Letter 2008/44, Annex 4, margin para. 40.

458 Under ISL Art. 51, para. 2, f., the FINMA can "demand the dismissal of the persons entrusted with the ultimate management, supervision, control or conduct of the business, or the general agent, as well as the responsible actuary and prohibit them from engaging in any further insurance activities for a maximum of five years."

459 Circular Letter 2008/44, margin para. 43.

possible.[460] The FINMA has the right to appoint (1) the liquidator of a supervised insurance business,[461] (2) a special bankruptcy administrator for the conduct of the bankruptcy proceedings and assign to it all of the powers of a meeting of creditors and (3) a person to represent the policyholders in the bankruptcy proceedings.[462] The FINMA has the same powers as a court to issue orders for the protection of the rights of creditors.[463] Claims from insureds which can be recognized by means of the books and records of the insurance business are deemed submitted.[464]

460 ISL Art. 53, para. 1.

461 ISL Art. 52.

462 ISL Art. 54, para. 1.

463 "The powers conferred by Article 170 of the Federal Law of 11 April 1889 on Debt Enforcement and Bankruptcy (DEBL) are available to the FINMA." ISL Art. 53, para. 2.

464 ISL Art. 54, para. 3.

IV. Criminal Prosecutions

A. Penalties

Among other offenses, the penal provisions of the FINMAG proscribe:

- engaging in an activity for which a "a license, recognition, admission or registration" is required under the Financial Market Laws without the requisite license, recognition, admission or registration;[465]
- the provision of false information to the FINMA, an audit firm or a designated third party;[466]
- the failure to have the annual financial statements prescribed by the Financial Market Laws audited by an admitted audit firm or the failure to have an examination ordered by the FINMA performed.[467]

For each of these violations, the FINMAG provides for imprisonment for up to three years or a monetary penalty for an intentional violation;[468] fines of up to 250,000 francs for a negligent violation;[469] and a monetary penalty equal to at least 45 day fines if the offense is repeated within five years after the date the previous judgment became legally binding.[470]

"Whoever fails to comply with an order issued by the FINMA under the threat of the criminal penalties under this article which has become legally binding or a decision of an appellate body shall be punished with a fine of up to 100,000 francs."[471]

B. Time Limit on Prosecutions

Prosecutions of violations of the FINMAG or the Financial Market Laws are barred after seven years.[472]

---

465 FINMAG Art. 44, para. 1.

466 FINMAG Art. 45, para. 1.

467 FINMAG Art. 47, para. 1.

468 FINMAG Art. 44, para. 1; Art. 45, para. 1; and Art. 47, para. 1.

469 FINMAG Art. 44, para. 2; Art. 45, para. 2; and Art. 47, para. 2.

470 FINMAG Art, 44, para. 3; Art. 45, para. 3; and Art. 47, para. 3.

471 FINMAG Art. 48.

472 FINMAG Art. 52.

C. Procedure

The Federal Law of 22 March 1974 on Administrative Criminal Law is applicable to criminal violations of the FINMAG or the Financial Market Laws if not otherwise prescribed by such laws. "The authority prosecuting and rendering judgment is the Federal Department of Finance."[473] "If a judicial determination has been sought or if the Federal Department of Finance considers that the prerequisites for imprisonment or another loss of liberty are present, then the punishable act is subject to the jurisdiction of the Federal Court. In this case, the Federal Department of Finance shall transfer the files to the Federal Prosecutor's Office for proceedings before the Federal Criminal Court."[474]

"If the Federal Department of Finance as well as the Federal Court or a cantonal court would have jurisdiction over a criminal matter, the Federal Office of Justice can order the consolidation of the criminal investigation with the criminal investigation authority that is already involved with the matter to the extent that there is a common factual basis, that matter is not yet pending before the responsible court, and the consolidation would not unreasonably delay the ongoing proceedings."[475]

473 FINMAG Art. 50, para. 1.
474 FINMAG Art. 50, para. 2.
475 FINMAG Art. 51 para 1.

Federal Law on the Federal Financial Market Supervision

SR 956.1

(Financial Market Supervision Law, FINMAG)

of 22 June 2007 (as of 1 January 2009)

The Federal Parliament of the Swiss Confederation,

on the basis of Articles 95 and 98 of the Federal Constitution[1] and after a review of the message of the Federal Council of 1 February 2006[2]

resolves:

Chapter 1: General provisions

Art. 1 Subject

[1] The Federal Government shall create an authority for the supervision of the financial market in accordance with the following laws (Financial Market Laws):

a. Pfandbrief Law of 25 June 1930[3];

b. Insurance Contract Law of 2 April 1908[4];

c. Collective Investments Law of 23 June 2006[5];

d. Banking Law of 8 November 1934[6];

e. Securities Exchanges Law of 24 March 1995[7];

f. Money Laundering Law of 10 October 1997;[8]

g. Insurance Supervision Law of 17 December 2004[9].

[2] This law specifies the organization and supervisory instruments of this authority.

Art. 2 Relationship to the Financial Market Laws

This law applies to the extent that the Financial Market Laws do not provide otherwise.

Art. 3 The supervised

Subject to financial market supervision are:

1 SR **101**
2 BBl **2006** 2829
3 SR **211.423.4**
4 SR **221.229.1**
5 SR **951.31**
6 SR **952.0**
7 SR **954.1**
8 SR **955.0**
9 SR **961.01**

a. persons who require a license, a recognition, an admission from, or a registration with, the financial market supervisory authority under the Financial Market Laws;
b. collective capital investments; and
c. audit firms.

Art. 4 Legal form, registered office and name

[1] The authority that shall supervise the financial market is a public law institution with its own legal personality and with its registered office in Bern.

[2] It shall bear the name "Federal Financial Market Supervisory Authority (FINMA)".

[3] It shall organize itself in accordance with the principles of a good corporate governance and self-financing operational management. It shall maintain its own financial accounts.

Art. 5 Objectives of financial market supervision

The financial market supervision aims, in accordance with the Financial Market Laws, for the protection of creditors, investors, insureds, as well as the protection of the ability of the financial market to function. It serves thereby to strengthen the reputation and competiveness of the Swiss financial marketplace.

Art. 6 Responsibilities

[1] The FINMA shall exercise its supervisory authority in accordance with the Financial Market Laws and in accordance with this law.

[2] It shall assume responsibility for international matters which are connected with its supervisory activities.

Art. 7 Principles of regulation

[1] The FINMA regulates through:

a. regulations, where this is provided in financial market laws and regulations; and
b. circular letters concerning the application of financial market laws and regulations.

[2] It regulates only to the extent needed in view of the regulatory objective. In this regard, it shall, in particular, take into account:

a. the costs to those subject to supervision and resulting from the regulation;
b. how the regulation affects competition, the ability to innovate and the international competitiveness of the Swiss financial marketplace;
c. the varying business activities and risks of those subject to supervision; and
d. international minimum standards.

[3] It shall support self-regulation and can, in the scope of its supervisory authority, recognize and enforce this as a minimum standard.

4 It shall ensure a transparent regulatory process and an appropriate involvement of those affected.

5 It shall issue guidelines for the implementation of these principles. In connection therewith, it shall consult with the Federal Department of Finance.

Chapter 2: Organization

Section 1: Governing bodies and staff

Art. 8 Governing bodies

The governing bodies of the FINMA are:

a. the board of directors;

b. the executive board;

c. the external auditors.

Art. 9 Board of directors

1 The board of directors is the strategic governing body of the FINMA. It has the following responsibilities:

a. It sets the FINMA's strategic goals and submits them to the Federal Council for approval.

b. It renders decisions on matters of great significance.

c. It issues the regulations delegated to the FINMA and adopts circular letters.

d. It supervises the executive board.

e. It appoints the internal audit function and ensures internal control.

f. It issues an annual report and submits it to the Federal Council for approval before it is released.

g. It appoints the director, subject to the approval of the Federal Council.

h. It appoints the members of the executive board.

i. It issues the by-laws and guidelines about information activities.

j. It approves the budget.

2 It comprises seven to nine professionally knowledgeable members who are independent from those subject to supervision. The board of directors will be appointed for a term of office of four years; each member can be reappointed twice.

3 The Federal Council appoints the board of directors. In so doing, it shall take into account an appropriate representation of both genders. It appoints the president and the vice president. It sets compensation. Article 6*a* of the Federal Personnel Law of 24 March 2000[10] shall apply by analogy.

10 SR **172.220.1**

[4] The president may neither engage in any other professional activity nor hold a federal or cantonal office, unless this is in the interest of the fulfillment of the FINMA's responsibilities.

[5] The Federal Council shall appoint the members of the board of directors and shall approve the termination of the employment relationship of the director by the board of directors if the prerequisites for holding this office are no longer fulfilled.

Art. 10 Executive board

[1] The executive board is the operational governing body. It is managed by a director.

[2] It has, in particular, the following responsibilities:

a. It issues decisions in accordance with the by-laws.
b. It prepares the materials needed for a decision by the board of directors and reports to it regularly, and in the case of special developments, without delay.
c. It fulfills all responsibilities that have not been assigned to another governing body.

[3] The by-laws shall specify the details.

Art. 11 Representation of specialist areas

[1] The FINMA is divided into specialist departments. The by-laws shall specify the details.

[2] The Federal Council and the board of directors shall ensure an appropriate representation of the various specialist areas in the board of directors and in the executive board.

Art. 12 External auditor

The Federal Audit Office is the external auditor and it shall issue a report on the result of its audit to the board of directors and the Federal Council.

Art. 13 Staff

[1] The FINMA shall employ its staff pursuant to public law.

[2] The board of directors shall provide rules for the employment relationship in a regulation. This shall specifically include regulations concerning compensation, fringe benefits, working hours, the duty of loyalty and termination. They must be approved by the Federal Council.

[3] Article 6a of the Federal Personnel Law of 24 March 2000[11] shall apply by analogy.

[4] The occupational pension fund for the staff shall be based on the laws and regulations on the Federal Pension Fund.

---

11 SR **172.220.1**

Art. 14 Confidentiality of official matters

1 The staff and the governing bodies are required to maintain the confidentiality of official matters.

2 The confidentiality obligation continues after the termination of the employment relationship or membership in a governing body of the FINMA.

3 The employees and the individual members of the governing bodies may not, without the authorization of the FINMA, as a party, witness, or expert in hearings or judicial proceedings, make statements about observations that they have made in the course of fulfilling their responsibilities and which relate to their official responsibilities.

4 All those appointed by the FINMA (appointed as investigators, rehabilitators, liquidators, receivers, other third parties) are subject to this confidentiality obligation.

Section 2: Funding and budget

Art. 15 Funding

1 The FINMA shall impose fees for supervisory proceedings in an individual case and for services. In addition, it shall impose an annual supervisory fee on those subject to supervision for each supervisory department and a supervisory charge for the costs to the FINMA that are not covered by fees.

2 The supervisory charge will be determined on the following criteria:

a. For those supervised under the Banking Law of 8 November 1934[12], the Securities Exchanges Law of 24 March 1995[13] and the Pfandbrief Law of 25 June 1930[14] the basis is total assets and the securities trading volume.
b. For those supervised under the Collective Investments Law of 23 June 2006[15], the basis is the amount of assets under management, gross revenue and the size of the business.
c. For an insurance business under the Insurance Supervision Law of 17 December 2004[16], the basis is its share of the total premium revenue of all insurance businesses; for insurance intermediaries under Article 43, paragraph 1 of the Supervision Law of 17 December 2004, the basis is their number and the size of the business.
d. For self regulatory organizations under the Money Laundering Law of 10 October 1997[17], the basis is gross revenue and the number of members; for financial intermediaries directly supervised by the FINMA under Article 2, paragraph 3 of

---

12 SR **952.0**
13 SR **954.1**
14 SR **211.423.4**
15 SR **951.31**
16 SR **961.01**
17 SR **955.0**

the Money Laundering Law of 10 October 1997, the basis is the gross revenue and the size of the business.

e. For audit firms that are subject to this law, the basis is the fees earned from audits of those subject to supervision.

[3] The Federal Council can provide for the division of the supervisory charge into a fixed basic charge and a variable supplementary charge.

[4] It shall specify the details, specifically:

a. the basis for assessment;
b. the supervisory departments under paragraph 1; and
c. the allocation of the costs to be financed by the supervisory charge among the supervisory departments.

Art. 16 Reserves

The FINMA shall establish reserves for the exercise of its supervisory activities in the amount of an annual budget within a reasonable period of time.

Art. 17 Treasury

[1] The Federal Finance Administration shall manage the liquid assets of the FINMA as part of its central financial management.

[2] It shall provide loans on market-based terms to the FINMA to ensure its ability to meet its payment obligations.

[3] The Federal Finance Administration and the FINMA shall amicably determine the details of this collaboration.

Art. 18 Financial reporting standards

[1] The FINMA's financial reporting standards shall fully present its asset, financial and income situation.

[2] It shall follow general principles of materiality, clarity, consistency and overall presentation and shall be guided by generally accepted standards.

[3] The reporting and valuation rules resulting from the financial reporting standards shall be disclosed.

Art. 19 Liability

[1] The liability of the FINMA, its governing bodies, its staff, as well as the FINMA's third-party agents is, subject to paragraph 2, governed by the Liability Law of 14 March 1958[18].

[18] SR **170.32**

The liability of the audit firms employed by it pursuant to private law is governed by the provisions of corporate law (Code of Obligations[19] Arts. 752-760).

² The FINMA and its agents are liable only if:

a. they have violated significant official obligations; and
b. losses are not attributable to breaches of duty by one who is subject to supervision.

Art. 20 Tax exemption

¹ The FINMA is exempted from every tax by the Federal Government, the cantons and the municipalities.

² Unaffected, however, remain the federal laws concerning:

a. the value-added tax;
b. the withholding tax;
c. the stamp duties.

Section 3: Independence and supervision

Art. 21

¹ The FINMA shall engage in its supervisory activity autonomously and independently.

² It shall establish with the Federal Council at least once annually the strategy of its supervisory activity, as well as the current issues in financial market policy.

³ It interacts with the Federal Council through the Federal Finance Department.

⁴ The *Ständerat* and the *Nationalrat* exercise the ultimate supervisory authority.

Section 4: Reporting to the public and data processing

Art. 22 Reporting to the public

¹ The FINMA shall report to the public at least once annually about its supervisory activities and supervisory practices.

² It shall not report about individual proceedings, unless there is a special supervisory need for it, in particular if the information is necessary for:

a. the protection of market participants or those supervised;
b. the correction of false or misleading information; or
c. the protection of the reputation of the Swiss financial marketplace.

³ If it has provided information about a proceeding, then it shall also give notice without delay of its termination. This may be omitted at the request of the affected party.

---

19 SR **220**

[4] It shall take into account the personal privacy rights of those affected in all of its information disclosure activities. The disclosure of personal data can be made in electronic or printed form.

Art. 23 Data processing and public registry

[1] The FINMA shall process personal data, including personal data especially deserving of protection and personality profiles, in the course of its supervision in accordance with this law and the Financial Market Laws. It shall specify the details.

[2] It shall maintain a registry of the supervised. This registry is to be made publicly available in electronic form.

Chapter 3: Supervisory instruments

Section 1: Examination

Art. 24 Basic principle

[1] In compliance with the Financial Market Laws, the FINMA shall conduct the examination itself, through third parties appointed by it or through audit firms appointed by the supervised.

[2] The supervised shall bear the costs of the examination.

Art. 25 Obligations of the supervised who are examined

[1] If, in accordance with the Financial Market Laws, an audit firm is employed or third parties are appointed, then the supervised are required to provide them with all information and deliver to them all documentation which they require for the fulfillment of their responsibilities.

[2] The choice of an audit firm must be approved by the FINMA.

Art. 26 Admission requirements

[1] An audit firm will be admitted if it:

a. is supervised under the Audit Supervision Law of 16 December 2005[20];
b. is adequately organized for audits in accordance with the Financial Market Laws; and
c. does not engage in any activity which requires a license under the Financial Market Laws.

[2] Lead auditors will be admitted if they:

a. have been admitted as audit experts under the Audit Supervision Law of 16 December 2005; and

[20] SR **221.302**

b. can demonstrate the necessary professional knowledge for audits in accordance with one of the Financial Market Laws.

3 The examinations are to be performed with the same degree of care as that used by proper and professionally knowledgeable auditor.

Art. 27 Reporting and measures

1 The audit firm shall deliver a report concerning its examinations to the ultimate management body of the one subject to supervision who is examined and to the FINMA.

2 If it determines that violations of provisions of supervisory law or other irregularities have occurred, then it shall set an appropriate deadline for the one subject to supervision who is examined to restore compliance. If the deadline is not met, then it shall inform the FINMA.

3 The audit firm shall notify the FINMA without delay in the event of serious violations of provisions of supervisory law or serious irregularities.

Art. 28 Supervision of the audit firms

1 The FINMA shall review the fulfillment of the admission requirements under this law and the audit activity of the audit firms in respect of the supervised in accordance with the Financial Market Laws.

2 The FINMA and the Federal Audit Supervisory Authority shall give each other all information and shall deliver all documentation which they require for the enforcement of the relevant laws and regulations. The shall coordinate their supervisory activities in order to avoid duplicate actions.

Section 2: Additional supervisory instruments

Art. 29 Information and reporting obligation

1 The supervised, their audit firms and external auditors, as well as persons who hold qualified or significant ownership interests in one subject to supervision, must provide the FINMA with all information and deliver to it all documentation which it requires for the fulfillment of its responsibilities.

2 The supervised must also report to the FINMA any circumstances which have material importance for the supervision.

Art. 30 Notice of the commencement of a proceeding

If there are indications of violations of provisions of supervisory law and the FINMA commences a proceeding, it shall give notice thereof to the parties.

Art. 31 Restoration of compliance

If one subject to supervision violates a provision of this law or of a Financial Market Law, or if other irregularities exist, then the FINMA shall ensure the restoration of compliance.

Art. 32 Findings of fact

If the proceedings establish that one subject to supervision has committed a serious violation of provisions of supervisory law and it is no longer necessary to order measures for the restoration of compliance, the FINMA may issue a decision setting forth its findings of fact.

Art. 33 Bar on employment

1 If the FINMA determines that a serious violation of provisions of supervisory law has occurred, it can bar the responsible person from holding a management position with one subject to its supervision.

2 The bar on employment may be imposed for a period of up to five years.

Art. 34 Disclosure of orders under supervisory law

1 If a serious violation of provisions of supervisory law occurs, the FINMA may disclose, in electronic or printed form, its final order including personal information therein after it has become legally binding.

2 The disclosure itself is to be ordered in the order.

Art. 35 Seizure

1 The FINMA may seize the profit that one subject to supervision or a responsible person in a management position obtained through a serious violation of provisions of supervisory law.

2 This rule applies by analogy if one subject to supervision or a responsible person in a management position had avoided a loss through a serious violation of provisions of supervisory law.

3 If the amount of the assets to be seized cannot be determined or cannot be determined without disproportionate effort, the FINMA can estimate it.

4 The right of seizure lapses after seven years.

5 A criminal seizure under Articles 70-72[21] of the Penal Code takes precedence over a seizure under this provision.

6 The seized assets are to be delivered to the Federal Government to the extent that indemnity is not paid to those who were harmed.

---

21 SR **311.0**

Art. 36 Appointed investigator

[1] The FINMA can appoint an independent and professionally knowledgeable person to investigate the facts relating to issues of supervisory law in respect of one subject to supervision or to enforce measures imposed under supervisory law (Appointed Investigator).

[2] It shall describe the responsibilities of the Appointed Investigator in the order of appointment. It shall specify to what extent the Appointed Investigator may act in the stead of the governing bodies of the one subject to supervision.

[3] The supervised must give the Appointed Investigator access to their facilities, as well as provide all information and documentation which the Appointed Investigator requires for the fulfillment of its responsibilities.

[4] The cost of the Appointed Investigator is borne by the supervised. They shall make an advance payment toward the costs if ordered to do so by the FINMA.

Art. 37 Withdrawal of the License, the Recognition, the Admission or the Registration

[1] The FINMA shall withdraw the license, the recognition, the admission or the registration of one subject to supervision if it no longer fulfills the prerequisites for the relevant activity or it seriously violates provisions of supervisory law.

[2] Upon withdrawal, the one subject to supervision loses the right to engage in the relevant activity. The other consequences of the withdrawal shall be determined under the applicable Financial Market Laws.

[3] These consequences apply analogously if one subject to supervision engages in an activity without possessing the relevant license, recognition, admission or registration.

Section 3: Cooperation with domestic authorities

Art. 38 Prosecuting authorities

[1] The FINMA and the criminal investigation authorities of the Federal Government and the cantons shall provide legal and official assistance to each other in accordance with the applicable laws.

[2] They shall coordinate their investigations to the extent possible and necessary.

[3] If the FINMA becomes aware of felonies or misdemeanors, as well as other violations of this law and the Financial Market Laws, it shall notify the responsible criminal investigative authorities.

Art. 39 Other domestic authorities

The [extent of the] FINMA's cooperation with other domestic authorities shall be determined, subject to Articles 40 and 41, in accordance with the Financial Market Laws and the [extent of the] other domestic authorities' cooperation shall be determined in accordance to the laws that apply to them.

Art. 40 Grounds for declining to cooperate

The FINMA can decline to make disclosure of nonpublic information and to deliver files to criminal investigation authorities and other domestic authorities to the extent that:

a. the information and the files serve only to develop internal opinions;

b. their disclosure or delivery would endanger a pending proceeding or adversely affect the performance of its supervisory activity;

c. it is not consistent with the goals of financial market supervision or its purpose.

Art. 41 Disputes

The Federal Administrative Court shall resolve differences of opinion between the FINMA, on one hand, and the criminal investigation authorities and other domestic authorities, on the other hand, upon the application of one of the affected authorities.

Section 4: Cooperation with foreign financial market supervisory authorities

Art. 42 Official assistance

[1] The FINMA may request information and documentation from foreign financial market supervisory authorities for purposes of enforcing the Financial Market Laws.

[2] The FINMA may only provide nonpublic information and documentation to foreign financial market supervisory authorities to the extent that they are required to observe governmental or professional confidentiality obligations and they:

a. use the information exclusively for the direct supervision of foreign institutions; and

b. forward the information to responsible authorities and bodies which are entrusted with the supervisory responsibilities in the public interest only on the basis of a general authorization in an international treaty or with the FINMA's consent.

[3] The FINMA shall refuse to consent if it is intended that the information will be forwarded to law enforcement authorities and legal assistance in criminal matters would be unavailable. It shall decide in consultation with the Federal Office of Justice.

[4] If the information to be provided by the FINMA relates to individual customers, the Federal Law of 20 December 1968[22] on Administrative Procedure is applicable.

Art. 43 Cross-border examinations

[1] For purposes of enforcing the Financial Market Laws, the FINMA can conduct direct examinations of foreign establishments of those supervised for which it is responsible for

22 SR **172.021**

consolidated supervision as part of home-country supervision, either on its own, through audit firms or designated third parties.

[2] It may permit foreign financial market supervisory authorities to conduct direct examinations of Swiss establishments of foreign institutions to the extent that these authorities:

a. are responsible for the consolidated supervision of the examined institution as part of home-country supervision; and
b. the prerequisites for official assistance under Article 42, paragraphs 2 and 3 are fulfilled.

[3] Only information which is necessary for the consolidated supervision of a foreign institution may be collected through a cross-border direct examination. Included, in particular, is information about whether an institution group-wide:

a. is appropriately organized;
b. appropriately recognizes, limits and monitors the risks of its business activities;
c. is managed by persons who offer the assurance that business is conducted in an irreproachable manner;
d. fulfills capital resources and risk-distribution regulations on a consolidated basis; and
e. properly fulfills its reporting obligations to supervisory authorities.

[4] The FINMA may accompany foreign financial market supervisory authorities in their direct examinations in Switzerland or allow them to be accompanied by an audit firm or designated third parties. The affected subjects of supervision may request that they are accompanied.

[5] Establishments organized under Swiss law must provide foreign financial market supervisory authorities and the FINMA with the information that is necessary for the performance of direct examinations or for official assistance by the FINMA and give them access to their records.

[6] Establishments are considered to be:

a. subsidiary corporations, branches, representative offices of those subject to supervision or foreign institutions; and
b. other businesses to the extent that their activities are subject to consolidated supervision by a financial market supervisory authority.

Chapter 4: Penal provisions

Art. 44 Activity without a license, recognition, admission or registration

[1] Whoever intentionally engages in an activity which requires a license, recognition, admission or registration under the Financial Market Laws without a license, recognition, admission or registration shall be punished with imprisonment for up to three years or a monetary penalty.

² Whoever does so negligently will be punished with a fine of up to 250,000 francs.

³ In the event of a repeat offense within five years after the date the previous judgment became legally binding, the monetary penalty shall amount to at least 45 day fines.

Art. 45 Providing false information

¹ Whoever intentionally provides false information to the FINMA, an audit firm or a designated third party shall be punished with imprisonment for up to three years or a monetary penalty.

² Whoever does so negligently will be punished with a fine of up to 250,000 francs.

³ In the event of a repeat offense within five years after the date the previous judgment became legally binding, the monetary penalty shall amount to at least 45 day fines.

Art. 46 Breaches of duty by audit firms or designated third parties

¹ Whoever, as auditor or designated third party, intentionally commits a gross breach of provisions of supervisory law by:

a. making material false statements or omitting material information in the audit report;
b. failing to make a required report to the FINMA;
c. failing to make a demand of the audited subject of supervision in accordance with Article 27;

shall be punished with imprisonment for up to three years or a monetary penalty.

² Whoever does so negligently will be punished with a fine of up to 250,000 francs.

³ In the event of a repeat offense within five years after the date the previous judgment became legally binding, the monetary penalty shall amount to at least 45 day fines.

Art. 47 Examination of the annual financial statements

¹ Whoever intentionally:

a. fails to have the annual financial statements prescribed by the Financial Market Laws to be audited by an admitted audit firm or fails to have an examination ordered by the FINMA performed;
b. fails to fulfill his or her obligations in relation to the audit firm or a designated third party;

shall be punished with imprisonment for up to three years or a monetary penalty.

² Whoever does so negligently will be punished with a fine of up to 250,000 francs.

³ In the event of a repeat offense within five years after the date the previous judgment became legally binding, the monetary penalty shall amount to at least 45 day fines.

Art. 48 Failure to comply with the FINMA's orders

Whoever fails to comply with an order issued by the FINMA under the threat of the criminal penalties under this article which has become legally binding or a decision of an appellate body shall be punished with a fine of up to 100,000 francs.

Art. 49 Violations by businesses

The investigation of punishable persons can be suspended and instead the business can be ordered to pay a fine (Article 7 of the Federal Law of 22 March 1974[23] on Administrative Criminal Law) if:

a. the investigation of persons who, under Article 6 of the Federal Law of 22 March 1974 on Administrative Criminal Law, are punishable would require investigative measures which would be disproportionate to the penalty which could have been imposed; and
b. for the illegal act in violation of the criminal penalty provisions of this law or the Financial Market Laws a fine of not more than 50,000 francs could be imposed.

Art. 50 Jurisdiction

[1] For illegal acts in violation of the criminal penalty provisions of this law or the Financial Market Laws, the Federal Law of 22 March 1974 [24] on Administrative Criminal Law is applicable to the extent that this law or the Financial Market Laws do not provide otherwise. The authority prosecuting and rendering judgment is the Federal Department of Finance.

[2] If a judicial determination has been sought or if the Federal Department of Finance considers that the prerequisites for imprisonment or another loss of liberty are present, then the punishable act is subject to the jurisdiction of the Federal Court. In this case, the Federal Department of Finance shall transfer the files to the Federal Prosecutor's Office for proceedings before the Federal Criminal Court. The transfer shall be deemed to initiate the prosecution. Article 73-83 of the Federal Law of 22 March 1974 on Administrative Criminal Law shall apply by analogy.

[3] The representatives of the Federal Prosecutor's Office and the Federal Department of Finance are not required to personally appear at the main hearing.

Art. 51 Consolidation of criminal investigation

[1] If the Federal Department of Finance as well as the Federal Court or a cantonal court would have jurisdiction over a criminal matter, the Federal Office of Justice can order the consolidation of the criminal investigation with the criminal investigation authority that is already involved with the matter to the extent that there is a common factual basis, that matter is not yet pending before the responsible court and the consolidation would not unreasonably delay the ongoing proceedings.

---

23 SR **313.0**
24 SR **313.0**

[2] The Appellate Chamber of the Federal Criminal Court shall determine any disputes between the Federal Department of Finance and the Federal Prosecutor's Office or the cantonal authorities.

Art. 52 Statute of limitations

The prosecution of violations of this law and the Financial Market Laws shall be barred after seven years.

Chapter 5: Procedure and legal protection

Art. 53 Administrative procedure

The procedure shall be based on the provisions of the Federal Law of 20 December 1968[25] on Administrative Procedure.

Art. 54 Legal protection

[1] The appeal of the FINMA's orders shall be based on the provisions concerning the federal administration of justice.

[2] The FINMA is entitled to appeal to the Federal Court.

Chapter 6: Final provisions

Section 1: Implementation

Art. 55 Implementing provisions

[1] The Federal Council shall issue implementing provisions.

[2] It can authorize the FINMA to issue implementing provisions for this law and the Financial Market Laws in matters of limited importance, specifically in matters that are primarily technical.

Art. 56 Implementation

The FINMA is responsible for the implementation of this law and the Financial Market Laws.

Section 2: Amendment of prior law

Art. 57

The amendment of prior law is addressed in the Annex.

---

25 SR **172.021**

Section 3: Transitional measures

Art. 58 Transfer of rights and obligations

1 The Federal Council shall determine the point in time when the FINMA shall have independent legal personality. From this point in time, it succeeds to the positions of the Federal Banking Commission, the Federal Office for Private Insurance and the Anti-Money Laundering Control Authority.

2 The Federal Council shall specify the rights, obligations and assets that are to be transferred to the FINMA, specify when the relevant legal effectiveness occurs and approve the initial balance sheet. It shall adopt all other measures necessary for the transition and shall issue the relevant regulations.

3 The FINMA shall assume responsibility for all proceedings of the Federal Banking Commission, the Federal Office for Private Insurance and the Anti-Money Laundering Control Authority which are pending on the date this law enters into force.

Art. 59 Transfer of employment relationships

1 The employment relationships of the staffs of the Federal Banking Commission, the Federal Office for Private Insurance and the Anti-Money Laundering Control Authority shall be transferred to the FINMA pursuant to Article 58, paragraph 1 and will be continued in accordance with this law.

2 There is no right to the continuation of the function, the field of work or the rank within the organization; there is, however, a right to the previous salary during a period of one year.

3 A job application procedure will be used only if it appears necessary because of a new organization or the availability of several candidates.

4 The FINMA shall endeavor to plan restructurings in a socially acceptable manner.

Art. 60 Responsible employer

1 The FINMA is considered the responsible employer for:

a. pensioners of the Federal Banking Commission, the Federal Office for Private Insurance and the Anti-Money Laundering Control Authority; and
b. their old age, disability and survivors benefits under the occupational pension fund which had become payable by the pension fund of the Federal Government before the entry into force of this law.

2 If the inability to work occurs before the entry into force of this law and its cause leads to disability at a later time and disability payments begin after its entry into force, FINMA is also considered the responsible employer.

Section 4: Referendum and entry into force

Art. 61

1 This law is subject to the right of the voters to petition for a referendum.

2 The Federal Council shall specify the effective date.

Date of entry into force:[26]

Articles 4, 7, 8, 9, paragraph 1 letters a–e and g–j, as well as paragraphs 2–5, Art. 10–14, 17–20, 21 paragraphs 3 and 4, 53–55, 58 paragraph 2 second sentence, 59 paragraphs 2–4; Annex: paragraph 4 (Administrative Court Law): heading before Articles 31 and 33 letter b: 1 February 2008

All other provisions: 1 January 2009

26 AS **2008** 5205

Annex
(Art. 57)

Amendments of prior law

The following federal laws are amended as follows:

1. Public Access to Governmental Records Law of 17 December 2004[27]

Art. 2, para. 2

...

2. Federal Law of 20 December 1968 on Administrative Procedure[28]

Art. 14, para. 1, provisions e and 2

...

3. Federal Law of 17 June 2005[29]

Art. 83, provisions u and v

...

4. Administrative Court Law of 17 June 2005[30]

Heading before Art. 31

...

Art. 33, provision b

...

Heading before Art. 35 and Art. 36a

...

Art. 36a

...

5. Criminal Court Law of 4 October 2002[31]

Art. 26, provision b

...

---

27 SR **152.3**. The amendment listed hereinafter is made in the mentioned law.
28 SR **172.021**. The amendments listed hereinafter are made in the mentioned law.
29 SR **173.110**. The amendments listed hereinafter are made in the mentioned law.
30 SR **173.32**. The amendments listed hereinafter are made in the mentioned law.
31 SR **173.71**. The amendment listed hereinafter is made in the mentioned law.

6. Pfandbrief Law of 25 June 1930[32]

Replacement of terms
The terms «Federal Banking Commission», «Banking Commission» *and* «Secretariat of the Banking Commission» *are to be replaced by* «FINMA» *throughout the law. Grammatical changes required by the change in terminology are to be made.*

Art. 5, subparagraph 3

…

Art. 32, para. 2

…

Art. 38a

…

Art. 38b

…

Art. 39

…

Art. 40

…

Art. 41 margin heading

Art. 42, 43 and 47
Repealed

7. Insurance Contract Law of 2 April 1908[33]

Art. 91, para. 3

…

Art. 92 margin heading and para. 2

…

8. Cartel Law of 6 October 1995[34]

Art. 10, para. 3

…

9. Financial Control Law of 28 June 1967[34]

Art. 8, para. 2

…

32 SR **211.423.4**. The amendments listed hereinafter are made in the mentioned law.
33 SR **221.229.1**. The amendments listed hereinafter are made in the mentioned law.
34 SR **251**. The amendment listed hereinafter is made in the mentioned law.

10. Road Transportation Law of 19 December 1958[35]

Art. 76a, para. 2

...

Art. 79e, para. 2

...

11. Accident Protection Contribution Law of 25 June 1976[36]

Art. 10, paras. 1 and 3

...

12. Federal Law of 18 March 1994[37] on Health Insurance[38]

Art. 21, para. 2

...

Art. 99, para. 2, third sentence

...

13. National Bank Law of 3 October 2003[39]

Art. 14, para. 2

...

14. Collective Investments Law of 23 June 2006[40]

Replacement of terms

The terms «Revision*» will be replaced with «Prüfung*», «auditor» will be replaced with «audit firm», «recognized auditor» will be replaced with «admitted audit firm», «Revisionsbericht**» will be replaced with «Prüfbericht**» *and* «supervisory authority» will be replaced with «FINMA». *Grammatical changes required by the change in terminology are to be made.*

[*Both words are best translated as "audit", so no change in the English translation is required.]

[**Both words are best translated as "audit report", so no change in the translation is required.]

---

35 SR **614.0**. The amendment listed hereinafter is made in the mentioned law.
36 SR **741.01**. The amendments listed hereinafter are made in the mentioned law.
37 SR **741.81**. The amendments listed hereinafter are made in the mentioned law.
38 SR **832.10**. The amendments listed hereinafter are made in the mentioned law.
39 SR **951.11**. The amendment listed hereinafter is made in the mentioned law.
40 SR **951.31**. The amendments listed hereinafter are made in the mentioned law.

Art. 2, para. 3, provision c

…

*Art. 14, para. 1bis*

…

Art. 47

…

Art. 50, para. 3

…

Art. 51, para. 6

…

Art. 126, para. 2
Repealed

Art. 127

…

Art. 128

…

Art. 130

…

Art. 131
Repealed

Art. 132

…

Art. 133

…

Art. 134

…

Art. 137
Repealed

Art. 139

…

Art. 141 and 142
Repealed

Art. 143

…

Art. 145, para. 2

...

Art. 148, para. 1, provisions a, c, g, subparagraph 4 and i
Repealed

Art. 148, para. 3

…

Art. 149, para. 1, provisions e, subparagraph 3, as well as paras. 3 and 4

…

4 Repealed

Art. 150

…

Art. 151
Repealed

Art. 152

…

15. Banking Law of 8 November 1934[41]

Replacement of terms

The terms «Federal Banking Commission» *and* «Banking Commission» *will be replaced by* «FINMA», «Revision*» *will be replaced by* «Prüfung*», «auditor» *will be replaced by* «audit firm» *and* «Revisionsbericht**» *will be replaced by* «Prüfbericht*» *throughout the law. Grammatical changes required by the change in terminology are to be made.*

[*Both words are best translated as "audit", so no change in the English translation is required.]

[**Both words are best translated as "audit report", so no change in the translation is required.]

Art. 1, para. 4

…

Art. 2, paras. 1 and 3

…

Art. 3d, para. 2

…

Art. 3h
Repealed

Art. 3bis, para. 1, introductory sentence

…

Art. 5
Repealed

Sixth Section (Arts. 11–14)

Repealed

41 SR **952.0**. The amendments listed hereinafter are made in the mentioned law.

Art. 18

…

Art. 19–22
Repealed

Heading before Art. 23

…

Art. 23

…

Art. 23bis, paras.1 and 2
Repealed

Art. 23ter

…

Art. 23^{quater}
Repealed

Art. 23^{quinquies}

…

Art. 23^{sexies}
Repealed

Art. 23^{septies}

…

Art. 23^{octies}
Repealed

Art. 24, para. 1
Repealed

Art. 26, para. 1, introductory sentence and provision b

…

Art. 38

…

Art. 39, para. 2
Repealed

Art. 46

…

Art. 47

…

Art. 48
Repealed

Art. 49

…

Art. 50–51bis
Repealed

16. Securities Exchanges Law of 24 March 1995[42]

Replacement of terms

The terms «supervisory authority» *and* «Banking Commission» *will be replaced by* «FINMA» *and* «auditor» *will be replaced by* «audit firm». *Grammatical changes required by the change in terminology are to be made.*

Art. 3 para. 1

…

Art. 11a

…

Art. 17

Art. 18 and 19
Repealed

Art. 23 paras. 3 and 4

…

Art. 28 provision g

…

Art. 32 para. 2 introductory sentence and 7

…

Art. 33a

…

Art. 33b

…

Art. 33c

…

Art. 33d

…

Heading before Art. 34

…

Art. 34
Repealed

Art. 35

…

---

42 SR **954.1**. The amendments listed hereinafter are made in the mentioned law.

Art. 35a

…

Art. 36

…

Art. 36a

…

Art. 38a

…

Art. 39 and 40
Repealed

Art. 41, para. 1, introductory sentence, as well as 3 and 4
1 *Introductory sentence: only affects the French text*

…

Art. 42

…

Art. 42a

…

Art. 43

…

Art. 44
Repealed

17. Money Laundering Law of 10 October 1997[43]

Art. 3 para. 5

…

Art. 12

…

Art. 13
Repealed

Art. 14 para. 1

…

Art. 15
Repealed

Heading before Art. 16

…

[43] SR **955.0**. The amendments listed hereinafter are made in the mentioned law.

Art. 16

…

Heading before Art. 17

…

Art. 17

…

Heading before Art. 18

…

Art. 18, subject heading, para. 1, introductory sentence, as well as paras. 2 and 3

…

Art. 18a

…

Art. 19
Repealed

Art. 19a

…

Art. 19b

…

Art. 20

…

Arts. 21 and 22
Repealed

Art. 24 para. 2

…

Art. 26 para. 2

…

Art. 27

…

Art. 28

…

Art. 29 paras. 1 and 3

…

Arts. 30 and 31
Repealed

Art. 34 para. 2

…

Art. 35 para. 2

…

Art. 36
Repealed

Art. 37

…

Arts. 38–40
Repealed

Art. 41

…

18. Insurance Supervision Law of 17 December 2004[44]

Replacement of terms

The terms «supervisory authority» *will be replaced by* «FINMA» *and* «auditor», *as well as* «external auditor» *will be replaced by* «audit firm». *Grammatical changes required by the change in terminology are to be made.*

Art. 2, para. 3

…

Art. 6, para. 2

…

Art. 22, paras. 2 and 3

…

Heading before Art. 27

…

Art. 27, para. 1, second sentence

…

Art. 28

…

Art. 29 Abs. 2 und 4
Repealed

Art. 47

…

Arts. 48 and 50
Repealed

Art. 61

…

44 SR **961.01**. The amendments listed hereinafter are made in the mentioned law.

Art. 73, para. 2

…

Art. 80

…

Art. 81–83
Repealed

Art. 86

…

Art. 87

…

Art. 88 para. 1

…

Federal Law concerning the Supervision of Insurance Businesses

SR 961.01

(Insurance Supervision Law, ISL)

of 17 December 2004 (as of 1 January 2009)

The Federal Parliament of the Swiss Confederation,

on the basis of Articles 82, paragraph 1, 98 paragraph 3, 117 paragraph 1 and 122 paragraph 1 of the Federal Constitution[1]

and after a review of the message of the Federal Council of 9 May 2003[2]

resolves:

Chapter 1: Subject, purpose and scope of application

Art. 1 Subject and purpose

1 This law governs the federal government's supervision of insurance businesses and insurance intermediaries.

2 It aims, in particular, for the protection of insureds against the insolvency risks of insurance businesses and against abuses.

Art. 2 Scope of application

1 Subject to supervision under this law are:

a. Swiss insurance businesses which engage in primary insurance or reinsurance;
b. insurance businesses domiciled in a foreign country, in respect of their insurance activities conducted in Switzerland or conducted from Switzerland, subject to any contrary provisions of an international treaty;
c. insurance intermediaries;
d. insurance groups and insurance conglomerates.

2 Excluded from supervision under this law are:

a. insurance businesses domiciled in a foreign country which only engage in reinsurance in Switzerland.
b. insurance businesses, to the extent that they are subject to special supervision under federal law to the extent of such supervision; considered as such, in particular, the occupational pension institutions recorded in the register of occupational pension plans.

1 SR **101**
2 BBl **2003** 3789

c. insurance intermediaries which have a dependent relationship to a policyholder, to the extent that they act in the interest of this policyholder and the companies controlled by it.

3 Insurance businesses, whose insurance activity is of slight economic importance or affects only a small group of insureds may be exempted by the Federal Financial Market Supervisory Authority (FINMA) from this supervision if special circumstances justify it.[3]

4 The Federal Council shall specify what is to be understood as engaging in insurance business in Switzerland.

Chapter 2: Commencing insurance business

Section 1: License

Art. 3 License requirement

1 Each insurance business which is subject to supervision under Article 2, paragraph 1, letters a and b (insurance business) requires a license from the FINMA[4] in order to commence engaging in the business of insurance.

2 Mergers, divestitures and changes in the legal form of insurance businesses also require an approval.

Art. 4 License application and business plan

1 An insurance business under Article 2, paragraph 1, letters a and b which wants to obtain a license to engage in the business of insurance must submit an application together with a business plan to the FINMA.

2 The business plan must include the following information and documentation:

a. the articles of incorporation;

b. the management structure and the geographic scope of the business of the insurance business and, if applicable, the insurance group or insurance conglomerate to which the insurance business belongs;

c. in the case of insurance business outside of Switzerland, the license from the responsible foreign supervisory body or an equivalent certification;

d. information about financial resources and reserves;

e. the financial statements for the last three financial years or the initial balance sheet of a new insurance business;

f. information about the persons who, directly or indirectly, own at least 10% of the capital or voting rights of the insurance business or who could, in another way, significantly influence its business activities;

---

3 Text in accordance with Annex para. 18 of the Financial Market Supervision Law of 22 June 2007, in force since 1 Jan. 2009 (SR **956.1**).

4 Terminology in accordance with Annex para. 18 of the Financial Market Supervision Law of 22 June 2007, in force since 1 Jan. 2009 (SR **956.1**). This change was made in the entire statute.

g. the identification by name of the persons entrusted with the ultimate management, supervision, control and conduct of the business or, for foreign insurance businesses, the name of the general agent [in Switzerland];

h. the identification by name of the responsible actuary;

i. the identification by name of the audit firm[5] and the persons responsible for the audit assignment and, to the extent that the insurance business is part of an insurance group or an insurance conglomerate, the organization of the audit assignment of the audit firm of the insurance group or insurance conglomerate;

j. the contracts or other arrangements through which any significant functions of the insurance business are to be out-sourced;

k. the intended lines of insurance and the nature of the risks to be insured;

l. if applicable, the statement of admission to the National Insurance Office and the National Guarantee Fund;

m. information about the means of providing legal assistance services to the extent that an license is requested for the "legal assistance" line of insurance;

n. the reinsurance plan, as well as the retrocession plan for reinsurance assumed;

o. the expected costs of establishing the insurance business;

p. the *pro forma* balance sheets and income statements for the first three business years;

q. information about the recognition, limitation and monitoring of risks;

r. the rating materials and general business terms and conditions which will be used in Switzerland for the insurance of all risks in occupational pension plans and supplementary insurance to the mandatory health insurance.

³ If an insurance business which already has a license for another line of insurance seeks a license for an additional line of insurance, then it only must provide the information and documents required by paragraph 2, letters a - l if they are different than those which already have been approved.

⁴ The FINMA can require further information and documents to the extent they are necessary for the consideration of the application.

Art. 5 Amendment of the business plan

¹ Amendments which relate to the elements of the business plan under Article 4, paragraph 2, letters a, h, i, k and r are to be submitted to the FINMA for its approval before they are implemented. In addition, amendments of the business plan which result from mergers, divestitures and restructurings of insurance businesses are to be submitted for approval.

² Amendments which relate to the elements of the business plan under Article 4, paragraph 2, letters b, c, d, f, g, j, l, m, n and q are to be notified to the FINMA; they are

5 Terminology in accordance with Annex para. 18 of the Financial Market Supervision Law of 22 June 2007, in force since 1 Jan. 2009 (SR **956.1**). The amendment was made in the entire text.

deemed approved if the FINMA does not initiate a review of the submission within four weeks.

Art. 6 Issue of the license

1 The license will be issued if the legal requirements are fulfilled and if the interests of the insured are protected.

2 If the insurance business is part of a foreign insurance group or a foreign insurance conglomerate, the license can be conditioned on the existence of an appropriate consolidated supervision by a foreign financial market supervisory authority.[6]

3 The license will be issued for one or more lines of insurance, It also authorizes the transaction of reinsurance in the relevant line of insurance. The Federal Council specifies the insurance lines.

4 The FINMA shall publicly disclose issued licenses.

Section 2: Prerequisites

Art. 7 Legal form

Insurance businesses must have the legal form of a corporation or a mutual corporation.

Art. 8 Minimum capital

1 An insurance business domiciled in Switzerland must have a minimum capital that, depending on the lines of insurance in which business is transacted, must amount to 3-20 million francs.

2 The Federal Council shall issue regulations concerning the minimum capital required for the individual lines of insurance.

3 The FINMA shall determine in each individual case the capital required.

Art. 9 Capital resources

1 An insurance business must have sufficient free and unencumbered capital resources in connection with all of its activities (solvency margin).

2 In determining the solvency margin, the risks that the insurance business is exposed to, the lines of insurance, the volume of business, the geographic scope of its business and internationally recognized principles are to be taken into account.

3 The Federal Council shall issue regulations concerning the creditable capital resources. The FINMA shall issue regulations concerning the calculation and the required amount of the solvency margin.

---

6 Text in accordance with Annex para. 18 of the Financial Market Supervision Law of 22 June 2007, in force since 1 Jan. 2009 (SR **956.1**).

Art. 10 Organizational fund

1 In additional to capital, an insurance business must have an organizational fund which allows it, in particular, to cover the costs of the establishment and development of its business or an exceptional business expansion. The amount of the organizational fund is, as a rule, at the commencement of business operations, an amount equal to as much as 50 percent of the minimum capital under Article 8.

2 The Federal Council shall specify the amount, the establishment and the duration for which the organizational fund is maintained and reestablished.

3 The FINMA shall determine in each individual case the required amount of the organizational fund.

Art. 11 Business purpose

1 An insurance business may, in addition to insurance business, only engage in businesses which are directly related to insurance business.

2 The FINMA can approve the conduct of other businesses if these do not endanger the interests of the insureds.

Art. 12 Transacting life insurance and other lines of insurance concurrently

Insurance businesses which engage in primary life insurance may, in addition, only engage in accident and health insurance.

Art. 13 Admission to the National Insurance Office and the National Guarantee Fund

Whoever wants to engage in the motor vehicle liability line of insurance must join the National Insurance Office and the National Guarantee Fund in accordance with Articles 74 and 76 of the Road Traffic Law of 19 December 1958[7].

Art. 14 Assurance of irreproachable conduct of business

1 The following persons must enjoy a good reputation and be able to provide assurance that business will be conducted in an irreproachable manner:

a. those who are responsible for ultimate management, supervision and control, as well as the conduct of business;
b. for foreign insurance businesses, the general agent [in Switzerland];

2 The Federal Council shall determine the professional qualifications that the persons specified in paragraph 1 must have.

3 If significant functions of the insurance business are delegated to other persons, paragraph 1 applies analogously.

7 SR **741.01**

Section 3: Additional prerequisites for foreign insurance businesses

Art. 15

1 A foreign insurance business which intends to engage in an insurance business in Switzerland must in addition:

a. be authorized to engage in insurance business in the country where it is domiciled;
b. establish a branch or subsidiary in Switzerland and appoint a general agent as its manager;
c. at its headquarters, have capital in accordance with Article 8 and a solvency margin in accordance with Article 9 which also takes into account the business activities in Switzerland;
d. have an organizational fund in Switzerland in accordance with Article 10 and appropriate assets;
e. provide a security deposit in Switzerland which is proportionate to the solvency margin related to the business in Switzerland. The FINMA shall determine the proportion and shall determine the calculation, the place of deposit and the assets which will be credited.

2 Contrary provisions in international treaties remain applicable.

Chapter 3: Engaging in the business of insurance

Section 1: Financial resources

Art. 16 Insurance technical reserves

1 An insurance business is required to establish sufficient insurance technical reserves for all of its business activities.

2 The Federal Council shall determine the principles for the determination of the insurance technical reserves. It can delegate the specification of the details concerning the manner and scope of the insurance technical reserves to the FINMA.

Art. 17 Restricted assets

1 An insurance business must secure claims under insurance contracts with restricted assets.

2 It is not required to provide security in accordance with paragraph 1 for its insurance portfolios outside of Switzerland if an equivalent security must be provided for them abroad.

Art. 18 Required amount of restricted assets

The required amount of restricted assets is equal to the insurance technical reserves under Article 16 and an appropriate surcharge. The FINMA shall specify the surcharge.

Art. 19 Application of restricted assets

[1] The assets in restricted assets will be used for the claims to be secured by the restricted assets.

[2] If an insurance portfolio is transferred to another insurance business, the restricted assets or equivalent assets shall be transferred to the assuming insurance business to the extent the FINMA does not order otherwise.

Art. 20 Regulations concerning restricted assets

The Federal Council shall issue regulations concerning the provision, location, coverage, alteration and control of restricted assets. It can delegate the specification of the technical details to the FINMA.

Art. 21 Ownership interests

[1] An insurance business with its domicile in Switzerland which intends to acquire an ownership interest in another business must report this to the FINMA when the ownership interest equals or exceeds 10, 20, 33 or 50 percent of the capital or voting rights of the other business.

[2] Whoever intends to directly or indirectly acquire an ownership interest in an insurance business domiciled in Switzerland must report this to the FINMA when the ownership interest equals or exceeds 10, 20, 33 or 50 percent of the capital or voting rights of the insurance business.

[3] Whoever intends to reduce an ownership interest in an insurance business domiciled in Switzerland below the thresholds of 10, 20, 33 or 50 percent of the capital or to reduce the voting rights or to so alter the ownership interest that the insurance business is no longer a subsidiary must report this to the FINMA.

[4] The FINMA can prohibit an ownership interest or subject it to conditions if the nature and scope of the ownership interest could endanger the insurance business or the interests of the insureds.

Section 2: Risk management

Art. 22

[1] An insurance business must be organized in a manner that, in particular, permits it to recognize, limit and monitor all significant risks.

[2] The Federal Council shall issue regulations about the objective, content and documentation of risk management.[8]

[3] The FINMA shall issue regulations concerning the monitoring of risks by an insurance business.[9]

Section 3: The responsible actuary

Art. 23 Appointment and function

[1] Insurance businesses must appoint a responsible actuary and provide this person with access to all business records.

[2] The responsible actuary must enjoy a good reputation, be professionally qualified and able to correctly assess the financial consequences of the activities of the insurance business. The Federal Council shall determine the professional qualifications the responsible actuary must have.

[3] An insurance business must notify the FINMA without delay of the termination or the resignation of the appointment of the responsible actuary.

Art. 24 Responsibilities

[1] The responsible actuary bears the responsibility for ensuring that:

a. the solvency margin is calculated correctly and the restricted assets meet the requirements of the supervisory regulations;
b. factually accurate accounting information is used; and
c. sufficient technical reserves are established.

[2] If the responsible actuary notes deficiencies, he or she is to notify the executive management of the insurance business without delay.

[3] In addition, the responsible actuary is to deliver a report at regular intervals to the executive management, or in the case of a foreign insurance business, the general agent [in Switzerland]. The proposed corrective measures, as well as any corrective measures already employed in respect of observed instances of non-compliance are to be reported.

[4] The FINMA shall issue more specific regulations concerning the responsibilities of the responsible actuary and the content of the report.

---

8 Text in accordance with Annex para. 18 of the Financial Market Supervision Law of 22 June 2007, in force since 1 Jan. 2009 (SR **956.1**).

9 Text added by Annex para. 18 of the Financial Market Supervision Law of 22 June 2007, in force since 1 Jan. 2009 (SR **956.1**).

Section 4: Reporting

Art. 25 Annual financial reports and regulatory reports

1 Insurance businesses shall produce each year, as of 31 December, a financial report, consisting of annual financial statements, an annual report and, if the law so requires, group financial statements. If the insurance business is part of an insurance group or an insurance conglomerate, then the group financial statements are, in each case, to be delivered.

2 In addition, they shall produce a regulatory report each year. The FINMA shall determine the requirements that this report must fulfill and shall specify the information and documents to be delivered with it.

3 Insurance businesses shall deliver the annual financial report as well as the regulatory report concerning the financial year then just ended to the FINMA not later than the following 30 April. Insurance businesses, which only are engaged in reinsurance shall deliver the reports not later than on 30 June.

4 Foreign insurance businesses shall deliver to the FINMA a separate annual financial report in respect of their business in Switzerland, as well as a separate regulatory report concerning the financial year then just ended.

5 The annual financial statements will be publicly reported in the report of the FINMA (Art. 48).

6 The FINMA can require interim reporting. It also can impose special requirements for the annual financial reports.

Art. 26 Special provisions concerning accounting standards

1 Insurance businesses must establish the general reserve required under Articles 671 and 860 of the Code of Obligations (CO)[10] in accordance with their business plans. The corporate law requirements concerning the establishment and release of undisclosed reserves do not apply to insurance technical reserves. Transparency and the protection of insureds remain assured.

2 The costs of incorporation, capital increases and business establishment and development costs during the financial year are to be charged to the organizational fund.

3 The Federal Council can, subject to the maintenance of transparency, issue other regulations for insurance businesses concerning the valuation of assets and liabilities, as well as the presentation of the annual financial statements.

10 SR **220**

Section 5: Audit[11]

Art. 27 Internal monitoring of business activities

1 An insurance business shall establish an effective internal control system, which takes into account all of its business activities. In addition, it shall appoint an internal audit function (Inspektorat)[12] which is independent from management.

2 The FINMA can exempt an insurance business from the requirement to appoint an internal audit function in individual cases when good cause is shown.

3 The internal audit function shall issue a report of its activities at least once each year and deliver it to the external auditors.

Art. 28 Audit firm[13]

1 An insurance business must appoint a licensed audit firm to review its conduct of its business.

2 The Federal Council shall issue implementation regulations for the requirements for the audit firm. It can authorize the FINMA to issue implementing regulations concerning technical matters.

Art. 29 Responsibilities of the audit firm

1 The audit firm shall review whether the annual financial statements conform, in respect of form and content, to statutory requirements, the articles of incorporation and the bylaws. In addition, it shall review, in accordance with the instructions of the FINMA, compliance with this law and the implementing regulations.

2 ...[14]

3 The FINMA can give additional assignments to the audit firm and require special reviews. The costs are borne by the insurance business.

4 ...[15]

Art. 30 Reporting obligation of the audit firm

The audit firm shall report to the FINMA without delay if any of the following are observed:

---

11 Text in accordance with Annex para. 18 of the Financial Market Supervision Law of 22 June 2007, in force since 1 Jan. 2009 (SR **956.1**).

12 Text of the second sentence in accordance with Annex para. 18 of the Financial Market Supervision Law of 22 June 2007, in force since 1 Jan. 2009 (SR **956.1**).

13 Text in accordance with Annex para. 18 of the Financial Market Supervision Law of 22 June 2007, in force since 1 Jan. 2009 (SR **956.1**).

14 Repealed by Annex para. 18 of the Financial Market Supervision Law of 22 June 2007, with effect from 1 Jan. 2009 (SR **956.1**).

15 Repealed by Annex para. 18 of the Financial Market Supervision Law of 22 June 2007, with effect from 1 Jan. 2009 (SR **956.1**).

a. criminal acts;
b. serious irregularities;
c. violations of the principles of an irreproachable conduct of business;
d. circumstances that may endanger the solvency of the insurance business or the interests of the insureds.

Section 6: Special provisions for individual lines of insurance

Art. 31 Restrictive regulations

The Federal Council can, for the protection of insureds, issue restrictive regulations for the various lines of insurance.

Art. 32 Legal protection insurance

1 An insurance business which wants to engage concurrently in legal protection insurance and other lines of insurance must:

a. delegate claims handling for claims in the legal protection insurance line to an independent business (claims adjusting business); or
b. grant to the insured the right, as soon as he or she can claim for the services of the insurance business under the insurance contract, to appoint an independent lawyer of his or her choice, or to the extent permitted by the applicable legal procedure, another qualified person who has the qualifications required by the relevant legal claim for the defense of his or her interests.

2 The Federal Council shall adopt rules governing the relationship between the insurance business and the claims adjustment business. It shall, in addition, issue regulations concerning the form and content of the legal protection insurance contract, specifically including the procedure to be used if the insurance business or the claims adjusting business cannot agree with the insured person on the measures for the resolution of the claim.

Art. 33 Natural hazards insurance

1 An insurance business may cover risks in Switzerland for fire risk only if coverage for natural hazards is included in the fire insurance.

2 The scope of coverage and the premium rating for natural hazards insurance are uniform and binding for all insurance businesses.

3 The FINMA shall review, on the basis of the rating materials and the related calculation materials provided by the insurance businesses, whether the resulting premiums are consistent with the risks and costs.

4 The Federal Council shall issue more specific regulations concerning:

a. the basis for the calculation of the premiums;
b. the scope of the natural hazards coverage and the limits of liability;

c. the nature and scope of the statistics to be provided by the insurance businesses.

5 It can:

a. if necessary, specify the terms of insurance;
b. impose measures in order to achieve an equal distribution of losses among the insurance businesses, in particular, membership in a private legal organization operated by the insurance businesses.

Art. 34 Motor vehicle liability insurance

Insurance institutions, which transact motor vehicle liability insurance must report to the FINMA the name and address of each claims adjustment organization appointed by them in each state of the European Economic Area in accordance with Article 79b of the Road Transportation Law of 19 December 1958.[16]

Art. 35 Reinsurance

1 Articles 15, 17-20, 32-34, 36, 37, 55-59 and 62 are not applicable to insurance businesses that engage exclusively in reinsurance.

2 The remaining provisions are to be applied by analogy.

Art. 36 Life insurance

1 The Federal Council shall issue regulations specifying the maximum technical interest rate for insurance businesses which engage in direct individual or group life insurance and which must fulfill obligations under life insurance contracts with interest rate guarantees.

2 Insurance businesses which engage in direct individual or group life insurance and which must fulfill life insurance contracts with rights to participate in surpluses must provide the insureds with a clear calculation of the policyholder surplus distribution each year. It must be especially clear from this on what basis the surpluses were calculated and under which principles they were distributed.

3 The Federal Council can issue regulations for insurance businesses pursuant to paragraph 2 concerning:

a. the method and manner in which the information which must appear in the statement is to be presented;
b. the basis for the calculation of the surpluses;
c. the basis and extent of the distribution of the surpluses.

Art. 37 Special rules for occupational pension plan business

1 Insurance businesses which engage in occupational pension plan business shall establish special restricted assets for their obligations in relation to occupational pension plans.

16 SR **741.01**

[2] They must keep separate annual financial statements for the occupational pension plan. These report in particular:

a. any release of reserves for future distributions of surplus;
b. premiums, including their allocation as savings, risk and cost premiums;
c. benefits payments;
d. any shares of surplus which were definitively allocated to insureds in the previous year and paid in the reporting year;
e. investment income, as well as unrealized gains and losses on investments;
f. the costs and income from derivative financial instruments;
g. the actual acquisition and administrative costs;
h. the actual costs of asset management;
i. the premiums paid for, and recoveries received from, reinsurance for disability, mortality and other risks;
j. the establishment and release of necessary technical reserves and specifically allocated equalization reserves.

[3] The Federal Council shall establish regulations concerning:

a. the method and manner in which the information which must be given in the separate annual financial statements must be presented;
b. the basis for the calculation of surplus distributions;
c. the principles for the distribution of the surplus distributions so calculated.

[4] The surplus distributions declared shall equal at least 90 percent of the surplus distributions determined under paragraph 3, letter b.

[5] If the financial statements show a loss, then no surplus distribution may be paid for the relevant financial year. The reported loss is to be carried forward to the next year and taken into account in the calculation of the surplus distribution.

Art. 38 Review of rating materials for which approval is required

The FINMA shall review in an approval procedure whether the expected premiums, based on the rating materials provided by an insurance businesses, are within a range that, on one hand, maintains the solvency of the individual insurance businesses and, on the other hand, maintains protection for insureds against abuse. Article 33, paragraph 3 shall not be affected.

Art. 39 Minimum benefits

Insurance businesses, to which the ownership of assets of the pension plans that were established by them and which are economically or organizationally dependent on them were transferred, must provide at least the benefits of a mandatory occupational pension plan.

Chapter 4: Insurance intermediaries

Art. 40 Definition

Insurance intermediaries, without regard for their title or description, are persons who offer or conclude insurance contracts on behalf of insurance businesses or other persons.

Art. 41 Prohibited intermediary activity

Insurance intermediaries are prohibited from engaging in an activity for the benefit of insurance businesses which are subject to this law, but are not authorized to engage in insurance activities.

Art. 42 Register

1 The FINMA shall maintain a register of insurance intermediaries (Register).

2 The Register is open to the public.

3 The Federal Council shall regulate the details.

Art. 43 Registration

1 Insurance intermediaries which neither legally nor economically, or in any other way are affiliated with an insurance business must be registered in the Register.

2 All other insurance intermediaries have the right to be registered in the Register.

Art. 44 Prerequisites for registration in the register

1 Registration is only possible for the person who:

a. demonstrates sufficient professional qualifications or, in the case of a legal entity, proves that it has sufficient employees who possess these qualifications; and
b. has obtained professional liability insurance or provided similar financial security.

2 The Federal Council shall specify the necessary professional qualifications and determine the necessary extent of the financial security. It can delegate the regulation of the technical details to the FINMA.

Art. 45 Disclosure obligation

1 As soon as insurance intermediaries contact insureds, they must inform the insureds of at least the following:

a. their identity and address;
b. whether the insurance coverage offered by the intermediary in a particular line of insurance is provided by only one or several insurance businesses and which insurance businesses are involved:

c. their contractual relationships with the insurance businesses on whose behalf they act, as well as the names of these businesses;
d. the person who can be held liable for negligence, mistakes or incorrect information in connection with their activities as insurance intermediaries;
e. the processing of personal information, in particular, the purpose, scope and recipients of the data, as well as the storage of it.

² The information under paragraph 1 is to be delivered in a form that is durable and accessible by the insureds.

³ The Federal Council shall regulate the details.

Chapter 5: Supervision

Section 1: General

Art. 46 Responsibilities

The FINMA has the following responsibilities:

a. It monitors compliance with the laws relating to insurance and insurance supervision.
b. It reviews whether the insurance businesses provide assurance that business is conducted in an irreproachable manner.
c. It monitors compliance with the business plan.
d. It monitors whether the insurance businesses are solvent, establish technical reserves in compliance with regulations and manage and invest assets properly.
e. It monitors the proper implementation of the claims handling regulations which are specified in the provisions of the Road Transportation Law of 19 December 1958[17] on motor vehicle liability insurance.
f. It protects the insureds against abuses by the insurance businesses and the insurance intermediaries.
g. It intervenes against improper circumstances which endanger the interests of the insureds.

² The FINMA can engage third parties to verify compliance with this law at any time. The costs are borne by the insurance business. The third parties so commissioned are exempted in relation to the FINMA from the secrecy obligation.

³ The Federal Council shall issue implementing regulations concerning the individual responsibilities.

---

17 SR **741.01**

Art. 47 Investigatory authority and reporting obligation concerning outsourcing [18]

[1] The FINMA can conduct investigations at any time.

[2] If an insurance business has delegated significant functions to other natural persons or legal entities, then these persons or legal entities are subject to the information and reporting obligations under Article 29 of the Financial Market Supervision Law of 22 June 2007[19].

Art. 48[20]

Art. 49 Publication of decisions

[1] The FINMA shall publish decisions concerning insurance law regularly.

[2] The Swiss courts must deliver to the FINMA, without charge, a copy of all decisions which address provisions of the Insurance Contract Law.

Art. 50[21]

Section 2: Protective measures

Art. 51 Principle

[1] If an insurance business or an insurance intermediary does not comply with the requirements of this law, a regulation or order of the FINMA, or if it appears that the interests of the insureds are otherwise endangered, then the FINMA shall adopt protective measures which seem to it necessary for the protection of the interests of the insureds.

[2] It can, in particular:

a. prohibit the unrestricted disposition of the assets of the insurance business;
b. order the deposit or restriction of assets;
c. assign in whole or in part the responsibilities and authorities of the officers and directors of an insurance business to a third person;
d. assign the portfolio of insurance policies and the related restricted assets to another insurance business with the consent of that insurance business;
e. order the liquidation of the restricted assets;
f. demand the dismissal of the persons entrusted with the ultimate management, supervision, control or conduct of the business, or the general agent, as well as

18 Text in accordance with Annex para. 18 of the Financial Market Supervision Law of 22 June 2007, in force since 1 Jan. 2009 (SR **956.1**).

19 SR **956.1**

20 Repealed by Annex para. 18 of the Financial Market Supervision Law of 22 June 2007, with effect from 1 Jan. 2009 (SR **956.1**).

21 Repealed by Annex para. 18 of the Financial Market Supervision Law of 22 June 2007, with effect from 1 Jan. 2009 (SR **956.1**).

the responsible actuary and prohibit them from engaging in any further insurance activities for a maximum of five years;

g. remove an insurance intermediary from the Register under Article 42.

Art. 52 Liquidation

If an insurance business becomes subject to liquidation, the FINMA may appoint the liquidator.

Art. 53 Commencement of bankruptcy proceedings

1 The commencement of bankruptcy proceedings in respect of an insurance business requires the approval of the FINMA. It shall issue the consent if rehabilitation is not possible.

2 The powers conferred by Article 170 of the Federal Law of 11 April 1889[22] on Debt Enforcement and Bankruptcy (DEBL) are available to the FINMA.

Art. 54 Conduct of bankruptcy proceedings

1 The FINMA can appoint a special bankruptcy administrator for the conduct of the bankruptcy proceedings and assign to it all of the powers of a meeting of creditors; it can, in addition, appoint a person to represent the policyholders in the bankruptcy proceedings.

2 For the notification of creditors, it can issue orders that depart from the provisions of the DEBL.[23]

3 Claims from insureds which can be recognized by means of the books and records of the insurance business are deemed submitted.

4 Claims under the insurance contracts for which security was provided pursuant to Article 17 will be first covered by the proceeds of the restricted assets. Any remaining proceeds are part of the bankruptcy estate.

Section 3: Additional protective measures for life insurance

Art. 55 Bankruptcy of an insurance business

1 Contrary to the terms of Article 37, paragraph 1 of the Federal Law of 2 April 1908[24] on the Insurance Contract, the life insurance policies which are secured by the restricted assets will not be terminated upon the commencement of bankruptcy proceedings.

2 In respect of the insurance policies referred to in paragraph 1, the FINMA can:

---

22 SR **281.1**
23 SR **281.1**
24 SR **221.229.1**

a. prohibit the repurchase of the polices and the making of loans against the policies, as well as advance payments and, in the situation covered by Article 36 of the Federal Law of 2 April 1908 on the Insurance Contract, the distribution of the reserves; or

b. grant a moratorium period to the insurance business for the performance of its obligations, as well the insureds for the premium payment.

3 During the moratorium period for premium payments, the insurance contracts can only be cancelled or converted to paid-up insurance at the written request of the insured.

Art. 56 Sale of restricted assets in bankruptcy

If the FINMA does not apply any special measures, then it shall direct the bankruptcy administrator to sell the restricted assets. When this direction is given, the insurance contracts expire. The insureds and the beneficiaries can no longer assert the claims permitted under Article 36, paragraph 3 of the Federal Law of 2 April 1908[25] on the Insurance Contract, as well as the claims under insurance policies which have become due and for credited shares of surplus.

Section 4: Additional protective measures in respect of foreign insurance businesses

Art. 57 Exclusion of the claims of third parties

In the case of foreign businesses, the investments constituting restricted assets as well as the security deposit are deemed pledged by operation of law for claims under insurance contracts which are included in insurance portfolios to be secured in accordance with this law. These investments can only be applied to meet obligations owed to third parties if the claims of all the insureds have been satisfied in full.

Art. 58 Venue for debt enforcement proceedings and forced sale

1 A foreign insurance business is subject to debt enforcement proceedings in respect of claims under insurance contracts which are included in insurance portfolios to be secured in accordance with this law where the Swiss branch or subsidiary is located (Arts. 151 ff. DEBL[26]). If the FINMA authorizes the sale of a real property, then the debt enforcement proceedings are to be continued where the real estate is located.

2 If an application for the sale of pledged property is made, the debt enforcement office is to notify the FINMA of this fact within three days.

3 If the insurance business fails to prove within 14 days after the submission of the application for the sale of pledged property that the relevant creditor has been satisfied in full, then after the insurance business has been heard, the FINMA shall inform the debt enforcement office which assets among the restricted assets or any security deposit are to be offered for sale.

---

25 SR **221.229.1**

26 SR. **281.1**

Art. 59 Limitations on authority

If the supervisory authority of the jurisdiction where the insurance business is domiciled has restricted or prohibited the disposition of assets of the insurance business, then the FINMA can, at its [the foreign supervisory authority's] request, impose the same measures on the [foreign] insurance business in respect of all [of its] Swiss business.

Section 5: End of insurance activities

Art. 60 Surrender of license

1 An insurance business which surrenders the license must submit a run-off plan to the FINMA for approval.

2 The run-off plan must provide details about:

a. the settlement of the financial obligations under the insurance contracts;

b. the funds that have been set aside for that purpose; and

c. the person responsible for these tasks.

3 If the insurance business does not comply with the approved run-off plan, then Article 61, paragraph 2 applies analogously.

4 An insurance business which has surrendered a license may not conclude any new insurance contracts in the relevant lines of insurance; existing insurance contracts may neither be extended nor may the scope of coverage be expanded.

5 The insurance business which has fulfilled its regulatory obligations will be released from supervision and the security deposit will be returned.

Art. 61[27] Revocation of the license

1 The FINMA can revoke the license to transact insurance business for individual or all lines of insurance if it ceased writing business more than six months earlier.

2 In connection with the revocation of the license under this law or under Article 37 of the Financial Market Supervision Law of 22 June 2007,[28] it shall adopt all measures that are necessary for the protection of the interests of the insureds, specifically those under Article 51.

3 After the revocation of the license, an insurance business may not conclude any new insurance contracts; existing insurance contracts may neither be extended nor may the scope of coverage be expanded.

27 Text in accordance with Annex para. 18 of the Financial Market Supervision Law of 22 June 2007, in force since 1 Jan. 2009 (SR **956.1**).

28 SR **956.1**

Art. 62 Transfer of an insurance portfolio

[1] If an insurance business transfers its Swiss insurance portfolio, in whole or in part, to another insurance business pursuant to a contractual arrangement, then this agreement requires approval by the FINMA. The FINMA shall approve the transfer only if the interests of the insureds are protected completely.

[2] If the FINMA approves a portfolio transfer, then it shall specify the conditions.

[3] The assuming insurance business is required to notify the assumed insureds individually about the portfolio transfer and the termination right within 30 days after the publication of the approval. An insured has the right to terminate the insurance contract within three months after the individual notice.

[4] The FINMA can order the exclusion of the termination right if the portfolio transfer does not result, economically, in a change of the contractual counterparty of the insured.

Art. 63 Publication

[1] The FINMA shall publish, at the cost of the insurance business, the surrender or revocation of the license to transact business.

[2] It shall publish, at the cost of the acquiring insurance business, the approval of a portfolio transfer.

Chapter 6: Special provisions concerning the supervision of insurance groups and insurance conglomerates

Section 1: Insurance groups

Art. 64 Insurance group

Two or more businesses constitute an insurance group if:

a. at least one is an insurance business;
b. they are, as a whole, primarily engaged in the field of insurance; and
c. they constitute an economic unit or otherwise, through influence or control, are connected to each other.

Art. 65 Imposition of group supervision

The FINMA can impose group supervision on an insurance group to which a business in Switzerland belongs, if the insurance group:

a. is actually managed from Switzerland;
b. is actually managed outside Switzerland, but is not subject there to an equivalent group supervision.

2 If foreign authorities simultaneously exercise complete or partial supervision over the insurance group, the FINMA shall consult with the foreign authorities concerning the responsibilities, methods and subject of the supervision, while preserving its own authority and taking into account any conglomerate supervision. Before rendering its decision, it shall consult with those businesses in the insurance group which have their domicile in Switzerland.

Art. 66 Relationship to individual supervision

The group supervision under this section is supplementary to the individual supervision of an insurance business.

Art. 67 Assurance of irreproachable business conduct

Articles 14 and 22 apply by analogy to the persons who are responsible for the ultimate supervision, control and conduct of the business of the insurance group, as well as its risk management.

Art. 68 Monitoring risks

The FINMA can issue regulations for the monitoring of group internal transactions and the group-wide risk concentration.

Art. 69 Capital resources

1 The Federal Council shall specify the group-wide creditable capital resources.

2 FINMA shall specify the required capital resources. In this regard, it shall make use of existing, internationally recognized principles in the insurance industry and take into account the significance of the other areas of business, as well as the related risks.

Art. 70 External auditors

Insurance groups must have an audit firm. Articles 28 and 29 apply analogously.

Art. 71 Reporting obligation

If insurance businesses belong to insurance groups, then the reporting obligation under Article 47 applies to all businesses of the group.

Section 2: Insurance conglomerates

Art. 72 Insurance conglomerate

Two or more businesses constitute an insurance conglomerate if:

a. at least one is an insurance business;
b. at least one is a bank or a securities dealer of economic significance;
c. they are, as a whole, primarily engaged in the field of insurance; and
d. they constitute an economic unit or otherwise, through influence or control, are connected to each other.

Art. 73 Imposition of conglomerate supervision

[1] The FINMA can impose conglomerate supervision on an insurance conglomerate to which a business in Switzerland belongs, if the conglomerate:

a. is actually managed from Switzerland;

b. is actually managed outside Switzerland, but is not subject to an equivalent group supervision.

[2] If foreign authorities assert complete or partial supervision of the insurance conglomerate, the FINMA shall consult with the foreign authorities concerning the responsibilities, methods and subject of the supervision, while maintaining its own authority and taking into account any group supervision. Before rendering its decision, it shall consult with those businesses in the insurance conglomerate which have their domicile in Switzerland.[29]

Art. 74 Relationship to individual and group supervision

The conglomerate supervision pursuant to this section is supplementary to the individual supervision and the supervision of an insurance or finance group by the relevant supervisory authorities.

Art. 75 Assurance of irreproachable business conduct

Articles 14 and 22 apply by analogy to the persons who are responsible for the ultimate management, supervision, control and conduct of the business of the insurance conglomerate, as well as its the risk management.

Articles 14 and 22 apply by analogy to the persons who are responsible for the ultimate management, supervision, control and the management of business of the insurance conglomerate.

Art. 76 Monitoring risks

The FINMA can issue regulations for the monitoring of the conglomerate's internal transactions and the conglomerate-wide risk concentration.

Art. 77 Capital resources

[1] The Federal Council shall specify the conglomerate-wide creditable capital resources.

[2] The FINMA shall specify the required capital resources. In this regard, it makes use of the existing, internationally recognized principles in the insurance and finance industries and takes into account the significance of these areas of business, as well as the related risks.

Art. 78 External auditors

Insurance conglomerates must have an audit firm. Articles 28 and 29 apply analogously.

---

[29] Text in accordance with Annex para. 18 of the Financial Market Supervision Law of 22 June 2007, in force since 1 Jan. 2009 (SR **956.1**).

Art. 79 Reporting obligation

If insurance businesses belong to insurance conglomerates, then the reporting obligation under Article 47 applies to all businesses of the conglomerate.

Chapter 7: Cooperation and procedure

Art. 80[30] National exchange of information

The FINMA is authorized to provide to other Swiss financial market supervisory authorities, as well as the Swiss National Bank, non-public information and documentation which is necessary for the performance of their duties.

Art. 81-83[31]

Art. 84 Procedure

1 If an order is issued concerning ratings that affects in force insurance policies, this is notified by publication in the *Bundesblatt*. The notice shall contain a summary presentation of the subject and the content of the order and, in respect of the insureds, is deemed to be the publication of the order under Article 36 of the Federal Law of 20 December 1968[32] on Administrative Procedure.

2 An appeal is to be submitted within 30 days after notice of the order.

3 Appeals against orders concerning rates do not suspend the effective date of the order.

Art. 85 Courts

1 Private law disputes between insurance businesses or between insurance businesses and insureds shall be decided by a court.

2 For disputes arising out of supplementary insurance to the social health insurance under the Federal Law of 18 March 1994[33] on Health Insurance, a simplified and expedited procedure is contemplated by the cantons in which the court officially determines the facts and evaluates the evidence in its sole and unfettered judgment.

3 In the case of disputes which are the subject of paragraph 2, administrative costs may not be imposed on the parties; in the case of proceedings conducted in bad-faith, the court may nevertheless impose costs, entirely or partially, on the responsible party.

---

30 Text in accordance with Annex para. 18 of the Financial Market Supervision Law of 22 June 2007, in force since 1 Jan. 2009 (SR **956.1**).

31 Repealed by Annex para. 18 of the Financial Market Supervision Law of 22 June 2007, with effect from 1 Jan. 2009 (SR **956.1**).

32 SR **172.021**

33 SR **832.10**

Chapter 8: Penal provisions

Art. 86[34] Violations

A fine of up to 500,000 francs will be imposed on the person who intentionally:

a. violates an obligation under Article 13;
b. violates a reporting obligation under Article 21;
c. fails to deliver the annual financial report and the regulatory report under Article 25 within the time period specified by law;
d. fails to establish the technical reserves required by supervisory law or approved in a specific case;
e. violates a reporting obligation under Article 45;
f. violates the requirement of a proper claims handling under Article 79c, paragraph 1 of the Road Transportation Law of 17 December 1958[35].

2 Whoever acts negligently will be punished with a fine of up to 150,000 francs.

3 In the event of a repeated offense within five years after the final legal judgment, the fine shall amount to at least 10,000 francs.

Art 87[36] Offenses

4 Imprisonment of up to three years or a fine will be imposed on a person who intentionally:

a. concludes or brokers insurance contracts on behalf of an insurance business that is not licensed to transact insurance business in Switzerland;
b. fails to submit for approval amendments to a business plan in accordance with Article 5, paragraph 1 or who does not report changes to a business plan to the FINMA in accordance with Article 5, paragraph 2;
c. removes or encumbers assets which are restricted assets, with the consequence that the required amount is no longer covered;
d. commits other acts which reduce the value of the restricted assets.

5 Whoever acts negligently will be punished with a fine of up to 250,000 francs.

6 In the event of a repeated offense within five years after the final legal judgment, the fine shall amount to at least 45 day fines.

---

34 Text in accordance with Annex para. 18 of the Financial Market Supervision Law of 22 June 2007, in force since 1 Jan. 2009 (SR **956.1**).

35 SR **741.01**

36 Text in accordance with Annex para. 18 of the Financial Market Supervision Law of 22 June 2007, in force since 1 Jan. 2009 (SR **956.1**).

Chapter 9: Final provisions

Art. 87 Implementation

¹ The Federal Council is charged with the implementation of this law.[37]

² Before the adoption of regulations, the Federal Council shall grant a hearing to interested organizations.

³ The cantons retain the right to issue public safety regulations concerning fire insurance. They can impose appropriate fees to be used for purposes of fire prevention and the prevention of loss from natural hazards on fire insurance businesses in respect of the Swiss portfolio and require them to provide, for this purpose, information about the policy limits of the fire insurance policies applicable to the territory of the canton.

Art. 88 Repeal and amendment of prior law

The repeal and amendment of prior law will be specified in an attachment.

Art. 89 Transitional measures

¹ Insurance businesses which have received a license for the transaction of business in insurance lines which are supplementary to other lines may, with the entry into force of this law and within its limitations, transact such business independently.

² The time limits for the delivery of the reports required by Article 25 are to be observed for the first financial year which follows the date of the entry into force of this law.

³ Insurance intermediaries under Article 43, paragraph 1 must apply to the FINMA for registration in the register within six months after the entry into force of this law.

⁴ The Federal Council can provide a transitional period for the acquisition of the professional qualifications required for the persons subject to Articles 23, 28 and 44.

⁵ Insurance businesses which have less capital than is prescribed by Article 8, must increase it within two years after the entry into force of this law.

⁶ Whoever, from within Switzerland, actually manages an insurance group or an insurance conglomerate, but does not transact insurance business in Switzerland, must give notice thereof to the FINMA within six months after the entry into force of this law.

⁷ Existing insurance groups or conglomerates must comply with the new provisions within two years after the entry into force of this law.

⁸ The FINMA can extend the time limits under paragraphs 5, 6 and 7 upon application and a showing of good cause for such an extension.

---

37 Text in accordance with Annex para. 18 of the Financial Market Supervision Law of 22 June 2007, in force since 1 Jan. 2009 (SR **956.1**).

Art. 90 Referendum and entry into force

[1] This law is subject to the right of the voters to petition for a referendum.

[2] The Federal Council shall specify the effective date.

Date of entry into force:[38]
Article 2, paragraph 2, letter c of the amendment to the Money Laundering Law (Annex para. II 8) will be entered into force on a later date
All other provisions: 1 January 2006.

[38] BRB of 9 Nov. 2005 (AS **2005** 5298)

Annex
(Art. 89)

Repeal and Amendment of Prior Law

I.

The following federal laws are repealed:

1. The Federal Law of 4 February 1919[39] on the Security Deposits of the Foreign Insurance Businesses;
2. The Security Law of 25 June 1930[40];
3. The Insurance Supervisory Law of 25 June 1978[41];
4. The Non-Life Insurance Law of 25 March 1992[42];
5. The Life Insurance Law of 18 June 1993[43].

II

The following federal laws are amended as follows:

1. Code of Obligations[44]

Art. 671, paragraph 6 and Art. 860, paragraph 4

Repealed

2. Accident Prevention Contribution Law of 25 June 1976[45]

Art. 10

...

3. Federal Law of 25 June 1982[46] on the Occupational Old Age, Survivors and Disability Fund

Art. 68, paragraph 2

Repealed

4. Federal Law of 18 March 1994[47] on Health Insurance

Art. 11, provision b

...

39 [BS 10 296; AS **1978** 1836 Art. 51 and Annex para. 1, **1992** 2363 Annex para. 3, **1993** 3209, **1995** 1227 Annex para.18]

40 [BS 10 303; AS **1978** 1836 Annex para. 2, **1992** 288 Annex para. 67 2363 Annex para. 4, **1993** 3211, **1995** 1227 Annex para. 19]

41 [AS **1978** 1836, **1988** 414, **1992** 288 Annex para. 66 733 SchlB Annex para. 3 2363 Annex para. 2, **1993** 3204, 1995 1328 Annex para. 2 3517 para. I 12 5679, 2000 2355 Annex para. 28, **2003** 232, **2004** 1677 Annex para. 4 2617 Annex para. 12]

42 [AS **1992** 2363, 1993 3247]

43 [AS **1993** 3221, **2004** 1677 Annex para. 6]

44 SR **220**

45 SR **741.81**. The change listed hereafter has been made in the referenced enactment.

46 SR **831.40**

47 SR **832.10**. The change listed hereafter has been made in the referenced enactment.

5. Federal Law of 20 March 1981[48] on Accident Insurance

Article 68, paragraph 1, provision a

...

6. Banking Law of 8 November 1934[49]

Art. 3b-3h

...

*Art. 3bis, paragraph 1 ^bis^*

...

Transitional provisions of the amendment of 17 December 2004

...

7. Securities Exchanges Law of 24 March 1995[50]

Art. 10, paragraph 5

...

Art. 14

...

8. Money Laundering Law of 10 October 1997[51]

Art. 2, paragraph 2, provision c and Art. 3, provision d

2 Financial intermediaries are:

c. the insurance institutions under the Insurance Supervision Law of 17 December 2004[52] (ISL), which engage in primary life insurance or distribute shares of an investment fund, as well as the insurance intermediaries under Article 43, paragraph 1 ISL;

3 ...

d. Repealed

Article 13, paragraph 2

...

Article 14, paragraph 1

...

48 SR **832.20**. The changes listed hereafter have been made in the referenced enactment.

49 SR **952.0**. The changes listed hereafter have been made in the referenced enactment.

50 SR **954.1**. The changes listed hereafter have been made in the referenced enactment.

51 SR **955.0**. The changes listed hereafter excluding Art. 2, para. 2 provision c have been made in the referenced enactment.

52 SR **961.01**.

Regulation on the Supervision of Private Insurance Businesses

SR 961.011

(Supervision Regulation, SR)

of 9 November 2005 (as of 1 January 2009)

The Swiss Federal Council,

based on the Insurance Supervision Law of 17 December 2004[1] (ISL), Article 15 of the Federal Personnel Law of 24 March 2002,[2] as well as the application of the treaty of 10 October 1989[3] between the Swiss Confederation and the EEA concerning direct insurance with the exception of life insurance and the treaty of 19 December 1996[4] between the Swiss Confederation and the Principality of Liechtenstein concerning direct insurance

orders:

Title 1: Scope of application

Art. 1 Insurance activity in Switzerland

[1] An insurance activity in Switzerland exists, regardless of the type of contract and where it is concluded, if:

a. a natural person or legal entity domiciled in Switzerland is among the policy holders or insured persons; or

b. property located in Switzerland is insured.

[2] Foreign insurance businesses with their domicile abroad which do not have a branch in Switzerland are not subject to supervision in Switzerland if they transact only the following lines of insurance business;

a. coverage of insurance risks in connection with marine transport, air transport and cross-border transportation;

b. coverage for risks located abroad;

c. coverage for war risks.

[3] Paragraphs 1 and 2 apply to insurance intermediation by analogy.

---

1 SR **961.01**
2 SR **172.220.1**
3 SR **0.931.1**
4 SR **0.961.514**

Art. 2 Reinsurance captives

1 Articles 41 - 53 are not applicable to insurance businesses that are owned by one or more trading, industrial or finance companies and that reinsure only the risks of these companies.

2 In the case of a complex risk structure or significant financial risks, the FINMA can declare Articles 41 - 53 applicable in an individual case.[5]

Title 2: Commencement of insurance business

Chapter 1: General

Art. 3 Scope of the license

1 The FINMA[6] shall issue the license to conduct business for one or more lines of insurance in accordance with Annex 1.

2 The license to conduct business for a line of nonlife insurance also authorizes the transaction of insurance lines B1–B13, B16 and B18, to the extent that the risks allocated to these lines:

a. are related to the primary risk or relate to the property that is insured against the primary risk; and
b. are covered by the same contract that covers the primary risk.

3 The risk allocated to the insurance line B17 may, under the conditions in paragraph 2, be covered without special consent to the extent this risk:

a. is related to the risks allocated to the insurance line B18; or
b. relates to disputes or claims which result from the use of sea-going vessels or connected with this use

4 The license to write insurance lines A1, A3, A4 and A5, as well as B1 and B2 also authorizes the writing of disability insurance.

5 The license to write primary insurance also authorizes the writing of reinsurance in the licensed lines of insurance.

Art. 4 Approval of mergers, divestitures and changes in legal form

1 The FINMA shall issue an approval pursuant to Article 3, paragraph 2 ISL if the protection of insureds, in particular protection against insolvency risks of the acquiring insurance business and abuse, is assured.

2 In the case of mergers, divestitures and changes in legal form, the affected businesses must ensure that existing insurance relationships are continued without change.

---

5 Text in accordance with Annex para. 11 of the Financial Market Audit Regulation of 15 Oct. 2008 in force since 1 Jan. 2009 (SR **956.161**).

6 Term in accordance with Annex para. 11 of the Financial Market Audit Regulation of 15 Oct. 2008 in force since 1 Jan. 2009 (SR **956.161**). This change was implemented throughout the regulation.

[3] Mergers, divestitures and changes in legal form may only be submitted for recording in the commercial register when the approval has been given.

[4] If mergers, divestitures and changes in legal form specified in Article 3, paragraph 2 ISL were recorded in the commercial register without the approval of the FINMA, it will take the action necessary to restore conformity with the law at the cost of the companies involved.

Art. 5 Notification obligation in the case of changes to the business plan

Changes in the business plan under Article 5, paragraph 2 ISL are to be notified to the FINMA within fourteen days from the occurrence of the relevant circumstances.

Chapter 2: License requirements

Section 1: Minimum capital

Art. 6 Basic principle

[1] If the business of an insurance business comprises multiple lines or multiple risks, in determining the minimum capital, the line or risk with the greatest amount is dispositive.

[2] ...[7]

Art. 7 Life insurance

The minimum capital for insurance business that engage in life insurance amounts to:

a. 5 million francs for the insurance lines A2.1, A2.4 and A7, as well as for the insurance lines A3.3, A3.4 and A6, to the extent only death or a premium exemption is insured;
b. 8 million francs for the insurance lines A2.2, A2.3, A2.5, A2.6, A3.1, A3.2, A4 and A5, as well as for the insurance lines A3.3, A3.4 and A6, to the extent that, in addition to insurance against death or a premium exemption, capital protection with guaranteed interest or other guarantees are issued;
c. 10 million francs for the insurance line A1;
d. 12 million francs for the insurance line A1, to the extent full protection is provided (conducting the savings process in the occupational pension plans with capital protection, minimum interest rate and pension conversion rate guarantee).

Art. 8 Nonlife insurance

The minimum capital for insurance businesses that engage in nonlife insurance amounts to:

a. 8 million francs for the insurance lines B1–B8 and B10–B15;
b. 3 million francs for the insurance lines B9, B16, B17 and B18.

---

[7] Repealed by para. 1 of the Regulation of 18 Oct. 2006, with effect from 1 Jan. 2007 (AS **2006** 4425).

Art. 9 Reinsurance

The minimum capital for insurance businesses that engage in reinsurance amounts to:

a. 10 million francs for the insurance lines C1 and C2;

b. 3 million francs for the insurance line C3.

Art. 10 Deviation from the minimum capital

Under special conditions, specifically if the risk exposure of the insurance business and the planned scope of business justify it, the FINMA can, within the statutory limits under Article 8, paragraph 1 ISL, deviate from the amounts under Articles 7-9.

Section 2: Organizational fund

Art. 11

1 The organizational fund, as a rule, amounts to 20% of the minimum capital. It may be used for purposes other than those specified in Article 10, paragraph 1 ISL no earlier than three years after its establishment and only with the approval of the FINMA.

2 For insurance businesses that are authorized to write insurance line C3, the organizational fund amounts to at least 300,000 francs.

3 The FINMA can require the increase or reestablishment of the organizational fund if a loss is reported in the annual financial statement or the insurance business plans an exceptional business expansion.

Chapter 3: Prudential rules

Art. 12 Board of directors

1 The board of directors must be chosen in a manner that ensures that, as a whole, it can fulfill its responsibilities to supervise and provide the ultimate management of the insurance business; in particular, it must be made certain that the necessary insurance expertise is available.

2 The curriculum vitae of each new member of the board of directors is to be delivered to the FINMA within 14 days after his or her appointment.

Art. 13 Double functions

1 The president of the board of directors may not simultaneously be the presiding officer of the executive board.

2 The FINMA can, in an individual case upon a showing of good cause, grant exceptions to an insurance business and subject these to conditions.

Art. 14 Management of the business

1 The persons who are responsible for the management of the business must have the necessary knowledge for the part of the insurance business that is under their control.

² The curriculum vitae of each new member of the executive board is to be delivered to the FINMA within 14 days after his or her appointment.[8]

Chapter 3: Supplementary regulations for foreign insurance businesses

Section 1: Solvency margin and security deposit

Art. 15

¹ An insurance business shall possess unencumbered assets in Switzerland in an amount equal to the required solvency margin which is required pursuant to Articles 23-32 for the conduct of business in Switzerland. The amount of the security deposit pursuant to paragraph 2 shall be included.

² It shall deposit with the Swiss National Bank assets as specified in Article 79, paragraph 1, letters a, b, e or g in an amount equal to 10 percent of the required solvency margin, however at least equal to the highest of the following specified amounts:

a. 600,000 francs for the insurance lines A1–A6, subject to letter b;
b. 450,000 francs for the insurance lines A2.1, A2.3, A2.4, A2.6 and A7 to the extent no capital, interest or longevity guarantees are provided, as well as for insurance businesses which engage in life insurance in the form of a mutual company;
c. 280,000 francs for the insurance line B14;
d. 80,000 francs for the insurance lines B10–B13, as well as B15;
e. 60,000 francs for the insurance lines B1–B8, B16 and B18;
f. 40,000 francs for the insurance lines B9 and B17.

Section 2: General agent

Art. 16 Requirements

¹ The general agent of a foreign insurance business shall reside in Switzerland and shall be charged with the actual management of the office for all of the Swiss business.

² He or she must possess the knowledge necessary for the operation of the insurance business.

³ Before the appointment of a general agent or a new general agent, the curriculum vitae and the power of attorney of the executive board are to be delivered to the FINMA.

Art. 17 Duties and authorities

¹ The general agent shall represent the foreign insurance business before the FINMA and in relation to third parties in all matters which relate to compliance with the insurance laws and regulations. In particular, he or she has the following duties and authorities:

---

8 Text in accordance with Annex para. II 1 1 of the Audit Supervision Regulation of 22 Aug. 2007 (SR **221.302.3**).

a. the acquisition or disposition of assets for the account of the insurance business for the purpose of establishing or modifying the security deposit or the restricted assets in accordance with the guidelines of the insurance business or the orders of the FINMA;
b. the maintenance of the files at the office for all Swiss business and the keeping of the books and register (Art. 19);
c. giving binding statements to the registers and land register offices needed to complete the legal transactions specified under letter a;
d. giving statements about the rating materials used in Switzerland and other insurance materials.

2 He or she shall represent the insurance business before Swiss courts and debt enforcement and bankruptcy offices and shall accept service of process on and notices to the insurance business with legally binding effect.

3 Not in his or her competence are statements about:

a. the expansion of the license;
b. forfeiting the license;
c. amendments of the business plan of the insurance business, subject to paragraph 1, letter d;
d. the annual financial report for all of the business of the insurance business;
e. the voluntary transfer of the Swiss insurance portfolio.

Art. 18 Power of attorney

1 The power of attorney is to include the rights and duties specified in Article 17.

2 The appointment of the general agent and the termination of the power of attorney will be published in the *Swiss Official Gazette of Commerce*.

Art. 19 Maintenance of records

1 The general agent shall maintain the records of the Swiss insurance portfolio at the office for all Swiss business and shall keep the relevant books and register.

2 Upon an application made upon a showing of good cause, the FINMA may permit the storage of the records at another location.

Art. 20 Foreign business

1 Foreign insurance companies that from Switzerland only conduct business abroad must provide proof that they are licensed to conduct insurance business in the country of their domicile and that the supervisory authority in the domiciliary jurisdiction has agreed to the establishment of a branch in Switzerland.[9]

9 Text in accordance with Annex para. 11 of the Financial Market Audit Regulation of 15 Oct. 2008, in force since 1 Jan. 2009 (SR **956.161**).

[2] The provisions applicable to the general agent apply by analogy.

Title 3: Solvency

Chapter 1: Basic principles

Art. 21 Financial security

Financial security is measured on the basis of solvency and insurance technical reserves.

Art. 22 Methods of determining solvency

[1] The solvency of the insurance business is evaluated on the basis of two methods:

a. Solvency I: The determination of the necessary capital resources in relation to the volume of business (required solvency margin) and the creditable capital resources (available solvency margin);
b. Swiss Solvency Test (SST): The determination of the necessary capital resources in relation to the risks to which an insurance business is exposed (target capital) and the creditable capital (risk-bearing capital).

[2] Both methods are to be applied independently from one another.

Chapter 2: Solvency I

Section 1: Required solvency margin for insurance businesses that write life insurance

Art. 23 Basic principle

The solvency margin required for the entire business operation of an insurance business is the sum of the required solvency margins under Articles 24-26.

Art. 24 Calculation for insurance lines A1 and A3

[1] The required solvency margin for insurance companies that write the insurance line A1 and A3 equals the sum of the first and second results.

[2] For the first result, 4 percent of the mathematical reserves will be multiplied with the quotient of the mathematical reserves reduced by the share reinsured and retroceded and the total of the mathematical reserves, subject to a minimum of 0.85.

[3] For the second result, the risk sum will be successively multiplied by the percentage determined under paragraph 4 and with the reinsurance factor.

[4] The percentage with which the risk sum is multiplied is for:

a. whole life insurance with a total term of up to three years, 0.1 percent;
b. whole life insurance with a total term of more than three and up to five years, 0.15 percent;

c. all other insurance 0.3 percent.

5 The reinsurance factor is the quotient resulting from the total risk amount reduced by the share thereof reinsured or retroceded and the total risk amount. It shall be at least 0.5.

Art. 25 Calculation for insurance lines A2, A6 and A7

1 The solvency margin required of insurance businesses that write insurance lines A2, A6 and A7 equals the sum of the first and second results.

2 The first result is calculated as follows:

a. for insurance for which the insurance business bears investment risk, 4 percent of the mathematical reserves are multiplied with the reinsurance factor applicable to these insurance products;
b. for insurance with a total term of more than five years for which the insurance business does not bear any investment risk, 1 percent of the mathematical reserves are multiplied by the reinsurance factor applicable to this insurance. To this product, 25 percent of the net administrative costs for the last financial year for this insurance are added, unless administrative cost reserves for five or more years are established.

3 For the calculation of the reinsurance factor, the mathematical reserves for the insurance under paragraph 2, letter a or for the insurance under paragraph 2, letter b is used. It equals at least 0.85.

4 The second result is calculated as 0.3 percent of the risk sum, multiplied with the reinsurance factor under Article 24, paragraph 5.

Art. 26 Calculation for insurance lines A4 and A5

The required solvency margin for insurance lines A4 and A5 is calculated in accordance with Articles 27–29.

Section 2: Required solvency margin for insurance businesses that write nonlife insurance

Art. 27 Calculation

1 The required solvency margin is calculated either according to the annual gross premium (Art. 28) or according to the median loss burden for the last three business years (Art. 29). The higher of the two calculation results is dispositive.

2 In the case of an insurance business that essentially only assumes credit, storm, hail or frost risks, the median loss burden is calculated on the basis of the last seven financial years.

Art. 28 Premium index

[1] The premium index is calculated either on the basis of the annual written or earned gross premium. The higher amount is to be used.

[2] If the premiums for the insurance lines B11, B12 and B13 cannot be determined exactly, then with the approval of the FINMA their allocation can be made on a statistical basis. The amounts of premium for these lines of insurance are in each case increased by 50 percent.

[3] The premium index will be determined as follows:

a. cancelled premiums and taxes and fees paid with premiums are deducted from the sum of the gross premium, including related charges, from primary insurance and reinsurance received in the course of the last business year;
b. 18 percent on the first 80 million francs of the amount under letter a and 16 percent of the amount in excess therereof are calculated and added;
c. the subtotal under letter b is multiplied by the quotient resulting from the claims borne by the insurer during the last three financial years, reduced by reinsured claims, and the amount of gross claims, but at least by 0.5.

Art. 29 Claims index

[1] The claims index is calculated on the basis of claims payments which were made during the time periods specified in Article 27 in primary insurance and in reinsurance business, plus the reserves for pending claims established in both business segments at the end of the last financial year.

[2] If the claims, reserves or recoveries in insurance lines B11, B12 and B13 cannot be determined exactly, then with the approval of the FINMA their allocation can be made on a statistical basis. The amounts for claims, reserves and recoveries in these insurance lines are increased by 50 percent in each case.

[3] The claims index is determined as follows:

a. the proceeds from recoveries during the time period specified in Article 27, as well as the reserves for pending claims in direct and in reinsurance business which were established at the beginning of the financial year two years preceding the last completed financial year are deducted from the amount determined under paragraph 1. If the time period is seven years, the amount to be deducted equals the reserves that were established at the beginning of the financial year which preceded the last completed financial year by six years;
b. on the annual average of the resulting amounts, 26% on the first 56 million francs and from the remaining amount in excess thereof 23% will be calculated and added together. The result is the subtotal;

c. the subtotal is multiplied by the quotient of the last three financial years resulting from the amount of paid claims after reduction for reinsured paid claims borne by the insurer and the gross amount of paid claims, but at least 0.5.

Art. 30 Reduction of the required solvency margin

[1] If the required solvency margin which results from the calculations under Articles 27-29 is lower than the required solvency margin in the preceding year, the required solvency margin equals at least the one of the preceding year, multiplied by the quotient of the amount of the amount of the reserves for pending claims at the end of the prior financial year and the amount of the reserves for pending clams at the beginning of the preceding financial year, but at most, 1.

[2] In calculating the reserves, the effect of reinsurance is ignored.

Art. 31 Health insurance

The percentages under Articles 28, paragraph 3, letter b and Article 29, paragraph 3, letter b for shall be reduced by one third for health insurance which is written in the manner of life insurance, if:

a. premiums are charged on the basis of probability tables in accordance with the principles of insurance mathematics;
b. an age-based reserve is established;
c. an appropriate security surcharge is imposed; and
d. the insurance business is not able to cancel the contract not later than after the lapse of the third policy year.

Art. 32 Travel assistance insurance

For insurance line B18 the amount of the claims payments used in the calculation of the claims index is equal to the costs incurred by the insurer for travel assistance services.

Section 3:
Required solvency margin for insurance businesses which engage in reinsurance

Art. 33 Nonlife reinsurance

For the reinsurance of the insurance lines B1–B18 the required solvency margin is calculated under Section 2 of this Chapter. The minimum quotient under Article 28, paragraph 3, letter c and Article 29, paragraph 3, letter c, however, is not used.

Art. 34 Reinsurance of the capital and pension insurance, as well as the unit-linked life insurance

[1] For reinsurance of the insurance lines A1–A3, the required solvency margin is the result of the sum of 4 percent of the mathematical net reserves and 0.1 percent of the net risk

amount. If no investment risks are assumed by the reinsurance, then the amount of the mathematical net reserves is 1 percent.

2 The mathematical net reserves are the result of the mathematical gross reserves minus the share ceded by retrocession.

3 The net risk amount is the result of the gross risk amount minus the share ceded by retrocession.

Art. 35 Reinsurance of other life insurance lines

1 The calculation of the required solvency margin for the reinsurance of the lines of insurance A4 and A5 is based on the provisions applicable to primary nonlife insurance. The minimum quotient under Article 28, paragraph 3, letter c and Article 29, paragraph 3, letter c, however, is not used.

2 The required solvency margin for the reinsurance of the insurance line A6 equals 4 percent of the mathematical net reserves.

3 For the reinsurance of the insurance line A7, the required solvency margin equals 1 percent of the assets of the communities.

Art. 36 Reinsurance of various insurance lines

If an insurance business writes reinsurance of nonlife insurance as well as life insurance, the required solvency margin equals the sum of the required solvency margins for the reinsurance of the relevant lines of insurance.

Section 4: Available solvency margin

Art. 37 Creditable capital resources

1 Creditable capital resources are, in particular:

a. the paid in capital;
b. the paid in surplus;
c. any non-voting share capital;
d. the statutory reserves prescribed by law and the free reserves;
e. the organizational fund;
f. the retained earnings from the preceding year;
g. the retained earnings of the then completed financial year;
h. in life insurance, the reserves for future shares of surplus, to the extent these have not yet been allocated to insureds.

2 On an application by the insurance business supported by good cause, the FINMA can permit credit for other categories as capital resources, in particular:

a. in life insurance and life reinsurance: the difference between the non- or partially 'zillmerized' coverage capital and the coverage capital 'zillmerized' with acquisition costs; this difference, for all contracts for which zillmerization is possible, may not exceed 3.5% of the difference between the insured amount and the unzillmerized coverage capital and must be reduced by the amount of any capitalized and unamortized acquisition costs;

b. reserves for future obligations and losses which cannot be unequivocally allocated to a specific transaction;

c. valuation reserves as the difference between the reported book value and the relevant market value for all assets with the exception of the insurance technical reserves and fixed income securities under Article 100, paragraph 1, provided that at least 50 percent of the required solvency margin must be covered by other capital resources;

d. hybrid instruments, to the extent that the prerequisites under Article 39 are fulfilled:

[3] To be deducted from creditable capital resources are:

a. the insurance business's own shares which are directly owned by it and held at its own risk;

b. intangible assets;

c. the loss from the preceding year;

d. the loss in the current completed financial year; and

e. planned dividends and returns of capital.

Art. 38 Special cases

For insurance businesses that write nonlife insurance or nonlife reinsurance and discount or reduce their insurance technical reserves, the available solvency margin is reduced in an amount equal to the difference between the undiscounted or unreduced insurance technical reserves and the discounted or reduced insurance technical reserves. An adjustment for the discounting of annuities in the insurance technical reserves is not necessary.

Art. 39 Hybrid instruments

[1] Loans, bonds and other liabilities with equity capital character (hybrid instruments) are creditable under the following conditions:

a. they are actually fully paid and not secured with assets of the insurance business;

b. they cannot be offset against debts owed to the insurance business;

c. their subordination to the claims of all other creditors in the event of the liquidation, bankruptcy or an arrangement among the creditors of the insurance business is contractually and irrevocably established;

d. the debt instrument or subscription agreement gives the insurance business the right to defer the payment of interest which has become due;

e. the debt and the unpaid interest must bear losses so that the insurance business is not compelled to cease writing business;

f. the contract may not have any clause which permits the debt to be repaid before the agreed repayment date under any circumstances other than in the case of the liquidation of the insurance business;

g. they cannot be repaid early upon the request of the bearer and then only with the prior approval of the FINMA. An application for approval must be made not later than six months before the proposed repayment date. The FINMA shall issue the approval if the insurance business proves that the repayment does have the consequence that the available solvency margin falls below the required solvency margin.

2 Credit for hybrid instruments is subject to the following limitations:

a. obligations collectively can be credited up to a maximum limit equal to 50% of the lesser of the amount of the available or the required solvency margin;

b. obligations with a fixed term can be credited up to a maximum limit equal to 25% the amount of the available or the required solvency margin. The amount of the credit during the last five years of the term will be reduced each year by 20 percent of the original nominal amount. If the creditor is granted a termination right, then the earliest possible repayment date is deemed the end of the term, subject to justified exceptions in individual cases for convertible bonds.

Art. 40 Control and reporting

1 An insurance business shall appoint an internal office to control the available solvency margin. It shall issue a report at the end of each financial year and submit it to the executive board and the FINMA within three months.

2 In special situations, the FINMA can require reporting during the year.

Chapter 3: Swiss Solvency Test (SST)

Section 1: Target capital

Art. 41 Definition

1 Target capital equals the risk-bearing capital that must be available at the beginning of the year in order for the average of the possible valuations of the risk-bearing capital at the end of the year which are below a certain threshold (value at risk) (expected shortfall in accordance with Annex 2) to be greater than or equal to the minimum amount under paragraph 4.

2 The risk-bearing capital is the difference between the market value of the investments and the discounted, best-possible estimated value of the insurance technical liabilities.

3 The threshold of the risk-bearing capital is the value it will sink below only with a certain occurrence probability. The FINMA shall define the probability. Changes in the de-

termination of the occurrence probability shall be announced by the FINMA at least a calendar year before taking effect.

4 The minimum amount is the cost of capital for the risk-bearing capital to be provided during the pendency of the development of the insurance technical liabilities.

Art. 42 Determination

1 The determination of the target capital is based on:

a. a model for the quantification of the relevant risks;
b. an evaluation of a series of scenarios; and
c. an aggregation procedure which brings together the results of the model and the scenario evaluation.

2 The FINMA shall specify the relevant risks; these are, as a rule, finance and insurance risks.

3 For the determination of the target capital, the assets will be valued at near market value and the liabilities by the best possible estimated value (Annex 3).

4 The near market value of the assets is the market value or, if one is not available, the market value of a comparable asset or a value in accordance with a calculation model. The near market value of debt capital is the sum of the discounted, best-possible estimated value and the minimum amount under Article 41, paragraph 4.

5 In the determination of the target capital, the effect of reinsurance or retrocession of risk will be fully recognized. The default risk of reinsurance is taken into account in the target capital calculation.

Art. 43 Model for the quantification of risk

1 Each insurance business must have a model for the quantification of risks.

2 The FINMA shall define a standard model that is uniformly designed for all insurance businesses in respect of financial risks and different in respect of the various types of insurance. If the standard model insufficiently takes into account the specific risk situation of an insurance business, it can require the appropriate adaption of the model or the use of an internal model.

3 Insurance businesses may use, partially or exclusively, their own models (internal models) for the quantification of risks, to the extent that these are approved by the FINMA. The approval shall be given if the qualitative, quantitative and organizational requirements of the FINMA are fulfilled.

4 The models for the quantification of the risks are to be reviewed regularly by the insurance business and adapted as appropriate.

[5] The selection of the model, changing models and significant changes to the model require the approval of the FINMA.

Art. 44 Scenarios

[1] The FINMA shall define hypothetical events or combinations of events (scenarios) whose occurrence within the period of a year is to be expected with a certain probability and which to a certain extent could have an adverse effect on the insurance business. It shall determine the occurrence probability of these scenarios.

[2] An insurance business shall define its own scenarios which take into account its individual risk situation.

[3] In the case of special risk situations, the insurance business shall submit a request for modifications of the prescribed scenarios.

Art. 45 Aggregation

The FINMA shall determine how the results of the assessments of the models for the quantification of risk and the results of the assessments of the models for the assessment of the scenarios are aggregated. For internal models, it can, upon request, approve other aggregation procedures.

Art. 46 Procedure for determination

[1] In determining the target capital, in particular for life insurance, significant guarantees and imbedded options are to be taken into account.

[2] The FINMA can, upon request, permit the diversification effects which result from the structure of an insurance group to be taken into account in the determination of the target capital. The calculation of these effects must take into account as well the limited fungibility of the capital.

Section 2: Risk-bearing capital

Art. 47 Definition

[1] Risk-bearing capital serves to cover the target capital and must be free and unencumbered. It equals the sum of the core capital and the supplementary capital.

[2] Supplementary capital can be credited up to a maximum of 100% of the core capital. Excluded is the lower supplementary capital under Article 49, paragraph 2, which can be credited up to a maximum of 50% of the core capital.

[3] The FINMA can, upon request, permit exceptions from the limitations under paragraph 2. An insurance business must, in particular, show how the risks, the security and the availability of the constituent elements of the risk-bearing capital are reflected in the internal model.

Art. 48 Core capital

[1] For the calculation of the core capital, the difference between assets valued at near market value and liabilities valued at near market value is added to the minimum amount under Article 41, paragraph 4. From which are deducted:

a. planned dividends and capital repayments;
b. the insurance business's own shares which are directly owned by it and held at its own risk;
c. intangible assets;
d. accrued property taxes.

[2] The core capital will be determined on the basis of market-value financial statements which take into account all economically relevant positions. The FINMA shall issue regulations concerning the preparation of the market-value financial statements on the basis of the statutory financial statements.

[3] An insurance business is permitted with the approval of the FINMA to credit to core capital debt instruments which only can be converted into equity capital of the insurance business and other similar innovative finance instruments.

Art. 49 Supplementary capital

[1] Hybrid instruments under Article 39, paragraph 1 which do not have a fixed repayment date are considered upper supplementary capital.

[2] Hybrid instruments under Article 39, paragraph 1 with an original term of at least five years are considered lower supplementary capital.

[3] The credit for the elements under paragraph two is made under the following conditions:

a. the credit will be reduced by 20 percent of the original nominal amount each year during the last five years of the term;
b. if the creditor is granted a termination right, then the earliest possible repayment date is deemed the end of the term, subject to justified exceptions in individual cases for convertible bonds.

Art. 50 Exceptions from coverage of the target capital

The FINMA may in exceptional cases partially exempt an insurance business from the coverage of the target capital with risk-bearing capital, if:

a. the insurance business is a subsidiary of another insurance business;
b. the other insurance business also calculates risk-bearing capital and target capital and the calculation can be verified by the FINMA;
c. the total amount of the risk-bearing capital of the subsidiary and the other insurance business is not smaller than the total amount of the target capital of the subsidiary and the other insurance business;

d. the subsidiary receives a guarantee or reinsurance coverage from the other insurance business the amount of which is equal to at least the difference between the target capital and the risk-bearing capital of the subsidiary;

e. the guarantee or the reinsurance is legally enforceable in Switzerland and the subsidiary or the other insurance business can prove that any capital flows under the guarantee or coverage specified under paragraph b cannot be restricted by a government agency or court;

f. there are cogent, economic reasons for not covering the target capital; and

g. the interests of the insureds are protected.

Section 3: Supplementary provisions

Art. 51 Frequency of the determination

1 Target capital and risk-bearing capital are to be determined annually.

2 If the risk situation of an insurance business changes significantly, then target capital is to be determined during the year by approximation and notified to the FINMA.

Art. 52 Data collection

An insurance business shall collect and record relevant data in a form which permits the calculation of target capital, risk-bearing capital, as well as the near market value reserves.

Art. 53 SST report

1 An insurance business shall prepare a report annually concerning the calculation of target capital and risk-bearing capital (SST Report). It is to be signed by the members of the executive board and to be submitted to the FINMA.

2 The SST Report shall include all relevant information which is needed to understand the calculation of target capital and risk-bearing capital, as well as the risk situation of the insurance business.

3 The FINMA shall set the date for the annual submission, subject to an appropriate notice period.

Title 4: Insurance technical reserves and restricted assets

Chapter 1: Insurance technical reserves

Section 1: Establishment and release

Art. 54

1 An insurance business shall demonstrate that it has sufficient insurance technical reserves. These comprise:

a. insurance technical reserves for the coverage of expected obligations;
b. volatility reserves to offset the volatility of the business, while taking into account the diversification, size and structure of the insurance portfolio.

[2] An insurance business shall release insurance technical reserves that are no longer needed.

[3] In the business plan, an insurance business shall specify the conditions for the establishment and release of insurance technical reserves. It shall document the reserving method used and the valuation of the insurance technical liabilities.

[4] The FINMA shall regulate the details concerning the type and scope of insurance technical reserves.

Section 2: Life insurance

Art. 55 Types of insurance technical reserves

[1] For the determination of the required amount of restricted assets, the following insurance technical reserves are to be established:

a. actuarial reserves for current insurance policies, after deduction of loans provided thereon, advance insurance payments and unpaid premiums;
b. reserves for unearned administrative cost premiums;
c. unearned premiums;
d. reserves for incurred but not yet paid claims;
e. increased reserves for annuities and reserves for longevity;
f. reserves for guarantees and the pension conversion factor;
g. reserves for interest guarantees;
h. reserves for rating changes and rating corrections;
i. shares of surplus allocated to the insureds;
j. reserves for claims for final shares of surplus;
k. inflations funds;
l. reserves to offset volatility over time on the liability side of the balance sheet to the extent prescribed by supervisory laws; and
m. reserves for other contractually provided guarantees and benefit elections.

[2] Excluded from insurance technical reserves used for the determination of the required amount of restricted assets are, in particular, reserves to offset volatility over time on the asset side of the balance sheet, as well as on the liability side to the extent these reserves are not prescribed by supervisory laws.

Art. 56 Required amount of restricted assets

The required amount of restricted assets comprises:

a. the insurance technical reserves under Article 55, paragraph 1;

b. the surcharge under Article 18 ISL.

Art. 57 Required amount for health and accident insurance

[1] If an insurance business writes health and accident insurance in addition to life insurance, then the amount of the required amount for these two lines is calculated under the rules for the required amount for health and accident insurance.

[2] In this case, the required amounts for life insurance, as well as for health and accident insurance shall be included together in restricted assets.

Art. 58 Basis for the individual calculation

[1] An insurance business shall calculate insurance technical reserves for each contract separately and in accordance with a cautious, prospective procedure.

[2] It can establish additional reserves which are not calculated individually which provide protection against general risks.

Art. 59 Gross principle

An insurance business shall establish all insurance technical reserves without taking reinsurance into account. The FINMA can permit exceptions in justified situations.

Art. 60 Interest rate for the calculation of technical reserves

An insurance business shall use a technical interest rate for the calculation of technical reserves which may not exceed the technical interest rate used for the rating.

Art. 61 Biometric basis for the calculation of technical reserves

For the calculation of technical reserves, an insurance business shall use the same or more conservative biometric data than those it used for the rating.

Art. 62 Increasing technical reserves

[1] An insurance business shall continuously monitor the rating materials and shall increase the insurance technical reserves as soon as these are shown to be insufficient on the basis of rating materials which are considered appropriate.

[2] The increase of insurance technical reserves is basically made from the surpluses produced by the individual portfolios. The FINMA can grant approval for scheduled increases of insurance technical reserves (increases of actuarial reserves) over a period of not more than ten years.

[3] Increases of actuarial reserves are to be made individually for each insured person, to the extent that these must be paid out when he or she withdraws from the collective [insurance plan].

[4] The FINMA can require additional increases in technical reserves in properly justified situations.

Art. 63 Coverage of redemption values

The technical reserves, less capitalized acquisition costs, must at all times cover the redemption values.

Art. 64 Unit-linked life insurance

If an insurance business grants a repurchase guarantee for unit-linked life insurance for its repurchase or for survival or death benefits, then it must establish reserves for these guarantees.

Art. 65 Zillmerization of actuarial reserves and capitalization of acquisition costs

1 The zillmerization of actuarial reserves is not permitted. Excluded are the actuarial reserves of the establishments of Swiss insurance businesses in countries in which the zillmerization is permitted under supervisory law.

2 The capitalization of not yet paid acquisition costs as an asset is fundamentally permitted. The FINMA shall issue guidelines concerning the scope and method of the capitalization. It can in properly justified cases prohibit capitalization.

Art. 66 Further technical reserves

1 An insurance business shall establish reserves for:

a. already allocated shares of surplus; and
b. the financing of final shares of surplus.

2 These reserves are to be established separately from each other and independently from surplus funds.

Art. 67 Volatility reserves

An insurance business shall establish sufficient volatility reserves for risk insurance.

Section 3: Nonlife insurance

Art. 68 Required amount of restricted assets

1 The required amount of restricted assets comprises:

a. insurance technical reserves established in accordance with the business plan without taking reinsurance into account;
b. other reserves established in accordance with the business plan and allocated to individual lines;
c. age reserves for health insurance in accordance with the business plan;
d. volatility reserves for credit insurance under Method No. 2 in Appendix 5 to the Treaty of 10 October 1989 between the Swiss Confederation and the EEA concerning primary insurance with the exception of life insurance, subject to paragraph 3;

e. additional reserves required under supervisory law for individual lines of insurance;
f. a surcharge pursuant to Article 18 ISL.

[2] Claims against reinsurers under reinsurance agreements can, upon request, be fully or partially included in restricted assets.

[3] Insurance businesses which write credit insurance are exempt from the establishment of volatility reserves under paragraph 1, letter d to the extent that their premium income from this line of insurance included in the calculation of the required amount of restricted assets is less than 4 percent of the total amount of premium income used in the calculation of the required amount of restricted assets and less than 4 million francs.

Art. 69 Types of insurance technical reserves

Insurance technical reserves include:

a. unearned premiums;
b. case reserves;
c. security and volatility reserves;
d. age reserves;
e. reserves for contractually agreed participations in surplus;
f. actuarial reserves for pensions;
g. additional technical reserves, which are to be identified precisely and their purpose is to be described.

Chapter 2: Restricted assets

Section 1: General

Art. 70 Minimum amount

When first established, the required amount of restricted assets is at least:

a. 750,000 francs for insurance businesses that write life insurance;
b. 100,000 francs for business that write nonlife insurance.

Art. 71 When the required amount of restricted assets is determined

[1] An insurance business is required to determine the required amount for each restricted asset as of the conclusion of the financial year.

[2] Upon the request of an insurance business supported by a showing of good cause, the FINMA can order that the requirement amount be determined as of another time.

[3] The FINMA can at any time require a new calculation or estimate of the required amount.

Art. 72 Reporting

[1] Within three months after the close of the financial year, an insurance business shall report to the FINMA the required amount for each restricted asset, together with an inventory of the assets covering them.

[2] An insurance business domiciled in Switzerland must in addition produce a report about each foreign insurance portfolio for which it is required to provide security in a foreign country.

Art. 73 Foreign insurance portfolio

A foreign insurance portfolio under Article 17, paragraph 2, ISL means all insurance contracts with an insured domiciled in a foreign country.

Art. 74 Coverage

[1] The required amount must be covered by assets (Art. 79) at all times.

[2] If an insurance business determines that there is a coverage shortfall, then it must immediately increase restricted assets. The FINMA can in special cases grant a cure period for the increase.

Art. 75 Securities lending

[1] The FINMA shall issue regulations concerning securities lending by insurance businesses, in particular concerning:

a. security methods;
b. contents of the agreements; and
c. the scope.

[2] Securities lending is considered a legal transaction similar to a loan through which an insurance business transfers certain securities to a borrower and the borrower is required to return securities of the same type, quantity and quality and to pay to the insurance business during the term of the securities loan any distributions received in respect of the securities.

Section 2: Establishment

Art. 76 General principles

[1] An insurance business establishes restricted assets through the allocation of assets. It lists and identifies these assets so that at any time, without delay, it can prove which assets belong to restricted assets and that the required amount of restricted assets is covered.

[2] The assets of restricted assets are, in the first instance, to be chosen on the basis of security, the actual financial situation, as well as the structure and the expected development of the insurance portfolio.

[3] In addition, while maintaining appropriate diversification, a market-competitive income stream is to be sought and anticipated liquidity needs are at all times to be secured.

Art. 77 Separate restricted assets

[1] Separate restricted assets are to be established for:

a. insurance under the occupational pension plans;
b. the savings component of insurance contracts in the insurance lines A2.1, A2.2 and A2.3; and
c. the savings component of insurance contracts in the insurance lines A2.4, A2.5 and A2.6.

[2] For contracts in the Swiss insurance portfolio which have been issued in foreign currencies, separate restricted assets can be established.

[3] For the insurance contracts in a foreign insurance portfolio for which an equivalent security in the foreign country is not required, segregated restricted assets can be established.

Art. 78 Management of capital investments

[1] An insurance business shall have:

a. an investment strategy;
b. an investment regulation which ensures compliance with the principles for the investment of capital assets under Article 76;
c. an organization that ensures that the persons entrusted with management and control have the necessary knowledge;
d. a risk management that is commensurate with the scope of business and the complexity of the investment activity.

[2] The executive board sets the investment strategy and shall submit it to the board of directors for approval.

Art. 79 Permitted investments

[1] The following assets may be allocated to restricted assets:

a. cash investments, specifically *Postcheck* deposits and bank deposits, as well as time deposits and other money market investments;
b. debt instruments for a fixed monetary amount, specifically, bonds and option bonds, as well as convertible bonds with debt character;
c. structured investment products, securitized obligations and credit derivatives;
d. other unconditional debt obligations;
e. equities, participation certificates, convertible bonds with equity character, share certificates of mutual companies and similar securities, if the issues are traded on a regulated market and can be sold on short notice;

f. residential and commercial buildings in Switzerland which are property of the insurance business, as well as ownership interests in companies which have as their sole purpose the acquisition and sale, as well as the leasing of residential and commercial buildings (real estate companies) to the extent these ownership interests amount to more than 50 percent;

g. obligations that are secured by a lien on real property in Switzerland;

h. alternative financial investments, such as hedge funds and private equity;

i. derivative financial instruments which serve hedging purposes and have no leverage effect on restricted assets if the underlying is in restricted assets and credit for them is adjusted in response to market fluctuations;

j. units in collective capital investments and single-investor funds.

2 Under certain conditions and to a certain degree, derivative instruments also can be allocated to restricted assets for purposes of preparing for an acquisition, increasing revenue and hedging cash flows from insurance technical obligations. The supervisory authority shall determine the permitted scope and conditions.

Art. 80[10]

Art. 81 Permitted assets for unit-linked life insurance

1 Restricted assets for the savings component of insurance contracts under the insurance lines A2.1, A2.2 and A2.3 may only be established with units of open-ended collective investment funds which are subject to the Collective Investments Law of 23 June 2006[11], [12].

2 Restricted assets for the savings component of insurance contracts under insurance lines A2.4, A2.5 and A2.6 may be established with assets specified in Article 79 under the following conditions:

a. if the benefits are linked directly to the value of an internal investment portfolio, then the insurance technical reserves must be established with the relevant shares, or if no shares are created, then by the underlying assets;

b. if the benefits are linked to an index or another benchmark, then the insurance technical reserves must be established by assets which correlate with the assets that are the basis for the benchmark.

Art. 82 Collective capital investments and single investor funds

1 An insurance business can credit units in collective capital investments to the extent that:

a. these are subject to effective supervision for the protection of investors; and

---

10 Repealed by para. 1 of the Regulation of 18 Oct. 2006, with effect from 1 Jan. 2007 (AS **2006** 4425).

11 SR **951.31**

12 Text in accordance with Annex para. 11 of the Financial Market Audit Regulation of 15 Oct. 2008, in force since 1 Jan. 2009 (SR **956.161**).

b. the units are traded on a regulated, liquid market or can be sold at any time.

[2] Units in single-investor funds may be credited to restricted assets to the extent that these single-investor funds:

a. are subject to an effective supervision;
b. will be held 100 percent by the insurance business;
c. the ability to take possession of the individual investments of the fund is assured at all times;
d. make investments in investments under Article 79; and
e. fulfill the requirements of Article 87.

[3] The organization of the collective capital investments or single-investor funds must be structured in respect of the specification of the investment policy, management authority, determination of the share of net asset value of the units, as well as the purchase and redemption of the units so that the interests of the insurance businesses participating therein are protected.

[4] Units in investment companies that are not listed on a securities exchange may be allocated to restricted assets if they fulfill the conditions set forth in paragraph 1 or 2.

Art. 83 Limits

The FINMA can set limits for individual categories of investments.

Section 3: Eligibility and control

Art. 84 Eligibility of assets

[1] The FINMA determines the suitability of investments included in restricted assets. It will set an appropriate cure period for the replacement of investments which it has determined to be unsuitable.

[2] The assets included in restricted assets must be unencumbered. Liabilities of an insurance business may not be offset against obligations that have been allocated to restricted assets. Article 91, paragraph 3 (derivative financial instruments) remains unaffected.

Art. 85 Verification by the FINMA

[1] The FINMA shall verify at least once each year whether:

a. the required amount is calculated correctly;
b. the investments allocated to restricted assets:
    1. are available,
    2. are allocated and physically maintained in accordance with regulations,
    3. equal at least the required amount,
    4. conform to the investment regulations under supervisory law.

[2] It can limit the examination to random tests.

[3] In the course of the examination, it can take into account the results of an examination by internal offices of the insurance business or by appointed third parties. For the examination of investments held by a custodian, it can rely on the inventory of the custodian.

[4] It can delegate the examination partially or fully to third parties.

Art. 86 Custody of investments

[1] Moveable investments allocated to restricted assets may be held at the headquarters of the insurance business in Switzerland or at the office for all Swiss business, as applicable, (own custody) or be held by a third-party custodian.

[2] Investments held in 'own custody' are to be kept segregated from the other assets of the insurance business and are to be marked as such. If stored in a safe, storage in segregated, locked compartments is sufficient.

[3] Whoever maintains investments with a third-party custodian shall maintain an inventory of the investments and shall mark them as allocated to restricted assets.

[4] The FINMA may at any time for important reasons order a change of the location of custody or the custodian or the manner of custody.

Art. 87 Notice and liability of the custodian

[1] An insurance business shall notify the location of custody, the custodian and the manner of custody to the FINMA, including any changes in respect thereof.

[2] A third party custodian is only permitted if the custodian is liable to the insurance business in Switzerland for the fulfillment of its obligations as custodian.

Section 4: Valuation of the assets

Art. 88 Fixed income securities

[1] For fixed income securities that must be repaid or amortized on a fixed maturity date and are denominated in a specified currency, excluding *Grundpfandtitel,* an insurance business shall determine the maximum creditable value in accordance with the scientific or linear amortized cost method.

[2] If the market value of a convertible bond is significantly greater than par value, then the FINMA can permit a valuation equal at most to market value. Bonds which are subject to mandatory conversion into equity may be allocated, at most, at market value.

[3] Structured products or combinations of financial instruments that are comparable to fixed income securities may be allocated to a certain extent and under certain conditions in accordance with the scientific or linear amortized cost method. The supervisory authority shall specify the extent and the conditions.

Art. 89 Amortized cost method

1 Under the scientific amortized cost method, the difference between cost and redemption value during the remaining term of the security, on each financial statement reporting date, is to be increased or reduced to the extent necessary that the original internal interest rate (return to maturity) can be maintained.

2 Under the linear amortized cost method, the difference between cost and redemption value during the remaining term of the security, on each financial statement reporting date, is to be distributed in equal amounts over the remaining term as depreciation or appreciation, as applicable.

Art. 90 Residential and commercial buildings, as well as real estate companies

1 An insurance business shall allocate residential and commercial buildings which are owned by it at not more than market value. The FINMA shall specify the procedure for the determination of market value.

2 For real estate companies in which an insurance business has more than a 50% ownership interest, the FINMA shall specify the creditable value. It shall rely on the estimated value of the properties and shall take into account any obligations.

Art. 91 Derivative financial instruments

1 Derivative financial instruments under Article 79, paragraph 1, letter i may be allocated, at most, at market value. If they are not listed on a securities exchange, a customary market valuation method will be used.

2 For derivative financial instruments under Article 79, paragraph 2, the FINMA shall specify the creditable value.

3 The offset (netting) of all derivative transactions under a master agreement is only permitted if a separate master agreement is made for each individual restricted asset. Negative positions which result from such agreements are to be deducted from restricted assets. The FINMA may specify conditions for the content of master agreements.

Art. 92 Collective capital investments

1 Collective capital investments under Article 82, paragraph 1 may, at the most, be allocated at market value or, if the share certificates are not listed on a securities exchange, then at net asset value.

2 For single investor funds under Article 82, paragraph 2, the individual securities of the fund's assets must be listed in restricted assets and be valued analogously in accordance with the requirements in this section.

Art. 93 Other investments

1 Investments under Article 79, paragraph 1, letters c, e and h, as well as money market book-entry obligations and securities with a variable interest rate without a fixed maturity

date will be credited, at most, at market value. If they are not listed on a securities exchange, then a customary market valuation method will be used.

[2] All other investments, including *Grundpfandforderungen* and time deposits will be valued, at most, at par value, taking into account the security and the distribution rate.

Art. 94 Investments denominated in a foreign currency

An insurance business may convert investments denominated in a foreign currency into Swiss francs, at most, at the median exchange rate at the time of the valuation.

Art. 95 Decision about valuation

[1] The FINMA shall determine the valuation of the investments in restricted assets.

[2] It can set lower crediting values for individual investments and investment categories if for reasons of protecting insureds it appears required.

[3] It can at any time require a valuation of restricted assets.

Title 5: Other regulations applicable to engaging in the business of insurance

Chapter 1: Risk management

Art. 96 Objective and content

[1] An insurance business shall ensure through a risk management appropriate to the characteristics of its business and through internal control mechanisms that it is able to:

a. recognize and evaluate potential risks early; and
b. implement early measures for the prevention or hedging of significant risks and aggregations of risk.

[2] Risk management comprises, in particular:

a. the selection and regular review by the management bodies of strategies and measures for all assumed risks;
b. a hedging policy which takes into account the consequences of the business strategy and which includes appropriate capital resources;
c. appropriate procedures which ensure that risk monitoring is integrated into the business organization;
d. identifying, monitoring and quantifying all significant risks;
e. an internal reporting system for the determination, evaluation and control of risks and risk concentrations as well as the related business processes.

Art. 97 Documentation

[1] An insurance business shall record its risk management in a document. This is to be updated constantly.

² The document includes, in particular, the following points:

a. description of the organization of risk management business-wide, as well as the related authorities and responsibilities;
b. the obligations of risk management;
c. the risk policy, including risk tolerance;
d. procedures for the identification of significant risks, as well as a description of the methods, instruments and processes for their measurement, monitoring and control;
e. description of the applicable limits system for risk exposures, as well as the control mechanisms;
f. business-internal guidelines for risk management and related processes.

Art. 98 Operational risks

¹ An insurance business shall record and evaluate operational risks on its own initiative.

² The FINMA shall periodically discuss the results of this evaluation with the insurance business.

³ It may, in support of the self-evaluation, issue questionnaires. These are to be returned to it completed, signed by the executive board, within three months after the close of the financial year.

⁴ If the self-evaluation reveals risks which could lead to inadequate solvency, then the FINMA may, in particular:

a. increase is supervision of the insurance business;
b. impose a surcharge on target capital.

⁵ An insurance business shall collect and analyze data concerning losses from operational risks.

Chapter 2: Responsible actuary

Art. 99

¹ The responsible actuary must have attained the qualification "Actuary SAV" or an equivalent qualification.

² The FINMA may, upon request, recognize relevant education, coupled with at least five years' professional experience as an actuary, as evidence of professional ability.

³ The responsible actuary must be knowledgeable about the Swiss situation (legislation, supervisory regulations, insurance market).

Chapter 3: Use of derivative financial instruments

Art. 100 Basic principle

[1] Insurance businesses may only use derivative instruments in order to reduce risks in respect of capital investments or its liabilities in relation to insureds, or in order to efficiently manage capital investments.

[2] All liabilities which could result from derivative financial transactions must be covered.

Art. 101 Investment strategy

Insurance businesses which use derivative financial instruments must adopt an investment strategy for these instruments. The executive board of an insurance business shall prepare the investment strategy, submit it to the board of directors for approval and monitor its implementation.

Art. 102 Content of the investment strategy

[1] The basic parameters for the use of derivative financial instruments must be specified in the investment strategy, in particular, the risk exposure limits and the basic principles of risk analysis.

[2] The investment strategy must, in addition, comply with the usual principles for capital investments, in particular those in respect of security, liquidity, return, diversification and allocation.

Art. 103 System of limits

Risk exposure limits are to be set in a manner commensurate with the financial and organizational capabilities of the insurance business.

Art. 104 Risk analysis

[1] Counterparty risks must be taken into account before the use of derivative financial instruments.

[2] The risks must be analyzed as often as the situation requires, however at least once per week for market risks and once per month for credit risks.

[3] The analysis of market and credit risks consists, among other things, of valuing open positions and comparing them with the established risk exposure limits.

[4] The result of the risk analysis is to be submitted to the executive board as often as the situation requires, however at least once per month for market risks and at least once every three months for credit risks.

Art. 105 Organization

An insurance business which uses derivative financial instruments, must have a suitable organizational structure; it observes, in particular, Articles 106-108.

Art. 106 Management and control

1 An insurance business must issue detailed guidelines to the persons entrusted with management, in particular, in respect of risk analysis.

2 It has a control system that is adapted to the scope of the business and the complexity of the derivative financial instruments.

3 The management of derivative financial instruments and the control must always be carried out by separate, independent persons.

Art. 107 Qualifications of staff

Whoever is entrusted with management and control, shall have the special knowledge and qualifications necessary for the task.

Art. 108 Activity report

An activity report about the use of derivative financial instruments must be submitted to the board of directors every six months.

Art. 109 Supervision

An insurance business shall submit a report annually to the FINMA about transactions in derivative financial instruments.

Chapter 4: Accounting

Art. 110 Securities and derivative financial instruments

1 Domestic insurance businesses may report in their financial statements fixed income securities denominated in a specific currency which could be repaid or amortized at a point in time fixed in advance at a value not greater than that under the scientific or linear amortized cost method in accordance with Article 89. Structured products comparable to fixed income securities are to be booked at a value not greater than that under the scientific or linear amortized cost method.

2 In the case of shares in a single investor fund under Article 82 paragraph 2, the direct investments of the fund assets will be booked in accordance with the provisions of this Article.

3 Payment obligations secured by security interests in land and all other securities, with the exception of those which serve to secure the savings component of insurance contracts in the insurance lines A2.1, A2.2 and A2.3, are to be booked in accordance with Article 667, paragraphs 1 and 2 of the Code of Obligations[13].

4 An insurance business may, with the approval of the FINMA, value the securities which relate to foreign business regions in accordance with the supervisory law valuation regulations of the individual countries.

---

13 SR **220**

5 Share certificates with a market value which serve to secure the savings component of insurance contracts of the Swiss insurance portfolio in the insurance lines A2.1, A2.2 and A2.3, are to be reported at the market value on 31 December or the most recent known market value before this date. Such share certificates without a market value are to be reported at net asset value.

6 Open positions in derivative financial instruments as of the financial reporting date may:

a. be taken into account with cautious assumptions for the valuation of the underlying assets, or
b. be reported separately in the balance sheet. In this case, they must be valued with cautious assumptions, however at the most, market value. In the case of derivative instruments that do not have a market value, the valuation may not exceed the value determined on the basis of recognized valuation models.

Art. 111 Risks in the valuation of securities

1 If the stability of the price of a security is at risk, then this must be taken into account in its valuation.

2 In the case of the valuation of securities which are issued by a debtor domiciled in a foreign country, then the difficulties which could arise in connection with the payment of principal or interest are to be taken into account.

3 The values determined under Article 110, paragraph 6 are to be appropriately adjusted to reflect the risk, in particular in respect of marketability, cancellation and performance costs, credit risk or the size of the position in relation to trading volume.

Chapter 5:[14] …

Art. 112-116

Chapter 6: Additional principles applicable to engaging in the activity of insurance

Art. 117 Abuse

1 Actions to the detriment of insureds or beneficiaries if they are repeated or affect a broad range of persons are considered abuses under Article 46, paragraph 1, letter f ISL, specifically:

a. an action of an insurance business or insurance intermediary that is calculated to significantly harm insureds or beneficiaries;

14 Repealed by Annex para. 11 of the Financial Market Audit Regulation of 15 Oct. 2008, with effect from 1 Jan. 2009 (SR **956.161**).

b. the use of contract provisions which violate the mandatory norms of the Insurance Contract Law or violate the mandatory norms of other regulations that are applicable to the contract;

c. the use of contract provisions which provide for an allocation of rights and obligations that is significantly contrary to the nature of the agreement.

2 It also is an abuse to disadvantage an insured or a beneficiary through significant unequal treatment that cannot be justified legally or for technical insurance reasons.

Art. 118 Insurance benefits with a waiting period

1 An insurance business shall not continue to charge a premium for an insurance product with a waiting period once the insured can no longer expect to receive insurance benefits.

2 This provision does not apply to the premium exemption for insurance benefits under collective insurance agreements.

Art. 119 Deposits in premium accounts

The balance in premium deposit accounts maintained by an insurance business for an individual insured may not exceed the sum of the future premiums.

Title 6: Provisions for individual lines of insurance

Chapter 1: Life insurance

Section 1: Rating

Art. 120 Basic principles

1 An insurance business that writes life insurance is required to use risk-based, biometric and capital markets-based underlying materials and calculation methods for the rating of its contracts. Binding validity periods are to be given in the business plan for the underlying materials and calculation methods used.

2 An insurance business shall review the adequacy of the rating materials annually on the basis of statistical evaluations. If the rating materials are shown to be insufficient, then they may not be used for new contracts.

Art. 121 Capital market-based principles for ratings other than for occupational pension plans

1 If life insurance contracts have an interest rate guarantee, then the technical interest rate that is used for ratings outside occupational pension plans may not exceed 60 percent of the rolling, ten-year mean of the reference interest rate. The FINMA shall specify the reference rate.

2 In justified cases, the FINMA can increase this limit.

[3] If guarantees are given whose rating relies on a capital market-based foundation other than technical interest rates, then this basis is, in accordance with the guarantees, to be determined carefully.

Art. 122 Mortality tables and other statistical tools

[1] An insurance business shall use mortality tables recognized by the FINMA and other recognized statistical tools in rating life insurance contracts. It may take into account statistical data from its own portfolio of insureds using an appropriate procedure recognized by the FINMA.

[2] An insurance business shall regularly revise its own statistical tools which are used for setting rates and shall conform them to the most recent state of knowledge at least once every ten years.

Art. 123 Rating classifications and experience rating

[1] An insurance business may only divide the insured risks in rating classes and use a rating based on the loss experience of individual contracts (experience rating) if this is agreed with the insured.

[2] Premium adjustments which result from an assignment to another rating class or experience rating are only permissible if the conditions on which the rating up or down will be made are agreed with the insured.

[3] If an insurance business uses rating classes or experience rating, it must also appropriately take into account the collective loss experience along with the individual loss experience in setting premiums.

[4] The rating must be performed in accordance with recognized actuarial methods.

Art. 124 Rating for credit life insurance

An insurance business may use premium calculation methods in the rating of credit life insurance that are not differentiated on the basis of age and gender (average premium methods) to the extent the following prerequisites are fulfilled:

a. a collective contract is involved in which a uniform maximum insured amount for each insured is provided;
b. the age of the insured at inception is limited to a maximum of 65 years;
c. the average premium rates will be reviewed and, if necessary, adjusted every three years.

Art. 125 Disability insurance

If an insurance business writes disability insurance as a line of life insurance, the regulations for life insurance also apply for disability insurance.

Art. 126 Increased coverage guarantee

[1] An insurance business may grant the insured the right to increase the insurance coverage during the term of the contract without a new medical examination (increased coverage guarantee).

[2] If an insurance business grants an increased coverage guarantee, then it must limit the increase of the insurance coverage and in addition address the following issues contractually:

a. the limit on each increase;
b. the limit on the possible increases in their entirety;
c. the age up to which increases are possible;
d. the frequency in which an increase can be requested or the events which give rise to the right to an increase.

[3] The prerequisites for an increased coverage guarantee must be included in the business plan.

Section 2: Settlement and redemption

Art. 127 Settlement values

[1] Settlement values are to be submitted to the FINMA for approval before they are used. Settlement values that an insurance business provides voluntarily are excluded.

[2] Settlement values will be approved under the following conditions:

a. they are appropriate;
b. they are based on the actuarial reserve which was calculated in accordance with the technical principles of the relevant insurance contract;
c. deductions from the actuarial reserve are only permitted for interest risk and for unamortized acquisition costs;
d. the converted insurance must be of the same type as the original life insurance; if an insurance business deviates from this, it must justify it;
e. the zillmerization percentage which was the basis for the deduction of the unamortized acquisition costs, may not exceed the percentage specified by the FINMA. These percentages take into account the differences among the contractual coverages;
f. the FINMA shall publish in an appropriate manner the percentages under letter e and the basis for their calculation;
g. the entire deduction for interest risk and unamortized acquisition costs may not exceed one third of the actuarial reserve to the extent that the insured had paid the premium for three years.

[3] The FINMA may rely on a report of the responsible actuary in granting its approval.

Art. 128 Capital option

If an insurance business grants a capital option, then the capital benefit is to be specified in the contractual documentation. In addition, the insurance business may not make any redemption deductions.

Art. 129 Limitation on policy loans

1 An insurance business may only provide policy loans on insurance contracts which can be redeemed (policy loans).

2 The aggregate amount of the policy loans which an insurance business provides to a policyholder may not exceed the current redemption value of the insurance contract.

Section 3 Requirements for life insurance contracts

Art. 130 Participation in surplus

If a right to participate in surplus is contemplated, then an insurance business shall provide information in the insurance contract documentation about:

a. the types of surplus allocations, in particular, about the portion which is credited annually and those credited only upon the expiration of the contract;
b. when the first surplus allocation will be made;
c. whether the allocation of surplus is made in advance or in arrear;
d. the application of the annual credited share;
e. the fact that the policyholder will be informed annually about the allocation and the status of the share of the surplus allocated to him or her;
f. how changes may be made in the surplus system during the term of the contract and the obligation to notify such a change to the FINMA in advance.

Art. 131 Insurance of children

1 If a child which is insured under a life insurance policy or an accident insurance policy dies before he or she is two years and six months old, then an insurance business may pay a death benefit in a maximum amount 2,500 francs. If the child dies before he or she has completed the twelfth year of life, then an insurance business may pay a death benefit under all of its policies which insure the life of that child in a maximum amount of 20,000 francs.

2 If the sum of the premiums that were paid for that child, credited with interest at 5 percent, is greater than the death benefit under paragraph 1, then the sum of the premiums plus such interest is to be refunded.

Art. 132 Premium adjustment clauses

1 An insurance business may adjust the premium for an in-force insurance contract on the basis of new circumstances if this is expressly permitted in the contract documentation.

2 No premium adjustment clause may be used that would suspend rate guarantees.

[3] There may be no provision for adjustments to annuities which are currently paid.

[4] Premium adjustments can only be made if there has been a significant change of the circumstances that were the basis for the premium calculation.

Section 4: Credit life insurance contracts

Art. 133 Definition

Temporary insurance policies against the event of death used to secure periodic installment payments in connection with purchase, credit, lease, or investment contracts (individual contracts) are considered credit life insurance policies. The risk of occupational disability also can be insured.

Art. 134 Content of the contract

[1] A collective insurance contract and the related individual contracts shall include all provisions concerning the rights and obligations of the insured persons. They shall govern, in particular, the effects the expiration, early termination or a suspension of the collective agreement, as well as the early repayment of the outstanding debt and the effect of a change in parties on an individual contractual relationship.

[2] In addition, in the collective insurance contract and in the related individual contracts, it is to be specified that:

a. the policyholder shall charge the insureds at most the premium amounts, including stamp taxes, calculated by the insurance business;
b. the policyholder can allow the insurance benefits claim of the insured person to be assigned to it only to the extent of the current outstanding debt;
c. shares of unearned premiums under Article 135 will be refunded to the insured person to the extent he or she had made payments in respect of the unearned premium;
d. the outstanding debt of the insured person shall be considered repaid to the extent of the payments by the insurance business.

Art. 135 Refund of unearned premium

[1] In the event of the early termination of an individual contract, an insurance business shall refund to the policyholder the unearned portions of the premium.

[2] The refund shall be paid directly to the insured person to the extent that the insurance business had agreed to do so in the collective contract.

Chapter 2: Regulations concerning surpluses in life insurance outside of the occupational pension plans

Art. 136 Surplus funds

[1] Insurance businesses shall establish a surplus fund for that part [of their business] which is outside of occupational pension plans. The surplus fund is a technical insurance balance sheet entry for the accrual of shares of surplus owed to policyholders.

[2] The part of the annual surplus collectively allocated to insured persons shall be retained in the surplus fund.

[3] Shares of surplus owed to the policyholders may only be paid from the surplus fund.

[4] At least 20 percent of the surpluses accumulated in the surplus fund are to be withdrawn and allocated to the policyholders annually.

[5] Shortfalls may only be withdrawn from the surplus fund if the revenues of the insurance business are insufficient to establish technical reserves in accordance with the business plan.

Art. 137 Allocation of shares of surplus

[1] The allocation of shares of surplus is to be made in accordance with recognized actuarial principles and in a manner that avoids abusive, unequal treatment.

[2] As soon as the shares of surplus have been allocated to the individual policyholders, these are deemed owed. They are to be distributed to the rightful claimants in accordance with the relevant contractual provisions or, if the accumulation of shares of surplus with interest was agreed, to be recorded in a balance sheet entry created specifically for that purpose.

[3] The system of participating in surplus may not be changed during the term of the contract to the detriment of the policy holders.

Art. 138 Final surplus

[1] If the life insurance contract provides for a final share of surplus, then a segregated reserve for each contract is to be established and funded annually. The share of the final surplus may not be based solely on the income situation [of the insurer] at the time of the expiration of the contract.

[2] The share of the reserves for the final share of surplus which becomes available in the event of the complete or partial termination of the life insurance contract before the expiration of the contract upon death or surrender is to be credited to the surplus fund to the extent that it is not paid to the policyholder.

[3] If the share of the final surplus is the most important surplus component of the contract, an insurance business must contractually assure the policy holder an appropriate share of

the accumulated share of the final policyholder surpluses in the event of death or the redemption [of the policy].

Chapter 3: Special provisions for the insurance under the occupational pension plans

Section 1: Annual operating account and information obligations

Art. 139 Annual operating account

1 For insurance benefits under an occupational pension plan, a separate operating account is to be maintained. Assets allocated to restricted assets in respect of the insurance under an occupational pension plan are to be included as an element of the operating account.

2 Assets can only be transferred at book value from the operating account for an occupational pension plan to that for other business and *vice versa*. The difference between book value and market value will be booked in the operating account for an occupational pension plan as profit or loss. If a market value is unavailable, an insurance business shall determine the near market value. The FINMA must approve the valuation method.

Art. 140 Disclosure obligations

An insurance business shall deliver to the policyholders within five months after the balance sheet date:

a. the operating account for insurance benefits under an occupational pension plan;
b. information about the determination of the credit to surplus and its allocation, and
c. all additional information which the policyholders require for the fulfillment of their statutory information obligations.

Section 2: Participation in surplus

Art. 141 Right to shares of surplus

1 The policyholders have a right to shares of surplus in accordance with this section.

2 The shares of surplus are to be allocated, subject to Article 152, paragraph 3, for the first time after the lapse of the first insurance year.

Art. 142 Basis of determination

1 The shares of surplus are to be determined on the basis of the operating account. In addition, the profit or loss is to be reported for the savings, risk and costs processes.

2 Shares of surplus are to be determined at least once each year.

Art. 143 Savings process and savings components

1 The savings process includes:

a. the accumulation of the old age credit balance;

b. the conversion of the old age credit balance into an old age pension;

c. the payment and management of current old age pensions and the related pensioner's children's pensions.

2 Income in the savings process (savings component) equals the income from capital in the operating account, reduced by the capital investment and capital management costs (net income from capital).

3 Expenses in the savings process are the expenses for the technical interest accrual at the guaranteed interest rate and for the payment and management of current old age pensions and the related pensioner's children's pensions, as well as for the management of the voluntary contribution policies.

Art. 144 Risk process and risk components

1 The risk process includes:

a. the payment of death benefits and their management in the form of capital payments, widow, widower and orphan pensions;

b. the payment of disability benefits and their management in the form of disability pensions, disability annuities and premium exemptions, and

c. the payment of the deferred benefits related to current old age pensions and the resulting survivor's pensions.

2 Income in the risk process (risk component) equals the risk premiums received.

3 Expenses in the risk process are the expenses in connection with insurance benefits and claims processing, in particular the expenses for the establishment of actuarial reserves for new disability and survivor pensions, for the management and payment of current disability and survivor pensions, as well as for inclusion in the reinsurance result.

Art. 145 Cost process and cost process components

1 The cost process includes the expenses for the administration and distribution of the insurance solutions of the occupational pension plans. The management and payment of current disability and survivor pensions are not included in the cost process.

2 Income in the cost process (cost component) equals the cost premiums received, without taking into account the capital investment and capital management costs, and also without taking into account the disbursement and management costs for current pensions.

3 The expenses in the cost process are the administration and operating costs of the insurance benefits of the occupational pension plans.

Art. 146 Special cases

1 Insurance contracts or parts thereof for which segregated income and expense accounting has been agreed will not be taken into account for the determination of the components under Articles 143–145.

[2] Insurance contracts or parts thereof for which the transfer of the capital investment risk to the policyholder has been agreed, will not be taken into account for the determination of the components under Article 143.

[3] Pure stop-loss contracts will not be taken into account for the determination of the components under Articles 144 and 145.

[4] The insurance contracts under paragraphs 1-3 are to be reported separately in the operating account for the relevant processes.

[5] For these contracts, Articles 152, paragraph 3 and 153, paragraph 1, second clause do not apply.

Art. 147 Minimum share and distribution share

[1] A part of the components under Articles 143-145 must be used for the benefit of the policyholders (distribution share). The distribution share must amount to at least 90 percent of the components (minimum share).

[2] If the savings component equals 6 percent or more of the actuarial reserve and the minimum interest rate established under Article 15 of the Federal Law of 25 June 1982[15] concerning the Occupational Old-Age, Survivors' and Disability Pension (BVG) is two-thirds or less than this rate in percent, the surpluses are to be distributed as follows:

a. the net income from capital in respect of the solvency margin, for the benefit of the insurance business;
b. 90 percent of the result for the benefit of the policyholders and 10% for the benefit of the insurance business. Result means the positive total balance under Article 149, paragraphs 1 and 3, less the establishment of reserves in accordance with the business plan under Article 149, paragraph 1, letter a.

[3] If an insurance business needs additional capital resources in order to fulfill the solvency requirements or if the share of the difference between the sum of the components and the distribution share which is attributed to insurer's assets is disproportionate to the allocation to the policyholder surplus fund, then this is to be reported to the FINMA. It can upon request or upon its own initiative make alternative rules.

[4] The distribution share is to be notified along with evidence of its application [to the FINMA] for approval.

Art. 148 Application of the distribution share

[1] The distribution share will be used first for the expenses in the savings, risk and cost processes.

[2] The total balance equals the distribution share, less the expenses in the savings, risk and cost processes.

---

15 SR **831.40**

Art. 149 Procedure in the case of a positive total balance

[1] A positive total balance will be applied in accordance with the business plan of the insurance business for:

a. the establishment of reserves for:
   1. longevity risk,
   2 future coverage shortfalls in pension conversions,
   3 reported, but not yet paid insurance claims, including increases in actuarial reserves for disability and survivors' pensions,
   4 incurred-but-not-yet-reported insurance claims,
   5 claims volatility,
   6 volatility in the value of the capital investments,
   7 interest rate guarantees,
   8 rating adjustments and restructurings;
b. Coverage of the costs for additional risk capital raised with the approval of the FINMA;
c. Funding the surplus fund.

[2] Reserves which were established under paragraph 1, letter a and which are no longer needed are to be allocated to the surplus fund.

[3] Risk capital under paragraph 1, letter b may only be raised with the approval of the FINMA; it can be used to fulfill supervisory law requirements or, in the interest of the insureds, for increasing income from capital investment.

Art. 150 Procedure in the event of a negative total balance

In the case of a negative total balance, the following measures are to be applied sequentially until the shortfall is covered:

a. Reserves which are no longer needed are to be released;
b. The distribution share must be increased;
c. The remaining shortfall is to be carried forward in an amount not to exceed the available surplus fund and to be set-off against the surplus fund in the following year;
d. The remaining shortfall is to be covered by free capital resources.

Art. 151 Surplus fund

[1] The surplus fund is a technical insurance entry in the balance sheet for the accrual of the shares of surplus owed to the policyholders.

[2] The amounts allocated to the surplus fund, subject to Article 150, letter c, may be used exclusively for the allocation of shares of surplus to policyholders.

Art. 152 Conditions for the allocation of shares of surplus

1 The shares of surplus for the policyholders are to be paid only from the surplus fund.

2 Funds which are credited to the surplus fund are to be allocated to the policyholders within five years.

3 In the case of a negative total balance, no shares of surplus may be allocated.

Art. 153 Principles for the allocation of shares of surplus

1 The shares of surplus accumulated in the surplus fund are to be allocated in accordance with recognized technical insurance methods, but in an amount of not more than two-thirds of the surplus fund.

2 The allocations of shares of surplus to pension plans shall be made in proportion to the actuarial reserve, the loss development of the insured risk and the incurred administrative costs, as well as in compliance with Article 68a BVG[16].

3 For exceptional reasons, the FINMA can order deviations from the two-thirds rule in paragraph 1.

Art. 154 Coverage for employee insurance institutions

Domestic or foreign insurance businesses without a license to engage in life insurance may reinsure the risks assumed by employee and association insurance institutions which are not subject to supervision, if:

a. the coverage is provided on a collective, nonproportional basis;
b. the coverage applies only to mortality and disability risk;
c. the employee or association insurance institution itself covers more than the full risk which is expected on the basis of technical insurance principals.

Chapter 4: Health and accident insurance

Art. 155 Transfer of age reserves

1 If an insurance business establishes age reserves for health insurance and retains the right to terminate [the insurance] after the occurrence of the insured event or is not required to continue the agreement after its lapse, then it must refund an appropriate portion of the age reserves for health insurance to the insured persons if one of the parties terminates the insurance contract or the insurance business does not continue the contract after its lapse.

2 It shall deliver a plan for the refund of the share of the age reserves for health insurance to the FINMA for approval. This plan shall include, in particular, the basis for the calculation and the amount of the share to be refunded. This information is to be included in the contractual documentation.

16 SR **831.40**

Art. 156 Closed blocks of business

[1] If an insurance business no longer adds any insurance contracts to an insurance portfolio (closed block of business), the policyholders in this portfolio have the right to obtain, as a replacement for their previous insurance contract, the most equivalent insurance contract in an open portfolio of the insurance business or one of the member companies of the same insurance group to the extent that the insurance business or the group company has such an open portfolio.

[2] An insurance business must inform the affected policyholders without delay about this right as well as the insurance coverage provided by the open portfolio.

[3] The age and health condition of the policyholder when the previous insurance policy was issued is controlling for the change from the previous to the new insurance contract.

Art. 157 Rating classes and experience rating in group health insurance disability insurance

Article 123 also applies to the group health insurance disability insurance.

Art. 158 Jurisdiction in group health insurance disability insurance

Insurance businesses are required in group health insurance disability insurance contracts with employers to provide, in addition to the specified jurisdiction, for jurisdiction at the location of the workplace of the employee.

Art. 159 Insurance of children

Article 131 applies by analogy to individual accident insurance or collective accident insurance for children.

Art. 160 Disability insurance

If an insurance business writes disability insurance along with health and accident insurance, the regulations for health and accident insurance also apply to the disability insurance.

Chapter 5: Legal protection insurance

Section 1: General provisions

Art. 161 Subject

Under a legal protection insurance contract, an insurance business assumes the obligation, in exchange for a premium, to reimburse costs resulting from legal matters or to provide services in connection with such matters.

Art. 162 Exceptions from the scope of applicability

Articles 163–170 of this regulation and Article 32, paragraph 1 ISL are not applicable:

a. to the activities of a liability insurance business in the defense or representation of person insured by it against liability claims in the course of a judicial or administrative proceeding if this activity, on account of this insurance, also is in the interest of the liability insurance business;

b. to disputes or claims in connection with the use of sea-going vessels.

Art. 163 Disclosure obligation

An insurance business which writes legal protection insurance simultaneously with other lines of insurance (composite insurers) and which does not assign the handling of claims to a legally independent business, shall inform the insured person without delay by letter with proof of delivery of the right to make a choice under Article 32, paragraph 1, letter b ISL.

Section 2: Claims handling businesses

Art. 164 Organization

1 Only insurance businesses which engage solely in legal protection insurance, as well as corporations or mutual corporations which do not provide any services in connection with claims handling for other lines of insurance, are permitted as claims handling businesses under Article 32, paragraph 1, letter a ISL.

2 The claims handling business must have its domicile or a branch in Switzerland.

3 The persons entrusted with the ultimate management, supervision and control, as well as conducting business and representing the claims handling business may not engage in any other activity for a composite insurance business.

4 The employees of the claims handling business which are entrusted with the handling of claims may not engage in any comparable activity for a composite insurance business.

Art. 165 Relationship between composite insurance businesses and claims handling businesses

1 The contract between the insurance business and the claims handling business must, in particular:

a. have a clause that gives the FINMA the right to review the management of the files of the claims handling business;

b. provide that the insured person may only assert claims under the legal protection insurance policy by submitting them to the claims handling organization.

2 An insurance business may not, in the event of conflicts of interest, give any instructions for the handling of insurance claims which could lead to disadvantages for the insured person.

3 A claims handling business may not, in the event of conflicts of interest, make any statements to the insurance business concerning the insurance claims handled by it which could lead to disadvantages for the insured person.

4 An insurance business is bound by a decision rendered against the claims handling business.

Section 3: Form and content of the legal protection insurance agreement

Art. 166 General provisions

1 The legal protection guarantee must be the subject of an agreement that is segregated from the other insurance lines or a separate chapter of a policy with the details of the legal protection guarantee and the relevant premium.

2 If the claims handling is assigned to a claims handling business in accordance with Article 32, paragraph 1, letter a, this business must be specified in the separate contract or separate chapter, along with its business name and the address of its domicile.

3 If an insurance business grants the insured person the right to consult an independent attorney or another person in accordance with Article 32, paragraph 1, letter b, then this right must be mentioned in the applications, policies, general terms of insurance and in the claims forms and it must be made especially conspicuous.

Art. 167 Choice of a legal representative

1 The insured person must be granted the right in the legal protection insurance contract to freely choose a legal representative who is qualified in the law applicable to the procedure:

a. if a legal representative is required in respect of the judicial or administrative proceeding;
b. in the case of conflicts of interest.

2 The contract may provide that if the chosen legal representative is not accepted by the insurance business or the claims handling business, the insured person has the right to nominate three other persons for the legal representation, one of whom must be accepted.

3 If a conflict of interest arises, then the insurance business or the claims handling business must make the insured person aware of his or her right.

Art. 168 Waiver of professional confidentiality

A clause in an insurance agreement requiring the insured person to release the legal representative from his or her professional confidentiality obligation *vis à vis* an insurance business may not be applied if a conflict of interest exists and the disclosure of the requested information to the insurance business could be to the disadvantage of the insured person.

Art. 169 Procedure in the event of differences of opinion

1 The insurance contract shall provide a procedure which provides a guarantee of objectivity comparable to an arbitration proceeding for the resolution of differences of opinion

between the insured persons and the insurance business or the claims handling business in respect of the measures to be used for the handling of the claim.

[2] If an insurance business or claims handling business declines to pay for a measure on the grounds that it has no chance of success, then the proposed solutions are to be justified immediately in writing and must make the insured person aware of the possibility of the procedure under paragraph 1.

[3] If the insurance contract does not provide for a procedure in accordance with paragraph 1 or if an insurance business or claims handling business fails to inform the insured person about it at the time of the declination of the policy benefit, then the need for legal protection for the insured person in the relevant case is deemed recognized.

[4] If a policy benefit is declined and the insured persons conducts proceedings at his or her own cost and obtains a judgment that is more favorable to him or her than the solution justified in writing by the insurance business or the claims handling business or the result in accordance with paragraph 1, the insurance business shall bear the costs thereof up to the maximum amount of the policy limit.

Art. 170 Success fees

An insurance business and claims handling business may not be promised a share of any success of an insured person.

Chapter 6: Natural perils insurance

Section 1: Insured losses and scope of coverage

Art. 171 Combined fire and natural perils insurance

[1] Insurance businesses which insure property (moveable property and buildings) in Switzerland against fire under insurance line B8 must also insure them for full value against natural perils.

[2] The insurance replaces insured property destroyed, damaged or lost as a result of natural perils.

Art. 172 Exceptions from the duty to provide insurance

[1] Damage to the following are not insured under the combined fire and natural perils insurance:

a. easily moved structures (such as display and party huts, large tents, carousels, display and trade show stands, inflatable structures and *Rautenhallen*) as well as their contents;
b. mobile homes, motor homes, boats and aircraft, including accessories;
c. motor vehicles as outdoor storage facilities or under a garden umbrella;
d. cog-wheel trains, cable cars, ski lifts, overhead electrical power lines and towers (except local power lines);

e. property located on construction sites;

f. green houses, greenhouse bed windows and plants;

g. nuclear power plants under Article 3, letter d of the Atomic Energy Law of 21 March 2003[17].

[2] A construction site is considered the entire area on which property is found which is there in connection with the construction, including before construction begins and after it ends.

Art. 173 Insured natural perils

[1] Natural perils damages are damages which result from flooding, storm, hail, avalanche, the weight of snow, falling rock, or landslide.

[2] A storm is deemed a wind of at least 75 km/h which uproots trees or tears off roofs in the area of the insured property.

[3] Natural perils damages are not:

a. damages caused by the subsidence of earth, poor building site, defective construction, inadequate building maintenance, omission of preventative measures, artificial earthquakes, snow slides from roofs, groundwater, the rising or flooding of lakes and streams, which, based on experience, recur at shorter or longer intervals;

b. without regard to the cause of the damages, those which result from water from lakes created by dams or other artificial bodies of water, reflux from blocked waste water pipes or changes in atomic structure;

c. operational or production damages which, based on experience, must be expected, such as damages associated with construction above and below ground, mine construction, quarrying stone or obtaining gravel, sand or clay;

d. damages caused by vibrations which have their origin in the collapse of artificially created hollow spaces;

e. vibrations which are caused by tectonic activity of the earth's crust (earthquakes) and volcanic eruptions.

Art. 174 Coverage exclusions

The following are excluded from the natural perils insurance:

a. damages caused by the weight of snow which only affect tiles or other roofing materials, chimneys or exhaust pipes;

b. storm and water damage to ships and boats on water.

---

17 SR **732.1**

Art. 175[18] Deductible

1 The insured shall bear the following deductible:

a. in respect of household insurance, 500 francs per event;
b. in respect of agricultural inventory insurance, 10 percent of the indemnity, but at least 1,000 francs and not more than 10,000 francs per event;
c. in respect of the insurance of other moveable property, 10 percent of the indemnity, but at least 2,500 francs and not more than 50,000 francs per event;
d. in respect of the insurance of buildings:
   1. which serve exclusively residential and agricultural purposes, 10 percent of the indemnity, but at least 1,000 francs and not more than 10,000 francs,
   2. which serve all other purposes, 10 percent of the indemnity, but at least 2,500 francs and not more than 50,000 francs.

2 The deductible will be deducted per event, one time each for movable property insurance and for building insurance. If an event affects several buildings of a policyholder, for each of which a different deductible as been provided, then the deductible amounts to at least 2,500 francs and not more than 50,000 francs.

Art. 176 Benefits limitations

1 If the indemnities determined for a single event and a single insured from all of the insurers which are allowed to engage in an insurance activity in Switzerland exceed 25 million francs, then these will be reduced to this amount. A further reduction under paragraph 2 shall not be affected.

2 If the indemnities determined for an insured event in Switzerland from all of the insurers which are allowed to engage in an insurance activity in Switzerland exceed 1 billion francs, then the indemnities due to the individual beneficiaries will be reduced in a manner that they collectively do not exceed this amount.[19]

3 Indemnities for moveable property and damages to a building may not be calculated together.

4 Damages which are separated in time and physical location constitute a single event if they can be traced to the same atmospheric or tectonic cause.

5 The prerequisite for the coverage of an event is that the insurance policy was in force at its commencement.

---

18 Text in accordance with para. 1 of the Regulation of 18 Oct. 2006, in force since 1 Jan. 2007 (AS **2006** 4425).

19 Text in accordance with para. 1 of the Regulation of 18 Oct. 2006, in force since 1 Jan. 2007 (AS **2006** 4425).

Section 2: Premiums and statistics

Art. 177 Basis of calculation

[1] Insurance businesses shall prepare a premium calculation system.

[2] They shall calculate the premium rates on the basis of the calculation system and in so doing shall take into account the expected change in loss requirements.

Art. 178 Approval of unit premiums and disclosure in the policy

[1] An insurance business shall submit the premium rate, including the calculation system to the FINMA for approval.

[2] The applicable premium is to be set out for the policyholder in the policy separately for the insured risks of fire and natural perils damages.

Art. 179 Statistics

[1] Insurance businesses shall deliver annually the data concerning the natural perils insurance to the statistics office specified by the FINMA.

[2] The statistics office shall process the data in accordance with the instructions of the FINMA to yield informative statistics, which provide information about the development of the natural perils insurance, in particular concerning premiums, claims expense (paid claims and case reserves, segregated by statistical year), the amounts insured and the losses that lead to a limitation of benefits under Article 176.

[3] The persons charged with the processing of the natural perils claims statistics are subject to a confidentiality obligation. In particular, they may not disclose the statistical information of the individual insurance businesses to other persons.

Art. 180 Exceptions

[1] Natural perils losses which are not covered by the insurance requirement under Article 172 shall not be included in the statistics.

[2] Pursuant to an application supported by good cause, the FINMA may exempt an insurance business from the duty to deliver data to the statistics office or exclude the data of an insurance business from inclusion in the statistics upon an application by the statistics office supported by good cause.

[3] An exemption or exclusion under paragraph 2 from participation in the statistics does not exclude the obligation to share in the costs pursuant to Article 181.

Art. 181 Costs

[1] Insurance businesses shall bear the costs of the evaluation of the premium rates and statistics.

[2] They shall prepare a plan for the cost allocation and shall submit it to the FINMA for approval.

[3] The approval will be granted if the plan provides for a balanced cost allocation.

Title 7: Insurance intermediaries

Art. 182 Exceptions from scope of application

Insurance intermediary activities abroad by an insurance intermediary with its headquarters or domicile in Switzerland are not subject to supervision in Switzerland.

Art. 183 Registration obligation

[1] No registration obligation exists under Article 43, paragraph 1 ISL for insurance intermediaries if:

a. the majority of the commissions they receive during a calendar year are predominantly from one or two insurance businesses;
b. they receive compensation or other financial advantages from insurance businesses that do not conform to customary compensation for insurance intermediation and therefore could affect their independence;
c. they have entered into cooperation agreements or other agreements with insurance businesses which affect their freedom to act on behalf of other insurance businesses;
d. they have a direct or indirect participation in more than 10 percent of the equity capital of an insurance business; or
e. they have a management function in an insurance business or otherwise exercise influence on the business processes of an insurance business.

[2] There is also no registration obligation under Article 43, paragraph 1 ISL if an insurance business:

a. owns directly or indirectly more than 10% of the equity capital of the insurance intermediary;
b. has a management function with the insurance intermediary or otherwise can exercise influence on the business of the insurance intermediary.

[3] The FINMA may order exceptions from the registration obligation under paragraphs 1 and 2 to the extent that special circumstances justify it.

Art. 184 Professional requirements

[1] The insurance intermediary shall demonstrate professional qualification by successfully completing an examination or through other equivalent evidence.

[2] The FINMA shall regulate the content of the examination. It can issue regulations for the conduct of the examination as well as the reasons for exemptions.

[3] The FINMA shall determine the equivalence of other professional certifications.

Art. 185 Personal requirements

Insurance intermediaries shall meet the following personal requirements:

a. they are not under any legal disability;

b. there are no penal judgments on account of actions which are incompatible with the business of an insurance intermediary and which have not been expunged from the penal register;

c. there are no outstanding certificates of unpaid debts against them.

Art. 186 Financial security

[1] An insurance intermediary shall have professional indemnity insurance against financial losses that covers its liability for violations of the professional duty of care. The annual policy limit for all claims must amount to at least 2 million francs.

[2] The obligation does not exist if a third party has obtained a professional indemnity insurance which includes the insurance intermediary in its coverage.

[3] Instead of a professional liability insurance, the insurance intermediary may provide equivalent financial security. The FINMA shall decide case-by-case what other financial security is to be viewed as equivalent.

[4] Anyone who wants to register under Article 43, paragraph 1, as well as Article 43, paragraph 2 ISL shall establish the existence of the required financial security for both forms of insurance intermediary business.

Art. 187 Register

[1] The register shall include the following items of information about the insurance intermediary:

a. name and address;

b. legal form;

c. the insurance businesses which are represented by the insurance intermediary pursuant to Article 43, paragraph 2 ISL;

d. the lines of insurance for which the insurance intermediary transacts business along with the relationship to the insurance businesses;

e. the employer, if the insurance intermediary is in an employment relationship;

f. the date of the initial registration;

g. the registration number.

[2] The insurance intermediary may be registered in the register under Article 43, paragraph 1 as well as Article 43, paragraph 2 ISL, but not for the same line of insurance.

[3] Legal entities which engage in a type insurance intermediary business defined in Article 43, paragraph 1 ISL shall be registered in the register in their role as insurance inter-

mediary. They must establish that they have enough employees which have the necessary qualifications and who also are registered in the register.

Art. 188 Public register

The data in the register are public and may be made accessible by data retrieval technology.

Art. 189 Changes in significant facts

[1] The registered insurance intermediaries are required to notify the following changes to the FINMA within 14 days after becoming aware of them:

a. change of name;
b. the loss of the financial security or failure to meet the minimum guarantee under Article 186;
c. replacement of a professional liability insurance with equivalent financial security, or *vice versa*;
d. termination of its activities as an insurance intermediary;
e. change from insurance intermediary business under Article 43, paragraph 1 ISL to insurance intermediary business under Article 43, paragraph 2 ISL, or *vice versa*;
f. change of the insurance business whose insurance contracts are intermediated by the insurance intermediary pursuant to Article 43, paragraph 2 ISL;
g. change of the insurance intermediary business for which the insurance intermediary works;
h. change of address.

[2] The insurance business from which the insurance intermediary has obtained professional liability insurance in accordance with Article 186, paragraph 1 must notify the FINMA without delay of the suspension or lapse of this insurance. The same applies if the coverage falls below the prescribed minimum.

[3] The same obligation applies to a person which has provided an equivalent form of financial security for the benefit of the insurance intermediary.

Art. 190 Disclosure obligations

To the extent that there are changes in the information under Article 45, paragraph 1 ISL, the insurance intermediary must inform customers about it at the time of the next contact with the customer.

Title 8: Insurance groups and insurance conglomerates

Chapter 1: Insurance groups

Section 1: Organizational structure, group structure and intra-group transactions

Art. 191 Organizational structure

1 An insurance group shall have an organizational structure that is consistent with the business activities of the insurance group and appropriate to the risks.

2 It shall submit an illustration of the organizational, control and management structure to the FINMA and any changes thereto within 14 days after they become effective.

3 The FINMA shall designate the entity that is its point of contact that is responsible for the supervisory law obligations of the insurance group.

4 It can request the submission of the articles of incorporation of the entity designated as the point of contact.

Art. 192 Group structure

1 An insurance group shall submit to the FINMA each year within three months after the close of the financial year a complete group structure chart in which all entities of the insurance group are shown. The FINMA may request this at more frequent intervals.

2 An insurance group shall report to the FINMA, not later than the execution of the contract, the creation, acquisition or the sale of a significant ownership interest by a member business of the group.

3 The FINMA shall specify, consistent with the size and complexity of the insurance group, what is to be understood as a significant ownership interest.

Art. 193 Group internal transactions

1 Group internal transactions are business and transactions, pursuant to which, the supervised businesses obtain support, directly or indirectly from another entity within the same insurance group for the purpose of fulfilling an obligation; in particular this applies to:

a. loans;
b. guarantees and off-balance sheet transactions;
c. business and transactions that are creditable capital resources under Article 37, paragraph 2, letter d;
d. capital investments;
e. reinsurance transactions;
f. cost-sharing agreements; and
g. other risk transfer transactions.

[2] Important group internal transactions are those which significantly change the financial condition of an individual entity or which significantly change, or will change, the insurance group as a whole and which exceed a minimum value specified by the FINMA.

Art. 194 Supervision of group internal transactions

[1] An insurance group shall submit a report about all important group internal transactions to the FINMA within 14 days after the legal effective date. In addition, the FINMA is to be informed annually, within three months after the close of the financial year, about all transactions. It can require reporting at more frequent intervals.

[2] If actions for the support of group entities are effected through natural persons or legal entities which are outside the insurance group, then a report also is to be made about this business and these transactions.

[3] The FINMA shall specify the nature and content of the reports and take into account the size and complexity of the insurance group in setting the minimum value.

Section 2: Risk Management

Art. 195 Purpose and content

Articles 96 and 98 apply by analogy for the purpose and content of risk management.

Art. 196 Documentation

[1] An insurance group shall submit the documentation concerning risk management to the FINMA within three months after the close of the financial year. Significant changes must be reported within a period of one month.

[2] In addition, Article 97 applies by analogy.

Art. 197 Report on group-wide risks and risk concentrations

[1] An insurance group shall submit a report to the FINMA within three months after the end of the financial year or, if it so orders, at more frequent intervals, about:

a. the group-wide risk situation;
b. the risk concentrations which present a solvency risk for the insurance group or an individual entity.

[2] The FINMA shall specify the form and content of the reports.

Section 3: Solvency

Art. 198 Applicable regulations

The solvency of an insurance group is evaluated by two methods in accordance with Article 22. This is done subject to the provisions of this section which shall be applied by analogy.

Art. 199 Required solvency margin

[1] The required solvency margin shall be calculated on the basis of the consolidated financial reports of the insurance group.

[2] The required solvency margin for the entire insurance group is the sum of the required solvency margins for life insurance operations, nonlife insurance operations and reinsurance operations, as well as for entities without supervisory law capital resources requirements.

[3] The solvency margins for specific operational areas shall be calculated by analogy in accordance with Articles 23 ff. For businesses without supervisory law capital resources requirements, the FINMA shall specify the required solvency margin.

[4] In exceptional cases, the FINMA may:

a. permit the calculation of the required solvency margin on another basis than that in paragraph 1, in particular the calculation by the addition of the required solvency margins of the individual business;
b. exclude certain business from inclusion in the calculation of the group solvency, to the extent that their inclusion would be unsuitable or misleading.

Art. 200 Available solvency margin

[1] If the financial statements are prepared in accordance with internationally recognized accounting principles, the creditable capital resources of an insurance group equals consolidated assets, subject to the following adjustments:

a. credit for minority interests;
b. deduction of all intangible assets;
c. deduction of planned dividends and returns of capital;
d. deduction of capitalized acquisition costs in nonlife operations.

[2] The FINMA may, upon request, allow credit for subordinated loans and other items with the same character as capital resources.

[3] If the financial statements are not prepared in accordance with internationally recognized accounting principles, the FINMA shall specify the creditable resources.

Art. 201 Methods for the calculation of risk-based solvency

[1] For the determination of the risk-based solvency calculation, an insurance group shall use an internal model for the identification and quantification of all significant types of risk.

[2] The model is to be submitted to the FINMA for approval. The FINMA shall issue regulations concerning the quantitative, qualitative and organizational requirements.

Art. 202 Reporting

The calculation of the Group Solvency I under Articles 199 and 200 and the risk-based solvency under Article 201 is performed semi-annually. It is to be submitted to the FINMA within three months after the close of the financial year or the financial half year. Upon request, for good cause shown, the FINMA can extend these deadlines.

Art. 203 External examination

1 An insurance group shall appoint an audit firm[20]. It shall examine annually whether the insurance group has complied with the obligations of this regulation and has implemented the risk management procedures described in the document [prepared] in accordance with Article 196. In addition, it shall prepare a report for delivery to the FINMA.

2 The FINMA shall issue directives for the examination. It can permit the examination to be performed by another qualified, independent third party.

Chapter 2: Insurance conglomerates

Art. 204 Applicable regulations

Articles 191–198, 200–203 and 216 concerning insurance groups apply to insurance conglomerates by analogy.

Art. 205 Allocation of businesses to the insurance and financial segments

1 The criteria for the allocation of business to the insurance or financial segments is the primary activity of the relevant business and the segment for which the business provides services. Businesses which cannot be unambiguously allocated, will be allocated to the insurance segment.

2 The allocation of the individual businesses to the insurance or finance segment is to be submitted to the FINMA for approval.

Art. 206 Required solvency margin

1 The required solvency margin is calculated on the basis of the consolidated financial statement of the insurance conglomerate.

2 The required solvency margin of the entire insurance conglomerate equals the sum of the required solvency margins in the insurance segment and the financial segment, as well as those for entities without supervisory law capital resources requirements in the financial segment.

3 The required solvency margin in the insurance segment is calculated on the basis of Article 199. In the financial segment, it is calculated on the basis of international or, with the consent of the FINMA, on the basis of nationally recognized principles in the banking segment. For entities without supervisory law equity capital resources requirements in the

20 Text in accordance with Annex para. 11 of the Financial Market Audit Regulation of 15 Oct. 2008, in force since 1 Jan. 2008 (SR **956.161**)

financial segment, the FINMA shall determine the calculation of the required solvency margin.

4 In exceptional cases, the FINMA may:

a. permit the calculation of the required solvency margin in the financial segment on the basis of equivalent methods, in particular, through the addition of the capital resources calculation in accordance with the requirements of an individual entity on the basis of the individual financial statements;
b. exclude certain entities from inclusion in the calculation of the required solvency margin to the extent their inclusion would be unsuitable or misleading.

Title 9:

Chapter 1:[21]

Arts. 207 and 208

Chapter 2:[22]

Arts. 209-214

Chapter 10: [23]

Art. 215

Chapter 11: Transition and final provisions

Art. 216 Transition provisions

1 and 2 ... [24]

3 Any portfolio of valuation reserves under Article 37, paragraph 2, letter c invested in fixed rate securities may, with the following limitation, continue to be credited during a period of not more than five years after entry into force: creditable during the transition period is the lowest value in the portfolio of valuation reserves on the last balance sheet date before entry into force and in the portfolio resulting from successive valuations at each year end.

---

21 Repealed by Annex para. 11 of the Financial Market Audit Regulation of 15 Oct. 2008, in force since 1 Jan. 2009 (SR **956.161**).

22 Repealed by the Art. 38, para. 2 of the FNMA Fees and Charges Regulation of 15 Oct. 2008 in force since 1 Jan. 2008 (SR **956.122**).

23 Repealed by Annex para. 11 of the Financial Market Audit Regulation of 15 Oct. 2008, in force since 1 Jan. 2009(SR **956.161**).

24 Repealed by Annex para. 11 of the Financial Market Audit Regulation of 15 Oct. 2008, in force since 1 Jan. 2009(SR **956.161**).

4 The following regulations apply in respect of target capital (Arts. 41–46) and risk-bearing capital (Arts. 47–50):

a.-c. ...[25]

d. They shall establish the risk-bearing capital needed for the coverage of the target capital within five years after entry into force.

e.-h. ...[26]

5 ...[27]

6 An insurance business shall report the details about the distribution of surplus under Article 130 to the insureds through an endorsement to the contract not later than the initial provision of information under Article 130, paragraph e. The endorsement must be consistent with the information in the business plan.

7 - 9 ...[28]

8 The conversion right under Article 156 must be granted to the insureds of closed blocks [of business] as of entry into force not later than two years after entry into force.

9 Insurance businesses which at the time of entry into force already have a license to transact business, must deliver a business plan to the FINMA within two years after entry into force. Changes in an existing business plan under ISL Article 5 are to be notified only after the submission of the new business plan.

10 Insurance business which are not authorized to engage in life insurance that at the time of entry into force had insurance with limited benefits for accident, illness and disability, such as, specifically, subscription insurance under which the payment of a death benefit is included, may maintain this death benefit provision only up to the expiration of the contract or until the occurrence of the insurance event. Article 14 of the Regulation of 27 June 1995 concerning Health Insurance[29] remains unaffected for the recognized health insurers.

11 - 15 ...[30]

16 Articles 175 and 176, paragraph 2 are, as of entry into force, applicable to all new and current insurance contracts.[31]

Art. 216a[32]

---

25 Repealed by Annex para. 11 of the Financial Market Audit Regulation of 15 Oct. 2008, in force since 1 Jan. 2009(SR **956.161**).

26 Repealed by Annex para. 11 of the Financial Market Audit Regulation of 15 Oct. 2008, in force since 1 Jan. 2009(SR **956.161**).

27 Repealed by Annex para. 11 of the Financial Market Audit Regulation of 15 Oct. 2008, in force since 1 Jan. 2009(SR **956.161**).

28 Repealed by Annex para. 11 of the Financial Market Audit Regulation of 15 Oct. 2008, in force since 1 Jan. 2009(SR **956.161**).

29 SR **832.102**

30 Repealed by Annex para. 11 of the Financial Market Audit Regulation of 15 Oct. 2008, in force since 1 Jan. 2009(SR **956.161**).

31 Added by para. 1 of the Regulation of 18 Oct. 2006, with effect from 1 Jan. 2007 (AS **2006** 4425).

Art. 217 Repeal of prior law

The following regulations are repealed:

1. Federal Council Resolution of 22 November 1978[33] on the Entry into Force of the Insurance Supervision Law and the Continuing Applicability of Federal Law (*Bundesratsbeschluss vom 22. November 1978 über die Inkraftsetzung des Versicherungsaufsichtsgesetzes und die Weitergeltung von Bundesrecht*);
2. Regulation of 19 November 1997[34] on the Use of Derivative Financial Instruments by the Insurance Institutions (*Verordnung vom 19. November 1997 über den Einsatz von derivativen Finanzinstrumenten durch die Versicherungseinrichtungen*);
3. Regulation of 11 September 1931[35] on the Supervision of Private Insurance Institutions (*Verordnung vom 11. September 1931 über die Beaufsichtigung von privaten Versicherungseinrichtungen*);
4. Regulation of 11 February 1976[36] on the scope of the Insurance Supervision Obligation (*Verordnung vom 11. Februar 1976 über die Abgrenzung der Versicherungsaufsichtspflicht*);
5. Regulation of 3 December 1979[37] on Engaging in Non-Insurance Transactions by the Private Insurance Institutions (*Verordnung vom 3. Dezember 1979 über den Betrieb versicherungsfremder Geschäfte durch die privaten Versicherungseinrichtungen*);
6. Federal Council Resolution of 22 November 1955[38] on the Subscriber, Buyer and Customer Insurance (*Bundesratsbeschluss vom 22. November 1955 über die Abonnenten- und die Käufer- und Kundenversicherung*);
7. Regulation of 18 November 1992[39] on the Legal Protection Insurance (*Verordnung vom 18. November 199236 über die Rechtsschutzversicherung*);
8. Regulation of 18 November 1992[40] on the Natural Perils Insurance (*Verordnung vom 18. November 1992 über die Elementarschadenversicherung*);
9. Regulation of 29 November 1993[41] on Direct Life Insurance (*Verordnung vom 29. November 1993 über die direkte Lebensversicherung*);
10. Regulation of 8 September 1993[42] on the Direct Insurance with the Exception of Life Insurance (*Verordnung vom 8. September 1993 über die Direktversicherung mit Ausnahme der Lebensversicherung*);

---

32 Added by Annex para. II 1 1 of the Audit Supervision Regulation of 22 August 2007 (SR **221.302.3**). Repealed by Annex para. 11 of the Financial Market Audit Regulation of 15 Oct. 2008, in force since 1 Jan. 2009(SR **956.161**).

33 [AS **1978** 1856, **1985** 885 Art. 4, **1986** 689 Art. 6, **1988** 116 para. II, para. 1, subparagraph c]

34 [AS **1998** 84]

35 [BS **10** 311; AS **1979** 1588, **1986** 2529. **1988** 116, **1990** 787, **1992** 2415, **1993** 2614, **1995** 3867 Annex para. 7, **1996** 2243 para. I 38, **1998** Annex para. 1, **1999** 3671]

36 [AS **1976** 239]

37 [AS **1980** 53]

38 [AS **1955** 1014]

39 [AS **1992** 2355]

40 [AS **1992** 2359, **1995** 1063 **2000** 24]

41 [AS **1993** 3230, **1996** 2243 para. I 39, **1998** 84 Annex para. 2, **2003** 4991, **2004** 1615, **2005** 2389]

42 [AS **1993** 2620, **1995** 5690, **1998** 84 Annex para. 3, **2001** 1286 para. II, **2003** 4999, **2005** 2389]

11. Regulation of 18 November 1992[43] on Volatility Reserves for Credit Insurance (*Verordnung vom 18. November 1992 über die Schwankungsrückstellung in der Kreditversicherung*).

Art. 218 Entry into force

This regulation enters into force on 1 January 2006.

43 [AS **1992** 2380]

Annex 1

Lines of Insurance

A. Life Insurance

A1 Group Life Insurance under an Occupational Pension Plan (*Kollektivlebensversicherung im Rahmen der beruflichen Vorsorge*)

A2 Unit-Linked Life Insurance (*Anteilgebundene Lebensversicherung*)

A2.1 Unit-Linked Capital Accumulation Insurance with Protection against Death or Disability (*Fondsanteilgebundene Kapitalversicherung mit Todesfall- oder Invaliditätsschutz*)

A2.2 Unit-Linked Capital Accumulation Insurance with Protection against Death or Disability as well as Guaranteed Benefits upon Maturity (*Fondsanteilgebundene Kapitalversicherung mit Todesfall- oder Invaliditätsschutz sowie Erlebensfallgarantie*)

A2.3 Unit-Linked Pension Insurance (*Fondsanteilgebundene Rentenversicherung*)

A2.4 An Internal Portfolio or other Reference Value-Linked Life Insurance with Protection against Death or Disability (*Interne Anlagebestände oder andere Bezugswerte gebundene Lebensversicherung mit Todesfall- oder Invaliditätsschutz*)

A2.5 An Internal Portfolio or other Reference Value-Linked Life Insurance with Protection against Death or Disability, as well as Guaranteed Benefits upon Maturity (*Interne Anlagebestände oder andere Bezugswerte gebundene Lebensversicherung mit Todesfall- oder Invaliditätsschutz sowie Erlebensfallgarantie*)

A2.6 An Internal Portfolio or other Reference Value-Linked Pension Insurance (*Interne Anlagebestände oder andere Bezugswerte gebundene Rentenversicherung*)

A3 Other Life Insurance

A3.1 Single Premium Life Insurance with Death Benefits and Guaranteed Benefits upon Maturity *(Einzelkapitalversicherung auf den Todes- und Erlebensfall)*

A3.2 Annuities (*Einzelrentenversicherung*)

A3.3 Other Individual Life Insurance (*Sonstige Einzellebensversicherung*)

A3.4 Group Life Insurance outside the Occupational Pension Plan (*Kollektivlebensversicherung ausserhalb der beruflichen Vorsorge*)

A4 Accident Insurance (*Unfallversicherung*)

A5 Health Insurance (*Krankenversicherung*)

A6 Capital Redemption Transactions (*Kapitalisationsgeschäfte*)

A7 Tontinen transactions (*Tontinengeschäfte*)

B. Nonlife Insurance

B1 Accident Insurance (*Unfall*) (including workplace accidents and occupational diseases)

- one-time benefits (*einmalige Leistungen*)
- recurring benefits (*wiederkehrende Leistungen*)
- combined benefits (*kombinierte Leistungen*)
- passenger transportation (*Personenbeförderung*)

B2 Illness (*Krankheit*)

- one-time benefits (*einmalige Leistungen*)
- recurring benefits (*wiederkehrende Leistungen*)
- combined benefits (*kombinierte Leistungen*)

B3 Land vehicle property insurance (excluding railway vehicles) (*Landfahrzeug-Kasko (ohne Schienenfahrzeuge)*)

All property damage to:

- Motor vehicles (*Motorfahrzeugen*)
- Land vehicles without motors (*Landfahrzeugen ohne eigenen Antrieb*)

B4 Railway stock property insurance (*Schienenfahrzeug-Kasko*)

All damage to railway stock (*Sämtliche Schäden an Schienenfahrzeugen*)

B5 Aircraft hull insurance (*Luftfahrzeug-Kasko*)

All damage to aircraft (*Sämtliche Schäden an Luftfahrzeugen*)

B6 Marine, inland marine and river transportation property insurance (*See-, Binnensee- und Flussschifffahrts-Kasko*)

All damage to:

- river watercraft
- inland lake watercraft
- ocean-going vessels

B7 Goods in transit (including goods, luggage and other goods) (*Transportgüter*)

all damage to goods regardless of the means of transportation used

B8 Fire and natural perils insurance (*Feuer und Elementarschäden*)

all damage (to the extent not covered under the lines B3, B4, B5, B6 or B7) caused by:

- Fire

- Explosion
- Storm
- Other natural perils excluding storm
- Nuclear energy
- Earth subsidence and landslide

B9 Other property damage (*Sonstige Sachschäden*)

All property damage (to the extent not covered by the lines B3, B4, B5, B6 and B7) caused by hail or frost, as well as causes of every other kind (such as, for example, theft), to the extent these causes are not included under number 8

B10 Liability for land vehicles with their own motors (*Haftpflicht für Landfahrzeuge mit eigenem Betrieb*)

Liability of every kind (including that of shippers) which results from the use of land vehicles with their own motors

B11 Aircraft liability (*Luftfahrzeughaftpflicht*)

Liability of every kind (including that of shippers) which results from the use of aircraft

B12 Marine, inland marine and river transportation liability (*See-, Binnensee- und Flussschifffahrtshaftpflicht*)

liability of every kind (including that of shippers) which results from the use of river boats, inland marine boats and ocean-going vessels

B13 General Liability (*Allgemeine Haftpflicht*)

All other types of liability which are not covered under the lines B10, B11 and B12

B14 Credit

- general insolvency (*allegemeine Zahlungsunfähigkeit*)
- export credit (*Ausfuhrkredit*)
- installment sales (*Abzahlungsgeschäfte*)
- secured loans (*Hypothekardarlehen*)
- agricultural loans (*landwirtschaftliche Darlehen*)

B15 Surety (*Kaution*)

- direct surety (*direkte Kaution*)
- indirect surety (*indirekte Kaution*)

B16 Various financial losses (*Verschiedene finanzielle Verluste*)

- occupational risks (*Berufsrisiken*)
- insufficient income (general) (*ungenügende Einkommen (allgemein)*)
- adverse weather (*Schlechtwetter*)
- lost profits (*Gewinnausfall*)

- current expenses of all kinds (*laufende Unkosten allgemeiner Art*)
- unexpected business expenses (*unvorhergesehene Geschäftsunkosten*)
- loss of value (*Wertverluste*)
- lost rent or revenue (*Miet- oder Einkommensausfall*)
- indirect commercial losses from the already mentioned (*indirekte kommerzielle Verluste ausser den bereits erwähnten*)
- noncommercial financial losses (*nichtkommerzielle Geldverluste*)
- other financial losses (*sonstige finanzielle Verluste*)

B17 Legal protection (*Rechtsschutz*)

Legal protection

B18 Travel assistance insurance (*Touristische Beistandsleistung*)

Assistance for the benefit of persons who experience difficulties during travels or absence from their place of residence

C. Reinsurance

C1 Reinsurance by insurance businesses which only engage in reinsurance

C2 Reinsurance in all lines of insurance by insurance businesses which engage in nonlife insurance

C3 Reinsurance by captives

Annex 2

Expected Shortfall

1. Definitions

ES Expected Shortfall

E Expected value (*Erwartungswert*)

X Stochastic variable for the modeling of losses in the relevant calculation

P Probability measure (*Wahrscheinlichkeitsmass*)

α occurrence probability (*Eintrittswahrscheinlichkeit*)

q Threshold value (*Schwellenwert*)

$q\alpha$ Threshold value for the occurrence probability α (*Schwellenwert zur Eintrittswahrscheinlichkeit* α)

2. Special case: distribution of X is constant (*Spezialfall: Verteilung von X ist stetig*)

Threshold value for the occurrence probability α is the number with the characteristic that X with the occurrence probability α is greater that $q\alpha$:

$$P[X > q\alpha] = \alpha. \qquad (1)$$

The Expected Shortfall of X with the occurrence probability α is the expected value of X under the condition that this value is greater than $q\alpha$:

$$ES[X] = E[\, X \mid X > q\alpha]. \qquad (2)$$

3. General case

The threshold value $q\alpha$ for the occurrence probability α is the lowest number which fulfills:

$$P[X > q\alpha] \leq \alpha \qquad (3)$$

The Expected Shortfall of X for the occurrence probability α is given by

$$ES[X] = 1/\alpha \bullet E[\, \max(X - q\alpha, 0)] + q\alpha. \qquad (4)$$

The case with the constant distribution is included in the general case. In the case with constant distribution, the formulae (2) and (4) are consolidated.

Annex 3

Near Market Value (*Marktnahe Bewertung*)

1. Definition

[1] The term near market value means market value, if this is available (Marking-to-Market).

[2] If a market value is not available, then the near market value will be determined on the basis of an appropriate model (Marking-to-Model).

2. Assets

[1] In the case of assets for which a market value is available, this is considered the valuation basis. This category includes, in particular, cash, government bonds and listed shares.

[2] In the case of assets for which a market value can be determined only with difficulty, the FINMA shall regulate the valuation. The near market value will, in any case, be derived from models based on similar, but listed financial instruments (Mix of Marking-to-Market and Marking-to-Model).

[3] Models for the determination of near market values may only be used if they:

a. are recognized by financial mathematics;
b. are based, as far as possible on observable market prices; and
c. are integrated in the internal processes of the insurance business.

3. Debt

[1] The near market value of the insurance obligations is composed of the estimated value of the obligations and the minimum amount under Article 41 paragraph 4.

[2] The best possible estimated value of the obligations is the expected value of the future contractually required payments, discounted on the basis of the risk-free interest rate (Swiss government bonds), subject to the following principles:

a. *Completeness*: all obligations will be valued, in particular implicit and explicit options and guarantees; in this regard, the following applies:
    1. Financial options are to be valued by methods recognized by financial mathematics, provided that characteristics of the options, such as term or behavior of the insureds is to be taken into account.
    2. For the valuation of embedded options, such as cancellation, repurchase options, guaranteed coverage increases and contract conversions with guaranteed rates, a rational insured must not be exclusively assumed, rather empirical data (such as observed exercise probabilities) may be applied for the modeling of the exercise of options. In each case, the correlation of the behavior of the insureds with the financial market is to be taken into account.

3. Allocated bonus and surplus payments, final bonus shares in the event of survival or from more favorable claims experience should be reserved on a near market basis with appropriate attention to their more or less binding guarantee.
4. Future, unguaranteed surplus benefits, as well as business taxes will not be taken into account.
5. Reinsurance options, such as profit participation clauses, are to be appropriately taken into account.

For claims events for which the loss amount is not known, a reserve in the amount of the expected value of the loss amount is to be established. For incurred, but not yet reported losses (IBNR), an appropriate reserve shall be established.

b. *The principal of the best possible estimated value*: The valuation does not include any implicit or explicit security, volatility or other adjustments for the insurance risk, rather is based only on the expected value of the obligations. Insurance risk adjustments are included in target capital. For example, one is to calculate with 2nd order biometric data or, in the case of loss reserves, the loss inflation is to be included.

c. *Timeliness*: The valuation is made on the basis of the most current available information.

d. *Transparency*: The models, parameters and deviations from standard principles are to be stated explicitly and submitted to the FINMA.

Regulation of the Federal Financial Market Supervision on the Supervision of Private Insurance Businesses

SR 961.011.1

(Insurance Supervision Regulation-FINMA, ISR-FINMA)[1]

of 9 November 2005 (as of 1 January 2009)

The Federal Financial Market Supervision (FINMA),[2]
on the basis of the Insurance Supervision Law of 17 December 2004[3] (ISL) and
the Supervisory Regulation of 9 November 2005[4] (SR),
as well as the application of the treaty of 10 October 1989[5] between the
Swiss Confederation and the EEA concerning Direct Insurance with the Exception of Life Insurance and
the Treaty of 19 December 1996[6] between the Swiss Confederation and the Principality of Liechtenstein concerning Direct Insurance
orders:

Section 1: Insurance technical reserves and restricted assets

Art. 1 Subject

[1] The surcharge under Article 18 ISL amounts to:

a. for life insurance: 1 percent of the insurance technical reserves used as the basis for the determination of the required amount;
b. for nonlife insurance: 4 percent of the reserves under Article 68, paragraph 1, letters a-c SR, but at least 100,000 francs.

[2] The surcharge does not apply for life insurance if the insurance business does not bear any investment risk.

---

1 Text in accordance with para. 1.7 of the Regulation of the FINMA of 20 Nov. 2008 on the Amendment of Government Agency Regulations to Conform to the Financial Market Supervision Law, in force since 1 Jan. 2009 (AS **2008** 5613).
2 Text in accordance with para. 1.7 of the Regulation of the FINMA of 20 Nov. 2008 on the Amendment of Government Agency Regulations to Conform to the Financial Market Supervision Law, in force since 1 January 2009 (AS **2008** 5613).
3 SR **961.01**
4 SR **961.011**
5 SR **0.961.1**
6 SR **0.961.514**

Section 2: Responsible actuary

Art. 2 Responsibilities

[1] The responsible actuary is responsible for the management of the technical part of the business plan. He or she shall decide which ratings are the basis for a product.

[2] He or she shall issue annually a comprehensive report to the executive board. The responsible management functions within the company shall deliver to him or her the necessary information.

[3] The responsible actuary shall notify the executive board immediately about any significant changes in the basis since the last report.

Art. 3 Content of the report

[1] The report shall present the current state of the possible developments in the company from an actuarial perspective, specifically insurance technical developments which endanger the financial condition of the business.

[2] The report shall contain all necessary information under Article 24, paragraph 1, letters a-c ISL. Further, it provides information on the technical result of the products.

[3] Along with the specific, material findings, the report shall make statements about:

a. which source materials, parameters and models were used; and
b. how sensitively the results respond to changes in the parameters.

Art. 4 Termination of the employment relationship

In the event of the termination of the employment relationship of the responsible actuary with an insurance business, both parties shall independently from each other inform the FINMA[7] about the reasons for the termination, resignation or dismissal.

Section 3: Accounting standards

Art. 5

The allocation to reserves required under corporate law (Arts. 671 or 860 CO[8]) must amount to at least, in the case of insurance business that engage in life insurance, 10% of the annual profit and, in the case of the other insurance businesses, 20% of the annual profit, [in each case] until the reserve fund equals 50% of the statutory capital [under corporate law] or again equals [such amount].

---

7 Text in accordance with para. 1.7 of the Regulation of the FINMA of 20 Nov. 2008 on the Amendment of Government Agency Regulations to Conform to the Financial Market Supervision Law, in force since 1 January 2009 (AS **2008** 5613).

8 SR **220**

Section 4: Final provisions

Art. 6 Transition provisions

[1] Insurance intermediaries which on 1 January 2006 had five years of primary occupational experience or eight years of part-time occupational experience as insurance intermediaries are considered professionally qualified under Article 185 SR.

[2] Insurance intermediaries required to register must attain any lacking professional qualification by 31 December 2007.

Art. 7 Entry into force

This regulation enters into force on 1 January 2006.

Circular Letter 2008/16

Responsible Actuary

Requirements for the Responsible Actuary

Reference:	FINMA-RS* 08/16 Responsible Actuary
Issued:	20 November 2008
Entry into force:	1 January 2009
Last amendment:	20 November 2008
Regulatory history:	Formerly FOPI Guideline 5.1/2006 Requirements for the Responsible Actuary of 1 March 2006
Legal basis:	FINMAG Art. 7, para. 1 provision b
	ISL Art. 23
	SR Art. 99
Annex:	Statement of Professional Ability

* Circular Letter

1 The FINMA issues the following circular letter on the basis of Art. 99 SR, as well as Art. 23 ISL and Art. 7, para. 1 provision b FINMAG (the sections without numbers serve as explanations). This circular letter is divided into the following sections:

2 1. An equivalent title under Art 99, para. 1 SR means a fully qualified actuary ("fully qualified member, "full member") of a foreign association of actuaries which has standards equivalent to the SAV [Swiss Association of Actuaries].

3 The list of foreign associations of actuaries which award such titles is to be found under: Europe: *www.gcactuaries.org* (under The Group Information / Member Associations); overseas: *www.actuaries.org* (under Membership / Full Membership).

4 2. An appropriate professional education under Art. 99, para. 2 SR is generally understood as an academic degree in mathematics or physics. In addition, candidates must submit a statement that they will only assume actuarial responsibilities for which they are qualified.

5 A model of this statement of professional ability accompanies this circular letter (see annex).

6 3. The knowledge of the Swiss situation under Art. 99, para. 3 SR is considered to exist if a person has, during at least the last three years, engaged in a wide range of actuarial activities in Switzerland in the lines of business engaged in by the insurance business. Persons who do not fulfill these conditions must prove that they possess equivalent knowledge commensurate with the scope of their duties.

7 Pursuant to Art. 23, para. 2 ISL, a responsible actuary must be able to correctly assess the financial consequences of the activities of the insurance business. If the responsible actuary holds a management position, then conflicts of interest may arise and under some circumstances endanger the ability of the responsible actuary to correctly assess the risks. This has caused the FINMA to issue paragraphs 4 and 5.

8 4. In the notice of the appointment of the responsible actuary, the relationship he or she has to the insurance business must be stated.

9 5. If the person proposed as the responsible actuary serves, in particular, simultaneously as a member of the management board or the board of directors, the FINMA reserves the right to impose conditions on the appointment.

Annex

Statement of Professional Ability

Statement of professional ability for a responsible actuary

I hereby declare that I am able professionally, and possess the necessary experience, in order to exercise the function of responsible actuary in accordance with Art. 23 of the Insurance Supervision Law (ISL).

Signature and date

Circular Letter 2008/18

Investment Guidelines for Insurers

Investments within Restricted Assets, as well as the Use of Derivative Instruments by Insurers

Reference:	FINMA-RS* 08/18 Insurer Investment Guidelines
Issued:	20 November 2008
Entry into force:	1 January 2009
Last amendment:	20 November 2008
Regulatory history:	Formerly FOPI Guideline 9/2006 Investment Guideline of 12 June 2006
Legal basis:	FINMAG Art. 7, para. 1, provision b
	ISL Arts. 17–20, 22, 37, 51, 56, 87
	SR Arts. 56, 57, 68, 70–95, 96, 97, 100–109, 139
	ISR-FINMA Art. 1
Annex 1:	Description of the valuation methods for real estate
Annex 2:	Example of a due diligence investigation for alternative investments
Annex 3:	Examples of derivatives transactions
Annex 4:	Model Agreement of the Swiss Bankers Association
Annex 5:	Listing of limits within restricted assets

* Circular Letter

Table of Contents

I. Scope of Application

A. Structure

This circular letter[1] is divided into the following text formats: 1

1. The text of the relevant laws and regulations (Times New Roman font)
2. The text of the circular letter (Ariel font)
3. Explanations of the text of the circular letter (*Arial italic font*)

B. Overview of the legal basis

The determination and establishment of restricted assets is governed, in particular, by the following sources of supervisory law: 2

- Federal Law concerning the Supervision of Insurance Businesses of 17.12.2004 (Insurance Supervision Law, ISL; SR 961.01)
  Art. 17 – 20, 22, 37, 51, 56, 87 ISL
- Regulation on the Supervision of Private Insurance Businesses of 9.11.2005 (Supervisory Regulation, SR; SR 961.011)
  Art. 56, 57, 68, 70 – 95, 96, 97, 100 – 109, 139 SR
- Regulation of the FINMA on the Supervision of Private Insurance Businesses of 9.11.2005 ([Insurance] Supervisory Regulation-FINMA, ISR-FINMA; SR 961.011.1)
  Art. 1 ISR-FINMA

C. Restricted assets

Relevant legal basis:

Art. 17 ISL Restricted Assets 3
[1] An insurance business must secure claims under insurance contracts with restricted assets.
[2] [. . .]

[1] The supervisory law requirements on which this circular letter is based are listed in the chapter "Scope of application", as well as, in addition, the other chapters which deal with the individual forms of investment.

4 Art. 20 ISL Regulations concerning restricted assets
The Federal Council shall issue regulations concerning the provision, location, coverage, alteration and control of the restricted assets. It can delegate the specification of the technical details to the FINMA.

5 This circular letter regulates - supplementary to the statutory and regulatory legal requirements - the details in respect of those assets that are allocated to restricted assets. There are no special regulations for assets that are not allocated to restricted assets - with the exception of the provisions concerning derivative financial instruments (see para. I.D.[2]). They are not within the scope of this circular letter.

6 *As part of its solvency supervision, the FINMA requires, however, that the unrestricted assets (free assets) are invested and managed in accordance with generally accepted investment principles. This also applies to the assets of Swiss reinsurance businesses which are not required to establish restricted assets.*

7 *Health insurance companies that offer supplementary insurance to the social health insurance pursuant to the ICL are, to that extent, subject to the FINMA's supervision. They must establish restricted assets for insurance policies that are subject to the FINMA's supervision. The investments that are allocated to restricted assets are subject to the requirements of this circular letter.*

a) Separate restricted assets

Relevant legal basis:

8 Art. 77 SR Separate restricted assets
[1] Separate restricted assets are to be established for:
a. insurance under the occupational pension funds;
b. the savings component of insurance contracts in the insurance lines A2.1, A2.2 and A2.3;
c. the savings component of insurance contracts in the insurance lines A2.4, A2.5 and A2.6.
[2] For contracts in the Swiss insurance portfolio which have been issued in foreign currencies, separate restricted assets can be established.
[3] For the insurance contracts in a foreign insurance portfolio for which an equivalent security in the foreign country is not required, segregated restricted assets can be established.

9 Each individual, separate restricted asset must comply with the requirements of this circular letter.

2 [References to] paragraphs without additional identification refer to [the paragraphs] of this circular letter.

For each individual, restricted asset, for example, the specified limits (see para. II. E.) or the coverage obligation (see para. II. C.) apply. 10

The insurance lines A2.1 through A2.3 relate to unit-linked life insurance and the insurance lines A2.3 through A2.6 relate to the life insurance linked to internal investment portfolios or other reference assets (see the Annex to the SR). 11

b) Foreign insurance portfolios

Relevant legal basis:

Art. 17 ISL Restricted assets 12
[1] An insurance business must secure claims under insurance contracts with restricted assets.
[2] It is not required to provide security in accordance with paragraph 1 for its insurance portfolios outside of Switzerland if an equivalent security must be provided for them abroad.

Art. 73 SR Foreign insurance portfolios 13
A foreign insurance portfolio under Article 17, paragraph 2, ISL means all insurance contracts with an insured domiciled in a foreign country.

Art. 77 SR Separate restricted assets 14
[. . .]
[3] For the insurance contracts in a foreign insurance portfolio for which an equivalent security in the foreign country is not required, segregated restricted assets can be established.

D. Use of derivative financial instruments

Arts. 100-109 SR regulate the use of derivative financial instruments for all insurance businesses which are subject to the supervision of the FINMA. The regulations apply regardless of whether the derivative financial instruments are allocated to restricted assets or free assets. The regulations mentioned under para. III.I.a. of this circular letter that regulate the use of derivative financial instruments therefore apply to all insurance businesses, including reinsurers. 15

II. Principles applicable to restricted assets

A. Definition, purpose and obligation to establish

Insurance businesses subject to supervision by the FINMA - with the exception of reinsurers - are legally required to establish certain assets for the purpose of securing insured claims, *i.e.*, so-called "restricted assets". The required 16 amount of restricted assets is determined by the amount of the insurance technical reserves and an appropriate surcharge pursuant to Art. 1 ISR-FINMA. Assets in the amount of this amount will be established by allocation, inventoried and marked with the notation "restricted assets".

B. Basic principles

a) Application

Relevant legal basis:

17 Art. 19 ISL Application of restricted assets
[1] The assets in restricted assets will be used for the claims to be secured by the restricted assets.
[2] If an insurance portfolio is transferred to another insurance business, the restricted assets or equivalent assets shall be transferred to the assuming insurance business to the extent the FINMA does not order otherwise.

18 Art. 54 ISL Conduct of bankruptcy
[. . .]
[4] Claims under the insurance contracts for which security was provided pursuant to Article 17 will be first covered by the proceeds of the restricted assets. Any remaining proceeds are part of the bankruptcy estate.

19 *Through the restricted assets, insureds acquire, in particular, a source of funds that ensures that their claims will be satisfied in priority to those of all other creditors in the event of the bankruptcy of the insurance business.*

b) Prohibition on encumbrance and offset

Relevant legal basis:

20 Art. 84 SR Allocation of assets
[1] [. . .]
[2] The assets included in restricted assets must be unencumbered. Liabilities of the insurance business may not be offset against obligations that have been allocated to restricted assets. Article 91, paragraph 3 (derivative financial instruments) remains unaffected.

21 The encumbrance of restricted assets through any kind of security interest, retention of title or offset or similar right is prohibited. (Exceptions, see para. III.I. Derivative financial instruments).

22 The assets in restricted assets may not in any way serve as security for the claims of third parties against the insurance business ("Collateral") (Exceptions, see para. III.I. Derivative financial instruments). The encumbrance of re-

stricted assets is also prohibited in connection with borrowing (*e.g.*, loans or repos) - including an indirect borrowing of debt (*e.g.*, short sales). No supplementary payment obligations may arise that are chargeable against the restricted assets.

C. Coverage

a) Continuous coverage obligation

Relevant legal basis:

Art. 74 SR Coverage 23
[1] The required amount must be covered by assets (Art. 79) at all times.
[2] If an insurance business determines that there is a coverage shortfall, then it must immediately increase restricted assets. The FINMA can in special cases grant a cure period for the increase.

An insurance business must ensure through appropriate organizational measures that the then current required amount under Arts. 56, 57 or 68 SR is covered with permitted assets under Arts. 79 and 81 SR. The amount of the then applicable required amount is determined on the basis of the current reserves. During the year, well-founded estimates may be used instead of actual reserves. 24

The obligation to verify the then current required amount has the purpose of ensuring that events occurring during the year which require additional technical reserves and therefore have an influence on the required amount, such as, for example, unexpected loss events, a need for additional reserves or the acquisition of new business, [will have the result that] additional assets for the coverage the required amount of restricted assets will be allocated immediately. 25

This obligation does not mean, however, that the required amount must be recalculated daily. As long as there are no indications that the required amount is no longer covered, careful estimates of changes since the last calculation will, as a rule, suffice in order to give an insurance business the certainty that the current required amount is covered. 26

b) Coverage obligation for unit-linked life insurance

Relevant legal basis:

Art. 81 SR Permitted assets for unit-linked life insurance 27
[1] Restricted assets for the savings component of insurance contracts under the insurance lines A2.1, A2.2 and A2.3 may only be established with units of open-ended col-

lective investment funds which are subject to the Collective Investments Law of 23 June 2006.

[2] Restricted assets for the savings component of insurance contracts under insurance lines A2.4, A2.5 and A2.6 may be established with assets specified in Article 79 under the following conditions:

a. if the benefits are linked directly to the value of an internal investment portfolio, then the insurance technical reserves must be established with the relevant shares, or if no shares are created, then by the underlying assets;
b. if the benefits are linked to an index or another benchmark, then the insurance technical reserves must be established by assets which correlate with the assets that are the basis for the benchmark.

28 It is not permissible for the claims of insureds under unit-linked life insurance policies for which reserves must be established to be secured otherwise than with the assets underlying the relevant contract because otherwise an insurance business would bear an additional investment risk (mismatch). This does not apply to the coverage of any surcharge on the required amount.

29 If a period after the premium becomes due has been fixed for the acquisition of the underlying assets in the relevant insurance contracts, then within this period cash in the amount of the uninvested premium can be allocated to restricted assets.

30 In an excess coverage situation, assets under Art. 79, para. 1 SR, which under no circumstances and at no time have a negative value, may be credited to restricted assets.

31 *Repealed*

D. Basic regulations for investments within restricted assets

a) General criteria for the allocation of assets to restricted assets

32 In order for an asset (hereinafter also referred to as "investment") to be allocated to restricted assets and to be considered a permitted capital investment (hereinafter also referred to as "investment"), the following criteria generally must be fulfilled:

33 • The investment is consistent with an investment strategy which takes into account the nature and complexity of the insurance business engaged in, as well as the financial situation of the insurance business (see para. II.F.a.).

34 • The investment is, as a rule, capable of being valued without difficulty and is, in relation to the relevant investment category, highly liquid.

- The insurance business has the necessary professional knowledge and applies appropriate processes and systems which are necessary for the professional selection, management and control of investments that have been made (see para. II.F.c.). 35
- The insurance business has the relevant professional knowledge and uses the processes necessary in order to understand the effects of an investment and its individual risk components and to be able at all times to assess the financial, legal and operational risks. 36
- The credit quality of the obligor can be verified (see para. II.F.e.). 37
- The investment may neither be encumbered nor set off against payment obligations owed by third parties (see para. II.B.b.). 38
- The investment may not include any insurance risks. 39

These fundamental principles will be made more explicit in the following sections. Supplementary provisions are issued for each investment category in section III. 40

b) Investment principles

Relevant legal basis:

Art. 76 SR General principles 41
[1] [. . .]
[2] The assets of restricted assets are in the first instance to be chosen on the basis of security, the actual financial situation, as well as the structure and the expected development of the insurance portfolio.
[3] In addition, while maintaining appropriate diversification, a market-competitive income stream is to be sought and anticipated liquidity needs are at all times to be secured.

The selection of the assets for purposes of allocating them to restricted assets is performed in accordance with the following investment criteria: 42

- Safety
- Return
- Diversification
- Liquidity

An insurance business must properly observe the investment principles established in its own investment strategy or in its investment regulation (Art. 78, para. 1, provisions a and b SR) in selecting the portfolio. 43

44 These investment principles apply for direct as well as indirect investments (*e.g.*, collective investments).

45 *Even if not all of these investment principles can be fulfilled to the same extent, an insurance business should appropriately take into account all of the investment principles in accordance with its own capacity for risk. Investments within restricted assets should aim for stable returns.*

aa) Safety

46 The investments for restricted assets must be chosen in such manner that they are safe, *i.e.*, that the ability to satisfy the claims of insureds is ensured at all times.

47 The selection of assets which could jeopardize the solvency of the insurance business (*e.g.*, assets pursuant to which additional payment obligations chargeable against restricted assets could arise) is not permitted.

48 *The safety of an investment is assured if it is secure from an economic and legal perspective. Economic safety is understood to mean the stability of principal or the value of an investment; legal safety of investments is measured by their availability and marketability. The requirement of economic and legal security applies equally to direct investments as well as indirect investments.*

49 *In regard to the stability of value of an investment, the following criteria will, for example, be observed:*
- *little volatility in the value of the restricted assets as a whole;*
- *a reliable valuation method for the investments;*
- *a listing on a regulated and liquid securities exchange or marketability at any time;*
- *the high quality of the creditworthiness of the debtor, confirmed by a recognized rating agency or an equivalent institution (see also para. II.F.e.).*

50 *The legal security of an investment refers, in particular, to the following criteria:*
- *The unrestricted ability to dispose of it;*
- *the unrestricted marketability and transferability of the assets.*

51 *In respect of the regulations to be observed under the principle "safety", reference is made to the special provisions for the individual investment categories.*

bb) Return

52 An insurance business shall select investments which are profitable and provide a stable return. Investments which do not provide income are unsuitable for restricted assets. This applies for direct as well as indirect investments. Investments should yield a market-return (*e.g.*, customary market interest rates).

cc) *Diversification*

Investments must attain sufficient and effective diversification. An appropriate mix in respect of the various investment categories, as well as an appropriate diversification among the obligors of the investments is to be achieved. 53

Investments in risky investment categories may only be made to a cautious degree and for effective diversification of the restricted assets. The risk capacity of the insurance business is to be taken into account in every case. Investments in assets with a credit rating lower than "investment grade (BBB/Baa)" are allowed only if the asset class is highly diversified and the necessary professional expertise in the area of credit risk permits it. 54

Risk concentrations are to be excluded. The exposure to a counterparty may not be greater than 5% of the required amount of restricted assets. If a greater exposure per counterparty occurs, this is to be notified to the FINMA immediately for approval (see para. II.E. Limits and Annex No. 5). 55
Obligations of the federal government, as well as the cantons, cantonal banks with cantonal guarantees, Swiss *Pfandbrief* institutions or of AAA-rated countries are excluded from the 5% limit. Also, obligations of foreign bodies whose obligations are at all times and completely guaranteed by a country with a AAA rating are excluded from this limit.

Obligations under insurance contracts / policies should be covered by investments in the same currencies. Investments in other reference currencies are to be limited to 20% of the required amount of restricted assets. The reference currency is considered the currency specified in the insurance contracts / policies issued by the insurance business. 56

The goal of diversification is to reduce the consequences of a default by one or more counterparties or the loss of value of an investment instrument. 57

An appropriate mix of the investments in respect of the various investment categories will, in particular, take into account the following criteria: 58
- *the specific risk profile and default risk of the obligor or the risk of loss of value of the investment classes;*
- *the expected return (income and prospects for capital gains);*
- *the investment horizon (i.e., term of the investment) of the investment;*
- *the correlation of the investment classes.*

An appropriate diversification of the investments in respect of the various obligors takes into account at least the following criteria: 59
- *different obligors;*
- *different geographic regions in which the obligors are domiciled;*
- *different industry branches and segments in which the obligors conduct their business activities.*

dd) Liquidity

60 The investments must be selected in a manner that the expected need of the insurance business for liquid assets is at all times assured.

61 *The liquidity of an investment depends, among other things, on the term of an investment (e.g., bonds, term deposits) or the possibility to assign (sell) the investment in the market or on a securities exchange.*

62 *Generally, an insurance business should select investments which can be liquidated quickly when necessary.*

c) Compliance with the investment principles for small required amounts

63 The investment principles of safety, return, diversification and liquidity (see para. II.D.b.) generally must be observed by small insurance businesses.

64 Small insurance businesses can request an exemption from the 5% counterparty limit in justified cases. The request shall include - along with the justification for the desired deviation from the rule - information about the obligor of the obligations which constitute more than 5% of the required amount of restricted assets, as well as the amount of the requested counterparty limit, taking into account the principles of appropriate diversification.

65 *In the case of small insurance businesses which have only a small required amount for restricted assets, strict compliance with the diversification principal is, under some circumstances, considered economically, unreasonable.*

d) Indirect investments; initial acquisition; restructurings

66 An investment, whether an initial acquisition, whether through a restructuring - in so-called indirect investments, such as e.g., in funds, ownership interests, structured products, or in bonds issued by special purpose vehicles (SPV), may not lead to a circumvention of the provisions concerning direct investments.

67 This circular letter contains investment requirements in respect of various indirect investments:

- Collective capital investments under para. III.J.b.;
- Single-investor funds under para. III.J.c.;
- Real estate investment companies under para. III.F.c.bb. (for an ownership interest > 50%) or under para. III.E.a. (as a listed real estate investment company);

- Structured products and securitized payment obligations under para. III.C.;
- Alternative investments under para. III.H.

The provisions for these investment instruments are designed in a manner that, depending on the instrument, either specific qualitative requirements and high liquidity for the entire investment instrument will be required or, alternatively, a so-called look-through method will be applied. An investment in an indirect investment, which includes a direct investment that is not creditable [to restricted assets] is only permitted of the specific provisions for the indirect investment are fulfilled and, because of its characteristics, the negative aspects which result in a lack of credit for the direct investment do not have an effect on the indirect investment. 68

Example: an investment in real properties which are relatively illiquid and have limited marketability as well and therefore are not permitted as investments in restricted assets, may then under this circular letter also not be credited as permitted investments if they are wrapped in new legal clothing. The only exception is the situation in which the risk situation for the investor is actually improved, as the following table shows in respect of a real property investment. 69

70

Structure	*Creditable?*	*Reason*
Direct investment: illiquid, difficult to value real property investment (e.g., a football stadium)	*No*	*The ability to value and sell it are limited (para. III.F.a.)*
Restructured into a single-investor fund	*No*	*Look-through method applied, treatment same as direct investment (para. III.J.c.aa)*
Restructured into a real property investment company	*No*	*Look-through method applied, treatment same as direct investment (para. III.F.c.bb)*
Constructed as a structured product that participates in real property	*No*	*Each individual element of the structured product as well as the underlyings of the derivatives transaction must be creditable individually (para. III.C.A.bb.)*
Formation of an alternative investment, e.g., a pri-	*No*	*Traditional investments which cannot be credited as direct investments may not be transferred to the alternative investments*

Structure	Creditable?	Reason
vate equity fund, i.e., in shares of a business organization that holds the relevant real property as an asset for its account		*category (para. III.H.a.)*
Formation of a collective capital investment pursuant to Art. 82, para. 1 SR	*Yes*	*For collective capital investments there are restrictive conditions: disposition at any time on a liquid market, as well a supervision by an effective fund supervisory authority (para. III.J.b.). This leads to a liquid, diversified and regulated real property portfolio.*

E. Limits

Relevant legal basis:

71 Art. 83 SR Limits
The FINMA can set limits for individual categories of investments.

72 On the basis of Art. 83 SR, limits will be prescribed for individual investment categories.

73 This means: an insurance business may hold investments in a specific investment category of not more than the limit, specified as a percentage of the required amount, for each individual restricted asset.

74 The limits that are generally to be observed - see para. II.D.b.cc. -- as well as the applicable limits per investment category are to be observed.

75 If there is excess coverage of the required amount, exceeding the prescribed limits is allowed.

76 An insurance business can, upon request, deviate from the specially specified limits in the table in Annex No. 5 for the categories III.E. (equities and other listed ownership securities), III.F. (real estate), III.G. (mortgage loans), as well as the limits for the net currency exposure (see para. II.D.b.cc.) and request its own limits for these categories. The approval of these individualized limits will be given by the FINMA under the following conditions:

- The insurance business makes a credible showing that no negative effects on the solvency of the business are to be expected as a result of the requested individualized limits. 77

- The insurance business shows that it has an appropriate risk management in respect of the relevant investment categories. 78

- The insurance business must at all times be able to demonstrate that the prescribed principles in this circular letter will continue to be fulfilled through the chosen limits and that the risk of insufficient coverage of the required amount of restricted assets as a result of significant losses of value in a specific investment category is adequately taken into account. In addition, the insurance business must credibly show with appropriate tests that stress scenarios [applied] to the restricted assets, even under the application of the individualized limits, will not lead to insufficient coverage of the required amount of restricted assets. The stress tests will be performed regularly. In these evaluations, the available free and unrestricted assets are to be included. 79

The conditions must be fulfilled at all times, even after approval. As soon as the requirements for the individualized limits are no longer met, an insurance business must comply with the prescribed limits. 80

For the other, not specifically mentioned investment categories, regardless of the satisfaction of criteria above, the specified limits in Annex No. 5 are to be observed because certain risks are insufficiently quantifiable (*e.g.*, alternative investments). 81

All limits within restricted assets are set out in Annex No. 5. Limits which can be superseded by individualized limits upon fulfillment of the criteria mentioned above are specially indicated. 82

The limits must be observed at all times. An insurance business must have appropriate control mechanisms in order that these requirements can be fulfilled. Securities which were loaned must be included in the calculation of the limits. 83

For the investment of assets within separate restricted assets under Art. 77, para. 1, provision b SR (unit-linked life insurance) no limits apply. For the investment of assets within separate restricted assets of internal investment portfolios or other reference assets, only the limits "net exposure to an Obligor / Counterparty", as well as "Securities Lending" are to be observed. These limits may, however, be exceeded if the policyholder has been expressly informed about possible deviations from these limits before the conclusion of the agreement. 84

F. Requirements for an insurance business

a) Investment strategy

Relevant legal basis:

85 Art. 78 SR Management of capital investments
[1] An insurance business shall have:
a. an investment strategy;
[. . .]
[2] The executive board sets the investment strategy and shall submit it to the board of directors for approval.

86 The investment strategy shall take into account, in an appropriate manner, the nature and complexity of the insurance business that is conducted.

87 *The investment strategy shall take into account, among other things, the financial situation of the insurance business, its liabilities, the risk and revenue profile of the insurance business, as well as the nature of the insurance business.*

b) Investment regulation

Relevant legal basis:

88 Art. 78 SR Management of capital investments
[1] An insurance business shall have:
a. [. . .]
b. an investment regulation which ensures compliance with the principles for the investment of capital assets under Article 76;
[. . .]

89 In the investment regulation, the entire investment process (the investment strategy, the investment principles, the organization of the investment process, control, reporting, etc.) will be defined and laid down in a document. An insurance business must, in particular, take into account the following topics in the investment regulation.

90 a. Principles and investment goals.

91 b. Methods of compliance with the investment principles, as well as this investment directive, as well as other decisions by the FINMA.

92 c. Description of the investment strategy.

93 d. Internal guidelines, limits and permitted assets which will be specified on the basis of individual risk capacity.

e. Investment techniques (*e.g.*, use of derivative investments, securities lending). 94

f. Description of the investment process. 95

g. Operational structure of the investment process: definition of tasks, authorities and responsibilities. 96

h. Description of the responsibilities of the investment management (see also para. II.F.c.aa.). 97

i. Professional knowledge of the staff; education. 98

j. Systems used. 99

k. Internal reporting to various organizational units and reporting periods. 100

l. Supervision and control of the investment process (risk management or control, see para. II.F.c.bb.). 101

c) Organization

Relevant legal basis:

Art. 78 SR Management of capital investments 102
[1] An insurance business shall have:
[. . .]
c. an organization that ensures that the persons entrusted with management and control have the necessary knowledge.
[. . .]

The management (investment management) and control (risk management) of the investment activity must be performed by persons who are independent of each other. 103

aa) Investment management

The investment management must ensure and perform at least the following responsibilities: 104

a. definition of the strategic and tactical investment strategy (composition of the capital investments); 105

b. the implementation of the investment strategy and the investment regulation; 106

107 c. the monitoring and the control of significant risks resulting from investment activities (market risk, credit risk, concentration risk, liquidity risk, currency risk, operational risk and legal risk);

108 d. the establishment of an investment process that is appropriate to the complexity of the investments;

109 e. the measurement and assessment of investment results, among other things, with benchmarks.

110 If an insurance business employs a third party for investment management, it will not thereby be released from responsibility for compliance with the requirements concerning investment management. In particular, an insurance business must at all times understand the investment process and monitor the prescribed investment strategy and investment principles, as well as be able to track the bookkeeping for all transactions. An insurance business is responsible for ensuring that the supervisory regulations, as well as the guidelines of the FINMA are observed.

111 The transfer of the investment management to a third party is subject, pursuant to Art. 4, para. 2, provision j ISL, to a FINMA approval obligation.

bb) Risk management and control under Arts. 78, 96 and 97 SR

Relevant legal basis:

112 Art. 78 SR Management of capital investments
[1] An insurance business shall have:
[. . .]
d. a risk management that is commensurate with the scope of business and the complexity of the investment activity;
[. . .]

113 Art. 96 SR Objective and content
[1] An insurance business shall ensure through a risk management appropriate to the characteristics of its business and through internal control mechanisms that it is able to:
a. recognize and evaluate potential risks early; and
b. [. . .]
[2] Risk management comprises, in particular:
a. the selection and regular review by the management bodies of strategies and measures for all assumed risks;
b. a hedging policy which takes into account the consequences of the business strategy and which includes appropriate capital resources;
c. appropriate procedures which ensure that risk monitoring is integrated into the business organization;
d. identifying, monitoring and quantifying all significant risks;

e. an internal reporting system for the determination, evaluation and control of risks and risk concentrations as well as the related business processes.

Art. 97 SR Objective and content 114

[1] An insurance business shall record its risk management in a document. This is to be updated constantly.

[2] The document shall include, in particular, the following points:

a. description of the organization of risk management business-wide, as well as the related authorities and responsibilities;
b. the obligations of risk management;
c. the risk policy, including risk tolerance;
d. procedures for the identification of significant risks, as well as a description of the methods, instruments and processes for their measurement, monitoring and control;
e. description of the applicable limits system for risk exposures, as well as the control mechanisms;
f. business-internal guidelines for risk management and related processes.

These requirements for risk management (-control) are to be applied by analogy for the management of capital investments. 115

Health insurance companies are excluded from Arts. 96 and 97 SR to the extent that their share of the supplementary insurance market amounts to less than 2% and they do not have a complex risk structure or significant financial risks (in accordance with the FOPI-"Circular Letter" 11/2006 New legal basis for private insurance of 1 November 2006 concerning ISL provisions for health insurers offering supplementary insurance). 116

d) Adequacy of the required measures

Relevant legal basis:

Art. 76 SR General principles 117

[1] An insurance business shall establish restricted assets through the allocation of assets. It lists and identifies these assets so that at any time, without delay, it can prove which assets are allocated to restricted assets and that the required amount of restricted assets is covered.

[. . .]

Organizational measures ensure that evidence of the coverage of the required amount of each separate restricted asset can be provided at any time. 118

e) Verification of creditworthiness of obligors

In the case of investments which have neither a customary market rating nor can be valued on the basis of a liquid market, an insurance business must at 119 least once each year verify the creditworthiness of the obligor (counterparty). This review process is to be documented internally.

120 The verification of creditworthiness may also be performed by an external party.

f) Ensuring stability of value

121 An insurance business must review the stability of the value of the individual investments on an ongoing basis and take into account in the valuation of an investment a reduction in value as a result of deteriorated creditworthiness. If the security of an investment is jeopardized ("necessity of an impairment"), then for credit to restricted assets a deviation must be made from the valuation methods prescribed and further listed below in the provisions in connection with the individual investment categories (*e.g.*, cost amortization method for bonds) and credit shall be given, at the most, for market value or near market value (see Art. 95, para. 2 SR). This can, in particular, affect the following categories in Art. 79 ISR:

122 a. Cash deposits (see para. III.A.)

123 b. Bonds, convertible bonds (see para. III.B.)

124 c. Structured products (see para. III.C.a.)

125 d. Other unconditional debt obligations (See para. III.D.)

126 e. Mortgage loans (see para. III.G.)

127 f. Derivative financial instruments (see para. III.I.)

G. Custody of assets

a) Custody in Switzerland

128 Moveable assets allocated to restricted assets may be held at the headquarters of the insurance business in Switzerland or the location of the business office for all Swiss business (own custody) or placed in third-party custody. In order that the claims of insureds are secured at all times by restricted assets, the assets allocated to restricted assets are to be held separately from the other assets of the insurance business and marked as such. If held in a safe, storage in separate lock boxes is sufficient. The account and custody account statements of the bank are to be marked with the notation "restricted assets" (Art. 86 SR).

Third-party custody is permitted only if the custodian is liable in Switzerland to the insurance business for the fulfillment of its custody obligations (Art. 87, para. 2 SR). The insurance business and the custodian must sign a so-called "form agreement" of the Swiss Bankers Association, revised attachment to Circular No. 771 D of the Swiss Bankers Association, see Annex No. 4). Under Art. 87, para. 1 SR, an insurance business must immediately report the location of the custodian, the custodian and the type of custody to the FINMA, including any changes in respect thereof. At the same time, it is compulsory that a copy of the form agreement be submitted to the FINMA. 129

In the form agreement, the limitations on the availability of the assets in restricted assets are expressly excluded. Accordingly, no security interest, retained title, offset and other rights may be asserted by the custodian. The assertion of such rights solely for claims in connection with the maintenance of the custody account or accounts (costs, fees, commissions, etc.) and claims in connection with collateral management in accordance with the special rules applicable to the legal framework for derivative transactions remains unaffected. Further, the form agreement provides that the assets in restricted assets may be maintained or booked by the custodian in its own facilities, with a domestic or foreign clearing house or with a foreign custodian, individually or collectively (collective custody). With regard to assets which the custodian bank delivers to a correspondent bank, clearinghouse or a custodian, it is liable to the depositor for their custody obligations in accordance with the principles of Art. 399, para. 2 Code of Obligations. 130

The FINMA may, for important reasons, order a change in the location of custody, the custodian or the type of custody (Art. 86, para. 4 SR). 131

b) Custody abroad

The maintenance of custody of investments abroad has certain inherent risks. Even if the foreign custodian has signed the form agreement mentioned above, it would not be certain in every case that the restricted assets could be used as security for the claims of insured. For one thing, the risk exists - as also in Switzerland - that a third party (not the custodian) could encumber the asset with a restriction on its disposition (security interest, etc.) or otherwise attach the asset. This can be especially problematic in the event of the bankruptcy of the insurance business if the relevant countries do not recognize the priority ranking of restricted assets under Swiss law and therefore subject them to general application by the bankruptcy administrator. As a result, the risk exists that the assets held by foreign custodians cannot be retransferred to Switzerland and will be set off against obligations abroad. The claims of the policyholders would not be secured in such a situation. 132

133 Therefore, foreign custodians are generally prohibited. The exceptions are the countries of Belgium and Luxembourg for which legal opinions are available in respect of the recognition of Swiss bankruptcies. A Swiss bankruptcy administrator could, as a consequence, sue the custodian for the release of the securities. The custodian is required to deliver securities of the same number and character to the Swiss bankruptcy administrator.
The form agreement also is to be unconditionally signed by Belgian and Luxembourger custodians.

H. Assets invested abroad

134 Assets invested abroad cannot be allocated to restricted assets to the extent that a payment obligation that has not been issued in the form of a security (debt certificates not issued as securities, deposits with banks such as time deposits, current accounts, etc.), as well as real property located abroad is involved.

135 The problem is that debt certificates are not considered securities and therefore, in the event of the bankruptcy of the insurance business, are to be treated as mere loan payment obligations. It can not be excluded that in the event of bankruptcy in certain countries that proceedings will be initiated in respect of assets located in such countries in which neither the Swiss nor the foreign preferences in respect of the restricted assets can be enforced. In addition, there is the risk that the obligors of the loans could be (partially) discharged from their debt through offset. Accordingly, the foreign debt certificate loans do not offer enough security in order to be allocated to the restricted assets of an insurance business. Residential and commercial buildings abroad are in the same situation.

136 Assets located abroad can only be allocated to restricted assets if a security is involved or a legal opinion is available concerning the recognition of Swiss bankruptcies and the related Swiss legal norms by the relevant foreign authorities. Exceptions to this principle are allowed only in the case of alternative investments in accordance with para. III.H.

137 *Repealed*

I. Reporting to the FINMA

Relevant legal basis:

138 Art. 72 SR Reporting
[1] Within three months after the close of the financial year, an insurance business shall report to the FINMA the required amount for each restricted asset, together with an inventory of the assets covering them.

[2] An insurance business domiciled in Switzerland must in addition produce a report about each foreign insurance portfolio for which it is required to provide security in a foreign country.

The FINMA shall annually specify the requirements and the process for the reporting about restricted assets. 139

III. Provisions for the individual forms of investment

For investments, in addition to the general principles set out above which are to be observed, the following requirements apply. 140

A. Cash investments

a) Permitted assets within restricted assets

Relevant legal basis:

Art. 93 SR Permitted assets 141
[1] The following assets may be allocated to restricted assets:
a. Cash investments, specifically *Postcheck* deposits and bank deposits, as well as time deposits and other money market investments;
[. . .]

Among other money market investments are short-term money market investments with a term of up to 12 months. 142

In respect of obligations (if the obligor is domiciled abroad) which are to be categorized as cash investments, the requirements of para. II.H. (Assets invested abroad) are to be observed. 143

b) Special requirements

The form agreement also must be signed by the counterparty in respect of cash deposits and account balances in accordance with para. II.G. (Custody of assets). In particular, every security interest, retention of title, offset and similar right of the obligor must be excluded in the form agreement. 144

c) Valuation

Relevant legal basis:

Art. 93 SR Other assets 145
[1] Investments under Article 79, paragraph 1, letters c, e and h, as well as money market book-entry obligations and securities with a variable interest rate without a fixed

maturity date will be credited, at most, at market value. If they are not listed on a securities exchange, the a customary market valuation method will be used.
[2] All other investments, including *Grundpfandforderungen* and time deposits will be valued, at most, at par value, taking into account the security and the distribution rate.

B. Bonds, convertible bonds

a) Permitted assets in restricted assets

Relevant legal basis:

146 Art. 79 SR Other assets
[1] The following assets may be allocated to restricted assets:
a. [. . .]
b. debt instruments for a fixed monetary amount, specifically, bonds and option bonds, as well as convertible bonds with debt character;
[. . .]

147 Generally, the following assets are allocated to this category:
Government bonds

- Bonds of cantons, cities / municipalities and other public law bodies
- Bonds of supranational organizations
- Bonds of Swiss Pfandbrief institutions
- Bonds of banks and finance companies
- Other corporate bonds
- Counter obligations of a Swiss-licensed banking institution
- Convertible bonds with debt character
- Synthetic bonds under para. III.I.b.ee.bbb.

148 Investments cannot be allocated to this category which are in fact issued as bonds, but because of their characteristics they are governed under another investment category in the investment guidelines.

149 *Examples: Cat bonds, bonds which are issued by an SPV, ABS / securitized obligations, CDOs (see para. III.C.b).*

150 In the case of convertible bonds, the following is to be observed: a distinction is to be made between convertible bonds with debt characteristics and convertible bonds with equity characteristics. If the value of the convertible bond is greater than 130% of its par value, it may be allocated to the category "equities" (Art. 79, para. 1 provision e SR). If the market price later falls below 130%, the convertible bond remains in the category "equity". Convertible bonds which must be converted into equity ("mandatory convertible") must be allocated to the category under Art. 79, para. 1 provision e SR.

In respect of convertible bonds of foreign counterparties, para. II.H. (Assets invested abroad) is to be observed. 151

b) Valuation

Relevant legal basis:

Art. 88 SR Fixed income securities 152
[1] For fixed income securities that must be repaid on a fixed maturity date (single repayment or amortization) and are denominated in a specified currency, excluding *Grundpfandtitel*, the insurance business shall determine the maximum creditable value in accordance with the scientific or linear amortized cost method.
[2] If the market value of a convertible bond is significantly greater than par value, then the FINMA can permit a valuation equal at most to market value. Bonds which are subject to mandatory conversion into equity may be allocated, at most, at market value.
[3] Structured products or combinations of finance instruments that are comparable to fixed income securities may be allocated to a certain extent and under certain conditions in accordance with the scientific or linear amortized cost method. The FINMA shall specify the extent and the conditions.

Art. 89 SR Amortized cost method 153
[1] Under the scientific amortized cost method, the difference between cost and redemption value during the remaining term of the security, on each financial statement reporting date, is to be increased or reduced to the extent necessary that the original internal interest rate (return to maturity) can be maintained.
[2] Under the linear amortized cost method, the difference between cost and redemption value during the remaining term of the security, on each financial statement reporting date, is to be distributed in equal amounts over the remaining term as depreciation or appreciation, as applicable.

Art. 93 SR Other investments 154
[1] Investments under Article 79, paragraph 1, letters c, e and h, as well as money market book-entry obligations and securities with a variable interest rate without a fixed maturity date will be credited, at most, at market value. If they are not listed on a securities exchange, then a customary market valuation method will be used.
[2] [. . .]

Convertible bonds which fall into the category of debt obligations under para. III.B.a. can be credited under the amortized cost method (Art. 88, para. 2 SR). Convertible bonds with equity characteristics will be credited at not more than market value (see para. III.E. Equities). 155

C. Structured products and securitized payment obligations

a) Structured products

aa) Definition

Relevant legal basis:

156 Art. 79 SR Permitted Assets
[1] The following assets may be allocated to restricted assets:
[. . .]
c. structured investment products, securitized payment claims and credit derivatives;
[. . .]

157 *Structured products are investments in the form of a bond or debt instrument through which a cash market instrument (e.g., a fixed interest security) is linked to one or more derivative financial instruments to make a single legal and economic instrument. Derivative instruments are linked to one or more underlying assets (e.g., shares, bonds, interest rates, exchange rates, alternative investments).*

bb) Permitted assets in restricted assets

158 The inclusion of structured products in restricted assets is subject to the following conditions:

159 a. The individual components (*e.g.*, cash market instrument and derivative) must meet the requirements of the relevant category of restricted assets.

160 b. The structured product may not have physical delivery or acceptance obligations.

161 c. There may not be any additional payment obligations or negative interest. Negative interest exists if the investor is required to make interest payments.

cc) Credit and valuation

162 Structured products may be valued and credited to restricted assets under one of the following 3 procedures. A procedure, once chosen, must be used until the sale or redemption of the structured product.

aaa) Valuation of a structured product as a whole at market value

163 If this procedure is chosen, there is no division of the structured product into its component parts for valuation. The structured product is, as a whole, subject to all provisions for the category to which it is allocated.

The structured product will be valued as a whole at market value and allocated only to a single category of restricted assets in accordance with the embedded risks. 164

Example. Index certificates consisting of a money market investment and long futures on an equity index can be allocated in their entirety at market value to the category "equity" (if a synthetic strategy is involved and all requirements under para. III.I.b.ee.bbb. are fulfilled). 165

If the structured product has various embedded risks, then under this valuation method it must be allocated as a whole to the most restrictive category (*i.e.*, the category which on the basis of the greatest risk results in the strictest requirements for allocation / credit). 166

Example. Cash market instruments combined with various derivatives which are linked to both equity indexes and commodity indexes will be allocated in their entirety to the category "alternative investments". 167

bbb) Division of a structured product into individual components

If a structured product is divided into individual components, then these may be allocated to the relevant categories and be valued and credited in accordance with the requirements of these categories. 168

Example. a zero-bond combined with a long call option may be allocated in parts to the categories "bonds" and "derivatives. The valuation of the zero bond is made at amortized cost, the option will be included at market value. 169

ccc) Valuation of a structured product as a whole at amortized cost

This method may be selected only if the following criteria are met: 170

a. The embedded derivative is linked solely to an interest rate or inflation. 171

b. The economic characteristics and risks of the derivative are closely connected with those of the cash market instrument. 172

c. There is capital protection equal to at least 90% of the purchase price. The capital protection seller has a minimum rating of A. 173

d. All cash flows are in the same currency and are not affected by fluctuations in currency exchange rates. 174

e. A significant leverage effect is excluded. The leverage effect of the embedded derivative is limited in respect of return so that the return the structured product can achieve may not be greater than twice the market return (a fixed interest rate bond of the same currency, term and creditworthiness) at the time of its purchase. 175

176 f. The term of the structured product amounts to a maximum of 12 years.

177 g. Structured products linked solely to interest rates or inflation may be included at the value determined by the scientific amortized cost method (in the category "debt obligations in a fixed amount"). The cost amortization is to be determined on the basis of the interest rate which is the internal rate of return resulting from the purchase price and the minimum cash flows (capital protection and any minimum coupons).

dd) Special requirements

178 The provisions concerning foreign counterparties must be taken into account (see para. II.H. "Assets invested abroad").

ee) Limits

179 A structured product or the individual elements of a structured product (in the case of division) fall under the relevant limits of the category to which they are allocated under para. III.C.a.cc.

b) Securitized obligations

aa) Definition

Relevant legal basis:

180 Art. 79 SR Permitted Assets

[1] The following assets may be allocated to restricted assets:

[. . .]

c. structured investment products, securitized obligations and credit derivatives;

[. . .]

181 *Securitized obligations are instruments of risk transfer (as a rule in the form of a bond) which transfer the credit risk of the assets contributed to a receivables pool to the purchaser of the securitized obligations. The securitized obligation can be divided into several tranches (senior, junior, equity tranche). The receivables pool can have a uniform or mixed composition and consist of physical or synthetic (structured) obligations. Examples of securitized payment obligations are asset-backed securities (ABS), mortgage-backed securities (MBS, RMBS, CMBS) and collateralized debt obligations (CDO, CBO, CLO, CMO, SFCDO).*

bb) Permitted assets in restricted assets

182 Only an investment in securitized payment obligations which can be evaluated on the basis of the special requirements imposed on an insurance business in

respect of transparency, complexity, stability of value (valuation) and risk listed in para. III.C.b.cc is permitted.

Not permitted are: 183

- Group internal transactions with securitized obligations (see para. IV.C. group relationships). 184
- Investments in insurance-linked securities (see para. II.D.a.). 185
- Investments in the high-risk tranches of a securitized obligation, accordingly, in particular, the equity tranches, junior tranches and mezzanine tranches. Investments in higher tranches (senior tranches, super-senior tranches) are also excluded if they, after considering all relevant aspects, do not comport with an investment-grade (BBB)-quality investment. This evaluation may not be based on external credit enhancement, such as guarantees, pledges, etc. (wrapped securities, monoliners, etc.). Consequently, the evaluation of the underlying assets is relevant. Structure-dependent credit enhancements (excess spread, reserve account, over-collateralization, etc.) may be taken into account in the analysis. The evaluation process must meet the requirements of para. III.C.b.cc. 186
- Investments in securitized obligations which have an obligation pool that is actively managed (managed CDO) if the insurance business is limited in this respect in the assessment of its risk and the stability of its value. If the investment guidelines and the management of the pools are designed in a manner that the insurance business can promptly track changes in composition and determine the effects on risks and the stability of value, then investments in managed CDOs are permitted. 187
- CDOs of CDOs and similar layered structures. 188

As a rule, securitized obligations have very complex structures which makes their detailed analysis indispensible. For this reason, the following general parameters and limitations for the inclusion of securitized obligations are defined. 189

cc) Special requirements

aaa) Organizational, know-how and investment process requirements for an insurance business

Because of the special characteristics of this investment category, an insurance business must have special qualifications and an investment process that takes into account the complexity of the investment, before it may invest in securitized obligations. The following requirements are to be fulfilled: 190

191 a. The insurance business must have a qualified staff that is able to adequately asses the stability of value and the risk-content of the investment and that also is in a position to be able to understand the risks that arise from the structure of the investment vehicle. It is to be specified internally which employees are entrusted with the investment in, and the later monitoring of, the securitized obligations. The authorities of these employees are to be specified.

192 *The evaluation of the inherent risks of securitized obligations generally should be based on the [insurance business's] own analysis and not exclusively on the assessment of rating agencies. The underlying pool of obligations must be examined in respect of its composition (nature/quality of the existing assets, actual diversification; the usual assumption of a simplified statistical correlation structure or even independent, equally distributed risk by the rating agencies can lead to the underestimation of the risks) and its stability of value (assumptions about the distribution of default probabilities, recovery rates).*

193 *In order to be able to provide an assessment of the development of the value of a securitized obligation, it is therefore necessary to have knowledge of the underlying markets of the existing assets in the pool of obligation (e.g., in the case of investments in an MBS, the regional concentration and credit practices of the banks whose mortgage loans were securitized should be scrutinized along with the developments in the real estate market.*

194 *In addition, whether the pool of obligations is physically available or created synthetically (e.g., with the aid of credit default swaps) must be taken into account, whether the securitization is linked to cash flows or market values, whether the pool is static or managed, etc. An exact analysis of the structure is absolutely necessary for the determination of stability of value and the risk of the securitized obligations. Analysis of the structure of the securitized obligations most of the time requires a division of the individual levels of the securitization. The risks and internal security measures must be examined closely in respect of their effect.*

195 *The relationship between the size of the purchased tranche and the portfolio covering it (subordination), the size of the subordinated tranches, as well as the waterfall structure must be examined closely.*

196 b. An insurance business shall have a well-documented investment process which is tailored to the special characteristics of this investment category.

197 c. Investment in securitized obligations must be anchored in the investment strategy of the business and included appropriately in the asset allocation.

It is to be noted that investments in securitized obligations also must be diversified in respect of the underlying risks so that an aggregation of risk does not result. 198

d. An insurance business shall have qualitative analysis instruments, as well as a due diligence procedure, so that the selection as well as the ongoing monitoring of investments is performed in accordance with qualitatively high standards. The ongoing monitoring is focused not only the change of a rating of the securitized obligations, but also on change in the underlying risks and market conditions. The frequency of the monitoring and its scope shall be specified. 199

bbb) Requirements for risk management (risk control)

An insurance business shall have the processes and instruments necessary in order to assess the risks of the securitized obligations in accordance with the minimum requirements of para. III.C.b.cc.aaa. The investments will be monitored continuously by risk management. 200

The risk profile of the investments will be integrated into the risk management of the insurance business so that the effects on the entire portfolio as well as the individual risk classes can be quantified. 201

Model risks of the structure of the securitized obligations and the liquidity risks will also be monitored by risk management. 202

ccc) Due diligence

An insurance business shall establish a due diligence process which guarantees a comprehensive and in-depth analysis of the structure, underlying risks and conditions of the securitized obligations. The availability of external ratings does not excuse an insurance business from the duty to investigate the risks in the investments. This investigation should ensure that the investment is only made in securitized obligations whose stability of value and risks can be tracked at all times and which conform to the risk policy of the insurance business. 203

dd) Limits

The investment in securitized obligations is limited to 10% of the required amount. The credited value per investment shall not exceed 1% of the required amount. 204

Securitized obligations have risk which, depending on the structure, are quantifiable only with difficulty. The complexity of the investment can have a negative effect on transparency. A quantitative analysis of the investment is subject to model risks. 205

ee) Valuation

Relevant legal basis:

206 Art. 93 SR Other Assets
[1] Investments under Article 79, paragraph 1, letters c, e and h, as well as money market book-entry obligations and securities with a variable interest rate without a fixed maturity date will be credited, at most, at market value. If they are not listed on a securities exchange, the a customary market valuation method will be used.
[2] [. . .]

207 The securitized obligations will be credited at not more than market value. In determining the value, the quality of the valuation (*e.g.*, in respect of the liquidity of the market) must also be investigated (see also Due diligence para. III.C.b.cc.ccc.).

D. Other unconditional debt obligations

a) Permitted assets in restricted assets

Relevant legal basis:

208 Art. 79 SR Other Assets
[1] The following assets may be allocated to restricted assets:
[. . .]
d. other unconditional debt obligations;
[. . .]

209 Permitted in this category are debt certificate loans to public law bodies, banks and other debtors domiciled in Switzerland to the extent that the latter are assigned a minimum rating of A (customary market rating).

210 The allocation of other debt certificate loans to restricted assets must be requested from the FINMA in advance.

b) Assets not permitted

211 The following unconditional debt obligations cannot be allocated to the category "other unconditional debt obligations":

212 a. Debt certificate loans made to foreign borrowers if the obligation has not been issued as a security (see para. II.H. Assets invested abroad).

213 b. Loans to private equity businesses which are to be handled under alternative investments in accordance with Art. 79, para. 1, provision h SR (see para. III.H. Alternative investments).

c. Policy loans because these were already deducted in determining the required amount. 214

d. Loans to debtors whose creditworthiness cannot be verified (see para. II.F.e. Review of creditworthiness of obligors). 215

e. Loans to group companies (see para. IV.C. Group relationships). 216

c) Special requirements

a. A written, legally valid debt acknowledgement must exist. 217

b. The obligor must explicitly waive all rights of set-off, retention of title and similar rights. 218

d) Valuation

The valuation is made at nominal value, taking into account the stability of value of the loan (see para. II.F.f. Ensuring stability of value). 219

E. Equities and other listed ownership interests

Relevant legal basis

a) Permissible assets in restricted assets

Art. 79 SR Permitted Assets 220
[1] The following assets may be allocated to restricted assets:
[. . .]
e. equities, participation certificates, convertible bonds with equity character, share certificates of mutual companies and similar securities, if the issues are traded on a regulated market and can be sold on short notice;
[. . .]

All securities in this category must be traded on a liquid market. Securities which, for example, are listed on a secondary securities exchange but are not regularly traded are not permitted. 221

In the case of convertible bonds, the following is to be observed: convertible bonds are divided into convertible bonds with debt character and convertible bonds with equity character. If the value of the convertible bond is greater than 130% of its par value, it may be allocated to the category "equities". If the market price later falls below 130%, the convertible bond remains in the category "equity". Convertible bonds that must be converted into shares (mandatory convertible) must be allocated to this category. 222

223 The provisions for this category apply as well to listed real estate companies. Para. III.F.b. is to be observed as well.

b) Assets not permitted

224 Unlisted equities, as well as shares in related businesses are not permitted assets within restricted assets (see also para. IV.C. Group relationships).

c) Limits

225 A maximum of 30% of the required amount of restricted assets may be invested in shares or other listed participating securities. The equity portion of collective capital investments and single-investor funds, as well as other instruments which increase the exposure to equities are to be added. Hedging is deducted from the exposure to equities under Art. 79, para. 1 provision i SR.

d) Valuation

Relevant legal basis

226 Art. 93 SR Other investments

[1] Investments under Article 79, paragraph 1, letters c, e and h, as well as money market book-entry obligations and securities with a variable interest rate without a fixed maturity date will be credited, at most, at market value. If they are not listed on a securities exchange, the a customary market valuation method will be used.

[2] [. . .]

227 Participating securities and convertible bonds with equity character are credited, at the most, at market value (Art. 93, para. 1 and [Art.] 88, para. 2 SR).

F. Real estate

a) Permitted assets within restricted assets

Relevant legal basis:

228 Art. 79 SR Permitted Assets

[1] The following assets may be allocated to restricted assets:

[. . .]

f. residential and commercial buildings in Switzerland which are property of the insurance business, as well as ownership interests in companies which have as their sole purpose the acquisition and sale, as well as the leasing of residential and commercial buildings (real estate companies) to the extent these ownership interests amount to more than 50 percent;

[. . .]

Generally, properties that are easily sold and whose valuation is subject to little uncertainty can be allocated to restricted assets. 229

aa) Types of buildings

If held in sole ownership, the following types of buildings can be allocated: 230

a. Residential buildings: single-family houses 231
multiple-family houses
condominiums

b. Commercial buildings: office and administration buildings 232

bb) Properties in Baurecht

Conditions of allocation: 233

a. The insurance business, as grantor of the *Baurecht* 234
   - The granted *Baurecht* yields regular, long-term, contractual secured income;
   - The acquirer of the *Baurecht* is creditworthy;
   - Only buildings built in *Baurecht* which are creditable under para. III.F.a.aa may stand on the real property

b. The insurance business, as acquirer of the *Baurecht* 235
   - The building built in *Baurecht* is creditable under para. III.F.a.aa

cc) Properties not allocable

Properties that are not allocable to restricted assets are those which are not easily saleable or whose valuation is subject to great uncertainty. 236

Generally, for example, the following properties are not allocable: 237
- Undeveloped land (which is a land reserve. On the contrary, a parcel [of land] on which a new building is constructed which is creditable under III.F.a.aa may be credited).
- Construction starts
- Production facilities
- Warehouses
- Factories
- Distribution centers
- Sport facilities
- Shopping centers, to the extent that they are not municipal center areas or those distinguishable by a peripheral use
- Hotels

- Properties acquired through debt enforcement auctions (if the insurance business has acquired the property as mortgagee)
- Restaurants
- Residences for the elderly or nursing homes
- Schools
- Buildings that will not attract a broad group of potential purchasers and luxury properties
- Vacation apartments or houses
- Properties that are jointly owned
- Properties environmental impairments under the Environmental Impairments Regulation (Art. 2 EIR, SR 814.680).

238 In addition, [the following] may not be included:

239 a. Properties abroad, regardless of whether these are held directly or indirectly.

240 b. Interests in real estate companies which are not listed on a securities exchange if the ownership interest is ≤ 50 %.

241 c. All properties which were encumbered for the purpose of securing debt.

242 In justified cases, upon request and on the basis of a plausible justification, an exception may be approved.

243 *Elaborations through three examples for requests for the approval of exceptions:*

244 *1. Residences for the elderly and nursing homes:*
Convertibility to another use is to be enumerated and taken into account in the valuation that is to be submitted.

245 *2. Properties acquired through debt enforcement auctions:*
Details of the valuation and [its] plausibility are to be submitted with the request.

246 *3. Properties with environmental impairments:*
The technical assessment of the expected clean-up costs is to be taken into account in the valuation. Both are to be submitted with the request.
If there are guarantees from the polluter or a governmental authority for the assumption of all clean-up costs, then these are to be submitted with the request for approval of an exception.

dd) Mixed use

247 Properties under para. III.F.a.aa. can, without regard for the extent of the residential or business use be credited.

Properties that in addition to a residential or business area have a use that is not creditable under para. III.F.a.cc. can, on the basis of the entire net rent of the entire property, be fully credited if the creditable part amounts to at least 70%. 248

Properties with a sales area of more than 30% may be credited if they are municipal center areas. 249

b) Limits

The investment in real properties is limited to 25% of the required amount. 250

A single property may not make up more than 5% of the required amount. 251

The categories of real property and mortgage loans are in their entirety limited to a maximum of 35% of the required amount. 252

In the calculation of these limits, the shares of listed real estate companies (REITs / Immo-AG) are to be included (see also para. III.E.a.). 253

c) Valuation

Relevant legal basis:

Art. 90 SR Residential and commercial buildings, as well as real estate companies 254
[1] An insurance business shall allocate residential and commercial buildings which are owned by it at not more than market value. The FINMA shall specify the procedure for the determination of market value.
[2] For investment companies in which the insurance business has more than a 50% ownership interest, the FINMA shall specify the creditable value. It shall rely on the estimated value of the properties and shall take into account any obligations.

Market value is considered the amount at which an asset could be exchanged between knowledgeable, willing to contract, and independent transaction parties. 255

The valuations are to be made annually. The principle of individual valuation is to be observed. 256

Real properties may be 100% credited if an audit firm in its report on restricted assets does not include a qualification stating that the rules for the plausibility of real property valuations prescribed in the Investment Guidelines were not observed. Otherwise, real properties in restricted assets may only be credited at 90% of the appraised value. 257

aa) Direct investments

258 In the case of financial investments (so-called investment properties) the audited market values used in the IFRS-/US GAAP or Swiss GAAP FER financial statements are mandatorily to be used.

259 In the case of owner-occupied properties, the US GAAP, IFRS- or Swiss GAAP FER balance sheet values are controlling. If valuations of that type are not available, the original purchase price, increased by any increases of value and reduced by any reductions in value, can be used, provided that this value is less than the market value of the property. If less than 50% of the surface area is owner-occupied, then the entire property is to be classified as a financial investment. If, however, the surface area is 50% or more, then it belongs in the category of owner-occupied real-estate.

260 If in the case of financial investments no audited market values can be applied, the properties are to be valued by one of the two following methods:

- Income capitalization calculation
- Discounted Cash-flow Method (DCF)

In unusual cases, an exception for another valuation method can be requested.

261 The chosen method is to be used consistently for all properties. The acquisition cost applies only for the initial valuation, taking into account transaction costs. For all further succeeding valuations, one of the two above-mentioned valuation methods is to be applied.In usual cases, an exception for another valuation method can be requested.
In unusual cases, an exception for another valuation method can be requested.

262 *A brief explanation of the two permissible valuation methods is to be found in Annex No. 1.*

bb) Real estate companies

263 Unlisted ownership interests with a share > 50% are credited at per share net asset value (NAV). The real properties held therein are, to the extent that they can be credited pursuant to para. III.F.a.aa., to be valued like a direct investment, taking into account any liabilities.

264 How any intra-group loans to non-listed real estate companies are to be treated is governed by para. IV.C.b.cc.aaa.

cc) Properties in Baurecht

265 The market value of a *Baurecht* that has been granted is to be determined either according to the DCF or the income capitalization method on the basis of the income and included in restricted assets. The near market valuation of all granted *Baurechte* must be performed uniformly with the same method.

dd) Testing the plausibility of the valuations

During a cycle of 10 years, all properties are to be valued individually, on a staggered basis, at least once completely – either internally or externally – by a professional real estate appraiser (including an on-site inspection) for the purposes of verifying the near market value reported in the financial statements. In this regard, it is to be ensured that the relevant land register extract is requested and included in the file. The same applies for an extract out of the plat book for the relevant location. An insurance business shall document internally the plausibility testing process and shall ensure that the results of the plausibility assessment, as well as the valuation of the individual properties and the specification of the model parameters, are included. In this concept, the testing methods used for the plausibility assessment will also be prescribed. The plausibility testing concept is a part of the investment regulation. 266

A hedonistic method will be accepted for the plausibility testing if it can produce reliable data. 267

If an insurance business has a different concept for the periodic value verification, it can submit it to the FINMA for approval. 268

The FINMA can request additional appraisal reports from insurance businesses at any time. 269

d) Complete file for each credited real property

Each insurance business is required to maintain a complete file for each credited property which includes the following: 270

- Schedule of lessees 271
- Extract from the land register 272
- Current extract from the plat book of the relevant location (mandatory for new entries, as well as after 1 September 2006 for valuations already subjected to the plausibility assessment) 273
- Current extract from the building insurance or a copy of the current building insurance policy 274
- Map of the area surrounding the property 275
- Current photo of the property 276
- Description of the building, which in particular includes: the year of construction, the dates of any renovations, the number of apartments and offices 277

278 • Statement of construction costs for newly constructed properties

279 • A copy of the purchase agreement for newly acquired properties

280 • The calculation of, and the basis for, the calculation of the current valuation

281 The FINMA reserves the right to require the submission of the relevant files for full review or random inspection.

G. Mortgage loans

a) Permitted assets within restricted assets

Relevant legal basis:

282 Art. 79 SR Permitted assets
[1] The following assets may be allocated to restricted assets:
[. . .]
g. obligations that are secured by a lien on real property in Switzerland;
[. . .]

283 Mortgage loans with variable as well as fixed interest rates and fixed terms can be credited to restricted assets.

b) Assets not permitted

284 Not creditable are mortgage loans for properties listed under the category real estate under para. III.F.a.cc. (Exception: mortgage loans on properties in joint-ownership are includable) and mortgage loans for properties located abroad.

285 In justified cases, upon request and on the basis of a plausible justification, an exception may be approved. The elaborations added under para. III.F.a.cc. for any requests for the approval of an exception under 1. [¶ 244] and 3. [¶ 246] shall be applied by analogy.

c) Limits

286 Mortgage loans are limited to 25% of the required amount.

287 The individual mortgage loans may not make up more than 5% of the required amount.

288 The categories real property and mortgage loans are together limited to 35% of the required amount.

d) Valuation

aa) Par value

Relevant legal basis:

Art. 93 SR Other investments 289
[1] [. . .]
[2] All other investments, including *Grundpfandforderungen* and time deposits will be valued, at most, at par value, taking into account the security and the distribution rate.

bb) Loan-to-value limits

Credit for restricted assets for each property can only be given subject to the following loan-to-value limits: 290

a. 66-2/3% of market value in the case of residential or commercial buildings. 291

b. 80% of market value for residential buildings*, if a regular amortization was agreed for the portion [of the debt] in excess of 66-2/3%% ([amortization] may also occur indirectly through a pledged policy). 292

c. 66-2/3% of market value in the case of properties, the portion of which subject to residential or commercial use is at least 70% and the non-creditable use (determined with reference to revenue value) as specified in the exclusion list (para. III.F.a.cc.) is 30% or less. In the case of properties in a municipal center area with a retail sales area of more than 30%, the maximum loan-to-value ratio is 66-2/3%, provided that the increased credit risk of such properties is to be taken into account. 293

d. 100% of market value if the additional 20% or 33-1/3% provided is fully covered by policies which have a redemption value that cannot suffer negative fluctuations in value. 294

*with a minimum residential percentage of 70%

An insurance business making loans may not be subordinated to other creditors with security interests in the real estate. If they rank equally, then credit can be given if all of the *pari passu* obligations secured by the real estate do not exceed the loan-to-value limits under para. III.G.d.bb. 295

In justified cases, upon request and on the basis of a plausible justification, an exception can be approved. 296

cc) Determination of the market value of the encumbered properties

aaa) Permitted valuation methods

297 The market value of an encumbered property can be estimated as follows:

- Income capitalization calculation;
- Discounted Cash Flow Method (DCF);
- Hedonistic methods;
- Practitioner methods.

298 The appraisal shall be performed by an internal or external, professionally qualified real estate appraiser.

bbb) Mortgage loans for properties in Baurecht

299 In determining the market value of a property in *Baurecht*, the payments for the *Baurecht* are to be deducted from rental income.

dd) Correction of the credit

300 If a debtor with an obligation secured by a mortgage that is [owed to] the insurance company is more than 7 months in default, an appropriate adjustment in value is to be made.

301 If the default is more than 12 months, the relevant mortgage loan is no longer creditable and consequently is to be removed from restricted assets.

ee) Verification of the market value of encumbered properties

302 An insurance business shall periodically verify (fully, at least every 10 years) the market value of the encumbered properties with an appraisal procedure listed under para. III.G.d.cc.

303 In this regard, it is to be ensured that in the case of each of these verifications the relevant land register extract for the encumbered property is requested and included in the file. The same applies for the extract from the plat book of the relevant location. The frequency and method are governed by criteria which the insurance business shall prescribe internally. An insurance business shall document internally the verification process. The review concept is a part of the investment regulation.

e) Complete file for each credited mortgage loan

304 Each insurance business is required to prepare complete files for the credited mortgage loans which include the following:

- A brief description of the encumbered property
- The loan contract

- Extract from the land register
- Current extract from the building insurance [institution] or a current copy of the building insurance policy
- Map of the area surrounding the property
- Current photo of the property
- Appraisal report (including the basis for the calculation of the loan-to-value ratio)

The FINMA reserves the right to require the submission of the relevant files for full review or a review of randomly selected files. 305

H. Alternative investments

a) Definition

Relevant legal basis

Art. 79 SR Permitted Assets 306
[1] The following assets may be allocated to restricted assets:
[. . .]
h. alternative financial investments, such as hedge funds and private equity
[. . .]

The hallmark of investments described as alternative investments is the "alternative investment character". Therefore, it is not permissible that investments of other categories, *i.e.*, the traditional investment categories which for the reasons specified in this circular letter can not be credited to restricted assets, notwithstanding the lack of alternative investment character, are credited to restricted assets under the investment category of alternative investments. 307

An insurance business has to define in its investment strategy which types of investments in this category may be made. 308

Based on current knowledge, the following investments are allocated to this category: 309

a. Hedge funds;
b. Private equity funds;
c. Currency-overlays;
d. Commodity indexes and baskets;
e. Structured products, which are linked to an alternative investment and, under the provisions of para. III.C.a., must be classified as alternative investments.
f. Collective capital investments which invest in traditional investments with increased risk or in alternative investments (*e.g.*, Arts. 68 ff. of the Collective Investments Law "other funds for traditional investments" and "other funds for alternative investments")

310 *For example, no derivatives can be allocated under "alternative investments" which in accordance with the provisions of para. III.I. (Derivative financial instruments) are not permissible.*

b) Permitted assets within restricted assets

311 Investment in single funds and fund-of-funds, as well as indexes or baskets is permitted.

312 Direct investments, for example, in individual private equity businesses generally may not be included.

313 *The investments should be made in diversified investments which are open to other investors (see also, para. III.H.c.cc.: Verifiability of manager quality).*

314 Investing in other forms of investment among the "alternative investments" must be requested and approved by the FINMA in advance. In this regard, the insurance business must prove to the FINMA that all the provisions listed in para. III.H. will be observed.

315 In order to be credited to restricted assets, alternative investments must have the following characteristics:

316 a. The portfolio of alternative investments is, as a whole, appropriately diversified.

317 b. Investments in commodity funds/indexes/baskets are only permitted for the purpose of further diversifying the entire portfolio of alternative investments.

318 c. An exit from the investment must be possible within market-customary periods (max. 24 months). This requirement does not apply to Private Equity Investments. In the case of these investments, care must be taken that the long-term nature of such investments is taken into account in the liquidity planning so that adequate liquidity is available at all times. In this regard, any "commitments" made also must be taken into account.

319 d. The highest possible loss is limited to the amount invested and any contractually assumed commitments are limited to a specific amount. An insurance business may not incur any additional payment obligations or other liability. This applies also on the case of an insolvency. The possibility of offset against the debts of the insurance business equally must be excluded.

320 e. In the event of an exit, the payment by the fund – if a payment-in-kind is made - may only be made in assets that under Art. 79, para. 1 SR may be included in restricted assets. If a hedge fund, for example, permits a pay-

ment-in-kind with commodities / precious metals, inclusion is, as a rule, not possible, unless the probability of such a payment-in-kind is exceptionally slight.

f. Investments based on indexes and baskets are permitted to the extent the investment is broadly diversified and has high liquidity. Transparency in respect of the underlying regulating system must be ensured so that the special requirements mentioned under point III.H.c. also can be fulfilled in respect of these investments by analogy. 321

g. Currency-overlays may not include any short sales (see the provisions for derivative financial instruments in para. III.I.). 322

c) Special requirements

This investment category should give insurance businesses the opportunity to diversify the investment portfolio more broadly through alternative investments and to achieve an optimization of stable returns. 323

Because, as a result of the market conditions, it is not appropriate to apply to the same extent the principles which are required for traditional investments, such as, for example, investments in the categories under Art. 79, para. 1, provision e (participating securities) or j (collective investments and single-investor funds), but an investment in alternative investments under the previously mentioned principles of diversification and return optimization is sensible, some of these principles apply only to a limited extent: alternative investments do not have to be issued in the form of securities, have a liquid market or be supervised by an effective supervisor for the protection of investors. 324

As a rule, alternative investments have very complex strategies and structures. This requires that an insurance business is able to understand the strategy and the consequences of the investment that is made and that it has appropriate control instruments in order to be able to asses the development of the investment. 325

Accordingly, the selection of the right funds, FoF managers, the investment strategies and a comprehensive analysis of the investment process and the investment team (Due Diligence) have a prominent position. For all of these reasons, parameters and limitations are defined below which an insurance business must fulfill for an investment in alternative investments. 326

aa) Organizational, know-how and investment process requirements for an insurance business

Because of the special characteristics of this investment category, an insurance business must have special qualifications and an investment process 327 that is appropriate to the complexity of the investments before it may invest in alternative investments. The following requirements are to be fulfilled:

328 a. The insurance business has qualified staff that is able to adequately asses the risk content of the investment and to understand the individual investment strategies of the investment vehicles. The responsible employees shall have excellent knowledge and contacts with specialists in the industry in which the investment is made. It must be specified internally which employees are entrusted with investment in alternative investments and what their individual authorities are.

329 b. The insurance business has a well-documented investment process which is tailored to the special characteristics of this investment category.

330 c. The investment in alternative investments must be anchored in the investment strategy of the entire business and properly incorporated into the asset allocation. The investment strategy shall provide for a reasonable distribution and diversification of the investments and shall specify in what proportion investments may be made in the various alternative investment styles or strategies. Care must be taken that the investments are diversified among a sufficient number of managers.

331 d. The insurance business shall have a quantitative analysis system, as well as a due diligence procedure, so that the selection as well as the ongoing monitoring of the investments is performed in accordance with high quality standards. The ongoing monitoring includes the manager, the strategy of the fund and the performance of the product (*e.g.*, income, volatility). The monitoring periods and its scope shall be specified.

332 e. A clear separation of staff is to be made between the investment process and risk management (control).

bb) Requirements for risk management (risk control)

333 An insurance business shall have the necessary processes and instruments to be able to asses the risks of alternative investments. The investments shall be continuously monitored by risk management.

334 The risk profile of the investments shall be integrated into risk management so that the effects on the entire portfolio, as well as on the individual risk classes can be quantified. An insurance business must have sufficient information so that the requirements of the SST can be fulfilled.

335 The model risks of the fund and the liquidity risks (exit problem) shall be monitored by risk management.

cc) Due diligence

An insurance business shall establish a due diligence process that guarantees a comprehensive and in-depth analysis of the management, strategy, structure, performance and terms and conditions of the fund. An insurance business shall also systematically question the manager and shall evaluate the documentation of the fund. This review should ensure that investments are made only in funds that fulfill the highest recognized qualitative standards. 336

The catalog in Annex No. 2 provides examples of a due diligence examination in the areas of management, strategy, structure, performance and terms and conditions. This list is not complete. 337

dd) Monitoring of legal risks

An insurance business must investigate legal risks in depth. The following points are to be taken into account: 338

a. The legal analysis must be performed by qualified persons who fully understand the legal form and the governing law under which the fund has been formed. 339

b. It must be ensured through legal measures that the conditions mentioned under para. III.H.b. (Permissible assets) actually will be observed. 340

The monitoring of legal risks is of central importance because the alternative investments in which investments will be made are often subject to foreign law. The contractual terms are, as a rule, complex and may provide for various obligations, as well as limit the exit options. 341

ee) Requirements for investments in a fund-of-funds

If an insurance business cannot fulfill all of the special requirements that are mentioned in this section, then it may only invest in funds-of-funds. An insurance business will, however, not be excused from the obligation to implement the processes mentioned in paras. III.H.c.aa. through III.H.c.dd. Individual steps may be omitted if these are already performed in sufficient detail by the fund-of-funds manager. The due diligence relates to the fund-of-funds and must be carried out in full. Investments in umbrella funds shall be diversified sufficiently among various managers. 342

The styles or strategies (in the case of private equity) in which the fund-of-funds invests must be understood by the insurance business. Investing in fund-of-funds shall be appropriately implemented in the investment process. 343

344 An insurance business shall have the necessary processes and instruments or shall receive sufficient support from the fund-of-funds provider in order to assess the risks of the planned alternative investments.

345 The monitoring of the legal risks (para. III.H.c.dd.), on one hand in relation to the fund-of-funds and, on the other hand, within the fund-of-funds must be ensured.

d) Limits

346 The following limits apply for this investment category:

347 a. The value of all alternative investments included in restricted assets may not exceed 10% of the required amount of restricted assets.

348 b. An insurance business shall set internal limits - subject to paras. III.H.d.cc and dd. - so that a risk diversification through sufficient funds / managers will be achieved.

349 c. The credited value for a single fund may not exceed 1% of the required amount.

350 d. The credited value per fund-of-funds may not exceed 5% of the required amount.

351 e. Care must be taken that "commitments" made for the succeeding years do not result in a breach of the listed limits.

352 f. Currency-overlays: The foreign exchange exposure is to be taken into account with the foreign currency limit (20%).

353 *Alternative investments have risks which, at the present time, can only be quantified with difficulty, if at all:*

354 • *The complexity of the investment can impair transparency (so-called black box). The strategies and investment decisions are changed with great speed. The decisive factor is the quality of the fund and of the fund manager upon whose decisions the insurance business must rely.*

355 • *Legal Risk: Most hedge funds / private equities are formed as types of legal entities that are not known under Swiss law (e.g., limited partnerships) and are domiciled offshore (e.g., Cayman / British Islands). Accordingly, legal uncertainties arise and a transfer risk. The effects of these risks in the event of the bankruptcy of an insurance business are difficult to assess.*

- *The ability to exit an investment is often available on a limited basis because the investments that have been made cannot be liquidated immediately.* 356
- *A qualitative analysis of the investments is subject to model risks. In addition, many investments do not have long track records.* 357
- *Crowding Effect: The more this category grows, the more limited are the advantages which arise through the exploitation of market inefficiencies.* 358
- *Compared to ordinary investment funds, hedge funds have greater freedom (short sales, leverage, lack of regulation and supervision).* 359

e) Valuation

Relevant legal basis:

Art. 93 SR Other assets 360
[1] Investments under Article 79, paragraph 1, letters c, e and h, as well as money market book-entry obligations and securities with a variable interest rate without a fixed maturity date will be credited, at most, at market value. If they are not listed on a securities exchange, the a customary market valuation method will be used.
[2] [. . .]

The NAV for hedge funds is calculated on the basis of the market value of the individual assets. It is to be ensured that an insurance business receives NAV valuations regularly (at least once per month). 361

In the case of investments in private equity funds, the quality of the valuation must be verified (see also Due diligence III.H.c.cc.). 362

f) Concept for alternative investments

Investments in alternative investments may only be made by insurance businesses which meet the requirements set forth in this document. Each insurance business must submit in advance to the FINMA a concept which shows how the criteria mentioned in paras. III.H.c. and III.H.e. will be fulfilled and how the relevant processes have been established. 363

Significant changes in a concept already approved are to be submitted to the FINMA for approval before the entry into force of the internal guidelines pursuant to which the concept will be implemented. 364

I. Derivative financial instruments

a) Basic principles

aa) Scope of application

365 The regulations in para. III.I.a. are to be observed in respect of all assets (including restricted assets).

bb) Use of derivative financial instruments

Relevant legal basis:

366 Art. 100 SR Basic principle
[1] Insurance businesses may only use derivative instruments in order to reduce risks in respect of capital investments or its liabilities in relation to insureds, or in order to efficiently manage capital investments.
[2] [. . .]

367 In the use of derivative financial instruments, an insurance business may not assume any risks which are not appropriate to the insurance business's volume of business and its ability to bear risk. The use of financial derivative investments should, in addition, be focused on stable returns.

cc) Coverage obligation when derivative financial instruments are used

Relevant legal basis:

368 Art. 100 SR Basic principle
[1] [. . .]
[2] All liabilities which could result from derivative financial transactions must be covered.

369 Obligations incurred must at all times and in the full amount (contract volume / notional) either be covered by the asset underlying the derivative (in the case of derivatives with obligations to sell) or through liquidity (in the case of derivatives with obligations to buy).

370 Cash as well as "cash equivalents" may be counted as liquidity. Bank deposits, time deposits, as well as government bonds with a credit rating of least AA, good liquidity and unrestricted marketability may be included as cash equivalents. In addition, the obligations mentioned under para. II.D.b.cc. [¶¶ 55, 56] which are excluded from the 5% counterparty limit may credited as cash equivalents. A negative leverage effect on restricted assets must be excluded at all times (*i.e.*, any sale of the bonds applied for coverage may not result in a deficit in the coverage of restricted assets, see para. III.I.b.bb.bbb. and para. IV concerning the derivatives in Annex No. 3). Other debt securities, as well as equities may not be considered cash equivalents.

The requirement for full coverage of the obligation at all times is satisfied if: 371

a. the liquidity or cash equivalents are available or 372

b. the underlying assets are in the assets of the insurance business and are available without restriction. Securities lending in respect of underlying assets and sale-and-repurchase agreements (repo, reverse repo) in connection with derivative transactions are not permitted. An exception exists for loaned securities if it is possible, without restriction, to require the return of these securities on short notice. 373

c. a double use of liquidity or underlying assets for the coverage of more than one transaction is excluded. Underlying assets or cash equivalents may be applied concurrently for the coverage of derivative positions if they include several risks, such as, e.g., a market, a credit or a currency risk, but they relate to the same underlying assets. 374

d. The market value of the cash equivalents or the number of underlying assets covers the entire obligation. In the case of payment obligations [owed to the insurance business] - with the exception of bank deposits and time deposits - only 90% of the market value of the payment obligation may be applied as coverage. 375

In the case of derivatives with the obligation to purchase or deliver an underlying (long futures, long forwards, short puts), such as, e.g., an equity, a financial index, a currency or an interest rate, the liquidity needed to fulfill the obligation must be available at all times. 376

In the case of derivatives with obligations to sell or deliver an underlying (short futures, short forwards, short calls), such as, *e.g.*, an equity, a currency or an interest rate, the underlying investment for the fulfillment of the obligation must be available, without restriction, at all times. In the case of index derivatives, the obligations are considered covered if there is a broad correlation between the underlyings and the index. 377
If there is a contractual right to settle an incurred obligation with a cash payment instead of the delivery of an underlying, the underlying must nevertheless be held so that market value fluctuations can be offset.

In the case of derivatives with an obligation to exchange payment streams (receiver or payer swaps), the payment stream which is to be paid (fixed or variable) must be secured with the necessary liquidity or "underlying". 378

In the case of combinations of derivatives, the obligations of the entire combination must be covered at all times by underlyings or liquidity in available assets for the fulfillment of the obligations. The underlyings of the combination must be identical to the underlyings applied for coverage. 379

380 See Annex No. 3, para. I. (Examples A1-A4).

dd) Investment strategy

Relevant legal basis:

381 Art. 101 SR Investment strategy.
Insurance businesses which use derivative financial instruments must adopt an investment strategy for these instruments. The executive board of an insurance business shall prepare the investment strategy, submit it to the board of directors for approval and monitor its implementation.

382 Art. 102 SR Content of the investment strategy.
[1] The basic parameters for the use of derivative financial instruments must be specified in the investment strategy, in particular, the risk exposure limits and the basic principles of risk analysis.
[2] The investment strategy must, in addition, comply with the usual principles for capital investments, in particular those in respect of security, liquidity, return, diversification and allocation.

383 Art. 103 SR System of Limits
Risk exposure limits are to be set in a manner commensurate with the financial and organizational capabilities of the insurance business.

384 The appropriate investment strategy for an insurance business will, in accordance with Art. 101 SR, be prepared by the executive board of the insurance business. The executive board is responsible [for ensuring] that the chosen investment strategy and the instruments used conform to the principles formulated in this circular letter.

385 The provisions mentioned here concerning the investment strategy are to be complied with mandatorily in the investment regulation under para. II.F.b (Investment regulation).

ee) Requirements for organization and staff

386 The following provisions concerning organization and staff are to be complied with mandatorily in the investment regulation under para. II.F.b (Investment Regulation).

aaa) Organization

Relevant legal basis:

387 Art. 105 SR Organization
An insurance business which uses derivative financial instruments, must have a suitable organizational structure; it observes, in particular, Articles 106-108.

Art. 106 SR Management and control 388
[1] An insurance business must issue detailed guidelines to the persons entrusted with management, in particular, in respect of risk analysis.
[2] It has a control system that is adapted to the scope of the business and the complexity of the derivative financial instruments.
[3] The management of derivative financial instruments and the control must always be carried out by separate, independent persons.

Art. 108 SR Activity report 389
An activity report about the use of derivative financial instruments must be submitted to the board of directors every six months.

bbb) Staff

Relevant legal basis:

Art. 107 SR Qualifications of staff 390
Whoever is entrusted with management and control, shall have the special knowledge and qualifications necessary for the task.

A qualified staff must be able to understand and track the nature of the effects 391
of the derivatives employed.

ccc) Risk analysis

Relevant legal basis:

Art. 104 SR Risk analysis 392
[1] Counterparty risks must be taken into account before the use of derivative financial instruments.
[2] The risks must be analyzed as often as the situation requires, however at least once per week for market risks and once per month for credit risks.
[3] The analysis of market and credit risks consists, among other things, of valuing the open positions and comparing them with the established risk exposure limits.
[4] The result of the risk analysis is to be submitted to the executive board as often as the situation requires, however at least once per month for market risks and at least once every three months for credit risks.

An insurance business must have a suitable risk management, which is able to 393
recognize and evaluate the risks from the use of derivative financial instruments. In the evaluation of counterparty risks, attention must be given both to the creditworthiness of the counterparty as well as the prevention of possible aggregations of risks.

The risk management of an insurance business shall ensure that the deriva- 394
tives strategies of the various business areas are recorded at a central location and are analyzed for mutual dependencies. In addition, various relevant sce-

narios are to be tested in order to ensure that the use of derivatives as a whole does not jeopardize the stability of the value of the restricted assets, as well as the solvency of the business. An insurance business shall ensure that in the various reports to the FINMA, the economic effects resulting from derivatives are correctly shown (*e.g.*, the reports on restricted assets, SST).

395 *Examples:*

- *In the case of bonds which are hedged against market value fluctuations, the duration must be adjusted.*
- *If a future swap transaction (e.g. the purchase of a swaption) is covered by an obligation due on the same date, this bond may not serve concurrently as cover for another transaction in preparation for an acquisition.*
- *If a transaction in preparation for an acquisition is concluded with respect to shares (e.g., long call), the equity exposure is consequently increased.*

b) Assets permitted within restricted assets

aa) Legal basis

Relevant legal basis:

396 Art. 79 SR Permitted Assets

[1] The following assets may be allocated to restricted assets:

[. . .]

i. derivative financial instruments which serve hedging purposes and have no leverage effect on restricted assets if the underlying is in restricted assets and credit for them is adjusted in response to market fluctuations;

j. [. . .]

[2] Under certain conditions and to a certain degree, derivative instruments also can be allocated to restricted assets for purposes of preparing for an acquisition, increasing revenue and hedging cash flows from insurance technical obligations. The supervisory authority shall determine the permitted scope and conditions.

bb) General provisions

397 The Supervision Regulation restricts the use of derivative instruments within restricted assets (Art. 79 SR). Derivatives generally are only permitted in restricted assets if:

398 a. the underlyings which are the basis for the derivatives are permitted investments under Art. 79, para. 1 SR;

399 b. they do not provide leverage for restricted assets, subject to the provisions of Art. 79, para. 2 SR;

c. they comply with the principles formulated in para. III.I.a. 400

in respect of a., Permitted underlyings

Permitted underlyings for derivatives within restricted assets are not only the direct investments, such as equity or debt instruments, but also assets which mirror indexes or interest rates. The prerequisite, however, is always that the actual underlying of this instrument is a permitted investment under Art. 79, para. 1 SR. The requirement that the underlying for a derivative is permitted in restricted assts is also to be met for index transactions. 401

Credit default swaps (CDS) are only permitted for the strategies precisely defined below. Other credit derivatives may not be allocated to restricted assets. In the use of CDS, increased demands are made on the knowledge and qualifications of the staff, as well as the risk analysis (para. III.I.a.ee. and para. III.C.b.cc.). The market liquidity of the relevant CDS is to be verified before it is employed and also continuously during its term. 402

in respect of b., Leverage

One speaks of leverage if the relative change in value of the derivative is greater than the change in value of the underlying asset. Leverage effects occur primarily in connection with derivatives and debt capital financings. In both cases, the investor participates with a small capital outlay on the change in value of a proportionally large asset. Leverage is defined as the relationship between the relative change in value of the derivative to the relative change in value of the underlying assets. In order to limit the financial effects of leverage on restricted assets, derivatives must be covered by liquidity or available underlying assets (see Annex No. 3, para. III.). 403

cc) Derivatives permitted for the hedging of asset portfolios

A hedging strategy serves to wholly or partially hedge the value of assets, for example against market or currency risks, *i.e.*, to reduce or completely eliminate the risks resulting from market price or currency fluctuations on the value of the investment within restricted assets. 404

Derivative instruments for hedging are only permitted if the following conditions are fulfilled: 405

a. The hedged underlying asset is included in restricted assets. 406

b. The obligations incurred are covered at all times by the underlying asset in restricted assets. 407

c. Market fluctuations are mirrored in the credit given for of the underlying asset in restricted assets. 408

409 d. The hedging instrument used makes an effective price hedge of the underlying asset possible, *i.e.*, the absolute price change of the underlying asset is offset by the absolute market price change of the hedging instrument. Through the use of derivative instruments, on a net basis, *i.e.*, after the offset of underlying asset and derivative positions, no short positions may be established (there may not be an over-hedge).

410 e. The instruments used shall not have a leverage effect on restricted assets.

411 Specifically, the following instruments, with which a "downside exposure" can be effectively hedged, are permitted:
a. Long put options
b. Short futures
c. Short forwards
d. Swaps

412 Instruments which serve to finance the hedging but which themselves do not provide effective hedging, such as short call options, explicitly may not be allocated to this category (see para. III.I.b.ff.).

413 Derivatives on indexes (*e.g.*, short SMI futures, long SMI put options) may be included for hedging restricted assets. In this regard it is to be ensured that the structure of the hedged portfolio is largely coextensive with the index and that the return on the portfolio closely correlates with the return on the index. This means that a broad correlation with the index must exist for the hedged position.

414 Foreign currency hedging via a third currency (a so-called proxy hedge) is not recognized as a hedge. If an insurance business can internally document and plausibly show that an intention to hedge exists with a proxy hedge it has entered into, the derivative can be included as an asset in the relevant category in which the reference currency is classified.

415 *Example: hedge of a USD bond with a USD/EUR instrument. The exposure is thereby converted from USD into EUR. Such a hedging transaction does not reduce the relevant exposure for the calculation of the foreign currency limit. The derivative is included with bonds.*

416 Interest rate hedging transaction for bonds which are valued under the amortized cost method generally may not be included in this category because they do not fulfill the condition set forth above "market fluctuations are mirrored in the credit given for of the underlying asset in restricted assets". If interest rate derivatives in such cases are transacted under the same master agreement (see para. III.I.e.) as that of restricted assets, the following procedure must be chosen:

Under Art. 88 and Art. 89 SR, a fixed income security may be included at not more than the value determined under the amortized cost method. The cost of the security is decreased or increased over the remaining term. Under Art. 79, para. 1, provision i SR, hedging instruments which hedge an underlying security whose credit in restricted assets does not mirror the hedged market fluctuations, may not be included. It must be extrapolated from this statutory provision that the value of a combined credit for a hedging instrument (derivative) and an underlying security (bond) may not exceed the value under the cost amortization method. 417

As a consequence:

If the hedged market value is greater than the value under the cost amortization method (or is the same), the interest rate derivative may be credited in restricted assets with a value of 0. Art. 79, para. 1, provision i SR, as well as Art. 88, para. 1 SR are, as a result, fulfilled. 418

If the hedged market value at the time the hedging transaction is made is less than the value included under the cost amortization method, then a reason for a value reduction arises which results from the purchase of the hedging instrument (see also Art. 95 SR, as well as para. II.F.f.). In this situation, the following variations may be applied: 419

a. The included value of the bond will be reduced to the hedged market value. This new initial value will be increased or decreased over the remaining term. The derivative is included with a value of 0. 420

b. Or: the derivative transaction is booked in free assets. 421

In Annex No. 3, para. VI, there are examples for both situations: "market value higher than AMC" and "hedged value lower than AMC". 422

When a macro-hedge is entered into, the adjustments on an individual security basis elaborated above can lead to technical problems. In these situations, it is therefore permissible to apply the procedure at the portfolio level by analogy. This is subject to the following conditions: 423

a. The hedged assets are held in restricted assets. The obligations that have been incurred are at all times covered by underlying assets in restricted assets. The hedging instrument that is used permits an effective price hedge of the underlying asset (see definition above). 424

b. The insurance business identifies the portfolio of hedged obligations on the internal inventory. 425

c. Credit is given for the derivative at a value of 0. 426

427 d. The insurance business shall verify when the derivative transaction is made whether a deficit in restricted assets would result if the hedged security is sold.

428 This test is performed as follows:
[sum of the hedged market values*] - [sum of all included assets at AMC*]
* only bonds which are affected by the macro-hedge are to be taken into account.

429 e. If the difference resulting from this test is negative, then there must be excess coverage in restricted assets in at least the amount of this difference on a continuous basis until the termination of the hedge.

430 f. In the annual report concerning restricted assets, the insurance business must disclose the results of this test (with current values) to the FINMA.

431 For the hedging of credit risk from asset portfolios, the following credit default swaps are permitted:

432 • CDS on individual securities, if the insurance business is the protection buyer (long protection)

433 • CDS on an index, if the insurance business is the protection buyer (long protection)

434 As a hedging instrument, a credit default swap may then only be allocated to restricted assets if it has been constructed with respect to "credit event payment", "credit event definition" and "reference obligation" in such a manner that a high level of hedging effect is achieved. If a portfolio is hedged with a CDS on an index, it must be ensured that there is extensive congruence between the portfolio to be hedged and the index portfolio in respect of their composition and the portfolio weighting. If the portfolio to be hedged and the index portfolio are different in respect of composition and/or portfolio weighting, such that a stable correlation relationship between them is not given and therefore the hedging effect is not ensured, rather only an approximation can be achieved (proxy hedge or cross hedge), the allocation of such a hedging instrument for this strategy is not permitted.

435 CDS on individual securities will only be credited at market value if the debt security (underlying security) suffers a long-term impairment in value (see para. II.F.f.) and as a result the CDS produces a hedging effect. If the underlying security is valued under the amortized cost method, credit for the CDS in restricted assets is given with a value of 0.

436 CDS on an index which serve as hedges will always be credited in restricted assets with a value of 0.

dd) Permitted derivatives for the hedging of cash flows from insurance technical obligations

This strategy has the purpose of hedging the long-term cash flows from insurance technical obligations. In addition, synthetic bonds (aaa.) and options (bbb., *e.g.*, swaptions) are permitted. 437

aaa) Synthetic bonds (time deposit combined with a receiver swap)

Synthetic bonds (see also Art. 88, para. 3 SR) are capital investments with the characteristics of fixed income securities. They are constructed from a combination of financial instruments. A receiver swap is superimposed over a time deposit with, e.g., a term of 20 years (variable interest rate, adjusted every 6 months). With the interest to be received on the time deposit, the variable interest to be paid on the swap is offset. The investor receives as a result a fixed interest rate over a term of 20 years. Through synthetic bonds, an insurance business can effect capital investments with durations which are not available on the market in the form of fixed income securities. 438

The provisions that apply to derivatives with a synthetic strategy apply to synthetic bonds (para. III.I.b.ee.bbb.) 439

bbb) Options (e.g., swaptions)

Swaptions and options which function similarly to a long swaption (options on bonds with a fixed coupon) may be included in restricted assets. Credit for other instruments is only allowed if notified in advance to the FINMA. 440

The permitted options (the need for hedging instruments can be determined on the basis of the entire portfolio; "macro hedge") are includable under the following conditions: 441

- A hedging of expected insurance technical liabilities is achieved. 442
- It is probable that the instruments can be held to maturity. Instruments that will be terminated before the maturity date must be justified in an internal report. 443
- The FINMA is informed about the transaction through the submission of documentation. It should be made especially clear therein that no overhedge exists at the conclusion of the transaction. 444
- The use of these instruments must be focused on stable returns; in particular, they may not be entered into with the intention of terminating them soon thereafter in order to thereby realize a gain. 445

ee) Permitted derivatives in preparation for an acquisition

446 A derivatives strategy can either provide for the acquisition of certain underlying assets on a date in the future (aaa. Acquisition preparation) or to substitute the acquisition of an underlying asset with derivatives pursuant to a synthetic strategy (bbb. Synthetic strategy; liquidity combined with a derivative).

aaa) Acquisition preparation

447 Only derivatives which fulfill the following conditions are permitted for acquisition preparation:
- The liabilities are covered by liquidity or cash-equivalents in accordance with para. III.I.a.cc.

448 Specifically, the following instruments are permitted:
- Long call options
- Short put options

bbb) Synthetic strategy

449 For a synthetic strategy, only derivatives which fulfill the following conditions are permitted:

450 • The combination between the derivative and liquidity has a similar market risk profile and at least the same liquidity as the replicated investment.

451 • The purpose of acquiring the derivative is to replicate the underlying assets. An insurance business shall document this in an internal report. The combination between the derivative and liquidity will be included in the relevant category (*e.g.*, money-market investments and equity futures will be allocated to the equities category).

452 • The contract volume or the nominal value is to be 100% covered by liquidity or cash equivalents (see also para. III.I.a.cc. / Coverage obligation).

453 • The transaction using derivatives does not produce more cost in comparison to the acquisition of the direct investment.

454 Specifically, the following instruments are permitted (see Annex No. 3, Example V):

- Long futures
- Long forwards
- Swaps

For purposes of replicating a corporate bond or a portfolio of corporate bonds, the following instruments are specifically permitted 455

- Credit default swaps on individual securities if the insurance business is the protection seller (sell protection) 456
- Credit default swaps on an index if the insurance business is the protection seller (sell protection) 457

A credit default swap, as an instrument of a synthetic strategy, may only be allocated to restricted assets if it has been constructed with respect to "credit event payment", "credit event definition" and "reference obligation" in such a manner that a corporate bond or a portfolio of corporate bonds is replicated with sufficient precision. In the selection of the relevant CDS or CDS indexes, the insurance business must bear in mind that the resulting position must comport with the investment policy of the insurance business. In particular, the resulting synthetic corporate bond or portfolio of synthetic corporate bonds may not have a rating that is worse than investment grade (BBB). 458

ff) Permitted derivatives for increasing income

The strategy of increasing income aims to generate additional income from existing assets, whether through tactical implementation of the investment strategy on the basis of market opportunities or market risk or through premium income from writing options. For this purpose, only derivatives which fulfill the following conditions are permitted: 459

- The incurred contract volume must be covered at all times in accordance with para. III.I.a.cc.

Specifically, the following instruments are permitted: 460

- Call and put options
- Credit default swaps on individual securities if the insurance business is in the position of the protection buyer (buy protection) and the CDS does not qualify as hedging. 461
- Credit default swaps on an index if the insurance business is in the position of the protection buyer (buy protection) and the CDS does not qualify as hedging. 462

gg) Permitted combinations

The combination of several basic forms of derivatives which have the same underlying assets is permitted. In this regard, the following conditions apply: 463

464 • The various components of the combined strategy must be disassembled and valued separately.

465 • The individual components of the combination - after their disassembly - must capable of being allocated to one of the above-mentioned strategies. The conditions mentioned for the various strategies must be satisfied.

466 The coverage obligations under para. III.I.a.cc must be satisfied.

hh) Structured products

467 In the case of structured products, the separate paragraph, III.C.a. Structured products, is to be observed.

ii) Assets and transactions not permitted

468 The following derivatives and transactions may not be allocated to restricted assets:

469 a. Short sales, *e.g.*, sales of underlying assets on a future date without the ownership of these when the contract is made.

470 b. Derivatives which are not covered by underlying assets or cash equivalents.

471 c. Derivatives which are derived from an underlying asset which is not permitted under Art. 79, para. 1 SR.

472 d. Transactions which have a leverage effect on restricted assets as a whole, subject to the provisions of Art. 79, para. 2 SR.

c) Limits

aa) Derivatives for hedging asset portfolios

473 For derivatives for the hedging of asset portfolios under para. III.I.b.cc. there are no limits.

bb) Derivatives for the hedging of cash flows from insurance technical obligations (under III.I.b.dd.bbb.)

474 The premiums of the open derivative instruments for the hedging of cash flows from insurance technical obligations (options under para. III.I.b.dd.bbb.) are limited to 5% of the required amount of restricted assets. The limit is to be met at all times. The open positions in swaptions and similar options are to be valued at amortized cost (see para. III.I.d.bb.aaa.).

cc) derivatives in preparation for acquisitions and for increasing income

The open derivative financial instruments for purposes of preparing for acquisitions and for purposes of increasing income are limited to 10% of the required amount of restricted assets. The limit is to be met at all times. 475
Excluded from this limit are derivatives used for the replication of a strategy (para. III.I.b.ee.bbb.), synthetic bonds (para. III.I.b.dd.aaa.) and the sale of call options (para. III.I.b.ff.) if all of the conditions in the relevant paragraph have been fulfilled.

The limit of 10% refers to the open contract volumes or the nominal values of the underlyings. The amount of the contract volumes results from the multiplication of the market value of the underlying asset, the number of contracts and the multiplier. In taking into account the value of options, a delta adjustment can be performed. 476

Synthetic bonds are credited to fixed income securities. In this case, there are no limitations. For the calculation of counterparty risk ("net exposure" in respect of an obligor: 5% limit), the value of the time deposit and any positive replacement value of the swap is to be taken into account. 477

dd) Crediting exposures to limits for underlyings

Commitment-increasing or commitment-reducing derivatives must be taken into account under the limits for the relevant underlyings. The limits mentioned above for derivative transactions are to be complied with cumulatively with the other limits within restricted assets. 478

Example: 479
Long call on shares: accounted for under the 10% limit under para. III.I.c.cc, as well as an increase of the equity exposure by the relevant contract volumes under the 30% equity limit (delta adjusted).

d) Valuation

aa) Market value and near market value

Relevant legal basis:

Art. 91 SR Derivative financial instruments 480
[1] Derivative financial instruments under Article 79, paragraph 1, letter i may be allocated, at most, at market value. If they are not listed on a securities exchange, a customary market valuation method will be used.
[...]

Derivative financial instruments generally may be included in restricted assets at not more than market value or securities exchange value. Specifically, this 481 means that the replacement value is considered market value. The replacement value is the price at which an open derivative position could be closed (terminated). Restricted assets must, therefore, be credited with the positive or negative replacement value (see Annex No. 3, para. II).

482 If a current market price is not available for derivatives or if market prices are not available for derivatives entered into OTC, then they must be valued on the basis of valuation models, which are appropriate and recognized in practice, on the basis of the market value of the underlying assets from which the derivative is derived. The valuations must be documented and capable of being tracked at all times.
The FINMA accepts generally recognized methods of financial mathematics for the valuation of unlisted instruments.

483 The credited derivatives position and the underlyings must reflect the actual value of the position: in the case of short call options, for example, the negative replacement value of the derivative will, at a minimum, be deducted from the underlying asset. This means that the combination of a credited derivative and a credited underlying may be credited in restricted assets at not more than the exercise or strike price.

bb) Special crediting rules

Relevant legal basis:

484 Art. 91 SR Derivative financial instruments
[1] [. . .]
[2] For derivative financial instruments under Article 79, paragraph 2, the FINMA shall specify the creditable value.
[3] [. . .]

aaa) Derivatives for hedging the payment streams from insurance technical liabilities

485 Swaptions and similar instruments for the hedging of insurance technical liabilities are included under the cost amortization method (the amortization is made from the acquisition date until the exercise date).

bbb) Replication of the strategy

486 The replicating strategies under para. III.I.b.ee.bbb. (and therefore also III.I.b.dd.aaa.) are valued according to the categories to which they have been allocated (see above).

487 In the case of synthetic bonds, the time deposit may be valued and credited at nominal value. Credit is given separately in a sub-category of fixed income securities. The receiver swap is credited (Art. 88, para. 3 SR) under the amor-

tized cost method (the amortization continues from the acquisition date until the maturity date). If the receiver swap has a value of 0 when it is concluded, then it is to be credited at 0 during the entire term. The swap may nevertheless be entered into under the same netting agreement as the other derivatives in restricted assets.

e) Legal parameters, netting agreements

aa) Statutory and regulatory provisions

Relevant legal basis:

Art. 91 SR Derivative financial instruments 488
[. . .]
[3] The offset (netting) of all derivative transactions under a master agreement is only permitted if a separate master agreement is made for each individual restricted asset. Negative positions which result from such agreements are to be deducted from restricted assets. The FINMA may specify conditions for the content of master agreements.

Art. 91, para. 3 SR gives an insurance business for the first time the opportunity to apply the close-out netting provided in an ISDA Agreement to restricted assets as well. The prerequisite is that master agreement conforms to the FINMA's circular letters and that the master agreement applies only to one restricted asset. 489

Because there is a general prohibition on offset in respect of restricted assets, it is therefore excluded that derivative transactions in free assets may be offset with derivatives transactions in restricted assets. It must always be clear to which master agreement the confirmations relate. 490

Collateral and margin accounts which must be provided in favor of a counterparty in connection with a master agreement mentioned under Art. 91, para. 3 SR must not be removed from restricted assets because the negative net position of the derivative transaction already must be deducted. Collateral received from the counterparty is legally a part of restricted assets, but will not be included in the calculation of coverage. The counterparty has an automatic right to the return of the collateral. 491

Security provided to the counterparty in the form of collateral and margin accounts from restricted assets is available to the counterparty without restriction as an enforceable asset to the extent that it can only be applied for the coverage of transactions in respect of the relevant restricted assets which relate to the relevant master agreement. 492

bb) Permitted master agreements (MA)

493 The only master agreements which are permitted are those for which the enforcement of close-out netting can be established (see para. III.I.e.dd., Netting opinions).

494 *The standardized master agreements most widely used in Switzerland are the Swiss Master Agreement for Over-the-counter (OTC) Derivatives (issued by the Bankers Association), as well as the ISDA Master Agreements (International Swaps and Derivatives Association Inc.).*

495 In all MAs which relate to restricted assets, it must be expressly provided that the counterparty waives the right to offset payment claims which are outside the scope of the MA. This waiver is to be expressly declared binding in the event of the insolvency of the insurance business.

496 If the 1992 ISDA MA is used, the "Second Method" is prescribed mandatorily for the calculation of the close-out amount.

497 In a MA, "automatic termination" is to be chosen in respect of a Swiss party. If the provision of security has been agreed, it must be specified contractually that the right to the return of the collateral is part of restricted assets. This is, however, not necessary if the security always is provided from free assets.

cc) Additional rules for transactions with foreign counterparties

498 The provisions set out above under paras. II.G. and II.H. are not affected.

499 In this case, the provision of security must be agreed.

dd) Netting opinions

500 Master agreements may only be entered into if it was confirmed by a relevant legal opinion that the netting provision is enforceable under the law applicable to the transaction and the netting agreement. In addition, a master agreement may only be made with a counterparty whose domicile is in a jurisdiction for which the enforceability of netting under the master agreement can be proved by a country-specific legal opinion. This also applies to Swiss counterparties because certain special situations are excluded in the netting opinions. For significant counterparties which are not covered by the general opinion, there are, in some instances, supplemental or industry opinions.

501 A netting opinion must confirm that the netting provision (close-out-netting) is recognized under the following laws and is enforceable:

502 a. under the law of the country in which the relevant counterparty is domiciled and in which any participating branch has its domicile;

b. under the law applicable to the transaction; and 503

c. under the law applicable to the netting agreement. 504

ISDA has arranged for the enforceability of the MA to be confirmed through legal opinions for a number of countries. These legal opinions may be examined by members and there is an annually updated compilation that is provided to banking supervisory authorities. 505

ee) Provision of security

If the provision of security is agreed, it must be ensured that this is provided as a mutual obligation. It must be ensured that the security is effectively available and can be fully taken into account in the close-out netting process. This must also apply in case of the insolvency of both parties. 506

A private sale, for example, would not be possible in a Swiss bankruptcy if the security is provided in the form of a normal security interest. 507

Threshold amounts which must be reached before there is even an obligation to deliver security must be kept as low as possible. If such thresholds are fixed, they must be specified for both sides in light of [credit] ratings. 508

Independent amounts which must be secured by proper security independently from actual netting obligations may not be included in a MA for restricted assets. A contractual provision that deviates from this may only be accepted if it is ensured that independent amounts provided out of restricted assets lead to an encumbrance of restricted assets to the smallest possible extent in excess of the actual netting obligations. Such a provision must be requested in advance from the FINMA and approved by it. 509

Minimum transfer amounts (MTA), which must be reached before the delivery or return of security must be made, are to be kept low. If minimum transfer amounts are agreed, they must generally be identical for both parties. Differing amounts of MTAs may only be provided on the basis of differing ratings. 510

Custody of the collateral is to be provided for in Switzerland or in a country permitted by the FINMA (analogously to the rules for custodians of restricted assets, para. II.G.). 511

Provision of security by an insurance business: the provision of security with assets from restricted assets is permitted. Because in this case the net value of the derivatives transactions in restricted assets is negative, the amount of the collateral must not be deducted. 512

Provision of security by a counterparty: the collateral received is legally part of restricted assets. The counterparty has, nevertheless, an automatic right to 513 withdraw it. The collateral may not be included in the calculation of the coverage for restricted assets because the positive net value of all derivatives transactions is credited. In the event of a claim against the collateral, the assets provided as security must be immediately transferred to restricted assets. The provision of security is to be identified so that third parties are able to recognize that is part of restricted assets.

ff) Prerequisites for standardized derivatives products

514 Para. III.I.e.aa. through III.I.e.ee. apply, in particular, for OTC derivatives. Insurance businesses are excluded from compliance with the mentioned provisions if they trade derivatives only on a regulated securities exchange (exchange-trade derivatives, ETD).

gg) Inventory of derivatives transactions in restricted assets

515 The underlying asset (underlying) is to be valued in accordance with the regulations in the SR.
The individual financial derivatives allocated to restricted assets will also be valued in accordance with the SR. In the inventory of restricted assets, the individual derivatives transactions will be listed (not the net amount). If the value of a financial derivative concluded under an MA of restricted assets is negative, then this negative value is to be listed in the inventory of restricted assets.

516 Upon the conclusion of a derivative transaction, an insurance business must specify the MA to which the relevant transaction belongs (MA "free assets" or MA "restricted assets increasing income or acquisition preparation..."). An insurance business must adopt the relevant organizational measures so that it is at all times possible to identify derivatives transactions that are governed by a specific MA. The inventories of restricted assets may only include derivative transactions which were concluded under the MA for the relevant restricted asset. An insurance business shall ensure that the counterparty can distinguish derivative transactions based on their destination ("restricted assets increasing income / acquisition preparation) . . . " or "free assets").

517 In this regard it is to be observed that the derivatives transaction as well as the underlying asset related to it always remain in the same pool of assets.

518 *If, for example, an underlying asset which is the underlying for a derivatives transaction is removed from a restricted asset, the relevant derivative transaction must first be ended or closed out. It is also possible that an insurance business agrees with a counterparty on an appropriate mechanism for shifting derivative transactions under the MA.*

J. Collective capital investments and single-investor funds

a) Permitted assets within restricted assets

Relevant legal basis:

Art. 79 SR Permitted assets 519
[1] The following assets may be allocated to restricted assets:
[. . .]
j. investments in collective capital investments and single-investor funds.
[2] [. . .]

The conditions for crediting these share certificates are listed in Art. 82 SR. 520

In the category under para. III.J.b. are collective capital investments which are regulated in accordance with the current regulations under the Collective Investment Law (CIL) and which are either allocated to the category securities funds under Arts. 53 ff. CIL or real estate funds under Arts. 58 ff. CIL (open-ended collected capital investments). The other funds for traditional and alternative investments under Arts. 68 ff. CIL, as well as investments in other alternative investments (*e.g.*, hedge funds, private equity funds, see para. III.H.) and the single-investor funds (see para. III.J.c.), however, are not included in this category. 521
For foreign collective capital investments, these distinctions are to be applied by analogy (*e.g.*, UCITS).

In the case of single-investor funds under para. III.J.c, this is a special form of collective capital investment in which onl a single investor has invested (see CIL). In this case, the right to access the direct investments of the funds must be ensured at all times. The direct investments of the fund, as well as the custodian of the fund must fulfill all the provisions concerning investments in restricted assets. 523

Under Art. 82, para. 4 SR, investments in investment companies which are not listed are only permitted if a fund under para. III.J.b. (collective capital investments) or para. III.J.c. (single-investor funds) is interposed. If the investment company is subject to meaningful supervision, then the interposition of a fund is not necessary. Listed investment companies are covered under the category in Art. 79, para. 1, provision e SR. 524

The term "meaningful supervision" means a supervisory body which in comparison to Swiss supervision (FINMA) is equivalent. 525

b) Special requirements for collective capital investments

Relevant legal basis:

526 Art. 82 SR Collective capital investments and single-investor funds
[1] An insurance business can credit interests in collective capital investments to the extent that:
a. these are subject to effective supervision for the protection of investors; and
b. the interests are traded on a regulated, liquid market or can be sold at any time.
[. . .]

527 The investment strategy of the collective capital investment must be set in accordance with the investment principles mentioned in para. II.D.b.

528 In the case of investments in foreign collective capital investments, the [fund] share certificate must have the character of a security.

c) Special requirements for single-investor funds

aa) General provisions

Relevant legal basis:

529 Art. 82 SR Collective capital investments and single-investor funds
[. . .]
[2] Interests in single-investor funds may be credited to restricted assets to the extent that these single-investor funds:
a. are subject to an effective supervision;
b. will be held 100 percent by the insurance business;
c. the ability to take possession of the individual investments of the fund is assured at all times;
d. make investments in investments under Article 79; and
e. fulfill the requirements of Article 87.
[. . .]

530 It must, in particular, be ensured at all times that direct access to the investments of the fund is possible (provision c), that the investments are made in accordance with Art. 79 SR as well as the FINMA's circular letters (provision d) and that the requirements under Art. 87 SR are fulfilled (provision e). The FINMA considers these requirements are fulfilled only if the requirements are both legally and organizationally are fulfilled.

531 In addition, the FINMA's general requirements for outsourcing are to be fulfilled.

532 An insurance business must prove, on one hand, on the basis of the fund regulation and, on the other hand, in making notifications concerning the busi-

ness plan that the entire structure of the single-investor fund conforms to the requirements of the FINMA.

bb) The fund regulation

The collective investment agreement must be terminable at any time and, in addition, must provide for the immediate return of the direct investments in kind. In addition, it must be specified in the fund regulation that the fund's management will comply with the investment regulations resulting from the mandatory provisions of insurance supervisory law (SR, regulations, circular letters or regulatory orders of the FINMA). 533

As a result, this form of investment will have the same liquidity as direct investments and will be placed on equal footing with direct investments in respect of security and return. 534

With respect to the constitutive documents of an investment fund, in particular the articles of incorporation of the fund management company, the investment regulation, the collective investment agreement, it must be specified that these must be notified to the FINMA (in accordance with Art. 4, para. 2, provision j ISL) before the effective date of these legal constitutive documents and therefore the establishment of the single-investor fund. Further, it is to be specified that all amendments to these constitutive documents also must be notified to the FINMA before their entry into effect. 535

In the case of a single-investor fund, the insurance business (legal entity) is the sole investor and no other investors can be included. 536

The fund may not make any investments with debt financing. The exception to this rule is for advances by the investor (*e.g.*, short-term liquidity financing). 537

The custodian bank of the fund must be located in Switzerland (or a country permitted in accordance with para. II.G.b.) and sign the Model Agreement of the Swiss Bankers Association (amended attachment to Circular No. 771 D of the SBA of 9.4.1987, see Annex No. 4). Arts. 86 and 87 SR are to be observed. 538

cc) Notifications concerning the business plan

The outsourcing of portions of restricted assets in single-investor funds is, under Art. 4, para. 2, provision j ISL, an outsourcing of a significant function of an insurance business and therefore an amendment of the business plan which must be notified to the FINMA. 539

The notice concerning the business plan must include the following information: 540

541 a. A description of the legal structure of the single-investor fund (which parties are involved, which contracts will be made, etc.).

542 b. The applicant shall state that it has ensured through service agreements or otherwise that service providers remain required to give information to the FINMA in respect of the outsourcing of significant functions (core functions) and that the intervention measures under supervisory law remain available. In particular, the FINMA must have the right to conduct on-site inspections of these service providers.

543 c. The applicant shall ensure that all contracts which relate to this fund structure take into account the relevant supervisory law regulations and do not have any contrary provisions.

544 d. Each amendment of the fund regulation will be notified to the FINMA. Changes in the parties involved (*e.g.*, custodian, investment management) are considered amendments to the business plan and are to be notified to the FINMA.

545 e. The fees which are paid to the parties involved are to be disclosed to the FINMA. The appropriateness of the fees must demonstrable at all times.

546 f. The applicant must explain to the FINMA in a statement pursuant to the business plan how the control function will be organized. This applies, on one hand, to the communication of the regulatory laws and guidelines, etc. to the service companies and, on the other hand, the monitoring of whether these companies comply with them. The statement must show where the responsibility for these control functions lies and what authority this function has and in which reporting interval the exchange of information will occur.

547 g. Concerning the valuation of a single-investor fund, the applicant must confirm that the individual securities of the fund are inventoried in restricted assets and are valued under the valuation regulations for direct investments (*e.g.*, amortized costs for bonds). The income from the investments in a single-investor fund is to be booked 100% in the income statement of the applicant - withheld profit is not permitted. This is also to be confirmed in the statement.

dd) Further information and documentation that is to be submitted to the FINMA with the notice concerning the business plan

548 a. Concerning fees (see below under para. III.J.c.cc., provision e), a comparative accounting is to be submitted which compares the previous fees for the investment and the future expenses. The basis for this accounting is the investments which will be transferred to the single-investor fund. In addition, the appropriateness of the fees is to be demonstrated, including any

basic documentation (*e.g.*, benchmark studies, if relevant for the calculation of the fees).

b. Model agreement with the custodian. 549

d) Limits

aa) Collective capital investments

For the control of the applicable limits in restricted assets (*e.g.*, currency, equity, real estate), the NAV of the collective capital investments will be distributed proportionally to the relevant categories. 550

An investment for each collective capital investment is limited to 5% of the required amount. This limit no longer applies if the collective capital investment fulfills all of the following criteria: 551

- The collective capital investment shall invest only in the categories money market, domestic bonds and foreign debtors, Swiss equities and foreign equities (explicitly excluded are investments with high risk, such as emerging markets equities and bonds, high-yield bonds, convertible bonds, hedge funds, private equity structured products, etc.). 552
- A withdrawal from the collective capital investment at NAV per share is possible at all times. 553
- The collective capital investment has segregated asset status (segregation in the event of bankruptcy for the benefit of investors). 554
- Compliance with the investment guidelines of the FINMA (in particular, the principles of the restricted assets, the exclusion of liability, encumbrance and offset of fund assets in relation to third parties, prohibition on borrowing) will be agreed between the parties. 555
- It will be contractually agreed, that the asset manager shall have duty to provide information to the FINMA analogous to that under Art. 29 FINMAG. 556
- An insurance business shall receive a report from the capital investment as of [each] 31.12. showing the individual securities positions. 557

An insurance business shall confirm to the FINMA that the points mentioned above have been contractually agreed or show the FINMA how they have been addressed. 558

bb) Single-investor funds

559 The investment per single-investor fund is not limited. The direct investments of the fund will be inventoried in restricted assets and thereby allocated to the relevant categories.

e) Valuation

aa) Collective capital investments

Relevant legal basis:

560 Art. 92 SR Collective capital investments
[1] Collective capital investments under Article 82, paragraph 1 may, at the most, be allocated at market value or, if the share certificates are not listed on a securities exchange, then at net asset value.
[2] [. . .]

561 In the inventory of restricted assets, an insurance business must allocate the interests in the mentioned collective capital investments on an aggregate basis in accordance with the investment classes mentioned in Art. 79 SR.

bb) Single-investor funds

Relevant legal basis:

562 Art. 92 SR Collective capital investments
[1] [. . .]
[2] For single investor funds under Article 82, paragraph 2, the individual securities of the fund's assets must be listed in restricted assets and be valued analogously in accordance with the requirements in this section.

563 For the crediting and valuation of single-investor funds in restricted assets under Art. 82, para. 2 SR, the basis is the direct investments of the fund (look-through principle). In the inventory of restricted assets, the individual securities of the fund must be listed and allocated to the categories under Art. 79 SR. The valuation is made in accordance with the principles specified in Arts. 88 through 95 SR.

IV. Supplementary provisions (concerning restricted assets)

A. Securities lending

a) Legal basis

Relevant legal basis

Art. 75 SR Securities lending 564
[1] The FINMA shall issue regulations concerning securities lending by insurance businesses, in particular concerning:
a. security methods;
b. contents of the agreements; and
c. the scope.
[2] Securities lending is considered a legal transaction similar to a loan through which an insurance company transfers certain securities to a borrower and the borrower is required to return securities of the same type, quantity and quality and to pay to the insurance business during the term of the securities loan any distributions received in respect of the securities.

b) Permitted transactions within restricted assets

aa) Parameters

Securities lending in possible only under the following conditions: 565

a. Master agreement 566
The insurance business enters into a master agreement with the counterparty (see para. IV.A.c.aa.).

b. Counterparty / Borrower 567
The borrower must have recognized and first class creditworthiness and it must agree to conduct these transactions only with a recognized clearing house (*e.g.*, Clearstream) or bank with first-class creditworthiness.

c. Rights in connection with the loaned underlyings 568
The insurance business shall remain the economic beneficiary (beneficial ownership) of the loaned securities. Interest and dividend payments made during the loan belong always to the insurance business. The insurance business is able at all times to require the return of the loaned securities, although the delivery of the security is subject to the applicable value dates / delivery periods. If a notice period for termination is agreed, its duration may not be more than ten banking days. The risks of the security's price fluctuations remain with the insurance business and are to be taken into account in restricted assets.

569 d. Provision of Security / Collateral
The right of the insurance business to require redelivery of the loaned assets (securities) must be secured by the pledge of securities or through the deposit with the intermediary of an appropriate amount of money or securities for the benefit of the insurance business (see para. IV.A.c.bb.).

570 e. Professional knowledge / Personnel
Insurance businesses that enter into lending transactions directly with the intermediary (bank) must have qualified and professionally knowledgeable personnel or obtain appropriate advice.

571 f. Term
Lending can be made only to the extent that the liquidity of the insurance business is not impaired. It must be possible at all times to terminate the loan within 10 bank working days.

bb) Transactions not permitted

572 Securities lending in connection with derivative transactions is not permitted. Exceptions are loaned securities if the unrestricted return of the securities on short notice is possible.

573 Securities from borrowing transactions may not be credited to restricted assets and may not be used for derivative transactions.

c) Special requirements

aa) Master agreements

574 The standardized master agreement between the insurance business and the borrower (*e.g.*, bank) must conform to customary international standards and, in addition, govern or include the following issues:

575 a. The restricted assets covered by a master agreement are to be specified. In addition, the underlyings which are available or excluded from securities lending are to be identified. The master agreement must refer to the restricted assets. The lending of underlyings which are in free assets under the same master agreement is not permitted.

576 b. The provision of security by the borrower is to be agreed for each transaction and the relevant provisions for the provision of security / collateral under para. IV.A.c.bb. are to be observed.

577 c. The borrower is liable for the prompt and unrestricted payment of the income (dividends and interest) paid during the loan, the exercise of other rights (*e.g.*, conversion rights and pre-emptive rights), as well as for the return [of the securities] in the same type, quantity and quality.

d. The ability to offset the loaned securities or the collateral with claims of any of the counterparties involved (*e.g.*, borrower, intermediary) must be explicitly excluded. It must be expressly stated that this exclusion applies in the event of the insolvency of the insurance business. 578

bb) Security / collateral

Securing the right to require redelivery with collateral: 579

a. In order to secure unsecured claims arising out of securities lending, collateral must be delivered to a separate custody account or account. The security can be established in the name of the insurance business or in the name of the bank, pledged for the benefit of the insurance business. The transfer of collateral shall be made simultaneously with the delivery of the [loaned] security. 580

b. The custodian (the depository bank) used for the provision of security / collateral must comply with the guidelines for the custody of securities (see Arts. 86 / 87 SR and para. II.H. Assets invested abroad). The depository bank must be in Switzerland and must have signed the relevant model agreement. 581

c. The value of the security provided must at all times amount to 105% of the market value of the loaned securities. The value of the security may amount to 102% of market value if a CHF bond with a credit rating of A or better is loaned. In this case, the security must be provided in CHF cash or CHF bonds with AAA creditworthiness. 582

d. The security must at all times fulfill all investment guidelines which apply to direct investments included in restricted assets. As security, only underlyings which are permitted as investments in restricted assets under Art. 79, para. 1 SR are accepted. As a rule, liquid assets should be provided. If a different form of security is agreed, it must be ensured, in particular, that the provision of security can be valued and traded daily and that it has a creditworthiness that is at least "investment grade" (BBB/Baa). Securities which are issued by the counterparty (principal, borrower) may not be used for the provision of security. 583

e. The security received may not be further pledged, loaned, sold or used in connection with derivative or repo transactions. 584

f. It must be made legally certain that the insurance business may access the security provided in full and unconditionally if the counterparty does not return or only partially returns the securities loaned. Claims by third parties against the insurance business may not affect access to the security provided. This also must apply in the event of an insolvency. 585

586 g. The security received will be credited legally to restricted assets. The counterparty, however, possesses a right to automatically retake possession. The security may not be credited in the calculation of the coverage of restricted assets because the security already is allocated to securities lending.

d) Limits

587 A maximum of 30% of the coverage value of the required amount of a restricted asset may be loaned. Loaned underlyings also must be taken into account in complying with the prescribed investment limits and be credited accordingly.

e) Valuation

588 The loaned underlying assets may be credited to restricted assets. Loaned portfolios of securities are to be included in the balance sheet in the same manner as [securities] not loaned. The loans made in a reporting year are to be disclosed to the external auditor in an appropriate manner. Loaned underlying assets are to be specially identified in the inventory of restricted assets.

589 Security or collateral received may not be credited to restricted assts because the loaned underlyings already are credited (see para. IV.A.c.bb.).

B. Repo Transactions (Repurchase Agreement, Reverse Repo)

a) Definition

590 *Repo: one party (securities provider) sells securities to a second party (securities recipient) and assumes at the same time the obligation to repurchase at a later time the same quantity and type of securities. In the interim, repo-interest is paid by the recipient of the securities and collateral is provided.*

591 Considered legally, a transfer of ownership occurs. From an economic perspective, a repo is a secured loan. As is customary for a loan, the securities recipient pays interest for the term of the transaction, a repo-interest (the difference between the purchase price and the sales price). The primary motivation for a repo transaction is temporary funding for the purpose of bridging liquidity shortages.

592 *Reverse Repo: a repo from the perspective of the counterparty (securities recipient).*

b) Creditability

Assets in restricted assets may not be used for repo transactions. 593
Securities from a reverse repo may not be credited to restricted assets and may not be used for derivatives transactions.

c) Rationale

a. Because of the transfer of ownership of the securities, an insurance business is no longer the legal owner (legal perspective). 594

b. Repo transactions lead to the borrowing of debt (borrowing of liquidity) and therefore the underlying assets may not longer be considered unencumbered (economic perspective). In addition, a repo does not lead to an increase in income from restricted assets, rather it burdens the existing income from the securities with costs. 595

C. Group relationships

a) Factual circumstances

Depending on the chosen organization or strategy, there are more or less close relationships between the individual corporate group companies. If there is a parent-subsidiary structure, the supervised parent company owns, as a rule, interests in supervised insurance businesses. 596

The parent may, for various reasons, provide loans to group companies: e.g., to provide regulatory capital to a subsidiary, to finance a real estate company, to finance an investment company, etc. 597

If the parent company of an insurance group is listed on a securities exchange, it is also possible that its own shares are repurchased in order to support the market price and then held as assets. In a different situation, a parent company may wish to let its insurance subsidiary repurchase bonds which will be held as assets of the insurance subsidiary until the repayment of the loan is due. 598

The obligations of an insurance business which is supervised by the FINMA must be covered with restricted assets. Included among the previously mentioned "group assets" are those which could be shown as unable to hold their value. If the supervised parent company comes into difficulty, the value of an investee company, a loan or another "group asset" could be impaired. 599

The problem areas are described below and individual questionable positions are addressed. 600

b) Investments not permitted within restricted assets

601 An investment is not suitable for restricted assets if the fulfillment of obligations under insurance contracts are not assured in accordance with Art. 17 ISL.

602 *This is especially the case with investments in group companies if the investment is closely correlated with the value of the business or if it results in double gearing effects.*

aa) [An insurance business's] own shares

603 The equity shares of an insurance business (supervised in Switzerland or abroad), whether they are listed or not, generally may not be applied to the coverage of restricted assets. The shares of other group companies in the portfolio of the supervised insurance business are also not suited as an investment for restricted assets because their value correlates directly with the supervised insurance business.

604 *From a business perspective, the repurchase or purchase of a corporation's own shares is the same as a reduction of shareholders' equity or a capital reduction.*

bb) [An insurance business's] own debt instruments

605 The debt instruments of the same insurance business, supervised in Switzerland or abroad, or another group company also are not suitable for restricted assets.

606 *The purchase of such debt instruments is practically the same as a repayment. To this extent, basically the same reasons are to be listed as with [an insurance business's] own shares.*

cc) Loans to group companies

Repealed

607 Repealed

608 *Repealed*

aaa) Loans to investment companies

609 Loans to investment companies may, under the following limiting conditions, be allocated [to restricted assets]:

610 A loan from a supervised insurance business to an investment company specified in Art. 82, para. 4 SR or a real estate company specified in Art. 79, pa-

ra. 1, provision f SR can be included if the borrower does not have any loans to group companies as assets in its books.

This should ensure that a double application in support of solvency for another supervised insurance business does not occur. 611

bbb) Other intra-group loans

All other intra-group loans which a supervised insurance business may provide are not suitable for restricted assets and therefore are not permitted. 612

dd) Ownership interests

Repealed

Repealed 613

Listed as well as unlisted ownership interests are not creditable. Excluded are all ownership interests in investment companies specified in Art. 82, para. 4 SR and all real estate companies specified in Art. 79, para. 1, provision f SR. All other unlisted ownership interests which are held by a supervised insurance business are not creditable to restricted assets. 614

c) Valuation

For crediting, suitable loans may be credited to restricted assets at nominal value, ownership interests at net asset value (NAV). 615

V. Transitional provisions

In the case of new investments, all conditions must be fulfilled from the entry into force of this circular letter. 616

This circular letter replaces the previous investment guidelines. 617

Annex 1

Description of the valuation methods for real estate

I. The Discounted Cash Flow Method (DCF)

Under the Discounted Cash Flow Method (DCF), the sum of all future net cash flows, discounted to the valuation date, establishes the current market value of the real property. 1

In practice, a 2-period model is, in most cases, chosen for use in which the net cash flows in the first period are estimated in detail over 10 years and for the second period after year 10, an always constant remaining net cash flow for the remaining useful life of the real property is used as the basis for the calculation. Here the irregularly occurring renovation costs for a property for the first 10 years will be accounted for on the basis of the investment budget and, for the period after year 10, estimated on the basis of the lifespan of the individual components of the building until the end of the term of useful life, converted into an annuity (constant amount during the relevant period) and deducted in arriving at the net payment flow in year 11. This net payment flow either will be capitalized (as perpetual payment) or, if only a limited period of use for the real estate is assumed, the present value (sum of the discounted value of the net payment flows from year 11 until the end of the period of use) is calculated as a so-called residual value. The sum of the discounted net payments during the first 10 years, as well as the residual value produces the near market value of the real estate.

A. Projecting the cash flows

On the basis of the schedule of lessees, the terms and conditions of the individual leasing relationships will be included in the DCF valuation. Here the principle applies that nonstandard contracts (*e.g.*, for office uses) will be listed individually, all other contracts (*e.g.*, residential uses, parking spaces) either will be combined completely or grouped according to other criteria, such as *e.g.*, apartment sizes. For the projections of the future rent income the following points are controlling: 2

- The positive or negative adjustment of the current rents to market rents at the next possible date. In the case of apartment rents, this may be distributed linearly or staggered over the entire calculation period because the date of the adjustment cannot be defined accurately enough. 3

4 • The adjustment of the rents to inflation. In the case of commercial use, in accordance with the lease contracts. In the case of residential use, roughly 40% of the inflation rate (as allowed under landlord-tenant law for the protection of the invested capital).

5 • For properties with vacancies in excess of the long-term vacancy rate (base vacancy rate) customary for the property, an occupancy scenario is to be projected, *i.e.*, in what time period and under what conditions can the vacancy rate be reduced to the base vacancy rate.

6 • If renovations (investments) are necessary within the calculation period of 10 years, the costs are to be projected and to be included in the calculation in the relevant year. If a part of the investments can be described as increasing value, this part is to be specified and the rents for the coming year are to be increased in accordance with the requirements of landlord-tenant law, but also especially taking into account the market situation.

B. Projecting Costs

7 Generally, the costs are to be determined on the basis of the income statements for the last 3 years for each property. Here this data must be verified with internal benchmarks (costs as a % of rents or in CHF/m2) and against the principle of sustainability. Special consideration is to be given to the previously mentioned maintenance and renovation costs.

C. Determining of the discount rate

8 The discount rate is especially significant in the case of the DCF-valuation because its variation leads to dramatic changes in value. The most commonly used method for determining this rate in real estate valuation is the risk component method. Here a base interest rate is assumed which corresponds to the long-term rate for riskless investments (Swiss government bonds) and which is increased with a surcharge for the illiquidity of the investment. Property-specific surcharges - or discounts for exceptionally good properties at good locations - for use, the micro- and macro-situation, as well as additional risks such as limited marketability as a result of condominiums, *Baurechte*, etc. will be added to this market-specific rate. In the determination of the discount rate, calculations may be made with factors.
In determining the residual value in year 11, the chosen discount rate is to be reviewed and adjusted, in particular, in respect of the continuing indexation of the rents. Depending on the use and the resulting amount of indexation of the rents, a discount in the discount interest rate is to be made in order to secure the indexation of the rents during the entire remaining period of use.

II. Income capitalization method

The income capitalization method proceeds on the basis that the value of real estate derives primarily from the present and future income streams generated by the property. The focus is not on the [physical] substance, rather the net present value of the income. The income capitalization method states that the value of a property primarily results from the sum of the realistically achievable rent payments, discounted to the date of the valuation. 9

A. Determining the rental income

The rental income of a real property is to be understood as the stable, attainable rent revenue (excluding utility costs). If there are special circumstances, the expected rent revenue is to be adjusted. Examples: 10
If the property is renovated and not occupied or only partially occupied, the currently attainable revenues are to be adjusted accordingly.
In the case of long-term lease contracts with fixed rents, there is a great probability that gross rents agreed at the time the contract was made no longer correspond to the current level of rent. For the determination of the stable, attainable rents, especially in the case of office properties and mixed-use properties, when the lease agreements expire and what rent revenue can be expected on a long-term basis is to be taken into account. If parts of the real property cannot be leased on a long-term basis, then the expected rent revenue is to be reduced to an appropriate extent.
If properties are in *Baurecht*, the relevant [Baurecht] rent payments are to be deducted from revenue.

B. Determining the capitalization rate

The rate for the capitalization includes all relevant risks which were not already taken into account in the rent revenue. As a rule, the following components are the relevant variables: 11

- Capital costs
- Surcharge for the type of property (*e.g.*, multiple family building, commercial building)
- Operating costs (type of construction, economic age of the building, size)
- Risk of vacancies
- Individual surcharge or reduction on the basis of the individual appraisals of the property (special characteristics, market conditions, use, micro and

macro-situation, limited marketability, *e.g.*, through condominium ownership, *Baurecht*, etc.)

12 The most commonly used method of determining this rate in real estate is the risk component method. The capital costs are the result of the base interest rate for long-term, risk-free investments (Swiss federal government bonds) and a surcharge for the investment's lack of liquidity.

13 The other property-specific and market-specific surcharges or deductions are added to this market-specific rate. For the determination of the capitalization rate, one may also calculate with factors.

14 The applicable capitalization rate so determined takes into account the property-specific characteristics, the area where the property is located and its location. One speaks of the so-called individual valuation principle.

Annex 2

Example of a due diligence investigation for alternative investments

I. Manager

- Review of the CV 1
- Is there a network with relevant contacts to the industry?
- Is the reputation above reproach?
- Are the fund's investments dependent on a single person?
- What degree of specialization does the team have?
- Does the manager have many years of experience and proven resistance to market risks in the past?
- Does the manager invest in the fund with his own funds?
- In the case of private equity: does the manager have specific experience in the development of businesses?
- Is the fund transparent with respect to decision-relevant information? What is the flow of communication? How frequently are reports or financial statements made available? Is it possible to receive an annual or half-year report?
- Verification by references

II. Strategy

- Is there a clearly defined investment strategy? 2
- Can this strategy be understood and is it reasonable?
- Is sufficient diversification available?
- What are the investment restrictions?
- How high is the maximum leverage factor?
- To what extent are short sales permitted?
- In what form will changes in strategy be reported?

III. Structure of the fund

- Are the investment and risk management processes clearly structured? 3
- Which risks are monitored? Is risk management adapted to the complexity of the strategy? Are liquidity risks analyzed? Are stress tests / future scenarios calculated?
- Is there ongoing monitoring?
- Does the fund have the necessary IT tools in order to adequately, quantitatively monitor the strategy pursued?
- Does the fund have a stable organization?

- How is the control process structured?

IV. Performance

4 - Is there a reliable track record?
- Valuation in the case of hedge funds: is NAV based exclusively on market fluctuations?
- Valuation in the case of private equity: is the valuation based on recognized standards? Is there a clearly prescribed process in respect of impairments? How are market transactions (sale / purchase of underlying companies) accounted for in the valuation?

V. Basic issues

5 - What are the exit options? Cost factors and time factors are to be taken into account.
- Reputation of the fund: are well-known investors invested?
- Which prime broker and other external parties does the fund work with?
- Is the reputation of the audit firm good and does it have the necessary know-how?
- Are there possible conflicts of interest with external parties? (In particular the relationships fund - prime broker - auditor must be investigated).
- Is the level of fees justified?

Annex 3

Examples for derivatives transactions

I. Examples for the coverage obligation under para. III.I.a.cc.

A1. Derivatives with purchase or delivery acceptance obligations 1

Example: Purchase obligation (long forward) on 500 UBSN in 3 months at a price of Fr. 140.- per share. So that the obligation is covered, the amount of Fr. 70,000.- must be reserved in cash equivalents until the exercise of the derivative. 2

A2. Derivatives with sale or delivery obligations 3

Example: sale obligation (short call) on 400 NESN at a price of Fr. 390.- per share. So that the obligation is covered, the 400 shares must remain unencumbered in the portfolio. Ownership of the shares must always remain with the insurance business. 4

Example: obligation to sell (short forward) EUR in the amount of Fr. 100,000.-. For the coverage of the obligation, a EUR debt instrument of Fr. 100,000.-, for example, must be applied. 5

A3. Derivative with an obligation to exchange payment streams 6

Example: an obligation to exchange a variable against a fixed interest rate (receiver swap). So that the variable payment streams can be paid at any time, a rolling money market investment must, for example, be applied. 7

A4. Combinations of derivatives 8

Example: bear-call-spread strategy 9
Purchase of a call on UBSN with an exercise price of 150.-
Sale of a call on UBSN with an exercise price of 130.-
In order that the obligation is covered at all times, an amount of FR. 20.- per share in liquidity must be available.

Example: replication of a short futures position 10
Sale of a put on NESN with an exercise price of 100.-
Sale of a call on NESN with an exercise price of 100.-
In order that the obligation is covered at all times, the underlying (NESN) must be held.

II. Valuation and limits

11 *Valuation of open derivatives as of 31.12.05 of Insurance Business X*

A. Initial position

12 Required amount as of 31.12.05 4,500,000.-

13 Insurance Business X has the following derivatives open on 31.12.05:

14 A 1,000 long call options on UBS N, exercise price Fr. 120.-, market value of the underlying asset on 31.12.05, Fr. 116.-, Ratio 5 : 1, option market price on 31.12.05, Fr. 0.63

15 B 2 long futures on the SMI, current index level at 31.12.05, 7204 points, forward price 7217 points, index multiplier Fr. 10.-

16 C 5,000 long call options on Nestlé N, exercise price Fr. 400.-, market value of the underlying on 31.12.05, Fr. 388.-, Ratio 40 : 1, option market price on 31.12.05., Fr. 0.52

B. Valuation or credit for open positions in restricted assets

17 A	1,000 x Fr. 0.63	= Fr.	630.-
B	2 x Fr. 10.- x (7,204 – 7,217 index points)	= Fr.	260.-
C	5,000 x Fr. 0.52	= Fr.	2,600.-
Total		**Fr.**	**2,970.-**

18 The market value of the open derivative positions in the amount of Fr. 2,970 will be credited to restricted assets.

C. Evidence of compliance with the limit under III.I.c.cc.

19 A	(1,000 : 5) x Fr. 116.-	= Fr.	23200.-
B	(5,000 : 40) x Fr. 388.-	= Fr.	48500.-
Total		**Fr.**	**71700.- (1.6% of RA)**

III. Leverage

A. Initial position

20 An insurance business buys two SMI futures contracts at 7204.

In exchange, it transfers to the margin account the amount of Fr. 14,408.- (approx. 10% of the value of the futures).
The corresponding value of the position is Fr. 144,000.-.

B. Scenario 1

In the first scenario, the SMI rises to 7300. This corresponds to an increase of approx. 1.33% of the original value. The new value of the position is Fr. 146,000.-. The derivative position increases by Fr. 2,000.–. Expressed as a percentage, this changes by 13.88%. 21

C. Scenario 2

In the second scenario, the SMI declines to 7100. This corresponds to a reduction of approx. 1.44% of the original value. The new value of the position is Fr. 142,000.-. The derivative position declines by Fr. 2,000.-. Expressed as a percentage, the additional margin changes by
-13.88%. 22

D. Conclusion

The problem of leverage can be eliminated through the coverage obligation. If the position is not merely covered by 10% but rather 100% of the value of the position, then the profit/loss position corresponds to the underlying investment. 23

IV. Negative leverage and the coverage obligation

A. Initial position

A bond X is in restricted assets, credited with 101% (AMC), Fr. 101,000.-. The market value (MV) of this bond is currently at 99%, Fr. 99,000.-. 24

Bonds may be applied as coverage at only 90% of market value (Fr. 99,000.- x 90% = Fr. 89,100.-). 25

B. Leverage effect test

The sale of the bond results in a loss of Fr. 2,000.- (2%) in restricted assets. 26

C. Scenario 1

27 Restricted assets cover 100% of the required amount. As a result of this sale, the required amount would not be fully covered.

D. Scenario 2

28 There is a surplus in restricted assets in at least the amount of the above-mentioned difference between the AMC and MV-values of the bond. As a result of this sale, the required amount would still be covered.

E. Conclusion

29 In scenario 1, there is a negative leverage on restricted assets, therefore in this scenario the bond X cannot be applied as liquidity coverage for derivative transactions.

V. Examples for the replication of a strategy

30

Replicated investment	Replicating strategy with derivatives
7-year bond	rolling money market investment and receive fixed under a 7-year swap
7-year bond	3-year bond and receive fixed under a 4-year swap with 3 year forward start
All equities of an equity index	money market and long equity index future
Corporate bond in EUR	corporate bond in USD and USD-currency swap EUR

VI. Treatment of interest rate hedging transactions for bonds which are included under the amortized cost method

Example 1: hedged market value is higher than the current AMC of the bond 31

	Year 1	Year 2	Year 3	Year 4	Year 5	Year 6
AW	105	105	105	105	105	105
AMC	105	104	103	102	101	100
MV	105	108	**115**	117	104	101
Hedge purchase			0	-2	11	14
Credit in RA - Bonds	105	104	103	102	101	100
Credit in RA - Derivatives	0	0	0	0	0	0

Example 2: hedged market value is lower than the current AMC of the bond

	Year 1	Year 2	Year 3	Year 4	Year 5	Year 6
AW	125	125	125	125	125	125
AMC	125	120	115	110	105	100
MV	125	118	**111**	113	98	99
Hedge purchase			0	-2	13	12
Credit in RA - Bonds	125	120	111	107	104	100
Credit in RA - Derivatives	0	0	0	0	0	0

Annex 4

Model agreement of the Swiss Bankers Association

Model Agreement[3]

Supplementary provisions for the business relationship (custody accounts/accounts) between Bank X (Custodian Bank) and insurance institution Y (Depositor) concerning the custody of assets which are part of the restricted assets of the Depositor Y.

This agreement supplements the above-mentioned business relationship, and takes precedence over any contrary provisions in the agreements between the parties.

1. The assets within restricted assets may be held or booked, individually or collectively (collective custody) by the Custodian Bank in its own facilities, with a domestic correspondent bank, with a domestic or foreign clearing house (examples: SIS SegaIntersettle AG, Euroclear Bank, Clearstream) or with a foreign custodian (Custodian).

   In respect of assets which the Custodian Bank delivers to a correspondent bank, a clearing house or a custodian, it is liable to the depositor for their custody obligations under the principles of Art. 399, para. 2 CO.

2. The Custodian Bank shall mark the custody accounts or accounts maintained by it which hold assets within restricted assets with the legend "Restricted Assets".

   The Depositor shall ensure that only assets within restricted assets are in such custody accounts or accounts.

3. The Custodian Bank acknowledges that the assets held or booked pursuant to para. 2 are intended to secure the claims or policyholders of the Depositor and it expressly states that it will not assert any security interest, retention of title, offset or similar rights in respect thereof, even if the Depositor becomes insolvent after the delivery of the assets or their allocation to restricted assets. The assertion of such rights solely for claims in connec-

[3] Revised Annex to Circular No. 771 D of the Swiss Bankers Association of 9.4.1987.

tion with the maintenance of the custody accounts or accounts (costs, fees, commissions, etc.) are excluded.

If claims are asserted in respect of the assets within restricted assets by third parties (including correspondent banks, clearing houses, custodians), the Custodian Bank shall immediately give notice thereof.

If the Depositor deposits assets in the "restricted assets" custody accounts or accounts which are already subject to a security interest in favor of the Custodian Bank, it can decline to effect the deposit or transfer thereof, demand provision of substitute security or the termination of the security interest.

4. The Depositor alone is solely responsible for compliance with regulatory requirements, in particular those concerning the minimum amount of restricted assets, the assets permitted therein and their composition.

Place/Date	Signed on behalf of the Insurance Institution	Signed on behalf of the Custodian Bank
....	....	....

Annex 5

Listing of limits within restricted assets

The limits are given as a percentage of the required amount of restricted assets

Chap./ Para.	Limit/Credit	Max %	Can a custom limit system be requested	Comment
II.D.b.cc.	**Net exposure per debtor / counterparty** In determining the net exposure, all obligations and capital investment instruments in restricted assets in respect of this party are to be aggregated. If the insurance business invests in more than one company of a group, then the total exposure in respect of this group is to be used. In determining the net exposure, guarantees provided to the insurance business, *e.g.*, in connection with structured products, are to be included. A deduction may be made for security received. Obligations of the federal government, as well as against cantonal banks with a cantonal guarantee, Swiss *Pfandbrief* institutions or AAA-rated countries are excluded from this limit. Foreign bodies are also excluded from this limit if the liability is at all times and in the full amount guaranteed by a country with AAA-rating. This limit may only be exceeded in justified, special cases with the approval of the FINMA. Such a request shall include the details of the investment instruments, as well as about creditworthiness (*e.g.*, rating) of the debtor/counterparty.	5%	no	*Sample calculation of net exposure:* Required Amount 1,000 UBS shares 10 Time deposit/Accounts UBS 5 Bonds UBS 20 Principal guarantee from UBS for a structured product 2 Net open derivatives transactions in respect of UBS Collateral received from UBS CDS (hedging the position) -10 ***Net exposure to UBS* 29 *(2.9%)***

Chap./ Para.	Limit/Credit	Max %	Can a custom limit system be requested	Comment
III.J.d.aa.	The investment per collective capital investment is also limited to 5%. Exceeding this limit is permitted if the prescribed criteria have been fulfilled cumulatively. (See para. III.J.d.aa.).			
II.D.b.cc. ccc.	**Currency Net Exposure** (reduced for FX-Hedging under Art. 79, para. 1, provision i SR) in currencies which are different from the reference currency for the required amount. The portion in foreign currencies which is present in the collective capital investments must be allocated to the exposure.	20%	yes	*Example* Required Amount 100 Direct investments CHF 75 Direct investments EUR 15 Direct investments USD 5 FX exposure in collective capital investments 5 Underlying assets hedged with FX hedging **Net FX exposure 20 (20%)** Required Amount USD Direct investments USD Direct investments CHF **FX Net Exposure: 15 (15%)**

Chap./ Para.	Limit/Credit	Max %	Can a custom limit system be requested	Comment
III.C.b.	**Securitized payment obligations**	10%	no	
	Securitized payment obligations may constitute max. 10% of the required amount.			
	A single investment may not constitute more than 1% of the required amount.			
III.F.b.	**Real Estate**			
	Max. for the entire investment category: 25% of the required amount.	25%	yes	
	A single property may not constitute more than 5% of the required amount.	5%	no	
III.G.c.	**Mortgage Loans**			
	Max. for the entire investment category: 25% of the required amount.	25%	yes	
	An individual mortgage loan may not constitute more than 5% of the required amount.	5%	no	

Chap./ Para.	Limit/Credit	Max %	Can a custom limit system be requested	Comment
	Real estate and mortgage loans combined	35%	yes	
II.E.c. (III.C.a.ee., III.I.c.dd., III.J.d.)	**Equities and similar securities**, which are traded on a regulated market and which can be sold on short notice (Art. 79, para. 1, provision e SR). To be included here are shares in collective capital investments and single-investor funds (provision j), as well as other instruments which increase the exposure to equities (see also, derivative financial instruments, para. III.I.c.dd and structured products, para. III.C.a.ee.). Hedging will be deducted pursuant to Art. 79, para. 1, provision i SR.	30%	yes	
III.H.d.	**Alternative investments** Under Art. 79, para. 1, provision h SR Limit per single fund Limit per fund-of-fund	 10% 1% 5%		For details, see III.H.d.

Chap./ Para.	Limit/Credit	Max %	Can a custom limit system be requested	Comment
III.I.c.	**Derivative Financial Instruments**			For details, see III.H.d.
	Derivatives for hedging payment streams from insurance technical obligations (under para. III.I.b.dd.bbb.) Premiums from open derivative financial instruments for hedging payment streams from insurance technical obligations (options under para. III.I.b.dd.bbb.) are **limited to 5% of the required amount.**	5%	no	
	Derivatives in preparation for acquisitions or to increase income The open derivative financial instruments for purposes of preparing for acquisitions and increasing income are limited to **10% of the required amount.** Derivatives for replication of the strategy (para. III.I.b.ee.bbb.), synthetic bonds (para. III.I.b.dd.aaa.) the sale of call options (para. III.I.b.ff.) are excluded from this limit if all of the conditions of the relevant para. have been fulfilled.	10%	no	

Chap./ Para.	Limit/Credit	Max %	Can a custom limit system be requested	Comment
	Crediting the exposures under the limits for the underlyings Derivatives which increase or reduce investments must be taken into account under the limits for the relevant underlyings. The limits for derivative transactions mentioned above must be observed cumulatively.			
	Securities lending A maximum of 30% of the coverage value of a restricted asset may be loaned. Loaned underlyings are to be taken into account in complying with the prescribed investment limits.	30%	no	

Circular Letter 2008/25
Reporting Obligation of Insurers

Self-reporting Obligation of Insurance Businesses concerning all Events Relevant to Supervision

Reference:	FINMA-RS* 08/25 Reporting Obligation of Insurers
Issued:	20 November 2008
Entry into force:	1 January 2009
Last amendment:	20 November 2008
Regulatory history:	Formerly FOPI Guideline 10/2006 Reporting Obligation of Insurance Businesses of 12 October 2006
Legal basis:	FINMAG Art. 7, para. 1, provision b, Art. 29

* Circular Letter

Table of Contents

I. Circumstances Required to be Reported

1. Events jeopardizing solvency. 1

2. Reduction of the ownership interest in another business below the thresholds of 10, 20, 33 or 50 percent of the capital or voting rights or a change in the ownership interest to such an extent that the business is no longer a subsidiary. 2

3. Criminal proceedings, as well as administrative law proceedings of a supervisory authority against an insurance business or members of its board of directors or its executive board. 3

4. Closing a portfolio in the supplementary health insurance segment. 4

5. Media-relevant events. 5

II. Rationale

A. General

In the Financial Market Supervision Law (FINMAG; SR 956.1), the obligation of the supervised to report to the FINMA is specified in Art. 29, para. 2 FINMAG. 6

With this circular letter, the self-reporting obligation established by Article 29 para. 2 FINMAG which is specifically applicable to insurance business in relation to the FINMA concerning all supervision-relevant events - as distinguished from the reporting obligations clearly defined in individual articles of the Insurance Supervision Law (ISL; SR 961.01) - is described and specified. 7

The Insurance Supervision Law governs, in a comprehensive manner, the reporting obligations of insurance businesses which primarily serve the protection of insureds. The FINMA therefore restricts itself to a few important circumstances in specifying additional reporting obligations based on this provision. This list is then extended to include additional events to the extent this seems necessary and appropriate for the protection of insureds. 8

B. Concerning individual points

Concerning I. 1: Art. 29, para. 2 FINMAG addresses circumstances that point to a possible development that could result in an impairment of solvency and which would not be recognized or would be recognized too late from the information to be submitted annually by insurance businesses. This applies in particular to developments such as a threatened shortfall in the coverage of the solvency margin, a threatened impairment of assets or an adjustment in the value of assets in an amount equal to at least 10% of capital resources or the occurrence of a large loss (e.g., significant civil litigation, especially abroad) 9 which exceeds an amount equal to 10% of capital resources. Also to be mentioned here is the novation / termination of reinsurance contracts to the extent the effect on the balance sheet exceeds an amount equal to 10% of [the insurer's] capital resources.

10 Concerning I. 2: This reporting obligation supplements the provisions of Art. 21 of the ISL in a reasonable manner by also imposing the reporting obligation on a reduction of an ownership interest by an insurance business (domiciled in Switzerland).

11 Concerning I. 3: The following events under point I. 3 must be reported to the FINMA if they have a direct or indirect relationship to the activities of the business or which relate to the business.

12 • The involvement of the business, a member of the board or directors or the executive board in an investigation by a supervisory authority. The application of administrative law measures against the insurance business or against members of the board of directors or the executive board.

13 • Criminal proceedings against an insurance business, involvement of a member of the board of directors or the executive board in criminal proceedings in connection with his or her activities on behalf of the insurance business.

14 • The imposition of penalties on the insurance business. The imposition of penalties on a member of the board of directors or the executive board, to the extent these penalties are related to his or her activities on behalf of the insurance business.

15 Concerning I. 4: The criteria on which the FINMA considers a portfolio to be closed are, above all, the number of new policies in the portfolio in question during a particular period of time, related thereto the age of the insureds and the nature of the risks. In addition, a closed portfolio can be presumed if an insurer offers products with nearly identical benefits, but which differ significantly from one another in the level of the premiums.

16 Concerning I. 5: If an insurance business wants to communicate with the media as of result of a development (communique), the FINMA should be contacted in advance and informed. Especially so if the FINMA is affected by the communication to the media.

Circular Letter 2008/27

Organization of Insurance Groups

Reporting about the Organization of Insurance Groups and Insurance Conglomerates

Reference:	FINMA-RS* 08/27 Organization of Insurance Groups
Issued:	20 November 2008
Entry into force:	1 January 2009
Last amendment:	20 November 2008
Regulatory history:	Formerly FOPI Guideline 13.1/2006 Reporting about the Organization 21 November 2006
Legal basis:	FINMAG Art. 7, para. 1 provision b
	ISL Arts. 22, 67, 75
	SR Arts. 194, 204

* Circular Letter

Table of Contents

I. Starting point

This circular letter describes minimum requirements for reporting about the organization of insurance groups (Groups) and insurance conglomerates (Conglomerates) that are subject to supervision. 1

The basis for this circular letter is Art. 191, para. 2 and para. 4 and Art. 204 SR, pursuant to which the Groups and Conglomerates are required to submit a description of the organization, control and management structure. Changes in one of these three reporting areas are to be reported within 14 days after becoming effective. 2

II. Purpose

The purpose of this notice is to provide the FINMA with comprehensive and timely information about the organization of the Group or Conglomerate. 3

III. Scope of application

This circular letter applies to all Groups and Conglomerates that were subjected to supervision pursuant to administrative order on the following legal basis: 4

- Insurance groups pursuant to Art. 65 ISL;
- Insurance conglomerates pursuant to Art. 73 ISL.

IV. Terms

A. Organizational structure

Organizational structure means the presentation of the division of the Group or Conglomerate in various business segments, such as for example life insurance, nonlife insurance, etc. or other separate major business areas as well as their description. 5

B. Control structure

The control structure comprises the designated members of the board of directors who are responsible for the supervision of the internal control system as well as the audit activities of the internal audit function and the audit firm. The internal control system (ICS) comprises the business-internal processes, methods and measures (group-internal / conglomerate internal directives) 6 which serve to ensure appropriate safety in respect of the risks of conducting business, in particular in respect of the efficacy of business processes, the reliability of financial reporting and compliance with laws and regulations.

C. Management structure

7 The management structure consists of the board of directors and the persons entrusted with management at the group management or conglomerate management level.

Their assigned areas, tasks and responsibilities are to be documented in the articles of incorporation, by-laws, regulations on the delegation of authority and code of conduct.

V. Minimum requirements for reporting

A. Staff organization of the Group/Conglomerate

8 A management structure chart of the management of the Group/Conglomerate showing the management structure and the subordinate level of management, including functional title and the specification of responsibilities where possible.

9 Name, date of appointment or the assumption of the role at that level of management, *curriculum vitae* and description of management duties within the Group/Conglomerate.

10 Name, *curriculum vitae*, description of duties and when the role at this management level was assumed.

B. Description of the organization

11 A description of the organization of the management structure, the tasks and responsibilities of management in the form of an organizational regulation. At a minimum it shall describe:

- Basis and scope of application
- Goals
- Function and procedures of the board of directors
  - Composition
  - Meetings and their frequency
  - Authority to adopt resolutions and the manner of their adoption
  - Minutes

    - Tasks and responsibilities
    - Compensation
    - Conflicts of interest

- Committees of the board of directors
    - Composition
    - Meetings and their frequency
    - Reporting to the board of directors

- Management
    - Appointment and organization
    - Tasks and responsibilities

- Internal audit
    - Appointment and organization
    - Tasks and responsibilities

- Common provisions
    - Signing authority
    - Recusal
    - Entry into force

- Annex 1: Assignment of responsibilities

- Annex 2: List of regular reports to the board of directors and committees

C. Group-internal/Conglomerate-internal directives

A table of the most important directives. This shall comprise, for example, underwriting guidelines for various product lines, claims management guidelines, etc. 12

VI. Initial submission and submission deadlines

The organization, control and management structures are to be submitted for the first time in accordance with requirements specified in the administrative order subjecting [the Group of Conglomerate] to supervision. 13

Circular Letter 2008/28

Structure of Insurance Groups

Reporting on the Structure of Insurance Groups and Insurance Conglomerates

Reference:	FINMA-RS* 08/28 Structure of Insurance Groups
Issued:	20 November 2008
Entry into force:	1 January 2009
Last amendment:	20 November 2008
Regulatory history:	Formerly FOPI Guideline 13.2/2006 Reporting about the Structure 21 November 2006
Legal basis:	FINMAG Art. 7, para. 1 provision b
	ISL Arts. 68, 76
	SR Arts. 192, 204
	CO Art. 665a

* Circular Letter

Table of Contents

I. Starting point

This circular letter describes the minimum requirements for reporting concerning the structure of insurance groups (Groups) and insurance conglomerates (Conglomerates) that are subject to supervision. 1

The basis for this circular letter is Art. 192 and Art. 204 SR. According to Art. 192, para. 1 and Art. 204 SR, Groups/Conglomerates must submit annually a complete group organizational chart to the FINMA. Upon the request of the FINMA, the frequency of the submission can be increased. 2

Pursuant to Art. 192, para. 2 and Art. 204 SR, the creation, the acquisition or the sale (including merger or liquidation) of significant ownership interests by a group or conglomerate company are to be notified to the FINMA. The notice must be given not later than the conclusion of the agreement. 3

Art. 192, para. 3 and Art. 204 SR, give the FINMA the opportunity to define what is to be understood as a significant ownership interest. In this regard, it has to be guided by the size and complexity of the Group or Conglomerate. 4

II. Purpose

The purpose of the notice obligation is to provide the FINMA with comprehensive and timely information about the structure of the Group or Conglomerate. In particular, the FINMA is to be informed about the scope and the change of the nature or geographic scope of business activities, as well as the ownership structure within the Group or Conglomerate. 5

III. Scope of application

This circular letter applies to all Groups/Conglomerates that were subjected to supervision pursuant to administrative order on the following legal basis: 6

- Insurance groups pursuant to Art. 65 ISL;
- Insurance conglomerates pursuant to Art. 73 ISL.

IV. Terms

A. Insurance group and Insurance conglomerate

Both terms are comprehensively described under Art. 65 ISL and Art. 72 ISL. 7

- Two or more business entities compose an economic unit or 8

- are linked to one another through influence or control and
- at least one of them is an insurance business and the Group or the Conglomerate is, taken as a whole, engaged in the business of insurance.

9 Influence or control over a business exists if there is majority voting control or joint management by the same management. 'Joint management by the same management' is understood as all ownership interests which are not held as capital investments.

B. Significant ownership interests

10 Under Art. 665a CO, ownership interests are shares in the capital of another business that are held for purposes of long-term investment and which provide controlling influence. The ownership interest of a group or conglomerate company in another business is to be considered significant when it exceeds thresholds set by the FINMA (see Point V).

C. Group structure chart

11 A group structure chart is to be understood as a tabular as well as a graphical presentation of all entities of the Group/Conglomerate. The hierarchical and functional structure should be listed and depicted in the form of an overview.

V. Principles and thresholds for significant ownership interests

12 The creation, the acquisition or the sale (including merger or liquidation) of significant ownership interests by one of the group or conglomerate companies is to be notified to the FINMA.

13 In determining the significance of an ownership interest for a Group/Conglomerate, the following principles are to be applied:

- The amount of the net assets (NAV) acquired or disposed of is CHF 100 million or more. Net assets is to be understood as the total of the assets minus the short- and long-term liabilities, as well as minority interests.
- The ownership interest's share of the NAV amounts to 1% or more of the reported equity capital of the Group/Conglomerate.

14 In addition, the following criteria apply:

- public interest
  The change in a significant ownership interest (purchase, sale, liquidation, merger, etc.) is often publicized by a news media release by the Group/

Conglomerate. The change is therefore of public interest in the opinion of the Group/Conglomerate, whether national or international. Changes in the structure which in the opinion of the Group/Conglomerate could be of public interest, are to be notified to the FINMA before the public disclosure.

- Changes in the composition of the shareholders of the Group/Conglomerate
  A direct or indirect ownership interest by natural persons or legal entities in the parent company of a Group/Conglomerate which fulfills one of the following conditions are to be notified to the FINMA:
  - A change results in the thresholds of 5, 10, 20, $33^1/_3$, 50 or $66^2/_3$% of the voting rights in the parent company being met, exceeded or reduced below,
  - there is a contractual agreement, pursuant to which a natural person or a legal entity acquires or can exercise significant influence on the parent company.

VI. Minimum requirements for reporting

A. Group structure chart

a) Tabular presentation

The presentation in tabular form shall include at least the following information: 15

- Name of the entity of the Group/Conglomerate;
- Address, including country;
- Function within the Group/Conglomerate: life, nonlife insurer or reinsurance company; holding company; other (to be specified);
- Responsible supervisory authority (if supervised);
- Companies which are part of the group, but which are not consolidated in accordance with the applicable accounting principles. The reasons for non-consolidation are to be given;
- Insurance conglomerates must, in addition, specify whether the company is part of the insurance or finance segment in accordance with Art. 205 SR.

b) Graphical presentation

The graphical presentation consists of an overview diagram, as well as a detailed presentation of the significant ownership interests and sub-groups. 16

In the overview diagram, the company which has the function of the strategic holding company of the Group shall be at the top. The significant ownership interests and sub-groups shall be presented thereunder and shall include a statement of the extent of the ownership interest in %. 17

18 The detailed presentation shall show the ownership interests and sub-groups by country or region with the legal entities that belong to them, again with a statement of the extent of the ownership interest in %.

19 The graphical presentation and the tabular listing are to be submitted in paper form; upon request, a submission in electronic form is possible.

B. Significant ownership interests

20 The creation, the acquisition or the sale a of significant ownership interest by one of the group companies is to be made through the following information:

- Name of the entity of the Group/Conglomerate;
- Address, including country;
- Parent company within the Group/Conglomerate;
- Purpose or function of the company within the Group/Conglomerate;
- Responsible supervisory authority (if supervised);
- Ownership interest in %;
- Value of the net assets

21 The notice must be made in each case in paper form; upon request, a submission in electronic form is also possible. The change of a significant ownership interest in accordance with the principle above which could be of public interest requires advance notice by telephone.

VII. Submission deadlines

A. Initial notice

a) Group structure chart

22 A current listing of the Group/Conglomerate structure is to be submitted for the first time in accordance with the requirements specified in the administrative order subjecting [the insurance business] to supervision.

b) Significant ownership interests

23 The notice obligation arises with inclusion under the Group or Conglomerate supervision.

24 A change in a significant ownership interest is to be notified not later than the conclusion of the agreement. The FINMA is to be informed about the altered structure before the media and the shareholders.

c) Changes in the composition of the shareholders

The notice obligation arises with inclusion under the Group or Conglomerate supervision. 25

Direct or indirect ownership interests or changes in accordance with the thresholds listed above are to be reported to the FINMA without delay. 26

B. Periodic notices

Groups and Conglomerates shall submit the current group organizational chart once each year within 3 months after the close of the year. 27

The legislative body has given FINMA the opportunity to require an increase in the frequency to more often than an annual notice. Reasons for this measure could exist, in particular, if: 28

- the Group/Conglomerate is in a period of accelerated change and therefore the structure changes rapidly;
- the creation, the acquisition, or the sale of significant ownership interests significantly influences the structure;
- the FINMA needs the current status of the structure in order to evaluate the total solvency situation of the Group/Conglomerate at a specific point in time.

Circular Letter 2008/29

Internal Business Transactions of Insurance Groups

Reporting on Internal Business Transactions by Insurance Groups and Insurance Conglomerates

Reference:	FINMA-RS* 08/29 Internal Business Transactions
Issued:	20 November 2008
Entry into force:	1 January 2009
Last amendment:	20 November 2008
Regulatory history:	Formerly FOPI Guideline 13.3/2006 Reporting on Internal Business Transactions of 21 November 2006
Legal basis:	FINMAG Art. 7, para. 1 provision b ISL Arts. 68,76 SR Arts. 193, 194, 204

* Circular Letter

Table of Contents

I. Starting point

This circular letter describes minimum requirements for reporting about the internal business transactions of insurance groups (Groups) and insurance conglomerates (Conglomerates) that are subject to supervision. 1

The basis for this circular letter is Art. 193 and Art. 194 SR and Art 204 SR. Pursuant to Art. 194, para. 1 and Art. 204 SR, Groups/Conglomerates must submit a report to the FINMA on all important group/conglomerate internal transactions within 14 days after their entry into legal force. In addition, the catalog of these group/conglomerate internal transactions is to be reported to the FINMA annually within 3 months after the close of the year. The FINMA can order a more frequent cycle for the submission. 2

According to Art. 193, para. 2 and Art. 204 SR, business and transactions are considered important if they significantly change or will change the financial situation of an individual business or a Group/Conglomerate or the thresholds specified by the FINMA will be exceeded. 3

Art. 194, para. 1 and Art. 204 SR specify that minimum notice periods must be observed for changes during the year and for the year-end notice. In addition, the FINMA may require more frequent reporting when needed. Art. 194, para. 3 and Art. 204 SR give the FINMA the opportunity to issue directions concerning the nature and content of the reporting and to define minimum values for the notice. In this regard, it has to be guided by the size and complexity of the Group or Conglomerate. 4

In Art. 193 and Art. 204 SR, the group/conglomerate internal transactions through which a business obtains support directly or indirectly from another business in the same group are listed. These comprise, in particular, loans, guarantees and off-balance sheet transactions, creditable capital resources, capital investments, internal reinsurance contracts and cost-sharing agreements. In an aggregated entry, all other risk transfer transactions are to be listed. This list forms the basis for the group/conglomerate transactions that must be notified. 5

II. Purpose

The purpose of the notification obligation is comprehensive, timely information, about group/conglomerate internal transactions, focused on the important transactions. 6

In this way it should be ensured that the FINMA has sufficient information to be able to evaluate the effects of the group/conglomerate internal [balance sheet] 7 positions and transactions on the financial situation of individual group/ conglomerate companies and the Group/Conglomerate as a whole.

8 The supervisory interest in group/conglomerate internal transactions is directed, in particular, at the following issues:

- Disclosure of dependencies and/or conflicts of interest of individual businesses in relation to other companies within a Group/Conglomerate;
- Recognition of contagious risks (the risk that one business's problem could affect another business or another part of the Group/Conglomerate);
- Recognition of the circumvention of sectoral regulations (risk of regulatory arbitrage, double gearing, etc.).

III. Scope of application

9 This circular letter applies to all Groups/Conglomerates that were subjected to supervision pursuant to administrative order on the following legal basis:

- Insurance Groups pursuant to Art. 65 ISL;
- Insurance Conglomerates pursuant to Art. 73 ISL.

IV. Terms

A. Group/conglomerate internal transactions

10 Group/conglomerate internal transactions exist if a business of the Group/Conglomerate obtains support directly or indirectly from another business within the Group/Conglomerate for the fulfillment of its obligations. In this regard it is irrelevant whether this is done in a contractual form or in another manner.

B. Categories

11 Under Art. 193, para. 1 SR, the following categories of group internal transactions exist:

Category	Example (not an exhaustive list)
Loans	• Direct and indirect loans between group/conglomerate companies, including the parent/holding companies without capital resource credit • Other forms of cross-financings similar to loans
Guarantees and off-balance sheet transactions	• Guarantees for supplementary capital contributions, for the coverage of losses, to secure financial obligations of subsidiaries (S)/parent companies (PC) • Letters of credit (LC) for the fulfillment of obligations of the S/PC • Letters of intent (LoI) for the fulfillment of obligations of the PC/S • Leasing obligations and contracts within the group • Securities lending, with and without transfer of ownership • Surety bonds • Credit lines for the benefit of potential group-internal obligations arising out of legal disputes with group internal companies.
Business and transactions which are creditable capital resources under Art. 37, para. 2, provision d SR	• Hybrid instruments which have been accepted as creditable capital resources for one of the companies involved, such as, for example, subordinated loans • Mandatory convertible bonds
Capital investments	• Investments in bonds or other instruments for short-term financing (current accounts, time deposits, etc.) through group internal companies • Shares of stock or equity-like securities from S or the PC as a financial investment

Category	Example (not an exhaustive list)
	• Bond placements by group companies in group companies • Options on the shares of companies within the group
Reinsurance transactions	• Group-internal reinsurance and retrocession agreements (pooling) • financial quota share • loss portfolio transfers
Cost-sharing agreements	• Service agreements between group companies (investments, IT-services, personnel costs, group internal outsourcing, etc. • Other mutual compensation
Other risk transfer transactions	• Letters of comfort • Group internal alternative risk transfer transactions • Balance sheet protection structures, as well as, e.g., holding CDS (credit default swaps), • CLN (credit-linked notes), • CDO (collateralized debt obligations) and • other ART instruments of group internal companies

12 There are transactions for which an allocation to more than one category is possible. These transactions are to be allocated to the category which corresponds most closely to the intended purpose.
Example: a subordinated loan belongs in the category "creditable capital resources" if the borrower actually credits it to creditable capital resources. On the other hand, it is to be allocated to "loans" if it does not function as a capital resource.

V. Basic principles

A. Notices about group/conglomerate-internal transactions

Important group/conglomerate-internal transactions are to be reported to the FINMA in the course of the year within 14 days after becoming legally effective. 13

Groups and Conglomerates are in addition required to submit an overview of the existing important group internal transactions once each year. 14

The legislative body has given FINMA the opportunity to require a more frequent submission. Reasons for this measure exist, in particular, if: 15

- the Group is in a period of accelerated change and the portfolio of group-internal transactions is therefore subject to rapid change;
- the change in important group-internal transactions has an effect on the solvency situation of an individual business in the Group/Conglomerate or the Group/Conglomerate as a whole;
- the FINMA needs the current status of the structure in order to be able to evaluate the financial situation of the Group/Conglomerate at a specific point in time.

B. Minimum thresholds for reporting

The [Federal Council] has delegated to FINMA the setting of the minimum thresholds for the notification of important group internal transactions in accordance with the size and complexity of the Group/Conglomerate (Art. 193, para. 2 SR). 16

Group internal transactions always must be notified if they significantly change, or could significantly change, the financial situation of an individual business or the Group/Conglomerate as a whole. 17

This focus on the solvency situation is to be taken into account at the group level, as well as at the level of an individual business. In determining the minimum thresholds, the available capital resources at the Group/Conglomerate level, as well as the capital resources situation of the involved parties is to be taken into account. 18

The following list sets forth the thresholds set by the FINMA: 19

1. A transaction equals or exceeds 1% of the available solvency margin at the Group/Conglomerate level. The basis is the calculation of the available

solvency margin at the end of the preceding financial reporting year. The relevant transaction is to be notified;

or

2. The sum of the nominal values (in the case of reinsurance, the premium) of all categories equals or exceeds 100% of the net assets of one of the involved companies. Net assets are to be understood as the total of the assets, minus the short and long-term liabilities, including minority interests. If this threshold is exceeded, all group/conglomerate internal transactions of this individual company which exceed 20% of net assets are to be reported.

VI. Minimum requirements for reporting

20 Reports must, at a minimum, include the following information:

A. Loans

21
- Names of the involved parties
- Capital resources of the involved parties
- Domicile of the involved parties (country)
- Size (amount, currency)
- Date advanced
- Term
- Interest rate
- Jurisdiction
- Purpose

B. Guarantees and off-balance sheet transactions

22
- Names of the involved parties
- Capital resources of the involved parties
- Domicile of the involved parties (country)
- Size (amount, currency)
- Date issued
- Term
- Place of performance and jurisdiction
- Purpose of the guarantee / off-balance sheet transaction
- Description of the guarantee / off-balance sheet transaction
- Conditions to exercise

C. Business and transactions which are creditable capital resources under Art. 37, para. 2 SR

- Names of the involved parties 23
- Capital resources of the involved parties
- Domicile of the involved parties (country)
- Size (amount, currency, interest rate (if applicable))
- Date issued
- Term
- Purpose

D. Capital investments

- Names of the involved parties 24
- Capital resources of the involved parties
- Nature of the capital investment
- Domicile of the involved parties (country)
- Size (amount, currency)
- Issuer
- Term (if applicable)
- Exercise conditions (if applicable)
- Purpose

E. Reinsurance transactions

- Names of the involved parties 25
- Capital resources of the involved parties
- Domicile of the involved parties (country)
- Size (gross written premium, currency, nominal amount of the risk)
- Type of reinsurance
- Line of primary insurance
- Purpose
- Term
- Retention of the involved parties

F. Cost-sharing agreements

- Names of the involved parties 26
- Capital resources of the involved parties
- Domicile of the involved parties (country)
- Size (amount, currency)
- Date of the agreement
- Term
- Place of performance

- Description of the services covered

G. Other risk transfer transactions

27 • Names of the involved parties
- Capital resources of the involved parties
- Domicile of the involved parties (country)
- Size (amount, currency)
- Description and
- Purpose

28 The annual reporting is to be submitted in the form of a letter; upon request, an electronic submission is possible.

29 The ongoing reporting of important group internal transactions is to be made in the form of a letter in every case; upon request, an additional submission in electronic form is possible.

VII. Initial submission and submission deadlines

A. Annual reporting

30 A current list of group/conglomerate internal transactions is to be submitted for the first time in accordance with the requirements specified in the administrative order subjecting [the insurance business] to supervision.

31 The report on important group/conglomerate internal transactions in accordance with this circular letter is to be submitted to the FINMA within three months after the end of the year (Art. 194, para. 1 AVO and Art. 204 AVO).

B. Ad hoc notices

32 The notice obligation arises with inclusion under the Group or Conglomerate supervision.

33 Notice of an important group-internal transaction is to be submitted within fourteen days after it becomes legally effective.

Circular Letter 2008/30

Solvency I Insurance Groups

Reporting on Solvency I by Insurance Groups and Insurance Conglomerates

Reference:	FINMA-RS* 08/30 Solvency I Insurance Groups
Issued:	20 November 2008
Entry into force:	1 January 2009
Last amendment:	20 November 2008
Regulatory history:	Formerly FOPI Guideline 13.4/2006 Reporting on Solvency I of 21 November 2006
Legal basis:	FINMAG Art. 7, para. 1 provision b
	ISL Arts. 69, 77
	SR Arts. 22-36, 39,198-200, 202, 204, 206
Annex 1:	Spreadsheet for the solvency of insurance groups [omitted]
Annex 2:	Spreadsheet for the solvency of insurance conglomerates [omitted]

* Circular Letter

Table of Contents

I. Starting point

This circular letter sets the minimum requirements for the calculation and reporting of the required, as well as the available, Solvency 1 for insurance groups (Groups) and insurance conglomerates (Conglomerates) for delivery to the responsible supervisory authority. 1

The basis for this circular letter is Art. 69 ISL, as well as Arts. 198-200 SR for Groups and Art. 77 ISL, as well as Arts. 204 and 206 for Conglomerates for the choice of the method and the calculation of both the required, as well as the available solvency margin. For the determination of the nature and manner of reporting to the FINMA, Art. 202 SR is the basis. 2

Under Art. 198 or Art. 204, as applicable, the solvency of Groups and Conglomerates is also to be assessed in accordance with two methods in Art. 22 SR. This circular letter addresses exclusively the first method under Art. 22, para. 1, provision a SR, Solvency I, the determination of the required capital resources based on the volume of business (required solvency margin) and the creditable capital resources (available solvency margin). 3

Under Art. 199, para. 1 AVO, the required solvency margin of a Group is to be calculated on the basis of the consolidated financial statement. Under para. 2, the required solvency margin is equal to the sum of the required solvency margins of the individual segments, such as life insurance, nonlife insurance and reinsurance, etc. Under para. 3, the segment-specific solvency margins of a Group are calculated by analogy in accordance with Arts. 23 ff. SR. Under para. 4, the FINMA may permit other calculations or exclude certain businesses of a Group/Conglomerate. 4

Under Art. 200, para. 1 AVO, the available solvency margin of a group equals, on the basis of a financial statement under internationally recognized accounting principles, the consolidated equity capital, adjusted for minority interests, all intangible assets, anticipated dividends and repayments of capital and capitalized acquisition costs in the nonlife segment. Further, items with the character of capital resources may be accepted by the FINMA upon request. Under para. 3, the FINMA shall specify the creditable capital resources in the case of an accounting standard that is not internationally recognized. 5

Under Art. 204 SR, Arts. 198 and 200 SR are to be applied by analogy for the calculation of the available solvency margin for Conglomerates. This also applies to Art. 202 SR in respect of reporting. The special differences are governed by Art. 206 SR. Under Art. 206, para. 1 SR, the consolidated financial statement is the basis for the calculation of the required solvency margin of a Conglomerate. According to para. 2, the required solvency margin equals the sum of the required solvency margins in the insurance segment and in the fi- 6 nance segment, as well as those for businesses without regulatory capital resources requirements in the finance segment. For the latter, the FINMA specifies the calculation of the solvency requirement. Art. 206, para. 4, provision b allows the FINMA to suspend the capital resources requirements for businesses not subject to supervisory rules to the extent that their inclusion would be inappropriate or misleading.

II. Purpose

7 Solvency I seeks to establish the adequate capitalization of a Group/Conglomerate in accordance with the scope of the business.

III. Scope of application

8 This circular letter applies to all Groups/Conglomerates which were subjected to supervision pursuant to administrative order on the following legal basis:

- Insurance groups pursuant to Art. 65 ISL;
- Insurance conglomerates pursuant to Art. 73 ISL.

IV. Terms

A. Solvency I

9 Under Art. 22 SR, the solvency assessment is made under two methods; on the basis of Solvency I and the Swiss Solvency Test. Under Solvency I, the relationship between the required capital resources based on the scope of the business (required solvency margin) to the creditable capital resources (available solvency margin) is to be understood.

10 The FINMA considers the Solvency I of a Group/Conglomerate is sufficient if the required solvency margin is covered by at least 100% of the available solvency margin.

11 The circular letter on intervention levels governs the resulting measures and provides for intensified supervision by the FINMA for a Group or Conglomerate solvency of less than 150%.

B. Required solvency margin

12 The required solvency margin of a Group is calculated on the basis of the consolidated financial statement of the Group and equals the sum of the required

solvency margins for the segments life insurance, nonlife insurance, reinsurance, plus the group businesses that do not have regulatory capital resources requirements. All consolidated group businesses are to be included in the calculation of the required solvency margin of the group. The FINMA shall specify the capital resources requirement for consolidated group businesses that do not have regulatory capital resources requirements.

The required solvency margin of a Conglomerate is also calculated on the basis of the consolidated financial statement of the Conglomerate. It equals the sum of the required solvency margin for the insurance segment, plus those for the finance segment, as well as those businesses in the finance segment that do not have regulatory capital resources requirements. The FINMA shall specify the calculation of the required solvency margin for businesses in the finance segment that do not have regulatory capital resources requirements. 13

C. Available solvency margin

The available solvency margin of a Group is calculated on the basis of a financial statement under internationally recognized accounting principles. Creditable capital resources are fundamentally considered the result of the following calculation: 14

Reported consolidated equity capital
- plus minority interests
- plus, upon request, approved subordinated loans and hybrid instruments
- plus, upon request, approved items with the characteristics of capital resources
- minus all intangible assets
- minus anticipated dividends and repayments of capital
- minus capitalized acquisition costs in the nonlife segment

Creditable capital resources

For financial statements under a recognized national accounting standard, the same conditions apply. 15

For the available solvency margin of a Conglomerate, the same conditions apply as for Groups. 16

D. Accounting requirements

The calculation of Solvency I is to be based on a financial statement in accordance with internationally recognized accounting principles. Internationally recognized accounting principles are considered to be the International Financial Reporting Standards (IFRS) and United States Generally Accepted Accounting Principles (US GAAP). 17

18 The national accounting standard, Swiss Professional Recommendation on Accounting Standards (Swiss GAAP FER), that also is applied can, upon request to the FINMA, be treated as equivalent to IFRS to the extent that the necessary elements for the calculation of the required and creditable capital resources on a consolidated basis can be separately established.

E. Reporting

19 The calculation of the required and available solvency margin for Groups and Conglomerates is made semi-annually. It constitutes the Group/Conglomerate Solvency 1 and is to be submitted to the FINMA within three months after the close of the relevant full-year or half-year reporting period. The Annexes 1 and 2 to this circular letter are to be used.

V. Principles for the calculation

A. Calculation of the interim (semi-annual) determination of Solvency 1

20 Although the solvency calculation that is to be submitted as of the end of the year is based on the audited consolidated annual figures in the income statement and balance sheet, an extrapolation of the relevant source data to an annual basis is necessary for required solvency margin in the semi-annual report. The company must separately prove the method of extrapolation to the FINMA. For the available solvency margin, however, the consolidated figures in the half-year balance sheet may, analogously to the annual balance sheet, be used.

B. Determination of Solvency 1 for insurance groups

a) The calculation of the required solvency margin

21 Consolidated basis:

For the calculation required solvency margin under Art. 199 SR, the relevant consolidated figures for the three individual primary segments, life insurance, nonlife insurance/health insurance and reinsurance are to be made available. Thereafter, the calculation of the required solvency margin for these three primary segments is made in accordance with the regulatory specifications in Arts. 23-36 SR. For the calculation of the reinsurance quotients only the group-external reinsurance may be credited.

Reinsurance business

Only assumed reinsurance is considered relevant reinsurance business within an insurance group. The group-internal assumed reinsurance is not included. Arts. 23-36 SR apply to the calculation of the required solvency margin. 22

Businesses without regulatory capital resources requirements 23

In the case of businesses in an insurance group without regulatory capital resources requirements, the required solvency margin is currently equal to 0% of net assets.

b) The calculation of the available solvency margin

In order to achieve the maximum possible uniformity, the creditable and non-creditable items for the calculation of the required solvency margin are specified below. 24

Creditable are: 25

1. Consolidated equity capital: This means reported consolidated equity capital on the basis of an internationally recognized accounting statement. For financial statements under a nationally recognized accounting standard, the same conditions apply.

2. Minority interests: If minority interests have not been included in equity capital, they shall be added.

3. Other items with equity capital character are creditable:
   a. Upon request, subordinated loans and loans, as well as hybrid instruments under Art. 200, para. 2 SR if they fulfill the conditions under Art. 39 SR. The evidence of fulfillment of the conditions is to be delivered to the FINMA with the request. For hybrid instruments of a Group, the relative limits under Art. 39 SR, para. 2 SR apply.
   b. Acquired present value of future profits (PVFP): the present value of future profits from acquired insurance contracts (PVFP of newly acquired portfolios included in the purchase price) is creditable analogously to the limits prescribed by the EU.
   c. The following assets, upon request and with persuasive evidence, may be credited for solvency purposes in relation to the FINMA to the extent they are not already reported in equity capital under IFRS/US GAAP. Included here in particular are:
      i. Shareholder dividends in life insurance business that have not been individually allocated.
      ii. Hybrid capital in the form of mandatory convertible securities which, by a certain date must be converted into equity capital, but which

currently have not or only partially have been converted into equity capital.

d. The FINMA may, upon request, in addition permit other items with equity capital character under Art. 200, para. 2 SR. Upon request, it shall decide on their credit.

26 Not creditable and, as applicable, to be deducted are:

1. The following intangible assets, if they have already been included in the calculation of equity capital, are to be deducted:
   a. Goodwill resulting from acquisitions.
   b. PVFP in the form of the present value of insurance contracts [the business] itself has written (PVFP from its own portfolios).
   c. Brands, licenses, trademarks and other intellectual property rights included in assets.
   d. Internally developed data processing programs (software) with limited market value and externally acquired programs without any meaningful resale value that have been included in assets.
   e. Tax credits from loss-carryforwards from earlier losses.

2. Anticipated dividends and repayments of capital (including minority interests): included are also reductions in par value or other types of transactions which target the goal of capital reduction. Anticipated dividends and analogous items are therefore to be deducted from equity capital when the resolution is submitted to the meeting of shareholders.

3. Capitalized acquisition costs in the nonlife segment (deferred acquisition costs non-life): because under Solvency 1 only the legally reclaimable acquisition costs under the redemption valuation rules are permitted, the capitalization effects from multiple-year acquisition costs in the non-life segment (property and casualty insurance, health insurance reinsurance) that already have been taken into account in equity capital are to be deducted.

C. Determination of Solvency I for Insurance Conglomerates

27 Under Art. 204 SR, Art. 198 SR and Arts. 200, 202 and 203 SR, which are controlling for the Solvency I of insurance groups, also are applicable in the case of insurance conglomerates.

a) The calculation of the required solvency margin

28 In the case of insurance conglomerates, the determination of the required solvency margin for the segments insurance, finance and businesses without regulatory capital resources requirements is calculated for each in accordance with the building-block approach. All companies that primarily or entirely serve

the insurance segment are included in the insurance segment, Businesses that cannot be unambiguously allocated are likewise included in the insurance segment.

Arts. 198-199 AVO, as well as the above provisions of this circular letter for the required solvency margin of insurance groups, apply for the specification of the insurance segment of an insurance conglomerate. 29

For the finance segment, the calculation is made in accordance with Art. 206, para. 3 SR on the basis of internationally or nationally recognized accounting principles. The required solvency margin in the finance segment is equal to the capital resources requirements for this segment. The FINMA shall specify which principles are to be applied. 30

b) The calculation of the available solvency margin

The preceding provisions for the calculation of the available solvency margin for insurance groups are also applied to insurance conglomerates. 31

VI. Minimum requirements for reporting

A. Form of reporting

For the Solvency 1 of the Group / Conglomerate, the following reports with the relevant reporting elements are to be submitted: 32

- Report template for insurance group XY → Annex 1
- Report template for insurance conglomerate XY → Annex 2

The reporting should, on one hand, present in detail the various elements of the required and available solvency margin and, on the other hand, show the figures for at least three half-year periods, i.e., the current [period], [the period] six months earlier, [the period] 12 months earlier. 33

Changes in the applied method of calculation, as well as the required and the available solvency margin are to be presented comparatively and explained. Changes in the basis of the calculation, such as the valuation method, changes in assets and liability positions, etc. are to be listed and presented comparatively. 34

B. Changes in the method of calculation

If an insurance group or an insurance conglomerate would like to change the method of calculation, it must submit an application which states the reasons 35 for the change and, in addition, shows the consequences in relation to the previous procedure. These changes require approval.

VII. Initial submission and submission deadlines

A. Initial submission

36 The solvency calculation is to be submitted for the first time in accordance with the administrative order imposing supervision.

37 Along with the initial report on Solvency 1, a comparative table is to be submitted to the FINMA. This presents the individual statements in detail and describes where the figures can be found in the consolidated reporting and how the required, as well as the available, solvency margin is calculated with the individual details. Adjustments in the consolidated figures also are to be shown.

38 The FINMA will state its views in writing on the comparative presentation before the method of calculation is officially accepted. The approval of the procedure does not, however, validate the entire calculation.

B. Periodic reporting

39 The prescribed reporting is to be submitted to the FINMA, in accordance with Art. 220 SR, twice each year within three months after the balance sheet date for the annual financial statements or the interim financial statement, in written as well as simultaneously in electronic form. Upon a justified request, the FINMA can extend this deadline.

VIII. Annexes

40 The reporting chart for Solvency 1 can be found in the Annexes 1 and 2.

Circular Letter 2008/31

Insurance Group Report

Preparation of the Group Report of Insurance Groups and Conglomerates

Reference:	FINMA-RS* 08/31 Insurance Group Report
Issued:	20 November 2008
Entry into force:	1 January 2009
Last amendment:	20 November 2008
Regulatory history:	Formerly FOPI Guideline 13.5/2006 Preparation of the Insurance Group Report of 21 November 2006
Legal basis:	FINMAG Art. 7, para. 1, provision b, Art. 27, para. 1 ISL Art. 25, para. 1, Art. 27, para. 3, Art. 29, para. 2, Arts. 70, 78

* Circular Letter

Table of Contents

I. Starting point

This circular letter describes the minimum requirements for the group report of insurance groups (Groups) and insurance conglomerates (Conglomerates) that are subject to supervision. 1

Under Art. 25, para. 1 ISL, insurance businesses shall issue a business report annually as of 31 December. This must be composed of an annual report and annual financial statements. If the insurance business is part of an insurance group (Group) or an insurance conglomerate (Conglomerate), then a group financial statement is to be submitted. 2

Under Art. 70 and Art. 78 ISL, Arts. 28 and 29 ISL apply by analogy for Groups and Conglomerates. Under Art. 27, para. 1 FINMAG, the audit firm shall issue a report on its audit and submit it to the FINMA. Under Art. 27, para. 3 ISL, the internal auditors shall issue a report at least once a year on their activities and shall submit it to the audit firm. The activity report of the internal auditors is an annex to the audit report of the audit firm in accordance with Art. 27, para. 1 FINMAG. 3

II. Purpose

The group financial statement and the related group report of the Group/Conglomerate should present the financial situation of the group transparently and convey a picture of the business activities of the Group/Conglomerate as accurately as possible. 4

III. Scope of application

This circular letter applies to all Groups/Conglomerates which were subjected to supervision pursuant to an administrative order on the following legal basis: 5

- Insurance groups pursuant to Art. 65 ISL;
- Insurance conglomerates pursuant to Art. 73 ISL.

IV. Terms

A. Group report

The group report consists of the group financial statements of the Group/Conglomerate and the explanatory report of the audit firm. 6

7 The group report addressed to the FINMA is based fundamentally on the consolidated Group/Conglomerate financial statements in accordance with one of the accounting standards approved by the FINMA.

B. Group financial statement

8 Under generally recognized business principles, a group financial statement consists of the annual report and the annual financial statements of the Group/Conglomerate.

9 The annual financial statements consist of the balance sheet, the income statement, the cash flow statement, the equity account, notes on accounting practices, the valuation and consolidation principles applied, as well as an annex with additional explanations on the principal balance sheet items, the income statement and the equity account. The confirmation report of the audit firm constitutes a part of the annual financial statements.

10 On the basis of the recognized accounting standards for the group report of the Group/Conglomerate, an interim report is to be submitted. The interim report of the Group/Conglomerate comprises a semi-annual balance sheet, the income statement for the period just ended, as well as the statement of the equity account.

C. Explanatory report

11 The explanatory report of the audit firm is to be submitted once each year with the group financial statements. The explanatory report of the audit firm consists of the detailed report on the audit results and the activity report of the internal auditors.

V. Basic principles – accounting standards requirements

12 So that the same basis is used universally, the same recognized accounting standards apply as well for the group financial statements as those applied for the calculation of the Solvency 1.

13 Internationally recognized accounting standards are the International Financial Reporting Standards (IFRS) and the United States Generally Accepted Accounting Principles (US GAAP).[1]

14 The national accounting standard, Swiss GAAP FER (Professional Recommendation on Accounting Principles), that also is applied may, upon a request

[1] For the definition of accounting standards requirements see also FINMA-RS 08/30 Solvency I Insurance Groups.

to the FINMA, be treated as equivalent. The request must be made in writing before the initial submission.

The proper application of, and compliance with, the applied accounting standards will be reviewed by the audit firm on the basis of corporate law. 15

The preparation of the interim report is performed in compliance with the chosen accounting standards. The interim report shall use the same valuation and presentation principles as the annual financial statements. Reliability, consistency and continuity are to be maintained. If in the course of the year appropriate periodic determinations are not made, then the relevant estimates and projections are only required to the extent necessary for compliance with the accounting standard for the interim report. 16

VI. Minimum requirements for the group report

A. Content of the group report

a) Annual group financial statements

The following information is part of the group financial statements that are to be submitted annually: 17

1. The annual report of the Group/Conglomerate
2. Audited financial statements, consisting of:
   a. consolidated balance sheet with a comparison of two years
   b. consolidated income statement with a comparison of two years
   c. consolidated cash flow statement
   d. consolidated statement of shareholders' equity, beginning two years before the end of the financial period
   e. An annex with explanations about, among others, the applied accounting standards, the principles of valuation and consolidation
   f. An annex with explanations about, among others, the most important items in the balance sheet, income statement, statement of shareholders' equity, as well as the other information to be provided in accordance with the applied accounting standards
   g. confirmation report of the group auditors.

b) Interim report

The FINMA refers, initially, to the information and explanations contained in the official, published periodic report. 18

19 The interim report must have at least the following elements:

- a half-year balance sheet;
- an income statement consistent with the reporting period;
- a statement of shareholders' equity for the half-year.

20 Explanations about the individual items of the interim report - to the extent they are available - also constitute an element of the report that is to be submitted.

B. Explanations by the audit firm

21 The minimum requirements for the explanatory report of the auditors consists of the detailed report of the audit firm on the examination of the annual financial statements of the Group/Conglomerate, including the activity report of the internal auditors.

VII. Initial submission and submission deadlines

A. Initial Submission

22 The group report is to be submitted for the first time in accordance with the requirements specified in the administrative order subjecting [the insurance business] to supervision.

B. Frequency of the reporting that is to be submitted

23 The group reporting is to be submitted in writing and electronically twice each year:

- as a financial report as of the end of the year and
- as an interim report as of mid-year.

24 They are to be submitted in each case within three months after the close of the financial year or half year.

Circular Letter 2008/32

Corporate Governance of Insurers

Corporate Governance, Risk Management and the Internal Control System for Insurers

Reference:	FINMA-RS* 08/32 Corporate Governance of Insurers
Issued:	20 November 2008
Entry into force:	1 January 2009
Last amendment:	20 November 2008
Regulatory history:	Formerly FOPI Guideline 15/2006 Corporate Governance of 21 November 2006
Legal sources:	FINMAG Art. 7, para. 1 provision b, Art. 29 ISL Arts. 14, 22 27, 67, 75, 76 as well as the related regulation provisions

* Circular Letter

Table of Contents

I. Legal basis, purpose and scope of application

A. Legal basis

This circular letter is based on the following legal basis: Art. 14 and Art. 22 ISL for corporate governance and risk management, Art. 27 ISL for the internal control system, as well as Arts. 67, 68, 75 and 76 ISL in respect of the insurance groups or conglomerates, as well as the related regulation provisions. 1

B. Purpose

This circular letter aims to specify the supervisory regulations for corporate governance (CG), risk management (RM) and the internal control system (ICS). It should establish, in summary and principles-based, a minimum standard for the areas CG, RM and ICS for the insurance businesses subject to supervision. 2

C. Scope of application

These provisions on corporate governance (CG), risk management (RM) and the internal control system (ICS) apply to all insurance businesses, insurance groups and conglomerates that have been subjected to Swiss insurance supervision pursuant to regulatory order in accordance with Art. 2, para. 1, provision a, b ISL, as well as in accordance with Art. 2, para. 1, provision d and Art. 65 and Art. 73 VAG (hereinafter "Businesses"). For health insurers with business subject to the Insurance Contract Law, the rules in the FOPI "Circular Letter" 11/2006 New Laws and Regulations for Private Insurance of 1 November 2006 apply. The provisions [of this circular letter] are applicable by analogy to the branches and offices in Switzerland of insurance businesses domiciled abroad. In the application of these provisions, the complexity and size of the relevant entity is to be taken into account and the principle of proportionality is to be respected. 3

For groups and conglomerates, the implementation in the highest group company is sufficient so long as the supervised individual companies are included in the group-wide control and management processes. 4

II. Definitions and goals

A. Definitions of corporate governance and objectives

Corporate governance includes the principles and structures on the basis of which a business is managed and controlled. Corporate governance aims for a 5 functional balance between the various bodies of the business ("checks and balances"), adequate transparency for business-internal transactions, as well as the reconciliation of the goals of the business with the expectations of the various interest groups. Among these are the policyholders and beneficiaries, the owners, the [insurance] supervisor, as well as the employees. The protection of the policyholders and beneficiaries is of special importance from a regulatory perspective.

B. Definition of risk management

6 Risk management includes the methods and processes which serve the identification, the evaluation, the risk strategies and the risk management measures, the monitoring and the reporting of risks.

C. Definition of internal control system

7 The internal control system comprises the prescribed business-internal processes, methods and measures that serve to ensure appropriate security in respect of the risks of conducting business, in particular in respect of the effectiveness of business processes, the reliability of the financial reporting and the compliance with laws and regulations.

D. Goals of risk management and the internal control system

8 An appropriate risk management (Art. 22 ISL, Arts. 96-98, as well as Art. 195 and 196, para. 2 ISR) and an effective internal control system (Art. 27 ISL) ensure that potential risks are recognized and evaluated early and that measures for the reduction or hedging of significant risks and risk concentrations are applied.

III. Provisions for corporate governance

A. General corporate governance principles

9 Businesses shall take into account the following corporate governance principles and adopt the necessary measures for their implementation:

- Clear documentation of the existing corporate governance structures and reporting processes, e.g., in the articles of incorporation, organizational regulation, as well as the regulation of appointed committees (see Art. 4, para. 2, provision a and b ISL, as well as 191 ISR);
- Compliance with the legal framework and the regulatory requirements relevant to the business's activities;

- Integrity and ethical behavior, as well as a culture of responsibility, for example through
  - the issue of guidelines and instructions which require ethical behavior by the employees of the Business;
  - the adoption of appropriate compensation and incentive systems which serve the long-term interests and the long-term fulfillment of the goals of the business and promote ethical behavior;
  - the recruitment of employees on the basis of the necessary qualifications.
- Compliance with principles for the avoidance of conflicts of interest and misconduct. They issue internal guidelines in this regard, among others in the area of capital investments and hedging instruments. For the latter, the code of conduct of the Occupational Pension Plans applies by analogy as the minimum standard;
- The appointment of a compliance function, to the extent this is appropriate to the size and scale of the Business;
- Periodic and hierarchically appropriate sensitizing of employees in respect of corporate governance, e.g., through training.
- The independence of the internal audit function as an important control function for the monitoring of business activities (Art. 27, para. 1, sentence 2 ISL);
- The creation of an appropriate environment in which the responsible actuary can perform his duties (see Art. 4, para. 2, provision h, Arts. 23-24 ISL, Art. 99 ISR, as well as Arts. 2-4 ISR-FINMA.

B. Board of directors

The following corporate governance principles apply to the board of directors 10
(for mutual companies, these are to be applied by analogy to the governing body).

- The board of directors is, in particular, responsible for the ultimate management , organization and supervision of the Business (Art. 716a, para. 1 CO, see also Arts. 894 ff. CO) and must be constituted so that, as a whole, it can fulfill these obligations (Art. 12, para. 1, first half-sentence ISR). This requires, among other things, an appropriate time commitment as well.
- The members of the board of directors must, collectively, display the necessary strategic insurance knowledge in addition to general professional

knowledge so that [the board of directors] can fulfill its responsibility for the supervision and ultimate management of the Business, in particular in order to understand and evaluate the business, the processes and the risks of the Business (Art. 12, para. 1, second half-sentence ISR);

- The members of the board of directors must be able to provide assurance that business will be conducted in an irreproachable manner, in that they possess appropriate professional knowledge (see above) and appropriate experience (fitness) and a good reputation (properness) (Art. 14 and 67 ISL);
- The members of the board of directors shall arrange their personal and business relationships so that conflicts of interest with the Business are avoided as much as possible;
- The president of the board of directors may not be, as a matter of principle, simultaneously the presiding officer of the executive board (prohibition on double functions under Art. 13 ISR);
- As part of its statutory organizational authority, the board of directors shall, depending on the size and complexity of the business, appoint committees of the board of directors for the purpose of improved management and monitoring (e.g., an audit committee, a nominating committee, or compensation committee);
- The board of directors shall adopt measures so that the principles of this circular letter are implemented.

C. Executive board

11 The following corporate governance principles apply to the executive board (for mutual companies with similar management structures, these apply by analogy).

- The members of the executive board must be able to provide assurance that business will be conducted in an irreproachable manner, in that they possess appropriate professional knowledge and appropriate experience (fitness) and a good reputation (properness) (Art. 14 and 67 ISL);
- The members of the executive board must have the necessary knowledge and appropriate experience for the management of the areas under their control (Art. 14, para. 1 ISR).
- The executive board of a Business must notify the FINMA without delay about all developments that are relevant for supervision (Art. 29, para. 2 FINMAG; see also, FINMA-RS 2008/25 Reporting Obligations of Insurers);

- The members of the executive board shall arrange their personal and business relationships so that conflicts of interest with the Business are avoided as much as possible.

IV. Provision for risk management and the internal control system

A. General principles

- The Business shall ensure a risk management system for all significant risks that is appropriate to [its] business situation and shall document it (Art. 22 ISL and Art. 96 and 97 ISR); 12
- The Business shall implement an internal control system that is appropriate to [its] business situation and effective and shall document it; 13
- The Business shall define the scope and suitability of [its] internal structures and processes, as well as the business-internal organization, responsibility and allocation of responsibilities between risk management and the internal control system; 14
- The Business shall review the processes in the area of the risk management and internal control system and shall promptly adopt important changes; 15
- The Business shall provide sufficient resources for risk management and the internal control system and shall define the reporting process. The Business shall sensitize employees in a hierarchically appropriate manner in respect of the tasks and responsibilities of the risk management and internal control system, e.g., through training; 16
- The Business shall establish a risk strategy that is appropriate to its size and scale and in doing so the risk appetite and risk tolerance shall be taken into account. The risk tolerance is limited by the loss of economic value that a Business is willing to bear or on the basis of appropriate measures is able to bear. It depends on the available resources (capital, HR, IT) and dictates the risk limits. The risk appetite constitutes the risk that the Business is willing to assume within the limit of its capabilities; 17
- The risk management processes and the internal control system comprise the following elements: 18
    - Risk recognition and evaluation (B.);
    - Risk management measures and control activities (C.);

- Information and documentation (D.);
- Monitoring for the purpose of identifying deficiencies and corrective measures (E.).

B. Risk recognition and evaluation

19 • The Business shall take appropriate measures concerning risk recognition and evaluation;

20 • An important part of the process of risk recognition consists of the classification of significant risks;

21 • Risk recognition and evaluation should be performed regularly;

22 • The significant risks are to be identified and evaluated;

23 • The methods for risk recognition and evaluation are to be reviewed regularly and amended as needed;

24 • The risk recognition and evaluation should take into account the current state of the art, in particular in respect of economic and actuarial methods;

25 • The risk recognition and evaluation should incorporate a prospective approach.

C. Risk management measures and control activities

26 • The Business shall adopt appropriate measures in respect of risk management measures and control activities (such as, e.g., guidelines and controls for underwriting, investments, reinsurance, insurance technical reserving, claims management, among others;

27 • The risk management measures should be compatible with the business-internal defined risk appetite and risk tolerance;

28 • The control activities should ensure that the defined measures are observed. Periodically, a report shall be issued about significant noncompliance with limits and measures, as well as the implementation of adopted control measures;

29 • Significant risks should be monitored;

30 • The methods used for risk management measures and control activities are to be reviewed regularly and amended as needed;

- The provisions for risk management measures and control activities should take into account the current state of the art, in particular in respect of economic and actuarial methods; 31

- There must be an appropriate separation of functions between operating and control activities for the prevention of conflicts of interest. 32

D. Information and documentation

- The goals of risk management and the internal control system are to be communicated business-internally on a timely basis to the proper recipients; 33

- The information is to be given to the relevant decision-makers. Information and escalation procedures are to be defined; 34

- The employees must be provided with all information necessary in order to be able to perform the responsibilities of risk management and the internal control system; 35

- Documentation for risk management and the internal control system: 36

    - The risk management and the internal control system are to be documented.

    - The documentation shall comprise, in particular:
        - Organization, including tasks, authorities and responsibilities;
        - Requirements for risk management and the internal control system;
        - Risk strategy, including risk tolerance;
        - Procedures for the identification of significant risks, as well as a statement of the methods, instruments and processes for their identification, measurement and monitoring;
        - Statement of the applicable system of limits for risk exposures, as well as the control mechanism;
        - Business-internal guidelines for risk management, the internal control system and the related procedures.

    - The documentation is to be updated as needed.

- Business internal risk reporting (Art. 96, para. 2, provision e ISR): 37

    - The reporting shall reflect the actual risk situation and risk concentration, including a statement of the methods, instruments and procedures that have led to these assessments;

    - The reporting shall be timely made to the relevant decision-makers;

- ○ The report shall include statements on the effectiveness and the weaknesses of risk management and the internal control system.

38 • Transparency internally and externally: the Business shall regularly inform the various stakeholder groups about:

- ○ Corporate governance;
- ○ The nature of risk management and the internal control system;

E. Monitoring for the purpose of identifying deficiencies and corrective measures (Monitoring)

39 The Business shall evaluate, on the one hand, the existence and functioning of the elements of the risk management and the internal control system and, on the other hand, the improvements in quality over time.

Circular Letter 2008/33

Capital Requirements for Reinsurance Captives

Risk-based Capital Requirements for Reinsurance Captives

Reference:	FINMA-RS* 08/33 Capital Requirements for Reinsurance Captives
Issued:	20 November 2008
Entry into force:	1 January 2009
Last amendment:	20 November 2008
Regulatory history:	Formerly FOPI Guideline 17/2006 Risk-based Capital Requirement of 21 December 2006
Legal basis:	FINMAG Art. 7, para. 1 provision b
	ISL Art. 9
Annex:	Factors for the calculation of the capital requirement for captives not subject to the SST

* Circular Letter

Table of Contents

I. Scope of application

This circular letter applies to all reinsurance captives which under Art. 2, para. 1 of the Supervision Regulation (SR) are exempt from performing the Swiss Solvency Test (SST). 1

II. Determination of the capital requirement

The capital requirement of a reinsurance captive is determined on the basis of insurance technical risk, market risk and credit risk. 2

The capital requirement for the assumption of the insurance technical risk equals the risk gap. The risk gap is understood as the difference between the contractually agreed maximum annual loss and the expected annual premium (after the deduction of any provisions, fees and other costs). If a maximum annual loss was not agreed or if it is unrealistically high, the maximum annual loss can be replaced with, for example, the claims expenses, which is the result of the estimate of 97.5% quintile of the loss ratio. For so-called long-tail business, the development risk must also be taken into account. In this case as well, the annual loss development on the basis of the 97.5% quintile is controlling. Diversification effects between different lines of insurance may be taken into account. 3

The capital requirement for the assumption of market and credit risk will be determined with the assistance of a factor model. The parameter table of the model is located in the annex to this circular letter. 4

The capital components defined in the paragraphs with margin paragraph numbers 2-4 will be added together. An appropriate diversification effect can be deducted from the resulting total. The amount of the diversification effect must be justified. The amount determined in this manner is the capital requirement determined on the basis of the balance sheet requirements. 5

In the case of new [captives], it also applies that the equity capital must be at least high enough so that a possible excess of liabilities over assets under Art. 725, para. 1 CO has no more than a 10% probability of occurring in the first year. The amount determined on this basis is the capital requirement on the basis of the balance sheet requirements. 6

III. Coverage of the capital requirement

If the capital requirement determined on the basis of the solvency requirements exceeds the maximum of the minimum capital and the required Solvency 1 solvency margin, then the FINMA may, upon a justified request, per- 7 mit the coverage of the difference through hybrid instruments with a term of at least 5 years. The hybrid instruments must satisfy the requirements of Art. 39, para. 1 SR.

8 If the capital requirement determined on the basis of the balance sheet requirements exceeds the capital requirement determined on the basis of the solvency requirements, then the FINMA may, upon a justified request, permit the coverage of the difference through hybrid instruments with a term of at least 5 years or through a guarantee from the owner of the reinsurance captive or a third party. A guarantee can only be credited if the guarantor has appropriate creditworthiness.

9 If obligations under the reinsurance contracts are due for which insufficient funds are available, the captive must be able to draw on the guarantee under margin paragraph 8 immediately. The FINMA shall determine the acceptance of the guarantee in each case.

IV. Exceptions

10 If a reinsurance captive is not in agreement with the result of the procedure defined above, then it has the opportunity to perform the SST. The business must prove in this case that it has a risk-bearing capital that equals at least the target capital.

V. Justification

11 Under Art. 2, para. 1 SR, most reinsurance captives are excused from the obligations to perform the SST. The motivation for this article of the regulation is the fact that the risk structure of a reinsurance captive as a rule is much simpler than that of another reinsurance business. Also, in the case of reinsurance captives, the principle that the capital requirement is derived from the risk of the business still applies. This circular letter serves to implement this principle. It is based on Art. 9, ISL, pursuant to which the determination of the necessary solvency margin -- generally understood as the required amount of capital resources under regulatory requirements -- is to take into account, among other things, the risks to which the insurance business is exposed.

12 The risk measure used in margin paragraph number 3 of this circular letter (97.5% quintile) was intentionally set less strictly than the risk measure under the SST (expected shortfall at the 1% level). In the case of reinsurance captives, a greater probability of insolvency can be tolerated than in the case of reinsurance businesses that assume risks from third parties.

Annex

Factors for the calculation of the
capital needs for captives not subject to the SST

1. Market risk	
a) Equities	% of risk capital
Europe & USA	25
Japan & others	30
b) Volatility risk	
Bonds with a term of up to three years	2
Bonds with a term of more than three years	5
Real properties and real estate	35
2. Credit risk	
a) Default risk of bonds	1
Bonds with a rating > "A"	5
Bonds with a rating between "A" and "BBB"	30
Bonds with a rating < "BBB"	to be determined
b) Reinsurance receivables	
Receivables from a reinsurer with a rating > "A"	2
Receivables from a reinsurer with a rating between "A" and "BBB"	10
Receivables from a reinsurer with a rating < "BBB"	60
Receivables from a reinsurer with without a rating	to be determined
3. Risk concentration	
For risk concentrations in respect of individual counterparties (equities, bonds, real estate, loans, etc.) which constitute more than 10% of the risk-bearing capital (equity capital + eligible equity capital components) risk capital must be set aside for volatility and default risks in addition to the capital requirement in accordance with the following factors. The amount of the capital requirement for default risks, volatility risks is limited to 100% of the relevant item.	

Between 10 and 20	15
Between 20 and 30	30
above 30	100

Circular Letter 2008/35

Internal Audit of Insurers

Internal Audit in Insurers

Reference:	FINMA-RS[*] 08/35 Internal Audit of Insurers
Issued:	20 November 2008
Entry into force:	1 January 2009
Last amendment:	20 November 2008
Regulatory history:	Formerly FOPI Guideline 1/2007 Internal Audit of 1 January 2007
Legal basis:	FINMAG Art. 7, para. 1 provision b
	FINMA-PV Art. 10, Art. 26, para. 2
	ISL Art. 4, para. 2, provision b, Art. 5, para. 2, Art. 14, para. 1, provision a, Art. 27, para. 1, sentence 2 and paras. 2 and 3, Arts. 67, 68, 75, 76
	ISR Art. 191, para. 1 and 2, Art. 204

[*] Circular Letter

Table of Contents

I. Starting point

Article 27 ISL directs insurance businesses to appoint an internal audit function[1] that is independent from management. The FINMA can, in justified individual cases, excuse an insurance business from the obligation to appoint an internal audit function. Internal audit is to issue a report on its activities at least once each year and to submit it to the audit firm. 1

The provision also included in Article 27 ISL on the internal control system is elaborated in the FINMA-RS 08/32 Corporate Governance of Insurers. 2

The obligation to establish an internal audit function also applies for insurance groups and conglomerates. In this regard, the FINMA relies on the authority in Articles 68 and 76 ISL to issue regulations for the monitoring of group internal processes and the group-wide risk concentration. 3

The complexity and size of the relevant insurance business or insurance group or conglomerate is to be taken into account in structuring the internal audit function and the principle of proportionality is to be taken into account. 4

II. Purpose

This circular letter aims to specify the supervisory regulations for the internal audit function. They should ensure principles-based, minimum standards for the internal audit function. 5

III. Scope of application

These provisions apply for all insurance businesses, insurance groups and conglomerates that are subject to Swiss insurance supervision. For health insurers with business subject to the Insurance Contract Law, the rules in the FOPI "Circular Letter" 11/2006 New Laws and Regulations for Private Insurance of 1 November 2006 apply. The provisions [of this circular letter] are also applicable to the branches and offices in Switzerland of insurance businesses domiciled abroad. 6

IV. Definition of terms

The internal audit function is an instrument of control of the board of directors. It conducts independent and risk-oriented examinations of the processes and structures of an insurance business, an insurance group or conglomerate. It 7

[1] "Internal audit office" and "inpektorat" (Art. 27, ¶ 1 ISL) , "internal audit" and "internal audit function" are synonyms. In this circular letter the term "internal audit function" is used.

supports the organization in achieving its goals by analyzing and evaluating the effectiveness of risk management, the internal control system, as well as the management and monitoring processes with systematic and goal-oriented methods and by issuing a report thereon.

8 It acts on behalf of the board of directors or the audit committee and issues a report to these bodies.

V. Provisions for internal audit

9 The following provisions, as well as the supplementary "Guidelines for Internal Audit" of the SVIR[2] apply as the standard for the structuring of the internal audit function.

A. Organization

10 The head[3] of the internal audit function shall be appointed by the board of directors. The internal audit function shall be directly subordinate to the board of directors and shall perform the control and review functions delegated to it.

11 In order to ensure collaboration between the board of directors and the internal audit function of insurance businesses, insurance groups or conglomerates, it may be desirable to establish an audit committee with composed of members of the board of directors that meets at regular intervals with the head of the internal audit function.

12 If an audit committee exists, it is recommended that it issues a report on the activities and findings of the internal audit function to the board of directors at least once each year.

13 It is recommended that the board of directors or, if applicable, the audit committee discusses the reports from the internal audit function. Processes should be established that ensure that the recommendations made in a report are addressed and any necessary measures are adopted within a reasonable period of time.

14 It is further recommended that the necessary basis for the internal audit function (meaning, purpose, scope of work and authorities, organization, responsibilities and functional requirements, reporting, etc.) is established in a regulation (audit charter) and that it be approved by the board of directors.

---

2 Swiss Institute of Internal Auditing

3 The functional titles, whether masculine or feminine are gender neutral and refer equally to men and women.

The internal audit function is organizationally independent from operational business activities. It shall operate independently from daily business activities. It shall have unlimited inspection and audit rights within the insurance business. All information is to be provided to it that is necessary for the performance of its audit duties. 15

The performance of the internal audit function cannot be combined with that of the responsible actuary. 16

B. Personnel requirements and professional standards

The internal audit function shall be knowledgeable and staffed with sufficient personnel. The audits are to be performed with the necessary professional care. The professional and management qualifications should fundamentally comport with the following principles: 17

- The members of the internal audit function must, as a group, possess fundamental knowledge, in particular about the business of insurance, insurance audits, corporate governance, risk management and internal control systems. The head of the internal audit function must ensure that business is conducted properly and that the appropriateness of the internal organization (including IT), risk management and internal control system will be evaluated by professionally qualified auditors.
- The internal auditors shall have, in particular, comprehensive knowledge of auditing principles, procedures and techniques, as well as accounting principles and procedures in the area of insurance.
- They understand the business management principles and concepts, the quantitative methods, as well as the computer-based information systems and their risks.
- They possess a basic understanding in the various areas of business management and economics, commercial and tax law.
- Internal auditors shall improve their knowledge, their skills and their other qualifications through regular continuing education.

C. Reporting

The internal audit function shall promptly issue a proper written report on all of the important findings of an audit to the board of directors or, if applicable, the audit committee. Serious deficiencies must be reported to the board of directors (or, if applicable, the audit committee) without delay. 18

19 Processes are to be established which ensure a prompt reporting to, and response from, the board of directors or, if applicable, the audit committee in the event of the discovery of significant problems.

20 The internal audit function shall issue at least once each year a complete report on its audit activities for delivery to the board of directors (or, if applicable, the audit committee). The report is thereafter to be delivered to the audit firm; vice versa, the audit firm shall deliver its audit report to internal audit (Art. 19 Financial Market Audit Firm Regulation). The audit firm and the internal audit function shall coordinate their activities (Art. 26, para. 2 Financial Market Audit Firm Regulation).

D. Quality assurance

21 It is recommended that the internal audit function has a quality review of its work performed by an independent, professionally qualified organization at regular intervals, but at least once every five years. This can be, for example, an audit firm authorized for insurance audits, the internal audit function of another insurance business or an organization to be designated by the Swiss Institute of Internal Auditing.

E. Outsourcing the business's own internal audit function

22 The responsibilities of the internal audit function or parts thereof may, subject to the approval of the FINMA, be outsourced:

a. to the internal audit function of the highest group company, to the extent that the supervised insurance business is included in the group-wide control and management processes;

b. to an audit firm recognized by the FINMA which is independent from the audit firm appointed by the insurance business in accordance with Art. 28 ISL;

c. to an external service provider which is independent from the audit firm appointed by the insurance business in accordance with Art. 28 ISL.

F. Exemption from the obligation to establish an internal audit function

23 Insurance businesses may, in justified cases, be exempted from the obligation to establish an internal audit function if the insurance business does not have a complex risk structure, for example, no significant operational risks, market

and credit risks (including group internal transactions), as well as insurance risks are present.

VI. Entry into force and transition provisions

Repealed 24

Repealed 25

Repealed 26

In the event of changes in the organizational structure or circumstances, applications may be submitted at any time. 27

Circular Letter 2008/39

Unit-linked Life Insurance

Unit-linked Life Insurance

Reference:	FINMA-RS* 08/39 Unit-linked Life Insurance
Issued:	20 November 2008
Entry into force:	1 January 2009
Last amendment:	20 November 2008
Regulatory history:	Formerly FOPI Notice Unit-linked Life Insurance of 20 May 2008
Legal basis:	FINMAG Art. 7, para. 1, provision b
	ISL Art. 23
	SR Arts. 25, 77, 81, 117 and Annex 1

* Circular Letter

Table of Contents

I. Starting point

With the introduction of the new supervisory law[1] on 1 January 2006, the provisions for unit-linked life insurance were fundamentally changed. There are still certain [matters] that are uncertain or unclear in respect of the interpretation of the new regulations. 1

II. Goal

The goal of this circular letter is the presentation of one of the approaches to be used by the FINMA in respect of unit-linked life insurance. In particular, the following questions should be answered: 2

- What requirements are imposed on life insurance in order for it to be classified as unit-linked life insurance? 3
- How is a license obtained for the unit-linked life insurance line of insurance? 4
- How is the required amount of restricted assets for unit-linked life insurance determined and with which assets are the restricted assets to be established? 5
- How is unit-linked life insurance taken into account under Solvency I? 6

The issue of the required minimum capital should, on the other hand, not be answered because this is answered unambiguously and in a manner incapable of being misunderstood in Art. 7 SR. It is also not the objective to specify the treatment of unit-linked life insurance under the Swiss Solvency Test (SST) or the settlement values of unit-linked life insurance. 7

III. Legal sources

The following listed articles of the SR contain, for this circular letter, relevant, specific regulations for unit-linked life insurance. 8

- Art. 25 (Solvency I) 9
- Arts. 77, 81 (restricted assets) 10

---

[1] Federal Law concerning the Supervision of Insurance Businesses of 17 December 2004 (Insurance Supervision Law, ISL; SR 961.01), Regulation on the Supervision of Private Insurance Businesses of 9 November 2005 (Supervisory Regulation, SR; SR 961.011) and the Regulation of the FINMA on the Supervision of Private Insurance Businesses of 9 November 2005 (Insurance Supervisory Regulation-FINMA, ISR-FINMA SR 961.011.1).

11 • Annex 1 (lines of insurance)

12 In addition, Art. 117 SR is relevant.

IV. Characterization of unit-linked life insurance

A. Definition

13 Unit-linked life insurance policies are life insurance contracts under which the survival benefits and the settlement values depend on the price change of securities, other assets or indexes. Here, the securities, other assets or indexes are known to the customer.

B. Explanation of the definition

14 In addition to the survival benefits linked to underlying assets, other contractual components are possible, or partially, even obligatory. Among them are, in particular, death benefits and additional guarantees in the event of survival.

15 Often, the policyholder can select the assets that underlie his or her contract freely, or from prescribed options.

16 Unit-linked life insurance is to be distinguished from classic life insurance with a specified participation in surplus linked to specified reference values. Although the amount of the benefit in the event of survival and the event of death is, depending on the design of the product, absolutely identical, the products are nevertheless distinguishable in that the classic life insurance is based on accumulated capital that earns a fixed rate of interest and not on underlying investments. The difference manifests itself then, in particular, in the calculation of the settlement value.

17 The terms "underlying assets" and "security assets" are used below. Among "underlying assets" are understood to be the assets on which the insurance is based and which determine the benefits under the contract. The "security assets" are, on the other hand, the assets which the insurer holds and with which it establishes restricted assets.

C. Categories

18 Depending on the nature of the assets underlying the contract, unit-linked life insurance is divided in two categories

- unit-linked life insurance for which the underlying assets consist exclusively of shares in open collective capital investments as defined in the CIL[2]; and 19
- life insurance policies linked to internal investment portfolios or other reference assets. 20

In the first category are the life insurance policies in the lines A2.1 through A2.3 under Annex 1 of the SR; in the second are those under the lines A2.4 through A2.6. 21

V. License for insurance line A2

The license is granted for the entirety of line A2 and not for the individual sub-lines A2.1 though A2.6. 22

If an insurance company had a license for the line A3 (unit-linked life insurance) as shown in the Annex to the Life Insurance Regulation (LIR; SR 961.611) as of 31 December 2005, i.e. immediately before the entry into force of the new insurance supervision laws and regulations on 1 January 2006, then this license is valid for the transaction of insurance business under the insurance line A2 under the new SR. 23

VI. Requirements for unit-linked life insurance

A. Underlying assets

For insurance policies under the lines A2.1 through A2.3, only "fund shares" under Annex 1 SR may be used as underlying assets. The SR does not impose any further limitations for the underlying assets. In contrast, it specifies in Art. 81 para. 1, that the security for these contracts may only be provided with shares of open collective capital investments "which fall under the Collective Investment Law of 23 June 2006". In the opinion of the FINMA, Art. 81 para. 1 SR is to be interpreted such that the restricted assets for the savings component of insurance contracts under the lines A2.1 through A2.3 may only be established with shares of open collective capital investments under the CIL. 24

The FINMA holds the view that it does not make sense to secure unit-linked life insurance policies through assets other than the assets which underlie the contract because otherwise an insurance business would bear an additional 25

---

2 Federal Law of 23 June 2006 on the Collective Capital Investments (Collective Investments Law, CIKL; SR 951.31). The open collective capital investments comprise, under Art. 8 CIL, the contractual investment funds and the investment companies with variable capital (SICAV). In particular, shares in foreign collective capital investments may be used as underlying assets for unit-linked life insurance to the extent an approval of the FINMA for it has been granted pursuant to Art. 120 CIL.

investment risk (mismatch). Accordingly, the FINMA considers it impermissible to offer insurance policies under lines A2.1 through A2.3 whose underlying assets are not shares of collective capital investments authorized under the CIL. This is, therefore, not a substantive limitation because insurance policies based on other collective investments can be allocated to the insurance lines the lines A2.4 through A2.6.

26 For the insurance lines the lines A2.4 through A2.6, generally all of the assets, as well as indexes, mentioned in Art. 79, para. 1 SR may be used as underlying and security assets. This results from Art. 81, para. 2 SR, pursuant to which, on one hand, only assets under Art. 79, para. 1 SR may be used for security and, on the other hand, the security must be provided directly with the underlying assets, shares of such assets or assets which are the basis for the index. In the regard, the qualitative requirements in the Investment Guidelines for Insurers (FINMA-RS 08/18) and the limits therein concerning "net exposure in relation to an obligor / counterparty", as well as "securities lending" must be observed. The limits in respect of "net exposure in relation to an obligor / counterparty" may, nevertheless, be exceeded if the policyholder is expressly informed thereof before the conclusion of the contract.

B. Bearing biometric risk by the insurance business

27 A life insurance business generally must bear a minimum biometric risk in respect of each insurance contract. Biometrics risks mean in this context those which are dependent on the duration of the life of the insured person or his or her disability or illness. A contract under which the insurance business does not bear any biometric risk is to be considered a capital redemption transaction (insurance line A6). The assumption of biometric risk can be made through various insurance policy components or constructions:

28 • death benefits insurance which exceeds a payment of the underlying assets

29 • a survival guarantee without or with limited death benefits

30 • disability insurance (in particular premium exemptions in the event of disability)

31 • annuities

32 The minimum biometric risk to be borne for unit-linked life insurance is defined in FINMA RS 08/40.

33 The requirements of the FINMA for the minimum assumption of risk are independent of those of the Federal Tax Administration. Compliance with the re-

quirements of the FINMA does not necessarily imply compliance with the requirements of the FTA for privileged tax status.

VII. Security for unit-linked life insurance

A. Establishment of restricted assets for unit-linked life insurance

Under Art. 77, para. 1, provisions b and c SR, separate restricted assets are to be established for each savings component of insurance contracts under the lines A2.1 through A2.3 and A2.4 through A2.6. E contrario, the components apart from the savings component of the insurance contracts are to be secured with general restricted assets. This applies in particular to the risk component for biometric risk, as well as any guarantees. In this regard, a reserve, calculated on the basis of actuarial principles, is to be established for guarantees which is to be included in the calculation of the required amount for general restricted assets. 34

Guarantees for which an insurance business mirrors the guarantee obligations with assets deserve particular attention. A distinction must be made between an exact mirroring of the guarantee and an approximate mirroring[3]. In the case of the exact mirroring, two situations are to be distinguished: 35

a. If the credit risk remains with the insurer (risk of default on the assets issued by third parties), then the guarantee is to be secured with general restricted assets. 36

b. If the credit risk is transferred to the policyholder, then the guarantee, together with the savings component, is secured in restricted assets for the lines A2.4 through A2.6. (also even if the savings component alone would be allocated to the lines A2.1 through A2.3). 37

Analogously to the exact mirroring, there are two situations to be distinguished in the case of approximate mirroring: 38

a. if the risk that the mirroring assets for the guarantee are insufficient or that the credit risk (risk of default on the assets issued by third parties) or both remain with the insurance business, the guarantee is to be secured with general restricted assets. 39

b. If the credit risk is transferred to the policyholder, then the guarantee, together with the savings component is secured in restricted assets for the 40

[3] Exact mirroring is understood as holding assets, in particular, derivatives, whose value in each case, with the exception of the default of the counterparty, corresponds exactly to the value of the guarantee or amount to be paid on account of the guarantee. Approximate mirroring means in this context the deposit of guarantee assets, whose price volatility is similar, but not in every case identical, with that of the mirrored guarantee.

lines A2.4 through A2.6. (also even if the savings component alone would be allocated to the lines A2.1 through A2.3).[4]

B. Calculation of required amounts of restricted assets for unit-linked life insurance

41 The required amounts of restricted assets for unit-linked life insurance, in accordance with Art. 56 SR, comprise the technical reserves under Art. 55, para. 1 SR and a surcharge in accordance with Art. 18 ISL. The surcharge, pursuant to Art. 1, para. 1, provision a, ISR-FINMA, amounts to 1% for life insurance.

42 According to Art. 1, para. 2 ISR-FINMA, the surcharge of 1% of the required amount does not apply if the insurance business does not bear any investment risk. This is true in every case for restricted assets for unit-linked life insurance. For restricted assets for insurance policies linked to internal investment portfolios or another reference value, this condition is only fulfilled if the establishment of restricted assets is made entirely with the assets underlying the contracts. This is, for example, not the case if an index is replicated not through a derivative, but instead through the assets underlying the index.

C. Establishment of restricted assets for unit-linked life insurance

43 The establishment of restricted assets for unit-linked life insurance, in accordance with Art. 81, para. 1 SR, is to be made with shares of collective capital investments approved pursuant to the CIL. As already mentioned under Section VI. A., the FINMA holds the view that a discrepancy between the underlying and the security assets is neither reasonable nor desirable. The FINMA considers it therefore impermissible that unit-linked life insurance is secured with assets other than the underlying assets because an insurance business otherwise bears an additional investment risk (mismatch). This does not apply to coverage for any surcharge on the required amount in accordance with Art. 1 ISR-FINMA.

44 For the establishment of restricted assets for the insurance lines A2.4 through A2.6, Art. 81, para. 2 SR provides clear requirements. In particular, congruence between the underlying and security assets is explicitly required.

45 For all unit-linked life insurance, the following exception provisions apply:

46 a. If a deadline is set after the due date for the premium for the acquisition of the assets underlying the contract in the contractual documentation, then

---

[4] In this case, one could speak of an exact mirroring because the guarantee of the policyholder is changed and the actual guarantee matches the mirroring exactly.

within this period cash in the amount of the uninvested premium may be credited to restricted assets.

b. if there is excess coverage, then assets under Art. 79, para. 1 SR which may not under any circumstances and at any time have a negative value may be credited to restricted assets. 47

D. Reporting to the FINMA about restricted assets

The general requirements for reporting about restricted assets apply to unit-linked life insurance as for the other insurance lines, but in any case with the following special rules: 48

- For restricted assets for unit-linked life insurance, only the first page (cover page) of the Form G2 is to be completed. 49
- For restricted assets for internal investment portfolios or unit-linked life insurance linked to other reference assets, only the first three pages (cover page and overview of coverage assets) are to be completed. 50

VIII. Treatment of unit-linked life insurance under Solvency I

Under Art. 25, para. 2 SR, the first result for the specification of the required solvency margin for insurance in the lines A2.1 through A2.6 is calculated fundamentally as 1% of 4% of the actuarial reserves, depending on whether the insurer bears an investment risk or not. In the opinion of the FINMA, the following four situations are to be distinguished: 51

- The insurer does not bear any investment risk (corresponds to provision b and d in Section VII. A.): 52
  If the insurer does not give any guarantees or if the risks of the mirroring (credit risk and risk of an inexact mirroring) are lodged with the policyholder, then the insurance for solvency [purposes] is to be taken into account with 1%.
- The insurer bears only the credit risk of the guarantee (corresponds to provision a in Section VII. A.): 53
  If the insurer has delivered a guarantee and mirrored it exactly, then the guarantee for solvency [purposes] is to be taken into account with 4% of the reserves for the guarantee – because the insurer bears an investment risk (specifically credit risk) on this part –, the remainder with 1%.
- The insurer bears the risk of the lack of a mirroring or an approximate mirroring of the guarantee (corresponds to provision c in Section VII. A.): 54

If the insurer has delivered a guarantee and has not mirrored it or only approximately, then for solvency the entire insurance is to be taken into account with 4%.

55 • The insurer cannot exactly mirror the reference asset of the insurance in restricted assets:
If the insurer cannot mirror the reference asset of the insurance in restricted assets, for example, because the insurance relies on an index for which an appropriate derivative is not available, then for solvency the entire insurance is to be taken into account with 4%.

IX. Information to the policyholder

56 An insurance business is required to inform the policyholder before the conclusion of the contract in accordance with the requirements that apply for information to be provided by a fund management to investors in open collective capital investments or by a SICAV under Art. 75 through 77 CIL. The relevant implementing provisions, specifically Arts. 106 and 107, as well as the Annexes 1 and 2 of the CCIR[5], are to be taken into account.

[5] Regulation on the Collective Capital Investments of 22 November 2006 (Collective Capital Investments Regulation, CCIR; SR 951.311).

Circular Letter 2008/40

Life Insurance

Life Insurance

Reference:	FINMA-RS* 08/40 Life Insurance
Issued:	20 November 2008
Entry into force:	1 January 2009
Last amendment:	20 November 2008
Regulatory history:	Formerly FOPI Guideline 1/2008 Life Insurance of 3 October 2008
Legal basis:	FINMAG Art. 7, para. 1 provision b, Art. 29
	ISL Arts. 4, 16, 25 para. 2, Arts. 36, 37
	SR Arts. 54–67, 117, 120, 121, 122, 123, 124, 125, 126, 127, 130, 136–138, 140–153
	ICL Arts. 90, 91
Annex 1:	The question of minimum biometric risk in life insurance
Annex 2:	Explanation of the formula for settlement values

* Circular Letter

Table of Contents

I. Introduction

Considering the existing requirements in the laws and regulations for the business of insurance, the life insurance circular letter sets forth the practice of the FINMA on: 1

- the rating of life insurance contracts not included in the occupational pension plans; 2
- the calculation of settlement values in the case of conversions and redemptions of life insurance contracts; 3
- participation in surpluses in life insurance. 4

Explanations are added in italic type. 5

II. Rating life insurance contracts outside the occupational pension plans

A. Art. 1 Purpose

[1]Arts. 1-9 of this circular letter have as their purpose, in particular, the implementation of Arts. 120-126 AVO. 6

[2]They set minimum requirements for the rating of life insurance contracts as well as the basis to be used for them. 7

B. Art. 2 Scope of Application

Arts. 1-9 of this circular letter apply for: 8

a. Unit-linked life insurance (insurance line A2), other life insurance (insurance line A3), as well as capital redemption transactions (insurance line A6) and tontines (insurance line A7). 9

b. Disability insurance, written as part of life insurance. 10

Arts. 1-9 of this circular letter do not apply to group life insurance written as part of the occupational pension plans (insurance line A1). The rules for this are in FINMA-RS 08/13 Rating Risk Insurance Occupational Pension Plans. 11

Arts. 1-9 of this circular letter also do not apply to accident insurance (insurance line A4), as well as health insurance (insurance line A5). 12

13 *On the other hand, Arts. 1-9 of this circular letter apply, in particular, to the restricted (pillar 3a) and the voluntary (pillar 3b) private pension plans.*

C. Art. 3 Basic principles (Art. 120 SR)

14 [1]In order that a life insurance product can be allocated to the insurance lines A2 and A3, a minimum biometric risk must be insured; that means a minimum part of the insurance benefit must be dependent on the disability, death or survival risk or other biometric risks of the insured person.

15 [2]The minimum share of the insurance benefit that is dependent on biometric risk amounts to 1% of the gross actuarial reserves before the 60th year of life of the insured person and, in the case of unit-linked life insurance, 1% of the value of the shares. From the 60th year of life of the insured person, the minimum share declines linearly to zero in the 80th year of life. In addition the maximum amount of the minimum share is subject to an absolute upper limit of CHF 100,000. Both of the average values for the basis calculation of the biometric risk for the ages 25 through 60 and insurance terms from 10 to 30 years calculated in Annex 1 may, in the case of a new product, be a maximum of 25% less. The requirement formulated in the first sentence of this paragraph for the minimum biometric risk is fulfilled if one of the two average values is met.

16 [3]An insurance business shall allocate life insurance with a savings component in respect of which the policyholder bears capital investment risk to the unit-linked life insurance, insurance line A2.

17 [4]For unit-linked life insurance (insurance lines A2.1, A2.2 and A2.3), it is to be noted that the shares identified under Art. 82, para. 1 SR as "shares of existing investment funds which are subject to the Investment Fund Law of 18 March 1994" are to be understood as open collective capital investments under the Federal Law on the Collective Capital Investments of 23 June 2006 (Collective Investments Law, CIL; SR 951.31).

18 [5]A capital redemption transaction (insurance line A6) is a contractual agreement between a life insurance business and the policyholder concerning the assumption of assets and their management pursuant to a mathematical procedure. It ends at an agreed time or upon the death of the insured person.

19 [6]In order that a life insurance product can be allocated to the insurance line A7 (Tontines), there must be a plan which provides that the amounts paid for the insurance contracts will be collectively capitalized and which governs how the assets so constituted will be distributed to the survivors or the legal successors of the deceased persons.

[7]An insurance business shall allocate contracts which insure too little biometric risk as defined in paragraph 2 to the capital redemption transactions, insurance line A6. Capital redemption transactions may not be described as insurance. 20

[8]An insurance business shall use only actuarially recognized rating models and rating source materials. 21

[9]An insurance business shall, in establishing the rating, appropriately take into account risk-equalization in the insured population, as well as across time. 22

[10]An insurance business shall apply the rating models so that at all times the following rules can be observed without restriction: 23

a. rules concerning insurance technical reserves in life insurance (on the basis of Art. 16 ISL and Arts. 54-67 SR); 24

b. rules concerning settlement values (on the basis of Art. 127 SR) in the following Arts. 10-26; 25

c. rules concerning the participation in surplus (on the basis of Arts. 136-138 SR) in the following Arts. 27-41. 26

Note about abuse: 27

Individual arrangements in the rating of life insurance contracts are permissible as specified in Art. 117, para. 2 SR. 28

Note about the issue of survival benefits guarantees: 29

The regulation in paragraph 3 has as its purpose that the life insurance business must either issue a survival benefits guarantee or grant the policy holder the right to determine the investment of the funds when it accepts funds for investment in the savings component of a life insurance policy. 30

In the case of products with a contractually prescribed link to an internal investment portfolio or in the case of fund products with only one offered fund, the decision of the customer to select that product is already considered the exercise of the determination right. 31

Tax aspects: 32

The allocation of a product to life insurance in the narrow sense does not mean that tax advantages or a tax exemption for credited interest (technical interest and shares of surplus) are simultaneously assured. The tax issues will be regulated by the Federal Tax Administration. 33

Note on the minimum biometric risk (para.2): 34

35 *Two methods for the measurement of biometric risk are explained in the annex to this circular letter which permit an approximate comparison of some different, commonly used life insurance models in respect of their biometric risk content.*

D. Art. 4 Capital markets basis for the rating outside of the occupational pension plans (Art. 121 SR)

36 [1]A maximum technical interest rate is to be observed. The FINMA shall calculate the maximum allowed technical interest rate on a monthly basis and shall post it on the FINMA website (www.finma.ch).

37 [2]If the FINMA lowers the maximum technical interest rate, then the adjustment of the technical interest rate for new policies must be made within 6 months.

38 [3]The FINMA can adjust the maximum technical interest rate if 60% of the rolling 10-year average reference interest rate is, for three consecutive months, 1/4% above or, for three consecutive months, 1/4% below the maximum technical interest rate.

39 [4]The reference interest rate is the spot interest rate of the Swiss National Bank for bonds of the Swiss Confederation with a term of 10 years.

40 *Comment:*

41 *Offers with a technical interest rate that exceeds the reduced maximum technical interest rate may only still be made to the extent the inception of the insurance is within the six-month adjustment period notified by the FINMA.*

42 [5]The FINMA can, upon a justified request of an insurance business, approve higher technical interest rates for specified policy terms or individual products. The FINMA will permit such exceptions, in particular, in the following situations:

43 a. for single-investment contracts with a term for which capital investments are available for the same time period and will be held for the relevant contract term;

44 b. for special offers with initial losses which are financed with free assets of an insurance business. The rules concerning reserves in life insurance and the source materials to be used for the calculation of the required reserve are to be observed;

45 c. for contracts with guarantees in the form of a formula for the technical interest rate that is understandable for the policyholder so that the technical

interest rate follows the movements of the interest rate curve or the interest rate of the underlying investment portfolio.

E. Art. 5 Mortality tables and other biometric and statistical source materials (Art. 122 SR)

[1]Acceptable statistical source materials are those recognized by the FINMA for mortality, disability and other measured biometric risks. An insurance business may also use statistical measurement data derived from its own insurance portfolio as well as segmented statistical measurement data. 46

[2]The measurement data derived from its own insurance portfolio are to be compared with statistical source materials recognized by the FINMA and, if necessary, to be adjusted in accordance with an appropriate statistical procedure recognized by the FINMA. The source materials derived therefrom must be cautious, but nevertheless take into account, in particular, any trends and the precision of the measurement. 47

[3]In the case of a segmentation of the statistical measurement data used, the FINMA is to be informed. 48

[4]The responsible actuary shall ensure that the biometric source materials used are reviewed regularly and replaced with new source materials adjusted on the basis of the most current knowledge as needed, but not later than after 10 years. 49

F. Art. 6 Rating classes and experience rating (Arts. 123 and 124 SR)

The use of rating classes and experience rating, the latter on the basis of the individual contract loss experience in group insurance, is permitted. The experience rating (income and payments accounting, profit formula, bonus/surcharge system) must take into account the structure of the contract, the insured benefits, the number of insured persons, the loss experience which has been tested for plausibility, as well as the expense history. The individual contract loss experience in individual life insurance cannot be taken into account. 50

G. Art. 7 Annual review of the rating source materials

Under Art. 120, para. 2 SR, insurance businesses must review the rating materials annually on the basis of statistical evaluations of their suitability. 51

52 *Note:*

53 *The FINMA selectively verifies compliance with this provision.*

H. Art. 8 Illustrative calculations for unit-linked life insurance

54 [1]If an insurance business gives a policyholder information before a unit-linked insurance policy is sold about the possible future value of the shares, then it must give the policyholder several illustrative calculations of the possible future value, taking into account the contractually specified payments from insurance technical reserves and various returns. One of the scenarios must be based on a defensible estimate of market returns. The other scenarios must show, in an equal number of favorable and unfavorable situations, the variability of the future returns. The assumptions about the return on the underlying capital investments that are made must be stated.

55 [2]An insurance business must give clear notice to the policyholder that the illustrative calculations are based on unreliable assumptions and past returns are not indicative of the future. Further, it must be clearly stated that a contractual obligation cannot be inferred from the illustrative calculations.

56 [3]To the extent that, in the case of unit-linked life insurance, the insured risk benefits and the risk premium are dependent on the actual return on the shares, the policy holder is to be made aware of the possible negative effects of this dependency in an understandable manner.

I. Art. 9 Additional information obligations for unit-linked life insurance (insurance lines A2.1, A2.2 and A2.3).

57 An insurance business must ensure that the prospectus published by the management of the fund or the SICAV is available at no charge before the conclusion of the contract (see Art. 75, para. 3 and Art 76, para. 4 CIL).

III. Calculation of settlement values for conversions and redemptions of life insurance contracts outside the occupational pension plans

A. General provisions

a) Art. 10 Purpose

58 [1]The rules under Arts. 10-26 of this circular letter have as their purpose the specification of the supervisory law requirements for the approval of settlement values.

[2]They do not apply to the settlement amounts which an insurance business offers voluntarily. 59

[3]For the approval of the settlement values, the rating materials and general insurance conditions necessary for the review are to be submitted to the FINMA. 60

[4]Approved settlement values are only to be re-submitted to the FINMA for approval if the definition of the settlement value has changed. 61

b) Art. 11 Scope of application

The rules in Arts. 10-26 of this circular letter apply to unit-linked life insurance (insurance line A2), to other life insurance (insurance line A3), for capital redemption transactions with the exception of disability insurance (insurance line A6) and for tontine transactions (insurance line A7). 62

Explanations: 63

Deferred life insurance in exchange for periodic premiums may not be redeemed, but instead be made premium-free. Therefore the rules under Arts. 12-14 and 17-20 with the general provisions apply to it, as well as Arts. 21-23 for the conversion. If the premiums have been paid for the remaining term, then the insurance coverage must be provided until the lapse of the contract. 64

Accident insurance (line A4) and health insurance (line A5) are not subject to Arts. 10-26 of this circular letter. 65

Group insurance under the occupational pension plans (line A1) is subject to special rules. At the time of the entry into force of this circular letter, it was, in this regard, FINMA-RS 08/12 Revolving Door Principle Occupational Pension Plans. 66

B. Settlement value

a) Art. 12 Definition

[1]The basis for the calculation of the redemption value is the actuarial reserve, calculated in accordance with the same technical basis as the premiums of the relevant contract. 67

[2]In the case of a conversion of a life insurance contract, the settlement value equals the actuarial reserve minus any deduction for unamortized acquisition costs (settlement value in the case of conversion). 68

69 [3]In the case of a redemption of a life insurance contract, the settlement value equals the actuarial reserve minus any deduction for unamortized acquisition costs, as well as any deduction for interest rate risk (settlement value in the case of redemption).

b) Art. 13 Principles, basis and calculation methods

70 [1]A settlement value is appropriate if a balance between the interests of the remaining group of policyholders and those of the surrendering policyholders exists.

71 [2]An insurance business shall include each component of an insurance contract in the calculation with the exception the components insured under the disability, accident and health insurance. For the latter, this can involve a deferred disability annuity or daily cash benefits in the case of illness, accident or a hospital stay.

72 [3]An insurance business may choose other technical source materials or other methods than those used for the calculation of the premium for the insurance contract to the extent that they result in at least equivalent results in all cases. An insurance business must demonstrate that this is so to the FINMA.

73 [4]In the case of a conversion or a partial redemption, a current disability annuity shall continue unless the insurance contract provides for a cash settlement of the annuity. In the case of a full redemption, the settlement amount for a current disability annuity must be appropriately taken into account unless the insurance contract provides for the continued payment of the current disability payments.

c) Art. 14 Deduction for unamortized acquisition costs

74 [1]An insurance business may make a deduction for unamortized acquisition costs in the case of a conversion or a redemption.

75 [2]The Zillmer interest rate that underlies the deduction for unamortized acquisition costs, relates to the present value of the gross premium. It may not exceed the interest rate for acquisition costs calculated in the rating and, in any case, a maximum of 5%. Only capital-accruing insurance policies with a choice of types of premium payments are affected by the limitation to a maximum of 5%.

76 [3]The present value of the gross premium is calculated on the same technical source materials as the premium for the relevant contract. For insurance policies for which the technical interest rate is not defined, the discount interest

rate equals the maximum interest rate permissible under Art. 121 SR when the contract was concluded.

[4]For the use of the maximum Zillmer deduction under para. 2, a modified gross actuarial reserve will be determined, which will be calculated with modified acquisition costs and administration costs. In this regard, the modified acquisition costs amount to a maximum of 5% of the present value of the gross premiums. The remaining part of the sum of the modified acquisition costs and administration costs will be defined as an annual constant during the entire term, such that its present value equals the present value of the total costs minus the present value of the modified acquisition costs. This rule applies regardless of the chosen type of premium payment. The procedure for the specification of the modified gross actuarial reserve is presented in Annex 2. 77

[5]The modified gross actuarial reserves have to take into account the limitation of the deductible acquisition costs under para. 4 for the deduction of the unamortized portion if the charges for costs are not distributed equally over the entire term. 78

[6]If the use of the rule of para. 5 yields results that cannot be justified because of the specific characteristics of a product, then the FINMA can in justified, exceptional cases approve a departure from this rule to the extent that a comparable appropriateness of the settlement is assured. 79

[7]In the case of a conversion or a partial redemption, the deduction is only permissible for the actually converted or redeemed part of the contract. 80

d) Art. 15 Deduction for interest rate risk

[1]In the event of a redemption, an insurance business may, in addition to the deduction under Art. 14, para. 1, make a deduction for interest rate risk, without regard to whether the insurance contract had been financed with periodic premiums or a single payment. The interest rate deduction allows an insurance business, in the event of a redemption, to compensate for losses resulting from rising interest rates which occurred when assets were sold. The interest rate risk deduction may not be made upon the redemption of unit-linked life insurance contracts without a capital guarantee at the end of the policy term. 81

[2]The deduction is determined in relation to the actuarial reserve. An insurance business shall in this regard take into account in particular: 82

a. current and historic 2nd order internal interest rates 83

or

b. current and historical capital market interest rates 84

and in both cases

85 c. the remaining term of the contract.

86 [3]All elements are, upon request, to be made available to the beneficiaries in a manner so that the interest rate deduction can be understood by a knowledgeable person.

e) Art. 16 Guarantee

87 If an insurance business promises financial guarantees in a unit-linked life insurance contract and these guarantees are included in the rating, then these guarantees are to be appropriately taken into account in the calculation of the settlement values.

f) Art. 17 Allocated shares of surplus

88 [1]The settlement value of allocated shares of surplus that are integrated in the actuarial reserve of the original insurance policy will be determined in the same way as the settlement value of the original insurance policy.

89 [2]If, in the case of the accumulation of interest on the allocated shares of surplus, a guaranteed interest rate is used which is at least as high as the technical interest rate for the insurance contract, then in the calculation of the settlement value, the value of the interest accrued up to the date of the calculation, less any applicable interest risk deduction under Article 15, is to be taken into account. If a guaranteed interest rate for the allocated shares of surplus is not provided or if the guarantee is below the technical interest rate, then a deduction for interest rate risk may not be made.

g) Art. 18 Unearned premiums

90 [1]The settlement value for the portion of the premium due during the period after the conversion or redemption is the same as the relevant portion of premium, to the extent this was not applied to the funding of the actuarial reserve.

91 [2]If the share of the premium had contributed to the funding of the actuarial reserve, then its settlement value equals the share of the costs and risk premium after the conversion or redemption date.

h) Art. 19 Pre-contractual information obligations

92 [1]An insurance business must inform the policyholder in writing about the following points before the conclusion of the insurance contract:

a. The forms of conversion and redemption, as well as the relevant legal consequences. 93

b. The specification of the biometric source materials, the technical interest rate and the rules for the determination of the settlement value in the case of conversion and redemption. 94

c. The method for the calculation of the deduction for interest rate risk in accordance with Art. 15. 95

d. A statement of the development of the redemption values and the conversion values before the deduction for interest rate risk and before deductions and costs of third parties. In the case of unit-linked life insurance policies, a statement of value development, with justifiable value projections, is to be produced. 96

e. The nature of, and information about, the extent of the deductions and costs of third parties which are imposed in connection with a redemption. 97

Explanation: 98

The specification of the biometric data under letter b must be designed in a manner so that it is clearly visible from which group of insureds the measurement data were drawn, as well as the measurement period. 99

Under letter e, the nature of the deductions and the costs of third parties and not the actual amount are intended because, in particular, the deductions and the costs of third parties are not predictable during the term. 100

i) Art. 20 Information obligations

[1]An insurance business shall inform the beneficiary, upon request, about the redemption value or the conversion value. If the beneficiary requests additional information for the determination of the redemption value or the conversion value, the following figures must be provided: 101

a. Actuarial reserve 102

b. Deduction for unamortized acquisition costs 103

c. Deduction for interest rate risk 104

d. Any accrued policyholder surplus amount 105

e. The pro rata share of the share of the surplus for the current insurance year 106

107 f. unearned premiums

108 [2]The information must be provided in a manner so that it can be understood by a knowledgeable person.

C. Conversion of the insurance contract

a) Art. 21 Conversion value

109 [1]When the premium payments are terminated, the conversion value equals the remaining, premium-free insurance benefits. For the calculation of the conversion value, the settlement value in the case of a conversion (Art. 12, para. 2) is reduced by the amount of the remaining premiums and used as a single payment for the premium-free insurance benefits.

110 [2]The settlement value in the case of a conversion, as well as the single payment will be calculated with the same technical source materials that were used for the premium calculation of the previous contract.

111 [3]To the extent that the insurance contract provides for it, a conversion may be made into an insurance policy of a different type. The single payment for the premium-free insurance benefits in this case can be made in accordance with the alternative basis provided in the general conditions of the contract to be converted.

b) Art. 22 The converted insurance policy

112 The converted insurance policy must be of the same type as the original life insurance policy. A deviation from this is only possible if:

113 a. the deviation can be technically justified to the FINMA; and

114 b. this deviation is provided for in the general insurance conditions.

115 *Note:*

116 *The general insurance conditions of the converted contract are the same as the general insurance conditions of the prior contract.*

c) Art. 23 Substitution of the conversion with a redemption

117 *The conversion right mandatorily must be provided pursuant to Art. 90, para. 1 of the ICL to the extent that the premiums had been paid for at least 3 years. If a positive actuarial reserve exists, then an insurance business must provide a conversion amount calculated with the assistance of Art. 21.*

An insurance business can offer the policyholder a redemption at the conversion value. If the policyholder accepts the redemption, then an insurance business can make an interest rate risk deduction under Art. 15 to the extent that this was mentioned in its offer. 118

D. Redemption of the insurance contract

a) Art. 24 Basic principle

[1]The payment amount equals the settlement value for a redemption, reduced by the amount of the remaining premiums. In order to avoid adverse selection, the settlement value for a redemption equals, at the most, the total of the benefits for events that are certain to occur. 119

[2]That portion of the settlement value for a redemption which cannot be paid as a consequence of paragraph 1 is to be converted. The provisions concerning a conversion are applicable to this portion. 120

[3]An interest rate risk deduction may only be charged in respect of the paid portion of the settlement value. 121

[4]The FINMA can approve a maximum amount up to which, in deviation from paragraph 2, a payment rather than a conversion can be made. 122

b) Art. 25 Partial redemption of an insurance contract.

[1]In the case of a partial redemption of an insurance contract with a reduction of the premium agreed when the contract was concluded, Art. 24 is applicable by analogy. The reduced premiums may not include acquisition costs which already had been repaid with the partial redemption. 123

[2]In the case of a partial redemption of an insurance contract without a reduction of the premium agreed when the contract was concluded, the acquisition costs already amortized through the partial redemption are to be taken into account in the determination of the new insurance benefits. 124

c) Art. 26 Settlement of the final share of surplus

In the case of a redemption or a conversion of a capital-accruing insurance contract, after half of the agreed contract term the policyholder must be credited a share of at least 50% of the reserves for the final share of surplus. This share increases linearly to 100% at to the end of the agreed contract term. 125

IV. Participation in life insurance surpluses

A. General provisions

a) Art. 27 Purpose

126 Articles 27-41 of this circular letter aim for the implementation of the supervisory law regulations for participation in surplus (Arts. 130-138, as well as 151-153 SR).

b) Art. 28 Scope of application

127 [1]Articles 27-41 of this circular letter apply to the insurance lines A1, A2 and A3 as set forth in SR Annex 1.

128 [2]Policyholder surplus participations within the meaning of this circular letter are only those for which the insurance business can influence the amount of the allocation to the policyholders.

129 *Basic principles:*

130 *In the case of a life insurance policy, a success-linked participation in surplus can be agreed contractually. The participation in surplus serves the purpose of allowing the policyholders to participate in the surpluses earned.*

131 *The participation in surplus will be drawn from the surplus fund of the insurance business and allocated to the insurance contracts entitled to surplus. The surplus fund has the function of smoothing the drawings for the participation in surplus over the years and not allowing them to fluctuate so widely as the annual business results. It can under special conditions serve as a risk absorber.*

c) Art. 29 Surplus plan (Arts. 137, para. 1 and 153, para. 1 SR)

132 [1]The allocation of shares of surplus to policyholders must be made in accordance with a surplus plan.

133 [2]For this purpose, an insurance business shall divide its portfolio of insurance contracts entitled to surplus into sub-portfolios of identical coverages. Distinctions can be made according to technical interest rates, varying types of risk, links to investments, and other criteria. Each sub-portfolio must receive a share of the surplus participation, determined in accordance with recognized insurance-mathematical methods, which takes into account the contribution of the sub-portfolio to the result.

[3]The allocation to the individual insurance policies within the sub-portfolios may not lead to significant inequalities that cannot be justified legally or from a technical insurance perspective (Art. 117, para. 2 SR). 134

d) Art. 30 Reporting to the FINMA (Art. 25 ISL)

An insurance business shall provide a detailed report on surplus in its annual regulatory report (Art. 25, para. 2 ISL). It shall include, in particular, information about the division of the portfolio into sub-portfolios, the system for the allocation of surplus to the sub-portfolios and within sub-portfolios, the selection of the surplus parameters and the amount of the surplus allocation to the sub-portfolios. A estimate of the sources of profit and loss must also be made. It can be made on the basis of a more general segmentation. 135

B. Participation in surplus outside the occupational pension plans

a) Art. 31 Surplus funds (Art. 136 SR)

[1]The surplus fund shall receive an allocation each year. It can also amount to the value zero. 136

[2]After the allocation, drawings of at least 20% are to be made annually from the surplus fund and distributed not later than the following year to the insurance contracts entitled to surplus. 137

[3]An insurance business may only use drawings from the surplus fund for the purpose of allocating the surplus or for the offset of shortfalls pursuant to Art. 136, para. 5 SR. 138

The annual drawings therefore reflect only partially the business results in the current year. A smoothing across the successful and less years occurs. 139

[4]Allocations to insurance contracts that are entitled to surplus, the amount of which cannot be influenced by an insurance business, are not made through the surplus fund. 140

b) Art. 32 Allocation of shares of surplus (Art. 137 SR)

[1]The allocation of surplus to the sub-portfolios must be performed in accordance with recognized actuarial methods. Permitted are: 141

a. a hierarchical specification of the sub-portfolios and a distribution of the surplus from the highest level to the smallest, lowest level in the hierarchy in accordance with the relevant sub-portfolio's share of the result; 142

143 b. a specification of the surplus parameters, such as interest, risk or cost surplus rates per sub-portfolio in relation to the specific characteristics of the sub-portfolio, such as, for example, loss experience or other factors that influence the result. In this regard, the differences between the sub-portfolios or in relation to the overall distribution must be justifiable actuarially;

144 c. other methods or variations to the extent that these are justifiable actuarially.

145 [2]The participation in surplus consists of interest rate, risk and cost components which must be specified per sub-portfolio for the allocation of surplus. The surplus components may be negative and offset against each other. For each sub-portfolio and each contract, however, the sum of the surplus components as well as the share for the current participation in surplus and the share for the final surplus must always be greater than or equal to zero.

146 [3]Within a sub-portfolio, the allocation of the participation in surplus to the individual contracts is generally made proportionally to the reference amounts for the death and disability risk premiums the cost premiums and the actuarial reserves.

147 [4]For exceptional reasons, in particular technical (*e.g.*, administrative systems) or systematic reasons (*e.g.*, surplus annuities), other procedures that deviate from these principles, such as, for example, mechanical procedures, can be applied. In each case, it must be ensured that within a sub-portfolio no significant inequalities arise that cannot be justified legally or from a technical insurance perspective (Art. 117, para. 2 SR).

148 [5]Changes in the allocation methods (such as, among others, the change from current participations in surplus to final shares of surplus or a change in the manner of application) are deemed to be system changes under Art. 137, para. 3 SR.

c) Art. 33 Terminal surplus (Art. 138 SR)

149 [1]A reserve for each contract shall be established for the final share of surplus specified upon the termination of the contract. It is created by drawings from the surplus fund.

150 [2]The claim upon the lapse of the full period of insurance equals the individual contract reserve for the final share of surplus at the time the policy lapses. The individual contract reserve cannot be reduced before the lapse of the policy.

151 [3]The reserve for the final share of surplus is an obligation that is included in the required amount of restricted assets and may not be credited to the coverage of the solvency margin.

[4]Reserves for final shares of surplus that are released as a result of death, redemption or conversion shall be reappropriated to the surplus fund to the extent that they were not credited to the policyholder. The appropriation does not have to be made on an individual contract basis, rather it can be made at the same time as the annual allocation to the surplus fund. 152

The settlement of the right to terminal surplus in the case of a redemption and a conversion is governed by Art. 26. 153

d) Art. 34 Various regulations

[1]In the allocation of surplus, an insurance business may take into account the product-specific relationship between the insurance obligations and the assets allocated to them (ALM[1]), in particular in the case of single premiums and periodic premiums. An insurance business may also calculate and include different guarantee costs, such as for high or low interest payment obligations or for contracts with or without a deduction for interest rate risk upon redemption (Art. 15). 154

[2]If an insurance business gives the policyholder information about the amount of possible future participations in surplus for capital-accruing insurance policies before the conclusion of the contract, then it must give the policyholder several illustrative calculations of the possible participation in surplus on the basis of different interest rates. One of the scenarios must be based on current parameters. The other scenarios must show the variability of the future returns in an equal number of favorable and unfavorable situations. The interest rates used must be disclosed. 155

If exclusively favorable or unrealistically exaggerated illustrative calculations are provided, then the policyholder is deceived about the realistic chances in respect of the total benefits under the contract. This would be abusive under Art. 117, para. 1, provision a SR. 156

[3]An insurance business must give clear notice to the policyholder that the illustrative calculations are based on unreliable assumptions and past returns are not indicative of the future. Further, it must be clearly stated that no contractual obligations can be implied from the illustrative calculations. 157

[4]An inflated allocation of surplus to other policyholders in order to comport with illustrative calculations delivered earlier constitutes an unjustifiable unequal treatment (Art. 117, para. 2 SR). The participation in surplus for current annuities may deviate from this principle. 158

---

[1] ALM: Asset Liability Management or management of assets and liabilities.

159 [5]In the case of single premiums, the participations in surplus for risk and expenses are based, as a rule, on the annually calculated risk and expense premiums. Approximations are permitted, subject to the prohibition abuse.

160 [6]An advance payment of a participation in surplus is permissible to the extent that it is based on relatively stable figures. The advance payment of a participation in surplus may be made only for a single year and must be fixed analogously to the deferred surplus rule.

161 *An advance payment of a participation in surplus is, for example, possible in the case of a pure death benefits insurance policy with annual premiums. the participation in surplus may be advanced and set-off against the annual premium.*

e) Art. 35 Information in the contract documentation

162 [1]An insurance business shall provide the information required by Art. 130 SR in its contractual documentation in a manner that is clear and understandable for policyholders.

163 [2]The information about the forms of surplus allocation shall include, in particular, a description of the principles of the allocation of the participation in surplus drawn from the surplus fund. In addition, the manner in which a participation in surplus is paid in the event of a redemption and death are to be described.

f) Art. 36 Annual information to the policyholder

164 An insurance business must deliver annually an understandable accounting concerning the participation in surplus to the policyholders. The following information is, in particular, to be provided therein:

165 a. the current basis for the calculation of the participation in surplus and the principles of their distribution;

166 b. the amount of the participation in surplus;

167 c. for contracts with terminal surplus: the status of the minimum entitlement to a final share of surplus upon the lapse of the complete contractual term, as well as the status of the reserve for the final surplus that is promised upon redemption;

168 d. for contracts with accrued shares of surplus with interest: the status of the surplus account and the currently accruing interest rate;

e. for contracts with a savings component: the itemization of at least the interest and balance components, as well as a statement of the interest rate for the total interest on the actuarial reserves. 169

It is recommended that, for all contracts for which is possible and useful, an itemization of interest rate, risk and expenses is made. 170

C. Participation in surplus within the occupational pension plans

a) Art. 37 Contractual counterparty in the occupational pension plans

The provisions of this section govern the allocation of surplus to the direct contractual counterparty of the insurance business (policyholder). 171

Included in this category are, in particular, the pension institutions and the holders of voluntary contribution policies. 172

b) Art. 38 Surplus fund (Arts. 151-153 SR)

[1]For transactions within the occupational pension plans, the surplus fund consists of a part for the contracts subject to the minimum quota obligation and a part for the special cases under SR Art. 146. 173

[2]The payment of the funds allocated to the surplus fund to the policyholders pursuant to Art. 152, para. 2 SR must be disclosed to the FINMA in an appropriate manner, such as a tranche accounting. 174

The allocation to the surplus fund for the minimum quota obligation contracts and the exceptional withdrawal for coverage of a negative balance pursuant to Art. 150 SR are governed by the FINMA-RS 08/36 Operating Account of the Occupational Pension Plans. 175

c) Art. 39 Allocation of the shares of surplus (Art. 153 SR)

[1]The allocation to the pension fund institutions should be made in accordance with a method that can consistently be subdivided into the included contracts and their insured policies. 176

[2]The surplus allocation is normally made analogously to the rules for transactions outside of the occupational pension plans as they were described in Art. 32. 177

[3]In the allocation of surplus, the loss experience of group [insurance] which has been tested for plausibility through the size [of the portfolio] and the duration of the observation period, as well as the cost experience may be taken 178

into account. In group insurance, negative surplus components may be offset with positive [components].

179 *The provisions of this section do not govern the distribution of a participation in surplus declared to a pension institution on the included contracts.*

d) Art. 40 Information in the contractual documentation

180 [1]An insurance business shall provide the information required under Art. 130 SR in its contractual documentation in a manner that is clear and understandable for policyholders.

181 [2]The information about the ways in which surplus is allocated includes, in particular, the description of the principles of the allocation of the participation in surplus withdrawn from the surplus fund.

e) Art. 41 Annual information to the policyholder

182 An insurance business must deliver annually an understandable accounting concerning the participation in surplus. The following information is, in particular, to be provided therein:

183 a. the current basis for the calculation of the participation in surplus and the principles of its distribution;

184 b. the amount of the participation in surplus;

185 c. for contracts with a savings component: an itemization of at least the interest and balance components, as well as a statement of the interest rate for the total interest on the actuarial reserve.

186 *It is recommended that an itemization by interest rate, risk and expenses be performed for all contracts.*

187 *The information for policyholders about the operating account is governed by the FINMA-RS 08/36 Operating Account of the Occupational Pension Plans.*

V. Final provisions

Art. 42 Entry into force and transition provisions

188 [1]This circular letter enters into force on 1 January 2009.

189 [2]It replaces all guidelines of the former FOPI on the technical interest rate in individual life insurance, in particular those of 11 June 2003.

[3]It applies to insurance contracts which were entered into for new products introduced to the market from 1 July 2009 to the extent that no contrary rules are defined in the following paragraphs. 190

[4]For insurance contracts on the basis of existing products as of 1 January 2009, the regulations in Arts. 10-26 apply to contracts concluded from 1 January 2011. 191

[5]The regulations concerning participation in surpluses in life insurance business apply, subject to the following paragraphs 6, 7, and 8 for contracts already in existence from 1 January 2010 as well. 192

[6]The rules for information to policyholders about the participation in surplus under Arts. 35, 36, 40 and 41 must be implemented for new and existing contracts by 1 January 2011. 193

[7]Information about the division of the portfolio into sub-portfolios, about the system distributing the surplus to the sub-portfolios, the selection of the surplus parameters and the amount of the surplus allocation to the sub-portfolios, as well as the estimate of the sources of profit and loss are to be delivered to the FINMA for the first time, along with the detailed surplus report (see Art. 30), for the year 2008 in the second half of 2009. If the surplus report cannot be delivered by the prescribed deadline, a request for a different procedure is to be submitted to the FINMA with a statement of reasons. 194

[8]The itemization of the surplus components by interest rate surplus and other surplus in connection with the calculation of the surplus allocation at the contract level (see Art. 32) and in connection with the annual reporting to the policyholders (see Art. 36) is not applicable - as an exception to para. 6 - in the case of mechanical surplus systems for contracts concluded before 1 January 2011. 195

[9]The rules for the illustrative calculations for unit-linked life insurance under Art. 8, as well as the illustrative calculations for the possible future participation in surplus under Art. 34, must be implemented by 1 January 2011 for new contracts to be made. 196

[10]For existing contracts with final surpluses, an insurance business shall establish reserves for the terminal share of surplus. This can be done incrementally over several years. An insurance business must submit a plan for the funding of these reserves to the FINMA by 30 June 2009. 197

Annex 1

The issue of minimum biometric risk in life insurance

I. Starting point

1 The basis for the minimum biometric risk approach is constituted by the mixed insurance for an annual premium, provided that the death benefits capital in each year is approximately 1% more than the net actuarial reserves. This means that the expenses for the biometric risk must correspond to a minimum relationship to the death benefits risk premium for a single payment or to the average actuarial reserves.

II Risk measurement for life insurance products

2 The measurement of risk for life insurance products is performed in accordance with 2 methods:

A. Risk premium in relation to gross premium

3

x	= age
n	= insurance policy term
t	= x. . .x + n
BWRP(t	= present value of the risk premium at age t
BP(t)	= gross premium at age t
BP	= leveled annual premium, gross
EP	= gross single premium

General formula for the relationship: $$\frac{\frac{1}{n}\sum_{t=x}^{x+n} BWRP(t)}{\frac{1}{n}\sum_{t=x}^{x+n} BP(t)}$$

Special cases:

Level annual premium: $$\frac{\frac{1}{n}\sum_{t=x}^{x+n} BWRP(t)}{JP}$$

single premium: $$\frac{\frac{1}{n}\sum_{t=x}^{x+n} BWRP(t)}{\frac{1}{n}EP}$$

B. Risk premium in relation to net actuarial reserves

4

x	= age
n	= insurance policy term
t	= x. . .x + n
BWRP(t	= present value of the risk premium at age t
NDK	= net actuarial reserves at age t

Formula for the relationship
$$\frac{\sum_{t=x}^{x+n} BWRP\ (t)}{\left(\frac{\sum_{t=x}^{x+n} NDK\ (t)}{n}\right)}$$

The calculation of the above parameters is performed for the succeeding age (x) and insurance term (n):

x/n	10	15	20	25	30
25	x	x	x	x	[x]
30	x	x	x	[x]	[x]
35	x	x	[x]	[x]	[x]
40	x	[x]	[x]	[x]	[x]
45	[x]	[x]	[x]	[x]	x
50	[x]	[x]	[x]	x	x
55	[x]	[x]	x	x	x
60	[x]	x	x	x	x
65	x	x	x	x	
70	x	x	x		
75	x	x			
80	x				

The basis for the minimum risk is constituted by the mixed insurance for an annual premium, provided that the death benefits capital in each year is approximately 1% more than the net actuarial reserves. From age 60 or later, the biometric risk may be set in linear increments sinking to 0 at age 80. From age 80, biometric risk in the product is no longer required. The following calculations include a linear reduction of the biometric risk from age 70 to age 80 (no remaining biometric risk). For the product, the risk of which is calculated, the above parameters for all required ages x and insurance terms n are to be calculated and to be compared with the basis (parameters of insurance product in question / parameter basis). From this comparison, an average value for the insurance terms 10 years (ages 45 to 60), 15 years (ages 40 to 55), 20 years (ages 35 to 50), 25 years (ages 30 to 45) and 30 years (ages 25 to 40) will be determined. 5

6 This average value, for the insurance product in question, in the case of the first method (risk premium in relation to gross premium), has to amount to at least 75% (in relation to the base mixed insurance for an annual premium, provided that the death benefit capital in each year is to approximately 1% greater than the net actuarial reserves. In the case of the second method, (risk premium in relation to net actuarial reserves) must also amount to 75% of this average value. It is sufficient if one of the two conditions is satisfied.

7 Below [are] the values of the base (mixed insurance for an annual premium), provided that the death benefit capital in each year is to be approximately 1% greater than the actuarial reserves. From age 70, the biometric risk sinks to 0 at age 80 in the following calculations):

8

RP / NDK	n		Average value		0.114%
x	10	15	20	25	30
25	0.012%	0.017%	0.025%	0.038%	0.059%
30	0.013%	0.021%	0.035%	0.058%	0.092%
35	0.016%	0.031%	0.055%	0.091%	0.144%
40	0.025%	0.050%	0.067%	0.142%	0.217%
45	0.040%	0.079%	0.137%	0.214%	0.278%
50	0.065%	0.124%	0.204%	0.268%	0.290%
55	0.101%	0.184%	0.248%	0.265%	0.206%
60	0.148%	0.214%	0.225%	0.175%	0.142%
65	0.159%	0.160%	0.117%	0.092%	0.074%
70	0.092%	0.061%	0.045%	0.035%	0.029%
75	0.014%	0.009%	0.007%	0.005%	
80	0.000%	0.000%	0.000%		
85	0.000%	0.000%			

9

RP / NDK	n		Average value		0.061%
x	10	15	20	25	30
25	0.006%	0.009%	0.013%	0.020%	0.032%
30	0.007%	0.011%	0.019%	0.031%	0.050%
35	0.009%	0.016%	0.029%	0.048%	0.078%
40	0.13%	0.026%	0.046%	0.076%	0.118%
45	0.21%	0.042%	0.072%	0.114%	0.151%
50	0.034%	0.065%	0.108%	0.144%	0.159%
55	0.053%	0.096%	0.131%	0.142%	0.113%
60	0.078%	0.112%	0.119%	0.095%	0.079%
65	0.084%	0.084%	0.062%	0.050%	0.041%
70	0.049%	0.032%	0.024%	0.019%	0.016%
75	0.008%	0.005%	0.004%	0.003%	
80	0.000%	0.000%	0.000%		
85	0.000%	0.000%			

III. Comparison of the biometric risk in the case of a customary life insurance rating with the minimum biometric risk pursuant to para. II

The figures in the following tables give the factor which exists between the basis above and the relevant insurance product under consideration. Accordingly, for example, a factor of 11.6 in the following table means that the biometric risk is this factor greater in relation to the basis above. 10

Mixed insurance for a single premium (death benefit capital = survival benefit capital): 11

RP / NDK			Average value		15.5
	n				
x	10	15	20	25	30
25	11.6	18.5	24.1	27.3	28.9
30	10.1	15.1	18.6	21.1	23.1
35	8.9	12.8	15.8	18.5	21.1
40	8.1	11.7	14.9	17.9	21.0
45	7.8	11.5	14.9	18.3	24.6
50	7.9	11.7	15.5	21.9	34.2
55	8.1	12.2	18.9	32.1	68.0
60	8.4	15.4	29.9	68.1	134.9
65	11.2	29.1	80.4	178.9	337.4
70	27.3	108.3	291.8	614.1	1091.1
75	273.5	1040.3	2596.1	5077.8	

RP / BP	Average value				24.7
	n				
x	10	15	20	25	30
25	20.1	31.8	40.3	44.4	45.2
30	17.3	25.8	31.1	34.1	35.8
35	15.3	21.8	26.3	29.6	32.1
40	13.9	19.8	24.4	28.0	30.9
45	13.4	19.3	24.0	27.8	34.5
50	13.4	19.4	24.2	31.9	45.1
55	13.5	19.6	28.5	43.8	81.1
60	13.7	23.9	42.4	84.4	138.1
65	17.8	43.0	103.7	189.6	279.3
70	41.7	145.9	321.0	520.6	694.9
75	383.0	192.3	2263.6	3258.2	

Mixed insurance for an annual premium (death benefit capital = survival benefit capital): 12

RP / NDK			Average value		15.5
	n				
x	10	15	20	25	30
25	277.8	351.7	379.3	362.1	321.3
30	224.6	256.5	251.8	229.3	203.8
35	189.6	199.7	190.2	175.4	161.1
40	165.1	171.1	165.9	157.8	151.3
45	157.3	166.1	165.3	163.0	181.0
50	160.9	174.1	179.3	207.3	271.1
55	169.0	190.3	235.8	330.3	584.7
60	183.1	258.7	407.0	762.3	1248.2
65	260.2	526.8	1168.2	2112.4	3316.1
70	662.0	2025.7	4358.4	7559.5	1.E+04
75	6890.9	2.E+04	4.E+04	7.E+04	

RP / BP	Average value				24.7
	n				
x	10	15	20	25	30
25	99.0	104.4	99.4	87.4	74.1
30	85.5	84.8	76.7	67.1	58.7
35	75.6	71.6	64.8	58.3	52.6
40	68.6	65.1	60.1	55.2	50.8
45	66.1	63.5	59.2	54.9	56.7
50	66.0	63.7	59.7	62.8	74.0
55	66.5	64.5	70.1	86.3	133.3
60	67.4	78.7	104.5	166.4	226.9
65	88.0	141.3	255.8	373.9	459.0
70	205.6	479.8	791.6	1027.0	1142.2
75	1889.8	3921.3	5583.0	6428.6	

13 Cash accumulation with premium waiver in the event of disability:

RP / NDK	n			Average value	132.9
x	10	15	20	25	30
25	876.5	661.2	485.4	336.9	225.5
30	810.2	535.1	347.3	223.1	145.0
35	618.6	365.8	223.4	141.4	92.9
40	406.2	230.0	140.2	90.3	61.5
45	251.3	143.5	89.5	60.1	48.0
50	156.7	92.0	59.9	47.9	46.0
55	101.0	62.1	49.2	48.5	64.8
60	68.7	53.4	54.4	73.3	94.0
65	64.1	71.4	104.2	140.4	179.9
70	110.0	185.6	270.7	364.7	467.2
75	719.4	1213.8	1770.8	2386.3	

RP / BP	n	Average value			60.7
x	10	15	20	25	30
25	518.9	336.0	217.5	134.9	81.3
30	479.9	271.9	155.4	89.1	52.0
35	366.0	185.4	99.5	56.0	32.9
40	239.7	116.0	61.8	35.2	21.3
45	147.5	71.6	38.8	22.8	16.1
50	91.1	45.1	25.3	17.6	14.7
55	57.9	29.7	20.0	16.9	19.2
60	38.5	24.6	21.0	23.6	25.1
65	35.0	31.4	37.2	40.5	42.0
70	57.7	75.6	85.8	90.2	91.6
75	349.4	432.1	468.1	479.3	

14 These 3 examples deal with 3 typical life insurance products which are sold in Switzerland and, subject to compliance with conditions imposed by the Federal Tax Administration, are tax advantaged as retirement savings products under voluntary retirement savings. The last two are also accepted for the 3a third pillar.

15 Mixed insurance for a annual premiums (death benefit capital = 105% of the net actuarial reserves):

RP / NDK	n			Average value	5.7
x	10	15	20	25	30
25	6.0	6.2	6.3	6.2	6.3
30	5.6	5.7	5.7	5.8	6.0
35	5.3	5.4	5.5	5.7	6.1
40	5.2	5.3	5.5	5.9	6.5
45	5.2	5.4	5.7	6.2	8.0
50	5.3	5.6	6.0	7.8	12.8
55	5.4	5.9	7.7	13.1	34.8
60	5.7	7.7	13.9	37.8	113.7
65	8.0	16.7	50.3	158.8	629.0
70	21.9	81.2	279.8	1119.0	6234.8
75	271.3	1107.8	4602.8	6.E+04	

RP / BP	n	Average value			5.0
x	10	15	20	25	30
25	5.0	5.0	5.0	5.0	5.0
30	5.0	5.0	5.0	5.0	5.0
35	5.0	5.0	5.0	5.0	5.0
40	5.0	5.0	5.0	5.0	5.0
45	5.0	5.0	5.0	5.0	5.7
50	5.0	5.0	5.0	5.8	8.0
55	5.0	5.0	5.9	8.6	17.6
60	5.0	6.1	9.6	20.3	38.6
65	6.6	12.2	29.0	58.7	103.5
70	17.2	50.8	113.5	210.5	345.4
75	185.5	496.9	1000.9	1712.1	

Mixed insurance for a annual premiums (death benefit capital = 110% of the net actuarial reserves): 16

RP / NDK			Average value	11.5
	n				
x	10	15	20	25	30
25	11.9	12.4	12.5	12.5	12.6
30	11.2	11.4	11.4	11.6	12.1
35	10.7	10.8	11.0	11.4	12.3
40	10.4	10.6	11.0	11.8	13.0
45	10.4	10.7	11.4	12.5	16.1
50	10.6	11.1	12.1	15.7	26.0
55	10.9	11.8	15.5	26.6	71.9
60	11.5	15.6	28.2	77.6	246.3
65	16.0	33.7	103.0	340.3	1787.4
70	44.1	165.6	592.3	2892.2	6240.8
75	550.7	2315.5	1.E+04	1.E+05	

RP / BP	Average value				10.0
	n				
x	10	15	20	25	30
25	10.0	10.0	10.0	10.0	10.0
30	10.0	10.0	10.0	10.0	10.0
35	10.0	10.0	10.0	10.0	10.0
40	10.0	10.0	10.0	10.0	10.0
45	10.0	10.0	10.0	10.0	11.3
50	10.0	10.0	10.0	115	16.1
55	10.0	10.0	11.8	17.2	35.3
60	10.0	12.2	19.2	40.6	77.3
65	13.2	24.4	58.0	117.3	207.1
70	34.5	101.6	226.9	420.9	690.7
75	370.9	993.8	2001.9	3424.2	

Both of these life insurance products are presented specially in connection with the accounting standards under IFRS 4. 17

Note on the accounting standard under IFRS 4: 18

The international accounting standard IFRS 4 divides life insurance contracts into two groups: 19
Contracts which include a significant biometric risk and others.

The Swiss Association of Actuaries recommends that significance should be estimated on the basis of a comparison between the insured benefit and the actuarial reserves. A risk amount equal to 10% of the actuarial reserves is identified as significant by the Swiss Association of Actuaries. In the gray area between 5 and 10%, the contracts first should be reviewed individually. If they do not pass this review, they must be accounted for as financial contracts under IAS 32/39 or they are covered by the exception rule for hybrid contracts with surplus rights under IFRS 4, §34 or §35. 20

Regardless of the method of financial reporting under IFRS 4, the rule under Chapter 2, Annex 1 sets a minimum standard. If it is fulfilled, then a life insurance contract for the private pension fund, 3a or 3b, classic or unit-linked exists. 21

Annex 2

Explanation of the formula for settlement values

I. Terminology and basis

1 For the purpose of this Annex, the term *settlement value* does not include the deduction for interest rate risk.

2 The calculations for the settlement value are based on the rating source materials when the contract was concluded.

3 The terms *gross* and *net* are used as substitutes for *with* and without *costs*.

II. Condition

4 The condition is especially dependent on the gross actuarial reserves for a modified product. In this regard, the acquisition costs of the modified product amount to 5% of the present value of the premium. The modified other costs are defined as an annual constant so that their present value equals the present value of the total costs, minus the modified acquisition costs. The excess costs therefore are distributed equally across the entire term.

The settlement value should then satisfy the following condition (+):

5 $\textit{Settlement value}_t \geq \max \{2/3 \cdot \textit{InventarDK}_t; \textit{BruttoDK}_t; \textit{BruttoDK}_t^{mod};\}$ (+)

6 In this regard, $\textit{InventarDK}_t$ is to be understood as the actuarial reserve for the normal product, *i.e.*, the net actuarial reserve plus the actuarial reserve for administrative costs, without taking into account the (negative) actuarial reserve for acquisition costs. $\textit{BruttoDK}_t$ is the total actuarial reserve for the contract, *i.e.*, the actuarial reserve plus the (negative) actuarial reserve for acquisition costs.

7 $\textit{BruttoDK}_t^{\text{mod}}$, is then defined for t<0 out of figures for the normal, unmodified product in the following manner:

$$\textit{BruttoDK}_t^{\text{mod}} = \textit{BruttoDK}_t + (KPBW_0 - 5\% \bullet PBW_0) \bullet \frac{\ddot{a}_{x+t:n-t}}{\ddot{a}_{x:n}} - KBW_t$$

8 With the following definitions

$\textit{BruttoDK}_1$ = Gross actuarial reserves at point in time t

$KPBW_0$	=	Cost premium present value at point in time t = 0 of the expected future cost premiums
PBW_0	=	Present value of gross premiums at the time of the conclusion of the contract t=0
KBW_t	=	Present value of costs at point in time t of the expected future costs

n is the term of the contract; in the case of contracts without time limits, it is infinity.

On the basis of the technical source materials and the requirements used in the rating. 9

If a technical interest rate is has not been defined for a product, then the maximum, allowable technical interest rate when the contract was concluded is used. If several technical interest rates are used, one of them may be chosen. If the development of the cost premium depends on future parameters not specified when the contract was concluded, then the development of the cost premium, must nevertheless, of necessity, be specified on the basis of a best estimate for the settlement value calculation. Further, it will be assumed that for the original product at point in time 0 that the present value of costs (= present value of the costs included in the benefits) equals the present value of the cost premiums (= present value of the costs included in the calculation of the premiums). 10

III. Options and guarantees

The value of options and guarantees must be taken into account in the actuarial reserve for the unmodified product. 11

IV Proof of the condition to the settlement value

The proof of compliance with the condition (+) is made through a direct calculation or through several illustrative developments of the settlement value and the comparative differences in the inequality. In many rating systems, the condition will be fulfilled automatically, as the examples below show. 12

V. Example 1

One considers a product with one-time acquisition costs ≤ 5% of the premium present value (PBW_0) and constant, annual other costs. Then [the following] always applies 13

$$BruttoDK_t^{mod} \leq BruttoDK_t$$

VI. Example 2

14 For products with one-time acquisition costs that can be amortized equally over the entire term and with constant, annual other costs, the following applies

$$BruttoDK_t^{mod} = InventarDK_t - 5\% \bullet PBW_0 \bullet \frac{ä_{x+t:n-t}}{ä_{x:n}}$$

for t > 0.

Circular Letter 2008/42

Reserves in Nonlife Insurance

Insurance Technical Reserves in Nonlife Insurance

Reference:	FINMA-RS* 08/42 Nonlife Insurance Reserves
Issued:	20 November 2008
Entry into force:	1 January 2009
Last amendment:	20 November 2008
Regulatory history:	Formerly FOPI Guideline 2/2008 Reserves in Nonlife Insurance of 6 November 2008
Legal basis:	FINMAG Art. 7, para. 1 provision b
	ISL Art. 4, para. 2, provision d, Art. 16, Art. 22, paras. 1 and 3, Art. 24, para. 1, Art. 25, para. 6, Art. 26, para. 3
	SR Art. 54, para. 4, Art. 69
	ISR-FINMA Art. 2
	Treaty of 10 October 1989 between the Swiss Confederation and the European Economic Area concerning Direct Insurance with the Exception of Life Insurance (with Annexes, Protocols, Exchanges of Correspondence, Declaration and Final Act)

* Circular Letter

Table of Contents

I. Purpose

This circular letter aims to regulate the establishment and release of insurance technical reserves for the statutory balance sheet on the basis of Art. 16 ISL, Art. 54, para. 4 and Art. 69 SR. 1

It sets the requirements in respect of the nature and scope of the insurance technical reserves, as well as the principles for their calculation. 2

II. Scope of application

This circular letter applies to claims under insurance contracts with the exception of foreign insurance portfolios for which security must be provided abroad pursuant to Art. 17 ISL. 3

This circular letter applies to the insurance lines B1 through B18 as defined in SR (Annex 1). Special issues concerning line B2 will be regulated separately. 4

III. Principles

Sufficient insurance technical reserves comprise insurance technical case reserves (Art. 54, para. 1, provision a SR) and volatility reserves (Art. 54, para. 1, provision b SR). 5

a. Insurance technical case reserves, as of the reporting date, are an estimate of the payments that will become due after the reporting date and the costs for all insurance claims under insurance agreements in existence as of the reporting date. The payments may not, with the exception of the actuarial reserves for pensions, be discounted. 6

   Expressed mathematically, the insurance technical case reserves are a provisional, unbiased estimate of the provisionally expected value of future cash flows on the basis of the information available at the time of the estimate. They are therefore considered a best estimate and are therefore neither on the cautious nor on the incautious side and specifically do not include any conscious reinforcement. 7

b. Volatility reserves are needed because of uncertainties in setting the case reserves (security or parameter risk), such as the probability volatility inherent in a loss event (volatility risk in the narrow sense). They serve to completely or partially offset unfavorable developments in the insurance technical case reserves. 8

Sufficient insurance technical reserves must nevertheless be at least as large as the near market value of the obligations. This value comprises the best- 9 possible estimate of the value of the obligations pursuant to Annex 3 SR and the minimum amount under Art. 41, para. 4 SR.

10 Insurance technical reserves are to be calculated gross and net, i.e., without and with allowance for recoveries from reinsurers under reinsurance agreements.

IV. Types of insurance technical reserves

A. Unearned premiums

11 Unearned premiums as of the reporting date comprise the portion of the premiums which is to be allocated to the period after the reporting date. It may not be set off against capitalized acquisition costs.

B. Case reserves

12 Case reserves as of the reporting date comprise all of the payments and costs that will be paid after the reporting date for all loss events that occurred before the reporting date. Included here are the claims pending as of the reporting date, the claims not yet reported as of the reporting date (incurred but not yet reported, IBNR) and the reopened closed claims as of the reporting date.

13 Claims adjustment costs are the costs incurred in connection with the adjustment of the claim. They comprise the costs directly allocated to the individual claims (allocated loss adjustment expenses, ALAE) and the costs that cannot be directly allocated (unallocated loss adjustment expenses, ULAE).

C. Security and volatility reserves

14 The security and volatility reserves comprise all amounts which serve to offset unfavorable [loss] development results in the insurance technical case reserves and fluctuations in claims costs.

15 Among the security and volatility reserves are, in particular:

16 a. The volatility reserves described under paragraph III., provision b which are not directly allocated to another type of volatility reserves.

17 b. The reserves under Art. 111, para. 1 of the Regulation on the Accident Insurance (UVV).

18 c. The volatility reserves for credit insurance under Method No. 2 in Annex No. 5 to the Treaty of 10 October 1989 between the Swiss Confederation and the European Economic Area concerning Direct Insurance with the

Exception of Life Insurance, subject to paragraph 2.3 of Method No. 2 in the above-mentioned Annex No. 5.

Methods and principles for the establishment and release of the security and volatility reserves are to be specified in the business plan. 19

D. Reserves for contractual policyholder surplus

Reserves for contractual policyholder surplus as of the reporting date comprise the share of the surplus that is owed after the reporting date which is to be allocated to the period before the reporting date. 20

E. Actuarial reserves for pensions

a) Actuarial reserves for pensions under the Federal Law on Accident Insurance of 20 March 1981 (UVG)

The actuarial reserves for pensions are to be calculated on the basis of the calculation basis in Art. 108 of the Regulation on the Accident Insurance of 20 December 1982 (UVV). 21

For reserves for the inflation adjustment, the following rule applies: 22

a. For the accident insurers which share in the fund for securing future pensions, the reserves for inflation adjustments equal the obligations to the fund. 23

b. For the accident insurers which do not share in the fund for securing future pensions, the actuarial reserves for pensions are to be increased by the estimated net present value of the declared and future inflation adjustments. 24

b) Actuarial reserves for pensions other than those under the Federal Law on the Accident Insurance of 20 March 1981 (UVG)

The actuarial reserves for pensions as of the reporting date comprise the payments in the form of a pension that are owed for all claims for which a pension right accrued before the reporting date. The payments include the inflation adjustments for pensions which are to be adjusted for inflation. The actuarial reserves for pensions may not be lower than those which result in the case of the discounting of the payments on the risk free interest rate curve. Departures from this principle must be justified in the business plan. 25

F. Other technical reserves

26 Other technical reserves are to be established as needed in accordance with the principles for sufficient insurance technical reserves described in paragraph III. Their designation and purpose are to be described in the business plan.

V. Processes and controls

A. Claims process

27 An insurance business shall specify the claims and reserving process at the level of individual loss reserves (case reserves) and shall specify an effective organization. It shall specify rules for the recording, adjustment, release and monitoring of the individual case reserves which takes into account the special characteristics of the various types of losses and reserving methods (individual case reserve, general reserve). It shall ensure the quality of the loss estimates and compliance with the guidelines on estimates and shall verify these in an appropriate manner.

B. Determining the case reserves

28 The data for the calculation of the case reserves must be current at the time of the calculation. An insurance business shall ensure that new knowledge and developments in the loss development are taken into account on a timely basis when loss reserves are set or changed.

29 The case reserves are to be determined on the basis of recognized actuarial principles. An insurance business must ensure an effective control of the development of the case reserves through loss triangles or other appropriate means.

C. Documentation

30 An insurance business must document the consistency of the data with the accounting rules, the applied method for the estimation of the insurance technical case reserves with a specification for uncertainty at the time of their establishment, the amount of the prudential and volatility reserves, as well as the received results.

31 The data to be documented in the supervisory report concerning insurance technical reserves will be specified by the FINMA.

VI. Transition provisions

The implementation of this circular letter by an supervised insurance business can be carried out in stages over several years. The relevant insurance businesses must submit a plan for the funding or adjustment of the relevant reserves or the implementation of this circular letter in general to the FINMA by 30 June 2009. 32

Circular Letter 2008/43

Life Insurance Reserves

Insurance Technical Reserves in Life Insurance

Reference:	FINMA-RS* 08/43 Life Insurance Reserves
Issued:	20 November 2008
Entry into force:	1 January 2009
Last amendment:	20 November 2008
Regulatory history:	Formerly FOPI Guideline 3/2008 Life Insurance Reserves of 20 November 2008
Legal sources:	FINMAG Art. 7, para. 1 provision b
	ISL Art. 4, para. 2, provision d, Arts.16, 24, 25, 26, 46
	SR Arts. 54, 55, 58-67
	SR-FINMA Art. 2
Annex:	Sub-portfolios for the annual review of insurance technical reserves under para. V.

* Circular Letter

Table of Contents

I. Purpose

This circular letter regulates the establishment and release of insurance technical reserves for life insurance on the basis of Art. 16 ISL, as well as Art. 54, para. 4, Art. 55 and Arts. 58-67 SR. 1

II. Scope of application

This circular letter applies to claims under life insurance contracts with the exception of foreign insurance portfolios for which security must be provided abroad pursuant to Art. 17 ISL. 2

This circular letter applies to the insurance lines A1 through A7 in accordance with Annex 1 SR. 3

III. Principles

Responsible Actuary 4
The Responsible Actuary is responsible for the establishment of sufficient insurance technical reserves.

Primary principle 5
The insurance technical reserves must be sufficient. This means, in particular, that the assumptions and methods for the determination of the reserves must be made in a manner that the permanent fulfillment of the obligations under the insurance contracts is guaranteed. In this regard, the reserves must be at least measured so that it is possible with an appropriate investment portfolio in the amount of the reserves to cover the benefit obligations as they arise with sufficient security.

Appropriateness and cautiousness of the assumptions and methods 6
The methods for the determination of the insurance technical reserves must take into account the complexity of the obligations. Uncertainty in the assumptions and methods is to be taken into account through the establishment of margins of safety. The relevant management rules and the behavior of policyholders is to be modeled cautiously.

Business plan 7
The assumptions and methods that are necessary for the determination of the insurance technical reserves must be described in the business plan. The details necessary for the calculation are to be recorded in an additional technical document in a transparent and understandable manner.

8 Amendments to the Business plan
New or altered assumptions and methods for the determination of the insurance technical reserves, whose effects on the reserves are not insignificant, are considered amendments to the business plan that must be notified to the FINMA in accordance with Art. 5, para. 2 ISL.

9 Monitoring the insurance technical reserves in sub-portfolios
At least once each year as of the balance sheet date, the insurance technical reserves for all sub-portfolios must be calculated with current, conservative assumptions. The minimum requirements for dividing the portfolio into sub-portfolios are specified in the annex. If the reserves for a sub-portfolio are not sufficient, then they must be increased.

10 Confirmation of sufficient insurance technical reserves in sub-portfolios
The analysis of whether the insurance technical reserves are sufficient is to be documented. Here, the responsible actuary evaluates the assumptions and methods for the determination of insurance technical reserves, the increase for each sub-portfolio and whether the amount of the insurance technical reserves is sufficient. If necessary, he or she shall recommend to the executive board measures for achieving sufficient insurance technical reserves. He or she shall confirm in a report to the executive board that the insurance technical reserves are sufficient or state that they are not sufficient.

11 Conformity of the volatility reserves with the plan
In order to ensure the long-term ability to fulfill the obligations, sufficient insurance technical volatility reserves are to be established. Here, a clear procedure is to be defined in the business plan pursuant to which the volatility reserves are to be established and released. The volatility reserves are divided among sub-portfolios and the total portfolio.

IV. Establishment of insurance technical reserves

12 In determining the insurance technical reserves, the specification of the assumptions – among others biometric data, technical interest rates, cancellation behavior, behavior in respect of the exercise of options and guarantees, the offset of fluctuations, surpluses in the case of contracts entitled to surplus, expected future costs for management and customer service, relevant management rules – and the methods must be made in accordance with conservative principles and through the inclusion of a margin of safety. The uncertainty of the methods also must be taken into account in an appropriate manner.

13 All material, relevant options and guarantees must be taken into account in determining the insurance technical reserves.

14 The basis for modeling the cash flows of the obligations is the projection into the future of the underlying, existing portfolio under conservative assumptions.

Simple, classic products can be modeled on a simplified basis, in that the their insurance technical reserves are determined as the value of the future cash flows under the application of a conservative technical interest rate and a conservative biometric basis. In this regard, simple, classic products are to be understood as pure risk insurance, mixed insurance, annuities or similar products, to the extent their modeling is based on an equivalent principle to conservative assumptions. Among the simple, classic products is unit-linked life insurance with or without interest rate or capital protection guarantees. 15

If insurance products have complex financial obligations, then these are, as a rule, to be addressed with stochastic models. 16

In the case of unit-linked life insurance, the insurance technical reserves for contracts or parts of contracts whose benefits equal exactly the value of a contractually specified portfolio of assets held by the insurance business are calculated on the basis of the value of these assets in the regulatory financial statements. For other obligations, such as in connection with death, survival or disability, segregated reserves are to be established. 17

For the determination of sufficient insurance technical reserves, it is necessary to appropriately take into account the possibility of very unfavorable changes in the behavior of the policyholder or the insured, in particular if the value of the obligation is closely correlated with their behavior. For the reserve at the inception of the contract, an especially unfavorable possible development must be taken into account. 18

The determination of insurance technical reserves for an insurance contract is based on technical interest rates which, under Art. 60 SR may not exceed the technical interest rate used in the rating. Outside of the occupational pension plans, the interest rate in accordance with Art. 121, para. 1 and para. 2 SR, as set at the inception of the contract, constitutes the upper limit. 19

The reserves are to be determined without credit for the unamortized acquisition costs. For foreign business, the foreign rules on zillmerization apply. 20

The insurance technical reserves must be calculated by taking into account each individual contract and, as a rule, be established on an individual contact basis. 21

It must be ensured that the insurance technical reserves for a contract – minus any capitalized acquisition costs – equal at all times at least the cash settlement value. 22

The assumptions and methods for the determination of the insurance technical reserves must be monitored product-by-product and, if applicable, adjusted for future new business. 23

24 If an insurance technical reserve is only sufficient if a complex management strategy for the covering investment is successful, then this concept is also to be described in the business plan.

V. Annual review

25 At least once each year as of the balance sheet date, a review must be made of whether the insurance technical reserves are sufficient. For the review, the requirements of paragraph III and IV apply with the additions and limitations set forth in margin paragraphs 26-32.

26 In performing the review, the portfolio is to be divided into at least the sub-portfolios in the Annex. Portfolios within these with a size that is not insignificant must be considered separate sub-portfolios if their insurance technical reserves are significantly below a sufficient reserve over a longer period of time. The insurance technical reserves must be sufficient for each sub-portfolio.

27 Current, conservative assumptions and methods must be applied to the review.

28 If the previous insurance technical reserves for a sub-portfolio in the aggregate are insufficient, then they are to be increased through additional insurance technical reserves until they are sufficient. The business plan is to be amended accordingly. The increase may be determined for the sub-portfolio in accordance with margin paragraph 26 rather than at the policy level. As a rule, the increase must be made not later than the balance sheet date. The responsible actuary must decide whether an increase is needed earlier. An increase over time in accordance with a plan can be approved by the FINMA in accordance with Art. 62 SR.

29 For the release of increases that are no longer required, rules which favor a minimal fluctuation in the level of the insurance technical reserves are to be specified in the business plan.

30 The insurance technical reserves set for contracts individually must, in any case, be just as large as if they were determined with the assumptions and methods applicable at the inception of the contract.

31 In the case of *simple, classic products* (margin paragraph 15), the insurance technical reserves are to be reviewed with conservative basic principles on a current basis and, if necessary, increases are to be made. In particular, interest rates must be used for the valuation of the cash flows of the obligations that with great certainty are below the return to be earned on the related investment portfolio after the deduction of costs.

If an insurance technical reserve is only sufficient if a complex management strategy for the covering investment is successful, then the success of this management strategy is to be reviewed at regular intervals, but at least once each year as of the balance sheet date. If it is not functioning, the insurance technical reserves must be adjusted in accordance with margin paragraph 5. The responsible actuary shall evaluate any irregularities which arise and shall note them in his or her report in accordance with margin paragraph 39. 32

VI. Additional provisions

In the case of the run-off of an insurance business or one of its large sub- 33
portfolios, in setting the insurance technical reserves, any increasing cost factors and the decreasing risk diversification must, in particular, be taken into account. The FINMA may specify the parameters for the reserving needs in an individual case.

The FINMA may also during the year have a review performed of whether the 34
insurance technical reserves are sufficient. It can have the review performed by an external actuary and it can prescribe the application of assumptions and methods for the determination of the reserves. The costs of any such review by an external actuary are borne by the insurance business.

The responsible actuary is also responsible for the determination of sufficient 35
gross insurance technical reserves in his or her insurance business if a part of the insurance technical obligations are ceded to another insurance business.

For advance premium payments or deferred payments of insurance benefits, 36
insurance technical reserves must be established and covered by restricted assets in accordance with Art. 17, para. 1 ISL.

From policyholder surplus funds, only that portion thereof whose payment 37
must be guaranteed in all situations for contractual or supervisory law reasons is to be covered as an insurance technical reserve with restricted assets.

Insurance businesses must cover the insurance technical reserves without 38
credit for reinsurance (gross) with restricted assets. The insurance technical reserves for assumed reinsurance are not part of the required amount [of restricted assets].

VII. Information about the reserves

The report of the responsible actuary to the executive board pursuant to 39
Art. 24, para. 3 ISL and Art. 2, para. 2 ISR-FINMA, as well as the supervisory report pursuant to Art. 25, para. 2 ISL shall include, among other things, the following information about the insurance technical reserves:

40 a. an assessment of whether business plan provisions for insurance technical reserves have been observed and whether the insurance technical reserves are sufficient.

41 b. the most important assumptions and methods for the for the determination of the insurance technical reserves. Here, the relevant changes in the assumptions and methods in comparison to the previous year are to be made transparent.

42 c. an assessment of the chosen assumptions and methods which also notes possible risks.

43 The FINMA shall receive key figures about the insurance technical reserves in the annual report under supervisory law. The details will be determined in connection with the collection of the data for this report.

44 The release of insurance technical volatility reserves and increases that are no longer required will be notified to the FINMA in advance.

VIII. Transition provisions

45 The rules for the insurance technical reserves in the business plan in accordance with this circular letter are to be submitted to the FINMA for approval by 31 December 2009.

46 The first annual review of the insurance technical reserves on the basis of the submitted business plans is to be performed not later than 30 June 2010 for the 2009 financial year. By this point in time, the results of the review are also to be submitted to the FINMA and any plans for increase in accordance with margin paragraph 28 are to be submitted for approval.

Annex

Sub-portfolios for the annual review of the insurance technical reserves under paragraph V.

Group insurance business

- Occupational pension plans
  - Business subject to a minimum surplus distribution obligation
    - current old-age and survivors pensions
    - current disability annuities and premium exemptions
    - pension account balances and deferred old-age pensions
    - inflation funds
    - all others
  - Business not subject to a minimum surplus distribution obligation
    - current old-age and survivors pensions
    - current disability pensions and premium exemptions
    - pension account balances and deferred old-age pensions
    - all others
- Other group business
  - current old-age and survivors pensions
  - current disability pensions and premium exemptions
  - additional group business (e.g., credit life insurance)

Individual insurance business

- Simple, classic products
  - pure risk insurance without further special guarantees
  - mixed insurance and the like without special guarantees
- Old-age pensions

current

deferred

Disability pensions

current

deferred

Unit-linked products without special guarantees

All others

Other products

Savings products with special guarantees grouped by portfolio with the same benefits

Other products grouped by portfolio with the same benefits

In addition, portfolios of not insignificant size within these sub-portfolios must be considered separate sub-portfolios if their insurance technical reserves are significantly below a sufficient reserve over a longer period of time (for example, in the case of older generations of ratings or improper product design). Sub-portfolios of insignificant size may be combined with other appropriate sub-portfolios. Various components of an insurance product may be taken into account in a single sub-portfolio to the extent the reserves for a component are not significantly below a sufficient reserve.

Circular Letter 2008/44

SST

Swiss Solvency Test

Reference:	FINMA-RS* 08/44 SST
Issued:	28 November 2008
Entry into force:	1 January 2009
Last amendment:	28 November 2008
Regulatory history:	Formerly FOPI Guideline 4/2008 Swiss Solvency Test of 28 November 2008
Legal basis:	FINMAG Art. 7, para. 1 provision b, Art. 29
	ISL Art. 9, para. 2, Arts. 22, 46, 51
	SR Arts. 2, 22, 41-53, 96, 198-202, 216, para. 4, as well as Annexes 2 and 3
Annex 1:	Near market value valuation under the SST
Annex 2:	Group model
Annex 3:	Credit risk in the standard model
Annex 4:	Intervention thresholds

* Circular Letter

Table of Contents

I. Starting point

1 Under the Federal Law concerning the Supervision of Insurance Businesses of 17 December 2004 (Insurance Supervision Law, ISL; SR 961.01), as well as the Regulation on the Supervision of Private Insurance Businesses of 9 November 2005 (Supervisory Regulation, SR; SR 961.011), both of which have entered into force on 1 January 2006, the solvency of insurance businesses is to be evaluated, subject to transition periods, under the Swiss Solvency Test (SST). At the same time, capital resources are evaluated under Solvency I.

2 This circular letter contains elaborations on the rules of the ISL and SR on the SST.

3 *Explanations have been added in italic type.*

II. Definitions

4 Valuation model

A valuation model is a financial mathematics or actuarial procedure for the determination of the values of assets or liabilities.

5 One-year risk capital

The one-year risk capital is the target capital reduced by the minimum amount.

6 Supplementary capital

Supplementary capital consists of hybrid instruments which fulfill the requirements under Art. 39, para. 1 SR and which were approved by the FINMA pursuant to Art. 37, para. 2, SR. This is divided pursuant to Art. 49 SR into an upper and lower supplementary capital.

7 Expected shortfall

This circular letter uses the term expected shortfall in accordance with the definition in Annex 2 of the SR.

8 Groups

Insurance groups and conglomerates under Arts. 64 ff. and 72 ff. ISL are referred to in the circular letter as groups.

9 Internal model

An internal model as used in this circular letter is a risk model used by an insurance business or group that deviates from the standard model. Deviations are greater than merely a change of the prescribed parameters.

Calibration test 10

The calibration test is identified as the verification of the FINMA-prescribed risk level and the parameters in respect of risk level, time line, confidence level, return above the risk-free counterparty interest rate curve for the determination of the minimum amount and – to the extent that internally determined interest rate curves under this circular letter are not used – the risk-free counterparty interest rate curve, which is used for the valuation.

Core capital 11

For the calculation of the core capital, the difference between the assets valued at near market value and debt capital valued at near market value is added to the minimum capital. The items mentioned in Art. 48, para. 1 SR are to be deducted therefrom.

Near market balance sheet 12

The near market balance sheet is a presentation of all of the near market rights and obligations, hereinafter assets and liabilities or total positions.

Method and parameter test 13

The method and parameter test is identified as the review of the appropriateness of the assumptions made, the method applied, the chosen parameters and the review of the presentation of the risk profile of the insurance business by the risk model. This test is called the "statistical quality test" by the International Association of Insurance Supervisors (IAIS).

Minimum amount 14

The minimum amount is the cost of capital for the risk-bearing capital to be provided during the term of the settlement of the insurance technical obligations.

Risk model 15

A risk model is understood as a mathematical-statistical procedure for the quantification of relevant risks and therefore the determination of the target capital.

Risk-bearing capital (RBC) 16

Risk-bearing capital is the sum of the core capital and supplementary capital to the extent the supplementary capital can be credited.

SST-Quotient 17

The SST-Quotient is determined by dividing the risk-bearing capital by the target capital.

18 Standard model

The standard model prescribed by the FINMA is a risk model consisting of sub-modules. The sub-modules relate to the insurance technical risks, market risks and credit risks.

19 Use test

The use test is identified as the verification of the application of the risk model by the insurance business for significant purposes of internal risk management.

20 Target capital (TC)

Target capital is defined as the sum of the discounted minimum amount in a year and negative one multiplied by the Expected Shortfall of the difference between the discounted Risk Bearing Capital in a year and the current Risk Bearing Capital (referred to as "Expected Shortfall of the Change of RBC"). The confidence level is specified in paragraph IX.

21 *Explanation:*

$$ZK_0 = \frac{Minimum\ amount_1}{1+r} - ES_\alpha \left[\frac{RBC_1}{1+r_0} - RBC_0 \right]$$

Where the confidence level equals (1 - α)

22 An insurance business may replace the term risk-bearing capital with core capital in the definition of target capital above. If this definition of target capital is chosen, then hybrid instruments under Art. 39, para. 1 SR are to be valued as follows: the future cash flows are to be discounted with the risk-free counterparty interest rate curve. The alternate rules in this circular letter do not apply.

23 The relationship between core capital, supplementary capital and the minimum amount is shown in an illustration in paragraph VI.

III. Scope of application and purpose

24 This circular letter applies to all insurance businesses and groups which are supervised by the FINMA pursuant to Art. 2, para. 1 provision a ISL, together with Arts. 65 or 73 ISL, with the exception of:

- branches of foreign insurance businesses as well as
- reinsurance captives under Art. 2 SR, to the extent they are not subject, on an exceptional basis, to the SST pursuant to Art. 2, para. 2 SR.

25 The purpose of this circular letter is to specify the requirements for the performance of the SST, as well as the reporting to the FINMA.

IV. Materiality

Under the SST, all material positions of the near market balance sheet and all relevant risks contemplated by this circular letter are to be taken into account. Non-material positions and irrelevant risks can be disregarded or presented in simplified form. Omissions and the simplified presentation of positions may only be made if the total effect of the omissions and simplifications leads to a relative change of the 26

- RBC or the TC

and the

- SST-Quotient

of less than 10%.

An insurance business shall document the analysis for the determination of non-material positions and irrelevant risks. 27

Explanation 28

As a rule, calculations of the – hypothetical – effects on RBC or TC should be based on substantiated estimates. The FINMA shall decide in individual cases whether the estimates were made with sufficient quality.

The FINMA reserves the right to require a more precise calculation of the RBC and TC. It will require this, in particular, if the SST-Quotient is less than 100% or could be less than 100% on the basis of a more precise calculation. 29

V. The near market balance sheet

A. Subject

An insurance business shall assess and value all assets and liabilities in accordance with economic considerations and near market, subject to any contrary specifications in the SR, to the extent that these are material under the definition above. Included therein are the so-called off-balance sheet positions as that term is used in accounting terminology. It also takes into account, in particular, all contingent liabilities and related rights. An insurance business shall prepare a near market balance sheet through the use of these valuations. 30

Explanation 31

At the current time, insurance businesses may submit the near market balance sheet in the form of the template integrated in the standard model or use the reporting format of the "List of Fundamental SST Data" made available on the FINMA website. In this regard, the balance sheet positions prescribed by the

FINMA show a minimal level of detail in the balance sheet. A more detailed presentation by an insurance business is permitted. The FINMA will publish any changes on its website not later than six months before the delivery date for the SST.

B. Basis of valuation

32 Generally, all existing assets and liabilities are to be valued in accordance with economic considerations and valued at near market. A near market valuation is based upon, and is not in conflict with, the information that can be obtained from trading in liquid financial markets. If a market value exists for an instrument, this will be used as the basis for the valuation ("marking-to-market"), and if not, the near market value will be determined on the basis of an appropriate model ("marking-to-model", see paragraph 1 of Annex No. 3 to the SR and paragraph V.C. of this circular letter).

33 For the near market valuation, assets and liabilities may be divided into their embedded sub-components. These may be valued in accordance with the marking-to-market or marking-to-model methods.

34 The near market balance sheet must pass the points of the calibration test that are relevant to it (see paragraph IX).

35 The reporting currency of the near market balance sheet and the presentation of the core capital generally may be freely chosen. A currency basket that provides an artificial currency derived from several other currencies may be chosen instead of a currency. If the near market balance sheet is prepared in a currency other than Swiss francs, it is, in addition, to be converted into Swiss francs.

C. Valuation methods

36 The near market valuation is to be structured in a manner such that independent, knowledgeable transaction parties would, as a rule, buy or sell at this price. If these requirements are not fulfilled, such as in markets under stress, procedures and estimated parameters are to be chosen credibly. Supplementary provisions for the near market valuation are to be found in Annex 1 to this circular letter, "Near market valuation under the SST".

37 The near market valuation of the obligations to policyholders and the near market value of the other liabilities will be determined, to the extent the liabilities are not hybrid instruments approved by the FINMA pursuant to Art. 39, para. 1 SR, under the assumption that the insurance business will fully discharge these obligations. In determining the near market value of all liabilities other than the hybrid instruments approved by the FINMA (see paragraph VI),

the creditworthiness of the insurance business may not be taken into account. This means that for the valuation of liabilities a marking-to-model often must be used. To the extent that a market value for these items is available, and an insurance business wants to use it, the effects of its own creditworthiness must be excluded from it.

Marking-to-market

To the extent that sufficient transactions in an asset or liability occur between independent, knowledgeable transaction parties or a sufficient number of securities dealers or brokers as transaction parties make offer prices for a potential transaction in good faith and on a binding basis and for significant [transaction] volumes, an insurance business shall use this price for the determination of the near market value of the position to be valued. If one or more of the conditions mentioned above is not fulfilled, an insurance business shall test the reasonableness of the appropriateness of the use of the observed transaction prices. The effort needed for the verification of the market price can be made dependent on the significance of the position to be valued. 38

Marking-to-model

In the situations in which marking-to-market is not possible, an insurance business must perform a marking-to-model. The marking-to-model must fulfill the following requirements: 39

- In the valuation by marking-to-model, an insurance business shall use both for assets as well as for liabilities fundamentally reliable finance and actuarial procedures. The models used shall be identified as valuation models. 40
- The valuation models are to be produced for all significant positions with the necessary care. The valuation of positions of limited significance can be performed with the aid of simpler valuation methods. An insurance business shall ensure that in this situation the valuation of each individual position or reasonably combined positions is performed. If the FINMA has doubts about the reliability of the simplified valuation models, it can require a more precise valuation. 41
- The valuation models and their parameters must be calibrated as far as possible on the basis of objectively observable data. 42
- The valuations models used for the determination of the near market values under the marking-to-model are to be documented sufficiently. 43
- To the extent that the basis for the determination of the near market value of insurance technical obligations represents the discounted best-possible estimated value, it must be increased in the amount of the minimum amount, so that in the event of the run-off of the insurance technical obligations, the costs of the equity capital employed are covered. 44

45 • To the extent that the near market value of insurance technical obligations can be made directly and without recourse to a discounted best-possible estimated value[1], this must not be divided into the discounted best-possible estimated value and the minimum amount. For the insurance technical obligations, a minimum amount must not be determined.

46 • The value of the liabilities which do not represent hybrid instruments approved by the FINMA under Art. 39 para. 1 SR will be determined through the appropriate application of the risk-free counterparty interest rate curve (see Annex 1 "Near market valuation under the SST").[2]

47 • Instead of the interest rate curves in common currencies prescribed by the FINMA, internally determined risk-free counterparty interest rate curves may also be used. The method for the determination of these interest rate curves is to be submitted to the FINMA in a suitable form for approval. If internally determined interest rate curves instead of those prescribed by the FINMA are used, the insurance business shall make a comparison of the internally determined interest rate curves with the FINMA prescribed interest rate curves. The insurance business shall perform a calculation or estimate of the difference between the present value of the expected cash flows from the obligations on the basis of the internally developed curves and the present value of the expected cash flows from the obligations on the basis of the curves prescribed by the FINMA. The FINMA reserves the right to impose a deduction from RBC in the event of significant differences in valuation which have their origin in the use of internal interest rate curves.

VI. Risk-bearing capital

48 Risk-bearing capital is the sum of the core capital and the supplementary capital to the extent that supplementary capital can be credited.

49 *Explanations:*

The minimum amount is a component of core capital. It is, however, not calculated explicitly for the determination of core capital because the near market value of the insurance technical obligations in most cases is the result of the best-possible estimated value and the minimum amount. Core capital is therefore determined by the assets valued at near market, less the best-possible

---

[1] Procedures which lead directly to a near market value of the insurance technical obligations are, e.g., a replicated portfolio.

[2] The FINMA makes available as of 01.01 and 01.07 of each year each risk-free counterparty interest rate curve in the most common currencies (CHF, EUR, USD, JPY). If the FINMA requires a insurer to calculate the SST during the year, it will provide the risk-free counterparty interest rate curves in the most common currencies. If other interest rate curves are needed, these are to be determined by the insurer itself.

estimated value of the insurance technical obligations and the other debt valued at near market in accordance with this circular letter.

50

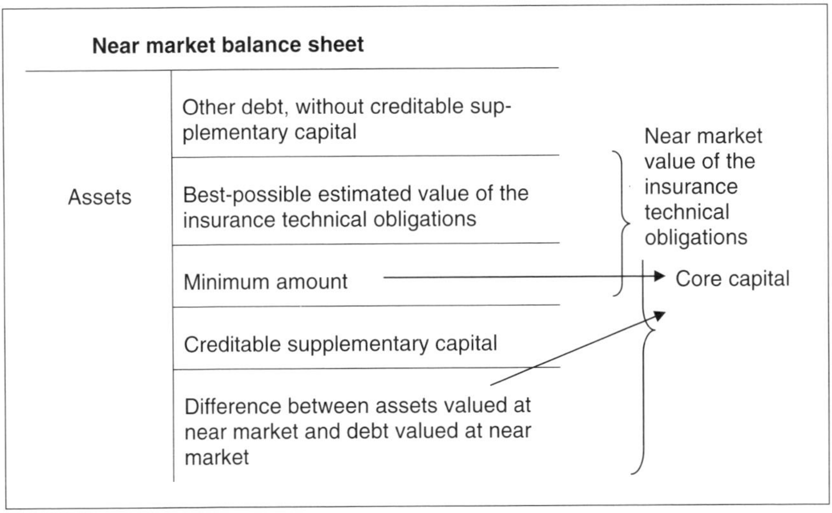

Illustration 1: Explanation of RBC

The expected shortfall of the change in RBC also determines the amount of the TC: The TC is specifically calculated so that the expected shortfall of the change in RBC in a year is greater than or equal to the minimum amount. The TC is therefore the result of two parts, specifically, first, the single-year risk capital as the expected shortfall of the change in RBC and, second, the minimum amount. 51

The minimum amount, as a part of RBC, is defined in Art. 41, para. 4 SR as the sum of the present values of the cost of capital for the RBC, including hedging costs in a run-off situation, totaled across all future years. The minimum amount, as part of RBC, does not itself result in any further capital costs. The present value of the cost of capital for RBC is therefore identical to the present value of the cost of capital for the single-year risk capital. The TC is therefore greater than the single-year risk capital by the amount of the minimum amount. 52

The upper and lower supplementary capital maybe credited to the RBC in the amount of the limits mentioned in Art. 47, para. 2 SR. Supplementary capital may be credited up to a maximum of 100% of the core capital. An exception is the lower supplementary capital under Art. 49, para. 2 SR which, under Art. 47, para. 2 SR – and under the conditions in Art. 49, para. 3 SR – may be credited up to a maximum of 50 percent of the core capital. 53

54 Hybrid instruments approved by the FINMA pursuant to Art. 39, para. 1 SR are credited at their market value, provided that the creditworthiness of the insurance business is taken into account. Whether the hybrid instruments can be credited to core capital within the limits under Art. 39, para. 2 SR is not relevant to their valuation. The procedure for the valuation of approved hybrid instruments differs from the approach for liabilities which are not approved hybrid instruments.

55 *Explanations:*

This approach to the valuation of hybrid instruments prevents a situation in which an insurance business, under certain circumstances, has to report a loss occurring immediately upon issue. Taking into account or excluding the [insurance business's] own creditworthiness has no influence on the amount of the RBC, at least with regard to hybrid instruments which can be credited as part of RBC.

56 *Taking into account guarantees received under the SST has both an effect on the RBC, as well as on the TC. As a rule, subject to sufficient capitalization of the insurance business and appropriate modeling, the present value of the received guarantee is relatively small and the effect of the modeling on TC is substantial and also has the effect of reducing risk.*

VII. The minimum amount

57 Under Art. 41, para. 4 SR, the *minimum amount* is the cost of capital for the risk capital to be provided during the loss development period for the insurance technical obligations.

58 For the determination of the minimum amount in practice, this definition is more specifically defined as follows:

59 *Explanation:*

For purposes of the minimum amount: Under Art. 42, para. 4 SR, the near market value of the insurance technical obligations is the result of the sum of the discounted, best-possible estimated value and the minimum amount.

60 For those cash flows from the insurance technical obligations for which the near market value cannot be determined directly, an insurance business shall proceed as follows: For each future year during the entire loss development period of the insurance technical obligations, a supporting-SST is to be performed and the single-year risk capital is to be determined. The supporting-SST to be performed includes, analogously to the actual SST, the methodical determination of the market, insurance and credit risks for the best-possible estimated value of the insurance obligations, as well as an assessment and aggregation of relevant SST scenarios.

Explanation: 61

Under the assumption that the near market value of the hedgeable risks is already fully included in the best-possible estimated value of the insurance technical obligations, the determination of the single-year risk capital is based on the unhedgeable risks.

The same parameters and assumptions are to be used by the businesses for the determination of the minimum amount as they used for the determination of the insurance technical obligations, this relates in particular to the assumptions 62

- about the [insurer's] own business policies,
- about the development of the [insurer's] own portfolio,
- about the [insurer's] own diversification of its own portfolio,
- about the [insurer's] own credit risk,
- about the behavior of customers.

Explanations: 63

For example, it would not be acceptable to the FINMA if:

- *instead of the cancellation assumptions used for the best-possible estimate, customer behavior with different cancellation behavior would be used,*
- *contrary to the assumptions that were made for the determination of the best-possible estimated value, a different business policy was assumed, such as an altered exercise of any management options,*
- *instead of the diversification in its own portfolio, a different diversification with a hypothetical portfolio would be used.*

The FINMA places great value on consistency between the determination of the best-possible value estimates on the one hand and the minimum amount on the other hand. In this regard, the assumptions for the minimum amount should follow those for the best-possible estimated value. If, for example, in determining the best-possible estimated value, a particular cancellation rate or, for example, in transactions under the Occupational Pension Plan Law a holding period of ten years is assumed, it is therefore a natural, compulsory assumption for the determination of the minimum amount. 64

Determination of the cost of capital / the minimum amount: The supporting-SST that is to be performed produces a single-year risk capital for each individual future year during the expected loss development period of the insurance technical obligations. In accordance with the materiality principle, an insurance business can omit the performance of a supporting-SST for each individual future year of the loss development period and instead determine the 65 single-year risk capital with assumptions. The approximation methods are to be justified to the FINMA and to be described in detail in the SST report.

66 The future single-year costs of capital are the result of the multiplication of the single-year risk capital with the return in excess of the risk-free counterparty interest rate curve, which is specified through the calibration test (paragraph IX). The future single-year costs of capital are to be discounted to the test date of the current SST with an interest rate curve that is free of counterparty risk. The sum of these present values produces the minimum amount.

VIII. Target capital

A. General

67 Insurance businesses shall use an appropriate risk model under the SST for the determination of the TC. In this regard, the issue is whether the FINMA's prescribed standard model is used or an internal model. An internal model is to be used if the standard model is not able to appropriately capture all relevant risks of the insurance business.

68 A risk model is considered suitable if it fulfills the requirements of this circular letter.

69 Until further notice, it is assumed that the credit risk standard model is to be considered suitable for all insurance businesses covered by this circular letter, although it does not meet the calibration test.

70 An insurance business must cover the minimum amount with sufficient risk-bearing capital not later than the lapse of the transition period in Art. 216, para. 4, provision d SR. If this requirement is not fulfilled at that time, the FINMA shall take the necessary action. Intervention thresholds and possible actions are specified in Annex 4, "Intervention thresholds".

71 An insurance business shall determine the TC and the RBC at least once per year and shall notify the result of its analysis to the FINMA.

72 Groups shall determine the TC and the RBC for the individual insurance businesses or clusters of the group or other relevant performance figures at the beginning of each semester.

73 If the circumstances justify it, insurance businesses shall also perform the SST during the year upon the request of the FINMA (see paragraph XIV. B).

Explanations: 74

In Art. 41, para. 1 SR, only the standard situation SST-calculation is mentioned in respect of the projection period of one year. For any calculation date during the year, the projection period of one year also applies.

The SR specifies in Art. 41 SR the test date on which the calculation must be performed. The test date is, in the usual case, 01.01 of each year. The positions as of 01.01 are often identical to those in the year-end balance sheet as of 31.12. of the preceding year. For the valuation and for risk measurement the positions as of 31.12. may be used, corrected for any changes, such as, for example, portfolio transfers. 75

B. Group modeling

The application of a suitable risk model for groups shall provide for the presentation of the individual legal entities, although under some circumstances several legal entities may be combined in a cluster. 76

Other elements for the modeling of groups are governed by Annex 2 "Group model". 77

C. Risk-generating positions

An insurance business shall take into account the relevant risks from all positions which are components of the near market balance sheet for the determination of the TC. In particular, it shall also take into account the risks from options, guaranties and other contingent liabilities and corresponding rights in an appropriate manner. 78

D. Risk categories

In the risk model, an insurance business shall include, to the extent relevant, at least the following risks: 79

1. Insurance technical risks 80
   - Nonlife insurance 81
     - Loss development risk
     - Risks of new claims
     - Risk aggregations

Both in the case of the risk of new claims as in the case of loss development risk, the parameters risk and random risk must be modeled, although not necessarily separately from each other.

82 ○ Life insurance

- Mortality
- Longevity
- Disability
- Reactivation
- Costs
- Cancellation and other options
- Risk aggregations

The risk model must, in addition, take into account both parameter risk as well as the random risk.

83 ○ Health insurance

The risk model must, in addition, take into account both the parameter risk as well as the random risk. It must distinguish between group daily benefits disability insurance and other health insurance business.

For the determination of the insurance technical risks, an insurance business must establish logical classes. In the event of the application of an internal model, it may choose in a reasonable manner to deviate from the standard classes prescribed by the FINMA in the standard model.

For all lines of insurance business, the risks generally must be determined on a gross basis. The effect of reinsurance must be modeled separately. In this regard, the credit risk of reinsurers is to be taken into account. The FINMA shall, upon request, permit a determination on a net basis if the insurance technical risks can be appropriately presented and the counterparty risk resulting from the reinsurance agreement is recognized and taken into account in the modeling.

84 2. Market risks

- Interest rate risk
- Spread risks

- Exchange rate risks

Explanations: 85

Insurance businesses are fundamentally free in the choice of currency for the preparation of the near market balance sheet. In this regard, it is to be taken into account that the free choice of currency can, in some circumstances, have consequences on which currency is used to measure the exchange rate risk. The currency should be chosen so that it takes into account the current and planned future business activities, the distribution of the assets and liabilities in various currencies, as well as the potential fluctuation in the value of positions.

In addition, it is possible in principle, for a an appropriate currency portfolio to be chosen for the RBC, which on account of the differences in the actual net currency positions, results in a foreign currency position. In the standard model, this portfolio consists entirely of Swiss francs. 86

- Real estate risks 87
- Equity risks
- Risks in connection with alternative investments (private equity, hedge funds, commodities, ...)
- Risks which result from changes in volatilities and correlations
- Risks which result from ownership interests in, or loans to, group companies are to be modeled in a manner that the specific volatility of these investments, as well as the dependency of the value fluctuations of these investments are taken into account with the other risks of the insurance business in the risk model.

Explanation: 88

As a rule, a large portion of the investments, as well as the insurance technical obligations, are subject to market risks, for example, in respect of interest rate risk and, in some circumstances, exchange rate risk. In life insurance, the insurance technical obligations are often, on account of the embedded options and guarantees, subject to a complex interest rate and equity risk.

3. Credit risks 89

Under the heading credit risks, the risk of a complete or partial default or of a creditworthiness / rating change of an obligor of the insurance business in respect of its obligations is to be modeled. An insurance business shall take into account all positions that have counterparty risk in the modeling 90 of the credit risk. In this regard, reliance is to be placed on the relevant documents of the FINMA and the Basel Committee, which is the basis for Annex 3 "Credit risk in the standard model". Affected are obligations owed by third parties, *e.g.*, under bonds and loans and, in particular, obligations owed by reinsurers, customers, brokers and agents, as well as contractual counterparties for derivative positions and securitizations. Positions which, under international standards (SA-BIZ) in the "Regulation on Capital and Risk Distribution for Banks and Securities Dealers" (Capital Regulation, CR; SR 952.03) and the FINMA Circular Letter 2008/19 "Capital Requirements for the Credit Risks of Banks" (Bank Credit Risks) of the FINMA, result in a capital charge and therefore to a risk weighting of 1250% under the credit risk standard model under the SST are not to be taken into account under market risk to the extent that the credit risk is determined with the credit risk standard model.

91 To the extent that an insurance business uses an internal model for the assessment of credit risks, it shall take the default risk and migration risk into account in the modeling.

92 4. Other types of risk

93 *Explanations:*

a) Operational risks: Up till now, an insurance business is solely responsible for monitoring and evaluating operational risks and it discusses the results of this evaluation periodically with the FINMA. At the current time, a quantitative assessment of operational risk is not generally required under the SST, unless an insurance business was expressly required to do so by the FINMA on account of grave circumstances. Operational risks are to be appropriately taken into account in risk management. The FINMA will study further development of the SST for purposes of [including] a systematic, quantitative monitoring of operational risks.

94 *b) Liquidity risks can only be partially monitored under a solvency system. They must be taken into account in the qualitative risk management of the company.*

95 *c) Risk concentrations are often not sufficiently taken into account in an analytical risk model. For this reason, they are given special treatment under "Scenarios". In addition, it must be ensured that this risk is recognized and evaluated in risk management and, if necessary, that measures for the prevention or hedging of significant risks or risk concentrations are applied.*

96 *d) Model risk: Model risk, up till now, apart from parameter risk in insurance technical risk, is not quantitatively addressed under the SST unless an insurance business was expressly required to do so by the FINMA on account of grave circumstances. Because model risk can never be ex-*

cluded completely, it is to be taken into account in risk management. It must be ensured, in particular, that the effects of any model deficiencies are recognized. This also requires, among other things, the monitoring of exposures and the establishment of limits on a nominal basis.

E. Scenarios

- An insurance business shall define, in addition to the scenarios defined by the FINMA, its own scenarios which take into account its own individual risk situation. The scenarios are to be documented appropriately and reviewed annually. The valuation of the relevant positions must be made in the scenarios with the assistance of a new valuation. In exceptional cases, the valuation may, for example, be approximated on the basis of sensitivities to the extent that no significant erroneous valuations are produced as a result. The results of the scenarios are to be analyzed and taken into account in risk management. 97
- An insurance business shall analyze, in particular, whether and to what extent the model used, as a result of its specifications, underestimates the probability of extreme occurrences in certain situations. If this is the case, an insurance business shall define the scenarios, evaluate them and take them into account in the determination of the TC. 98
- An insurance business shall analyze, in particular, whether and to what extent, the model used underestimates the effects of risk concentrations on the capital requirement. An underestimation of this type occurs, for example, if in the case of a potentially solvency-jeopardizing exposure in relation to a counterparty, the model relies only on the default probability suggested by the rating of the counterparty. If this is the case, specific scenarios are to be defined, evaluated and taken into account in the determination of the TC. 99

F. Applicability of standard models and internal models

An insurance business shall use a risk model for the determination of the TC that shows all of its relevant risks in an appropriate manner. The FINMA shall make a standard model available as a possible modeling tool for the determination of the TC. Groups, as well as reinsurance businesses, must develop an internal model, subject to individually approved exceptions. 100

If the standard model is used, the parameters used must be adjusted by the insurance business if they do not correlate sufficiently with the specific risk situation of the insurance business. The adjustments are to be documented. They are to be justified to the FINMA in an understandable manner and will be approved by it to the extent they are appropriate. 101

102 In addition, insurance businesses may, upon request and after approval, use internal models, partially or entirely, instead of the standard model to the extent that these fulfill the supervisory law requirements of the ISL, the SR and this circular letter and therefore are suitable for the measurement of relevant risks under the SST. The request for approval of the internal model must by signed by a member of the board or directors or a member of the executive board.

103 If an insurance business cannot develop an internal model for its relevant risks with reasonable effort because of its structure and the standard model is not appropriate for the relevant risks, then the FINMA may impose a capital charge which excuses the insurance business from the obligation to completely model risks that are not shown by the standard model. The FINMA shall determine the capital charge, which shall be reviewed annually, with the aid of a conservative estimate performed on the basis of an appropriate procedure, taking into consideration the protection of the policyholder. An insurance business shall show that it is able to adequately monitor and manage these risks without the quantitative measurement of risks not shown by the standard model. The FINMA shall review regularly the appropriateness of the estimate and the method for the management of the risks not shown. It shall in addition review whether changes have occurred that make the effort required for the development of an internal model appear required.

G. Standard model

104 If an insurance business uses the FINMA standard model for the determination of the TC, it shall submit the standard model with its underlying data to the FINMA together with the SST report.

105 If the parameters of a standard model used by an insurance business have been altered to the extent that the FINMA is no longer able to assess the appropriateness of the approach during the annual review process, the FINMA may use the review mechanisms which it used for the approval of the internal models.

106 The template and the explanatory documents will be updated by the FINMA at least annually and shall be available in a timely manner.

107 *Explanations:*

As assistance for the use of the standard model, the FINMA shall make available on the website a template, as well as various explanatory documents and instructions for the use of the template, as well as for the documentation of adjustments of the parameters and other commentary. Significant changes in the structure of the model shall be notified by the FINMA not later than six months before the SST submission deadline.

The FINMA shall adapt the parameters used in the standard model based on the latest information from time to time at annual intervals. 108

H. Internal models

The general requirements for risk models under paragraph VIII.A through VIII.E also apply to the use of internal models. 109

a) Approval requirements and approval

The approval of the internal model constitutes the release of the internal model by the FINMA for its use for purposes of supervision. The approval of the internal model does not excuse an insurance business from the obligation to regularly review the suitability and appropriateness of the model. 110

The FINMA shall grant the approval upon request to the extent that the requirements set forth in this circular letter in respect of 111

- the methodology and parameters,
- the qualitative aspects, as well as the organization, especially governance,
- the implementation, as well as
- the documentation of the internal model

are fulfilled.

The FINMA shall review, subject to the materiality definition under paragraph IV of this circular letter, whether simplifying assumptions in the modeling are appropriate in the case of an insurance business and consistent with the circumstances of the relevant insurance business. 112

The approval can be made subject to conditions. For the duration of the review process, an insurance business may use the not-yet finally approved internal model for purposes of supervision to the extent notice to the contrary from the FINMA is not sent to it. 113

Explanation: 114

The FINMA relies on the documentation submitted by the insurance business, on on-site inspections and the documentation requested in connection therewith, as well as on the results of its audits or audits by third parties that it has arranged for its decision about the approval of the internal model for a particular insurance business. The FINMA may, in addition, rely on the results of ex-

aminations by knowledgeable independent experts, as well as foreign supervisory authorities.

b) Methodology and parameter testing

115 Insurance businesses have to fulfill the requirements mentioned in this section in respect of the methodology and the parameters.

aa) General

116 The internal model must pass the calibration test under paragraph IX of this circular letter and in addition, the methodology and parameter test. For the methodology and parameter test, the following points are, in particular, to be fulfilled:

117 • An insurance business shall establish the significant positions in accordance with this circular letter and take into account the relevant risks in accordance with this circular letter. In addition, it shall show which risks it is exposed to and which relevant risks result from the individual positions and their combined effects.

118 • Unknown variables, such as, for example, the value of a risk factor, of a position, or a financial instrument or of the RBC at the end of the year are, as a rule, to be modeled with random variables. The risk model shall specify, in particular, the common distribution function of these risk factors, define the functional dependency between the risk factors and the positions or the financial instruments and permit a determination of the probability distribution factor of a loss of RBC during the year.

119 • The methods for the determination of the probability distribution of a loss of RBC must be based on established actuarial and finance mathematical methods. The choice of the common distribution function of the risk factors, as well as the calibration of this distribution function must be based on realistic and credible assumptions. The modeling of dependencies between the risk factors is to be taken into account. Simplifications may be made under paragraph IV, as well as VIII.H.b)bb) of this circular letter.

120 • The change in the near market value of the assets and liabilities in relation to the risk factors must be capable of being understood.

121 • The risk factors, as well as the estimation procedure for their distribution parameters are to be shown.

122 • If the modeling is performed in sub-models, the aggregation of the sub-models or the results from the sub-models is to be explained.

- If it is possible and appropriate, the model parameters will be determined with the assistance of established statistical estimation methods. The data used must be complete, correct and recent. If insufficient relevant data are available, expert opinions may be employed. The FINMA can require insurance businesses to use more conservative parameters to the extent the parameters previously used are not sufficiently suitable for the presentation of the risks. The data set used and the parameters derived from it must, subject to materiality, be verified and, if necessary, updated at least once each year before the calculation of the SST. 123

bb) Simplifications and omissions

If an insurance business makes simplifications in respect of the requirements of paragraph VIII.H.b)aa), it must, in particular, prove that the simplifying internal model leads to a well-founded and, in case of doubt, conservative capital requirement. If simplified internal models are used, then the inclusion of dependencies or diversification effects, is, as a rule, subject to a certain latitude. An insurance business shall demonstrate that the quantification of diversification effects is well-founded and conservative. 124

Simplifications and omissions in risk measurement which fulfill the materiality requirements under paragraph IV of this circular letter may be used by insurance businesses. The FINMA may prohibit the use of simplifications and omissions or subject them to conditions if thereby the risk situation of an insurance business would become non-transparent. 125

c) Model changes and changes in the risk profile

An insurance business shall submit significant model changes to the FINMA for approval and shall show significant changes in the risk structure of its business immediately after their determination. It shall submit the relevant documentation in which the changes have been marked. In the event of significant model changes, their effects on the risk calculation are to be tested and documented. 126

The FINMA shall approve significant model changes to the extent the requirements for internal models have been fulfilled. 127

The FINMA shall, in addition, regularly review whether general progress in modeling techniques has been taken into account in the internal models. If necessary, the FINMA may issue an order requiring the adaption of the internal model to the current state of the art. 128

An insurance business may only substitute the standard model for an approved internal model only upon a showing a sufficient cause and after approval by the FINMA. 129

d) Documentation of the internal models

130 An insurance business shall deliver to the FINMA documentation of the various modules of the internal model, as well as the relationships between these modules. The documentation must be self-contained. It should permit a knowledgeable third party to understand, within a reasonable period of time, whether the regulatory requirements for the approval of the internal model have been fulfilled.

131 The documentation shall explain the method (theories and assumptions) which are the basis for the internal model, as well as their use within the insurance business. It shall describe the limitations and weaknesses of the internal model. The documentation shall state which positions and financial instruments or which risks were not taken into account.

132 The documentation shall explain the empirical basis for the internal model. It shall describe, in particular, how the model parameters were estimated and the data sets and other information sources were used.

133 The documentation must include [a statement of] whether the insurance business is, in its opinion, in compliance with the calibration test, as well as the methodology and parameter test.

134 The documentation shall state how data quality and, in particular the quality of information about positions and exposures, is assured.

135 For the review of the internal model, the FINMA may require from an insurance business the evaluation of certain pre-defined scenarios and the exclusion of certain parameters.

e) Modular review of internal models

136 The FINMA shall publish on its website a review concept for the approval of internal models. The review is performed as a modular and risk-oriented system review. As a result, a model can be approved partially. This is, for example, the case if the review is performed only for a part of the area under review or only for individual modules. The FINMA can give review assignments to third parties.

f) Provisional use of unapproved internal models

137 Internal models requested by an insurance business before this circular letter enters into force and which are sufficiently documented may be used provisionally until they have been given approval with legal force, subject to any contrary order by the FINMA.

g) Capital charge until model approval

The FINMA may impose an appropriate capital charge on insurance businesses which were required to develop an appropriate internal model during the period before the approval of the internal model. 138

The FINMA shall determine the capital charge with the assistance of an estimate that is to be reviewed annually. The FINMA shall set the capital charge in a conservative manner. 139

IX. Calibration test

The calibration test establishes minimum framework which an insurance business must use in the application of risk models and in the valuation of the near market balance sheet and it includes the following: 140

- Risk measure: The relevant risk measure is established by the expected shortfall of the change in RBC, as defined in Annex 2 SR and paragraph II of this circular letter, at a confidence level of 99% and a time period of one year. 141
- Return: The return across the risk-free counterparty interest rate curve for the determination of the minimum amount will be published on the FINMA website. 142
- Interest rate curves: The risk-free counterparty interest rate curve specified in the standard model or an internally-determined risk-free counterparty interest rate curve under paragraph V.C. of this circular letter is to be used for the valuation in the near market balance sheet under the SST to the extent interest rate curves in the relevant currency for the valuation are needed. The valuation with the mentioned risk-free counterparty interest rate curve is to be performed without regard for how interest rate risk is modeled. 143

X. Qualitative and organizational requirements

A. Responsibilities of the directors and officers of the company or the group

The responsibility for the use of an appropriate risk model lies with the board of directors of the company. It can delegate to the executive board the responsibility for the development – so long as the standard model is not used – and the implementation and the further use of the internal model. 144

145 In the case of groups, the directors and officers of the business identified under Art. 191, para. 3 SR must ensure that the provisions under paragraph X of this circular letter are implemented analogously in the company which the group manages from Switzerland.

B. Use test

146 Under the use test, an insurance business ensures that it uses the risk model appropriately.

147 An insurance business shall ensure that the exposure limits at the business level are set in conformity with the risk model.

148 The executive board and the board of directors shall have sufficient understanding of the risk model, its outputs and its limitations in order to appreciate the implications of the risk model in connection with risk management and the capital requirement of the insurance business. They shall know and take into account the results of the risk models in their decision-making.

149 The FINMA may, in justified cases, for example, if it requires the use of an internal model, give the insurance business a reasonable deadline to integrate the risk model into the processes of the business.

150 *Explanation:*

If an internal model is used in many applications within an insurance business, then the FINMA has a strong indication that the insurance business has an inherent interest in the quality and maintenance of the internal model. This can have an effect on the FINMA's audit effort under its risk-oriented approach.

C. Regular validation

151 An insurance business shall ensure that compliance with the supervisory law requirements of the SST is verified and that the results of this verification are given to the board of directors or the executive board. In particular, on the occasion of the issuance of the annual SST-report, compliance with the supervisory law requirements shall be validated.

152 An insurance business shall, in particular, review:

- the suitability and appropriateness of the applied risk model and its internal scenarios
- the fulfillment of the qualitative and organizational requirements
- the requirements for implementation

If the risk profile of the insurance business changes or if deficiencies in methods are discovered, then the insurance business shall adjust the risk or valuation model or shall use an internal model. 153

XI. Implementation requirements

An insurance business shall have a documented, internally reviewed and internally approved procedure that ensures that all transactions and business concluded are completely, correctly and timely recorded and prepared for valuation and risk measurement. 154

An insurance business shall ensure the physical security of the data storage to a sufficient extent. 155

Under the internal control system, the implementation risks of the SST are also to be taken into account. 156

XII. SST Report

A. Frequency

Under Art. 53 SR, an insurance business shall prepare a report on the calculation of the TC and the RBC annually (SST Report). This is to be signed by the executive board and to be submitted to the FINMA. As from the business year 2011, the result of the SST must be delivered to the FINMA not later than 30 April of each year. The FINMA shall adopt a transition plan. In this regard, the submission date will be brought forward in stages, notified at least six months in advance, from the end of July to the end of April. 157

If the FINMA requires an SST[3] during the year, it shall notify the submission date. 158

Under Art. 202 SR, groups issue an SST Report each semester. The FINMA shall align the submission date with the submission dates for the legal entities belonging to the group and shall give timely notice of these. 159

B. General

Under Art. 53, para. 2 SR, the SST Report includes all relevant information that is needed for an understanding of the calculation of the TC and the RBC, as well as for the assessment of the risk situation of the insurance business. 160

---

[3] See para. XIV.B.

161 The SST Report must put the FINMA in a position to be able to understand the risk situation of the insurance business.

162 The SST Report shall address at a minimum the following topics and explain them:

163 ▪ The application of the methods for the determination of the near market values or the best-possible estimated values for all positions in the near market balance sheet. An insurance business shall show, with the assistance of a suitable analysis, which positions are not material. The simplified valuation methods and summaries used for these positions are to be shown

164 ▪ The elements of RBC, including the core capital and the supplementary capital

165 ▪ A presentation of the data inputs in the relevant risk models for the determination of the market, credit, life insurance, nonlife insurance and health insurance risks, as well as the modeling of capital and risk transfer instruments

166 ▪ The scenarios prescribed by the FINMA and those defined by the insurance business

167 ▪ The determination of the minimum amount

168 ▪ The TC

169 ▪ Risk concentrations/risk aggregations

170 ▪ Ceded reinsurance

171 ▪ Other relevant risks

172 ▪ Deviations from the standard model: in the event of the use of the standard model, deviations from sub-elements of the standard model are to be documented, to be justified in a factually correct manner and presented in an understandable manner so that they can be approved on the basis of these materials

173 The FINMA may, as needed, specify other elements of information and shall notify these in a suitable manner to the insurance businesses.

C. Review of the SST Report

174 To the extent that an insurance business correctly uses a suitable risk model, the FINMA shall confirm in writing, within six months after the submission

deadline for the SST Report and upon fulfillment of the requirements under Art. 41 ff. SR, that the insurance business does not, in the opinion of the FINMA, require any additional RBC. This confirmation can be given subject to conditions.

To the extent that the applied internal model is a model previously submitted to the FINMA and approved by it, an insurance business shall design the SST Report so that it is apparent why and which changes in the internal model were made and the extent to which the risk structure -- compared with the circumstances at the time of the approval of the internal model -- has changed. 175

The FINMA may, in the event of material weaknesses in the performance of the SST calculation, require an insurance business in writing, within a reasonable period of time, to submit an improved recalculation and, if necessary, to revise the report. To the extent that these weaknesses cannot be corrected within a reasonable period of time, the FINMA can impose a conservatively calculated capital surcharge and, if necessary, impose other measures to secure solvency. To the extent it is necessary for the protection of policyholders, the FINMA shall, in the event of material weaknesses, immediately impose a capital surcharge or impose other measures. 176

If the FINMA comes to the conclusion that a confirmation of the SST Report cannot be considered, it shall order appropriate measures for the improvement of the SST Report. These may be accompanied by a surcharge on TC and / or a deduction from RBC. 177

If material weaknesses exist, such as, *e.g.*, significant mistakes in the application of the standard model, obvious and serious mistakes in the application of an internal model or serious deviations from the requirements for an internal model, the SST is considered not fulfilled. In such a case, the TC and the RBC will be estimated by the FINMA and so ordered. 178

XIII. Data to be submitted

The FINMA sets the following minimum requirements for data which are to be submitted together with the SST Report as part of the SST: 179

- If the SST standard model is used for the SST calculation, then the SST template is to be completed and submitted to the FINMA. 180
- If the SST calculation is not, or only partially, based on the standard model, then the template should not even be completed or only partially completed. In this case, the set of the fundamental SST data, together with any portions of the SST template that were used, is to be submitted. 181

182 In addition to these minimum requirements, the FINMA may in individual cases require additional data.

XIV. Reporting exceptional events

A. Required loss reporting

183 An insurance business shall report to the FINMA on aggregated losses on the basis of the thresholds defined below as a near market assessment of the entire economic balance sheet. If events become known which could have led to relevant losses, then an estimate of these losses is to be notified without delay. A new estimate of the RBC is to be notified not later than two weeks after such losses become known. Losses which must be notified under this regulation are:

184 ▪ In the case of an SST quotient of more than 150%: losses of one third or more of the RBC as determined under the last SST calculation or any revised RBC determined after a loss that was required to be reported.

185 ▪ In the case of an SST quotient between 100% and 150%: losses of 20% or more of the RBC as determined under the last SST calculation or any revised RBC determined after a loss that was required to be reported.

186 ▪ Losses which lead to a SST quotient of 100% of less.

187 ▪ As soon as the SST quotient at the beginning of the year or its current estimate in the course of the year in the event of an exceptional loss falls below 100%: losses that equal 10% of the RBC or its estimate during the year.

188 An insurance business shall re-estimate the TC after a loss that is required to be reported and, if warranted, in a simplified manner. This estimation is generally prepared as of the same day on which the RBC is re-estimated.
The estimates may be limited to the effects of significant, determinative factors which lead to a change in the RBC or the TC. This also means that for components of the target capital calculation that are not materially different than on 1 January a new estimate is not required. The simplifications are to be disclosed to the FINMA.

B. Significant change in the risk profile

189 The FINMA is to be notified pursuant to Art. 51, para. 2 SR without delay of significant changes in the risk situation of an insurance business. Significant changes in the risk situation exist at least if the TC changes by 20% or more since the last calculation.

The FINMA shall determine whether a re-estimate of the RBC and / or the TC must be performed. The supervisory authority shall set the relevant measurement date in consultation with the insurance business. 190

For a re-estimate, the simplification principles under paragraph XIV apply. 191

XV. Test phase

The rules set forth in paragraphs XIV.A and XIV.B apply as from 1 January 2010. The time until 1 January 2010 is considered a test phase in which in the mentioned situations the simplified estimates of the RBC or the TC are to be submitted. 192

The rules set forth in paragraph XII.C, first section relating to the confirmation of the FINMA apply as from 1 January 2011. 193

Annex 1

Near market valuation under the SST

I. Principles of near market valuation

The principles of near market valuation are stated in Annex 3 of the SR. as well as in the circular letter on the Swiss Solvency Test. A distinction is basically made between the application of market values (marking-to-market) and valuation model values (marking-to-model). In the use of valuation model values, the FINMA may involve independent third parties for the verification of the procedures at the cost of an insurance business. 1

The obligation of near market valuation, as stated in the circular letter on the Swiss Solvency Test, constitutes an overriding, autonomous principle. IFRS valuations may be used if they fulfill this principle. The FINMA shall publish on its homepage, at irregular intervals, a current list of the balance sheet positions and categorizations for which IFRS values are generally not consistent with this principle; the IFRS valuation can also be inappropriate in other circumstances. 2

Valuation methods for selected balance sheet positions currently viewed as appropriate are listed below; the focus in this regard is on positions for which market values cannot be regularly determined. To the extent that market values exist, they are to be used preferentially for the relevant positions. The list under paragraphs II and III should not prevent an insurance business from using proven, better methods for the mentioned positions. 3

II. Near market value of assets

A. Loans, including secured loans with variable and fixed interest rates

Set forth below are the principles for the valuation of loans granted with variable and fixed interest rates and analogously for secured loans that are to be addressed. 4

a) Risk-adjusted interest rate

The risk-adjusted interest rate is understood as the nominal interest rate, corrected by the amount of the risk premium. The risk premium takes into account, in particular, the general risk aversion of the market, the term of the debt obligation, the liquidity of the debt obligation, the priority of the debt obli- 5 gation, the creditworthiness of the obligor, as well as the existence and quality of any security instruments.

b) Loans, including secured loans with fixed interest rates

6 An insurance business shall discount the payment streams from loans and secured loans with fixed interest rates with risk-adjusted interest rates. To simplify, risk-adjusted interest rates may be used on a portfolio basis for portfolios of the same types of secured loans.

c) Loans and secured loans with variable interest rates

7 An insurance business shall value loans, including secured loans, with variable interest rates in accordance with procedures that are customarily used in financial mathematics for bonds with variable interest rates.

Explanation:

8 *Influential on value is, in addition to the effect of the changed interest rate since the last fixing date, in particular, the effect of a changed spread (risk premium) for a product with otherwise comparable characteristics (remaining term, reference interest rate, priority, ...). Most of the time, such a product does not exist, so the actual spread has to be estimated.*

d) Secured loan security interests

9 An insurance business shall determine the value of secured loan security interests, including the property used as security, on the basis of market value. The market value of the security for a secured loan shall be reviewed by an insurance business periodically (at least every 10 years). The frequency and estimation method shall be based on criteria which depend on the type of property and which an insurance business shall internally specify and document.

10 *Explanation:*

A hedonistic valuation procedure can be used to the extent that the available data quality and the valuation model used permit reliable real property valuation.

e) Group-internal loans and obligations

11 Group internal loans are also to be valued by an insurance business pursuant to the marking-to-market method, subject to the use of risk-adjusted interest rates.

B. Real property

a) Principles for the valuation of real property

An insurance business shall value all properties and land annually. The principle of individual valuation is to be observed. 12

Various valuation methods are explained in the following chapters. 13

Analogously to the Investment Guidelines of the FINMA for Insurers (FINMA-RS 08/18), all real properties are to be valued, in a cycle of at least once every 10 years, on a staggered basis, individually at least once completely -- either internally or externally -- by a knowledgeable real estate appraiser (as a verification of the market value, including an on-site inspection). In this regard, it is to be ensured, in the case of each of these verifications, that the relevant extract from the land register is ordered and added to the file. The same applies for the extract from the register of environmentally impaired sites under Art. 32c, para. 2 of the Federal Law on Environmental Protection. 14

b) Methods for the valuation of real properties

Current methods of near market valuation for real properties are the discounted cash flow method (DCF), the income capitalization method and the hedonistic method. The DCF and the income capitalization method are explained in greater detail in the annex to the Investment Guidelines of the FINMA for Insurers; the hedonistic method, in this annex. In addition, other methods may be used to the extent that they produce a near market value. 15

An insurance business shall notify the valuation model or the methodology chosen by it to the FINMA. It shall document the specification of the value-determining factors. 16

Explanations 17

Hedonistic valuation procedures

The hedonistic valuation method is based on the characteristics of the property (size, micro and macro situation, age, construction quality, ...).

It is only appropriate for those real properties for which a sufficiently good data pool ensures the high quality of the valuation. In Switzerland, the data situation is insufficient in particular for many office and industrial real properties, as well as real properties in certain rural regions. 18

C. Ownership interests

19 *To the extent available and qualitatively sufficient, for ownership interests the market value of the relevant business is to be used.*

20 For ownership interests that are not quoted on a securities exchange or for which the trading volume of their shares is very low, then in most situations an observable market value for valuation purposes is not available. In these cases, the near market value of the business is therefore determined on the basis of a valuation model (marking-to-model), for example, on the basis of the following valuation concepts:

21 • value of an ownership interest in an insurance business = core capital (under Art. 48 SR) minus the minimum amount

22 • value of an ownership interest not in an insurance business = "net asset value" (NAV) at the near market value, excluding intangible assets

23 *Explanations:*

The FINMA is aware, that under the valuation concepts for an insurance ownership interest in an insurance business above, that not all debt liabilities of the ownership interest can be valued at near market.

24 *In particular, under Annex 3, Art. 3, para. 1 of the SR*
- *the liabilities also are to be valued excluding the [insurer's] own counterparty risk.*
- *the future, unguaranteed participations in surplus and business taxes are not taken into account in the valuation of the liabilities.*

25 *It therefore results in a simplification that is nevertheless consistent with the valuation of the [insurer's] own liabilities, as well as the treatment of the subsidiary in the group model.*

26 The FINMA has the ability to require a near market valuation of ownership interests which cannot be performed under the simplification above. This, in particular, is so if significant undisclosed liabilities exist which would result in an overvaluation of the value of the ownership interest.
An insurance business has the choice of valuing the liabilities at near market, without taking into account the limitations in Annex 3 SR. It is to be ensured that the risk modeling is consistent with the chosen valuation methodology.
A company may, upon request, take into account intangible assets in the calculation of the NAV of the ownership interest. It must, in this regard, show that the volatility of intangible assets is fully taken into account in the risk model.

27 In this regard, the value of an ownership interest is, as a rule, not negative because of the limited liability of the shareholder. Risk transfer instruments, such

as informal guarantees, as well as links to the reputation of the owner of the ownership interest may, in practice, have the result that the owner of the ownership interest offsets the negative value of an ownership interest through capital injections. Any supplementary payment obligations of a parent company in respect of a subsidiary are nevertheless only taken into account to the extent they are legally binding (see para. III.C.d) of this Annex)
An [insurer's] own shares (shares of the parent company which are held by the investee company) must be deducted from NAV.
Upon request to the FINMA, a different valuation is possible in special cases (e.g., in the case of service companies).

Explanation: 28

To the extent that such a supplementary payment obligation exists, it affects not only the valuation, but also reduces the target capital of the subsidiary and increases the target capital of the parent company.
In the case of a company, for which the expectation of profit-making business exists, the value so determined shall include a deduction because the value of future business is not taken into account. This treatment is consistent with the fact that ([the insurer's]) own intangible assets must be deducted in the calculation of risk-bearing capital.

D. Guarantees and surety bonds received

The near market valuation of guarantees and surety bonds received by an insurance business means that both the expected value as well as a risk premium are to be taken into account. The ability to value guarantees and surety bonds requires that these are legally binding and enforceable. In the evaluation of the enforceability of these guarantees and surety bonds, the characteristics of the relevant applicable law (specifically, private law, bankruptcy law and supervisory law) are to be observed. In the event of doubts in this regard, the FINMA may require the preparation of a high-quality, independent legal opinion to the extent the guarantees and surety bonds are significant. 29

Explanation: 30

A valuation concept appears, for example, as follows: value of the guarantee / surety bond equals the expected value of the benefit, including capital costs saved by the recipient (minimum amount). This concept is consistent with the valuation of a received reinsurance coverage.
Guarantees and surety bonds produce, as a rule, a greater effect on the TC than on the RBC.

The default risk of the guarantor / surety is to be taken into account in the valuation. 31

E. Hedging transactions

32 Hedging transactions may not, as a rule, be offset against the hedged transaction by an insurance business.

33 Assets and liabilities may be offset by an insurance business if the transactions are offset by an identical offsetting position and the counterparty risk in relation thereto can be excluded by a securities exchange or through another mechanism. Offset positions do not have to be listed individually.

III. Near market valuation of liabilities

A. [An insurer's] own creditworthiness

34 For the determination of near market values for liabilities which are not hybrid instruments approved by the FINMA under Art. 39, para. 1 SR, the creditworthiness of the obligor is not relevant.

35 *Explanations:*

This rule is a deviation from the market value principle, however, for purposes of simplicity, the valuation under this rule is also described as a near market valuation.

36 *This rule means that for the valuation of these liabilities a marking-to-model frequently will be applied. Otherwise, a market value, to the extent available, must be adjusted to remove the effects of the [insurer's] own creditworthiness. A consequence of this is that the value of borrowings at the time of the borrowing is, as a rule, higher than the nominal value. The FINMA uses, therefore, the label "near market" because this valuation should be distinguished from the valuation under other accounting standards (*e.g.*, nominal value) and all valuation parameters used, apart from spread based on the [insurer's] own creditworthiness, must be chosen near market.*

B. Near market valuation of insurance technical obligations

37 The rules in Annex 3, Art. 3 of the SR apply, as well as the relevant provisions of this circular letter on the Swiss Solvency Test. The provisions in the technical document have an explanatory character.

C. Near market valuation of non-insurance technical obligations

a) Fixed and variable interest rate valuations

The rules under paragraph II.A of this annex apply, with the exception that the risk-free counterparty interest rate rather than the risk-adjusted interest rate for the valuation must be applied. 38

If a securities exchange price is available, an insurance business either must correct it for the effect of the risk premium or perform a valuation under the appropriate application of the risk-free counterparty interest rate curve; for example, a discounting of the cash flows. In the case of variable [interest rate] liabilities with a fixed term, the risk premium is to be set at zero. 39

b) Reserves for employee retirement plans

An insurance business shall use the same valuation methods for reserves for employee retirement plans as for the insurance technical reserves (completeness, principle of the best-possible estimated value, timeliness and transparency). 40

c) Accrued tax liabilities

Accrued tax liabilities are, under SR Annex 3, para. 2, provision a and para. 4, not to be valued. 41

d) Issued guarantees and surety bonds

In contrast to many accounting standards, there are no off-balance sheet positions in the near market balance sheet. All guarantees and surety bonds, as well as comparable instruments are to be valued by an insurance business at near market. In this regard, both the expected value of the benefits (without taking into account a possible default of the guarantor), as well as, in particular, the volatility of these, are to be taken into account. 42

e) Hybrid capital

Instruments which fulfill the requirements for hybrid instruments under Art. 39, para. 1 SR are to be valued at near market value, taking into account the spread on the basis of the [insurer's] own creditworthiness. 43

Explanations: 44

In contrast to the valuation of insurance technical obligations, the change in the spread on the basis of the [insurer's] own creditworthiness for hybrid instruments in supplementary capital has no influence on the amount of the RBC as long as the limits on supplementary capital are not reached. Spread changes shift only the allocation between core and supplementary capital.

45 *Hybrid instruments which do in fact fulfill Art. 39, para. 1 SR but nevertheless cannot be credited because of the limitations provided in Art. 47, para. 2 SR, are, subject to taking into account the spread for the [insurer's] own creditworthiness, to be valued. It thereby will be ensured that an instrument, without regard to its allocation to RBC, will be valued uniformly. In addition, with this valuation, it will be avoided that financing with instruments which the FINMA assumes potentially protect an insurance business leads to a direct reduction of the RBC.*

Annex 2

Group model

I. Introduction

Groups use their structure in order to create capital efficiency and business efficiencies. Bound with this can be risks for the insureds, as well as for the financial stability of the group. 1

Groups must, in addition to the individual businesses belonging to the group, under the regulations under the ISL, the SR, as well as the circular letter on the Swiss Solvency Test (hereinafter the "SST Circular Letter"), fulfill the legal requirements in respect of group solvency. This annex makes clearer the requirements for the design of the group models; in addition, their evaluation and the measures resulting therefrom are addressed. 2

Two concepts are currently used internationally for the modeling of all relevant risks of groups. 3

The first concept presents the risk of a group on a consolidated basis, as though the group were a legal entity ("consolidated group modeling"). In this way, the lead supervisor can determine whether the group fulfills the capital requirements on the basis of its external liabilities. Group internal liabilities will not be presented because it is implicitly assumed that the assets within the group are freely transferable. 4

The second concept is based on the risk modeling of the individual legal entities of the group, although sometimes combined in a cluster, and therefore shows, in addition to the external relationships, the relationships between the entities ("granular group modeling"). With the second method, the risks of the assets and liabilities of the individual legal entities are evaluated from a risk perspective in accordance with uniform guidelines and, in addition, the risks that result from relationships within the group. On the basis of the second method, the FINMA, as lead supervisor of the group, can determine if any potential exists for the jeopardization of the insureds and the financial stability of the group from individual parts of the group, for other parts of the group or for the group as a whole, and whether the individual parts of the group provide necessary assistance to the others as needed or whether other risk-reducing measures are available. 5

For the SST, the granular group modeling will be assumed, provided that in addition a consolidated group modeling can be allowed upon the request of 6 the group or required by the supervisor. The "Group SST" is based on the granular group modeling which may be supplemented through the consolidated group modeling.

II. Basis

7 Under Art. 69 and 77 ISL, the FINMA specifies the necessary capital resources for the entire group. In addition, Art. 201 and 204 SR prescribe that groups must use a suitable model for the determination and quantification of all relevant risks.

8 In addition to the statutory basis for the SR, the SST circular letter and its annexes are relevant. Not relevant are:

- Paragraphs VIII.E., X.B, as well as XI and XIV in the circular letter on the Swiss Solvency Test.
- Annex 4 "Intervention Thresholds".

III. General principles

A. General

9 The granular modeling consists of the near market valuation of all assets and liabilities of each legal entity belonging to the relevant group and the modeling of all relevant risks of these legal entities. This also includes all capital transfer and risk transfer instruments between the relevant entities which fulfill the requirements described below. Simplifications under para. III.B of this Annex remain unaffected.

10 The methods for the valuation and the risk modeling are the same as the procedures for individual companies under Swiss supervision. In particular, the valuation is to be made near market. For the determination of the minimum amount, diversification effects in the granular group model may only be taken into account within the clusters under para. III.B.b). The capital transfer and risk transfer instruments taken into account in the model must be specified and their modeling is to be documented.

11 *Explanation:*

Because capital transfer and risk transfer instruments, such as loans, guarantees, reinsurance contracts and other instruments are frequently used between the legal entities of a group, the correct presentation of these instruments and their effects on the RBC and TC of the individual entities in accordance with the valuation and risk-modeling principles of the SST is especially important.

Examples: 12

A hybrid loan from one group company to another group company is, in respect of the claim for repayment, to be accounted for as an asset by the loan lender. The risk which this financial instrument is subject to affects the target capital of the loan lender in a manner corresponding to the underlying risks of the loan recipient. To the extent that the conditions of the SR for the hybrid instrument are fulfilled and the limits for the supplementary capital have not been exhausted, the loan will be credited to the RBC of the loan recipient. An ownership interest between two group companies has a similar effect.

A group internal reinsurance contract, in addition to the effects on the near market balance sheet, leads, as a rule, to an increase in the TC of the reinsurer and to a reduction of the TC of the reinsured. A guarantee has a similar effect. 13

For the SST, only capital transfer and risk transfer instruments which are legally binding and enforceable may be taken into account for the group-internal relationships. In evaluating the enforceability of the capital transfer and risk transfer instruments, the special features of the relevant applicable law (specifically, private law, bankruptcy law and supervisory law) are to be reviewed and, upon request by the FINMA, to be set out in high-quality, independent legal opinions. 14

Explanation:

Because the Group SST only takes into account legally binding instruments, nonbinding statements from the directors or officers of a group company, as well as the strategic significance of a group company, will not be reflected in the quantitative model. 15

Generally, each legal entity of a group determines a RBC and calculates a TC through the application of the granular group model, while taking into account the group structure. Omissions and simplifications under para. III.B of this Annex may be made if the total effect of the omissions and simplifications of the positions influences the SST quotient of each legal entity by less than 20%. 16

For each legal entity, the FINMA is to be notified of at least the RBC and its components, the balance sheet amount and the amount of the capital investments, as well as the TC. To the extent the FINMA requires additional / other data, it will timely notify this on its homepage in the document "List of Fundamental SST Data". 17

B. Permitted simplifications

a) General

18 Upon a justified request, the FINMA shall allow insignificant legal entities not to be taken into account under the granular group model. In such a case, only the significant legal entities will be included in the granular group model.

b) Cluster

19 Upon a justified request, the FINMA shall approve the combining of several legal entities into a hypothetical entity for the purpose of the risk modeling, hereinafter referred to as a cluster. Clusters are necessarily smaller than the entire group. The FINMA shall, for example, permit the simplification if the structure is so complex that a correct depiction of all legal entities would result in disproportionate expense. A logical assemblage of clusters is based, as a rule, on the ownership structure of the group. The FINMA shall review whether the documented assumptions are realistic and whether, under these assumptions, a sufficient fungibility of capital within the clusters exists. The capital transfer and risk transfer instruments between the clusters must be reflected in the model.

Explanation:

20 *The creation of clusters has the effect that within a cluster complete fungibility of capital and a higher degree of diversification than in the sum of the individual entities is implicitly assumed. Attention is to be given to these effects in the selection of the composition of the cluster. Good cluster selection keeps the distortions from the mentioned effects as slight as possible.*

21 The clusters are to be modeled on the basis of the partial consolidation.

c) Symmetrical valuation

22 Upon a justified request, the FINMA may permit a symmetrical valuation to the extent that no significant distortions result from it. This means that the companies which have obligations in relation to other companies of the same group may value these under the Group SST and the SST for individual legal entities without regard for the creditworthiness of the counterparty.

Explanation:

23 *In the valuation of liabilities which do constitute supervisory law non-creditable hybrid instruments under Art. 39, para. 1 SR, the [insurer's] own creditworthiness fundamentally may not be taken into account. This has the consequence that upon an exchange of rights and obligations between group companies, the company which reports its obligation as a liability reports a higher absolute*

value than the company for which this instrument constitutes an asset. This asymmetrical treatment of rights and obligations can under some circumstances cause a disproportionate expense for groups.

IV. Evaluation of group solvency

a) To the extent all legal entities or clusters in the granular group model have an SST quotient of more than 100%, the requirements of the Group SST are met. 24

b) The group may ask to produce, in addition, a consolidated group model. The same may be ordered by the FINMA. 25

If a consolidated group model is produced, it must be demonstrated by the group that an SST quotient of at least 100% will be achieved on the basis of the consolidated group model. The requirements for the Group SST will also be met in this case. 26

Explanation: 27

The Group SST on the basis of the granular group model does not lead to a single SST quotient, rather to a number of SST quotients which in a given case result in an SST quotient on a consolidated basis.
The determination of the group solvency on the basis of a consolidated group model constitutes a further perspective for the determination of the RBC and TC on the basis of the granular group model of the legal entities or clusters.

V. Group risk management

Each group has to demonstrate how its group model is embedded in risk management in order to protect the financial stability of the group and interests of the insureds. 28

If individual, significant legal entities or cluster in the Group have a SST quotient of less than 100% and risks exist for the financial stability of the group or the interests of insureds, then the risk management of the group must show which measures will be implemented in order to guarantee the financial stability of the group and protect the interests of the policyholders. These measures may consist of a reduction of risks, a transfer from surplus fungible capital or other suitable measures. In this regard, special attention is to be given to the liquidity and transferability of the assets within the group. 29

VI. Measures by the FINMA

30 The FINMA may, on the basis of information acquired through the Group SST, impose measures in order to bring the risks of the group into a reasonable relationship to available capital. These may include, among others, that risks are reduced or additional capital is provided.

Annex 3

Credit risk in the standard model

I. Introduction

The FINMA is required in Art. 43, para. 1 SR, to make available a uniform, standard model for the quantification of financial risks. Under financial risks, both market and credit risks are understood. 1

This Annex to the circular letter on the Swiss Solvency Test specifies the standard model for credit risks – hereinafter referred to as Credit Risk Standard Model – under the SST. 2

II. Basis

The Credit Risk Standard Model is based on, subject to the provisions under paragraph III, the "Regulation on Capital and Risk Distribution for Banks and Securities Dealers" (Capital Regulation, CR; SR 952.03) and the circular letter "Capital Requirements for the Credit Risks of Banks" (Bank Credit Risks) of the FINMA. These will be referred to hereinafter as "CR, as well as the mentioned circular letter". 3

The CR, as well as the mentioned circular letter, implement in national law the revised framework agreement concerning "International Convergence of Capital Measurement and Capital Standards" of the Basel Committee for Bank Supervision of June 2006 (hereinafter: framework agreement). To the extent that the CR, as well as the mentioned circular letter, do not sufficiently govern situations, the rules of the framework agreement are given supplementary application. The CR, as well as the mentioned circular letter, and the framework agreement together are referred to hereinafter as "Basel II Basis". 4

The FINMA shall, in addition, make available a brief instruction for the explanation of the approach for important positions under the Credit Risk Standard Model – hereinafter the "Brief Instruction", as well as a template (hereinafter "Template Basel II"). 5

III. Modifications in respect of the SST

A. General

6 The Basel II Basis also regulates along with the supporting capital for credit risks, the supporting capital for market risks, risks that are not related to a counterparty and operational risks. In addition, it regulates the determination of capital resources.

7 The Credit Risk Standard Model of the FINMA for the SST relates exclusively to those parts of the mentioned documents which govern credit risk. The rules in the Basel II Basis are modified for the purposes of the SST in the respects mentioned below. A revision of the Basel II Basis, in addition, can later become the occasion for a revision of this Annex.

B. Near market values

8 The Credit Risk Standard Model of the FINMA does not apply the risk weightings for credit positions and positions subject to counterparty risk on the basis of balance sheet values determined under accounting rules, but rather the near market values in accordance with Annex 1 "Near market valuation under the SST" to the circular letter on the Swiss Solvency Test.

9 The extent that the application of near market values for certain positions on the basis of the Brief Instruction and the Basel II Basis reasonably cannot be performed, the insurance business is to contact the FINMA for approval of an alternative.

C. Capital deduction

10 Positions for which a capital deduction is prescribed in the Basel II Basis, disregarding Art. 23, para. 1, provision a CR, are, under the Credit Risk Standard Model, subject to a 1250% risk weighting. This corresponds to complete coverage with risk-bearing capital under the SST.

D. Equities and ownership interests

11 Individual credit risks which result from positions for ownership interests are, as a rule, not to be taken into account because the risks of the shares in this business most of the time can be modeled as a whole. Credit risks under this paragraph are to be taken into account in the standard model if an insurance business has isolated the underlying risks of the business in which it holds participating securities and has modeled these risks.

E. Collective capital investments

Hedge funds, in the Credit Risk Standard Model, are not a collective capital investments under the CR. Collective capital investments are, whenever possible, to be divided into their component parts which then can be taken into account under the credit risk model. 12

F. Ceded reinsurance and retrocessions

Ceded reinsurance and retrocessions are forms of risk reduction from which counterparty risk results. 13

Already existing receivables under reinsurance agreements are to be supported as ordinary receivables at their risk-weighted market value. 14

Under the credit risk standard model, the expected value of the payments on future losses which are already covered by concluded reinsurance agreements, is considered a receivable owed by the reinsurance business which is to be taken into account as a risk-weighted asset. This approach is to be applied by an insurance business without regard for whether the expected value of the payments on future losses is actually reported as an asset or it reduces target capital. 15

The approach described above may lead, in some situations, to a relevant underestimation of risk if the occurrence of the insured event could be causally linked to the default of the reinsurer. The FINMA reserves the right in such cases to prescribe a different approach. 16

G. Pledged life insurance

In addition to the [forms] of security listed in the Basel II Basis, such as, e.g., life insurance with a redemption value, a pledged life insurance policy may be taken into account for security at not more than redemption value. If the obligee of the debt is also the issuer of the policy, it shall receive for the part of the debt secured by the policy a risk-weighting of 0%. 17

H. Multiplier

The FINMA waives the application of the use of the multipliers listed in Art. 64 CR. 18

Annex 4

Intervention thresholds

I. Introduction

This Annex specifies the measures which the FINMA may impose depending on various thresholds to the extent that an insurance business has not fulfilled the solvency requirements of the SST. 1

The Annex is limited to the measures in respect of individual legal entities. Measures in respect of groups are dealt with in Annex 2 "Group model". 2

II. Basis

To the extent that an insurance business does not fulfill the solvency requirements under the SST, the FINMA has the obligation under Art. 46 ISL, in particular under Art. 46, para. 1, provision d ISL, to obtain information pursuant to Art. 29 FINMAG or Art. 47 ISL and / or to adopt protective measures under Art. 51 ISL. 3

III. Thresholds

The FINMA defines three thresholds which rely on the SST quotients. The thresholds are specified as follows: 4

- Threshold 1 states the solvency requirement under the SST. It is met if the RBC equals the TC. This means an SST quotient of 100% and thereby a confidence level of 99%. 5
- Threshold 2 is met if the RBC equals 80% of the TC. 6
- Threshold 3 is met if the RBC equals 33% of the TC. 7

If the RBC of an insurance business is above Threshold 1, then the insurance business is in the so-called green zone. If the RBC of an insurance business is between Threshold 1 and Threshold 2, then the insurance business is in the yellow zone. With a RBC between Threshold 2 and Threshold 3, then the insurance business is in the so-called orange zone. If the RBC is below Threshold 3, then the insurance business is in the so-called red zone. 8

The required amounts for the various thresholds will be set during the review of the SST report and are binding until the conclusion of the review of the next 9

SST report. In justified cases, e.g., in the case of extraordinary losses, the FINMA may require a determination of RBC from an insurance business during the year and, if necessary, a new estimate of the TC. Thereafter it performs an interim assignment of the insurance business to the green, yellow, orange or red zone and, if applicable, makes an adjustment of the required amounts for the various thresholds.

IV. Measures

A. General

10 The content and extent of the measures to be imposed by the FINMA pursuant to the non-exhaustive list in Art. 51 ISL are based on the solvency situation, i.e., in particular on falling below the thresholds defined above.

11 Transactions that have the immediate consequence that the SST quotient is below the above-mentioned thresholds require approval.

Important note:

12 **The following description of measures are to be understood as general guidelines which may neither bind the FINMA to a specific measure – unless it is stated as an obligation below – nor does it give third parties a right that a particular measure will be imposed. In addition, it is possible that depending on the concrete situation of an insurance business, even outside of the SST, that other – more extensive or less extensive – measures are to be imposed than those which are assigned to a particular zone.**

B. Measures in the green zone

13 To the extent an insurance business is in the green zone, the FINMA does not impose measures on the basis of the SST solvency situation.

C. Measures in the yellow zone

14 If an insurance business is in the yellow zone, an increased risk exists for the interests of the insureds as a result of the solvency situation. In this situation, the FINMA will intensify the risk dialogue with the insurance business with the goal of reducing the risk for the insureds.

a) Cause analysis and action plan

The FINMA, in addition, requires from insurance businesses which are in the yellow zone an analysis of the causes which have led to falling below the threshold. In this situation, it requires the insurance business to prepare an action plan, as a rule, within two months after the determination of the coverage deficit, which is based on realistic assumptions. The action plan – to be approved by the FINMA – shall specify in binding form the content and the timing of the measures for the improvement of solvency. The action plan is to be designed so that the green zone will be reached, as a rule, one year after the notice to the FINMA. 15

The action plan consists of:

- immediate measures for the improvement of the SST quotient (for example, an increase in capital, risk reduction, obtaining reinsurance). These are, as appropriate, to be implemented before the action plan is submitted; 16
- a strategy for the improvement of the SST quotient in the medium term; 17
- a list of important, long-term individual measures as components of this strategy; 18
- a time plan for the implementation of the measures; 19
- a projected income statement, a projected balance sheet with a projected time line of at least four quarters from the completion of the rehabilitation plan. 20

The FINMA shall regularly verify compliance with the action plan. If the action plan is not observed, then the FINMA reserves the right to impose additional measures pursuant to Art. 51 ISL. 21

b) Approval obligation for certain transactions

Resolutions by the company that lead to dividend payments, returns of capital, voluntary redemptions of its bonds, group-internal transactions, including the issue of guarantees, as well as the allocation of surpluses to policyholders and similar transactions are to be submitted to the FINMA in advance for approval. 22

c) Other possible measures

Upon an evaluation of the insurance business's situation, the FINMA may order additional measures. The FINMA may, in particular: 23

- have examinations performed by independent experts which verify the valuations for the near market balance sheet or the appropriateness of the procedures for the determination of the TC. 24

25 • require that important ratios are measured during the year and reported to the FINMA.

26 • order supplementary scenario analyses which permit the review of the effectiveness of the rehabilitation measures in the prescribed time period with various assumptions about the development of the risk factors.

27 The mentioned measures do not excuse an insurance business from the fulfillment of obligations under corporate law to the extent that the prerequisites in this respect are met (in particular, Art. 25 CO).

D. Measures in the orange zone

28 If an insurance business is in the orange zone, the FINMA may impose measures in addition to those pursuant to para. IV.C of this Annex and / or, if necessary, make the measures adopted pursuant to para. IV.C of this Annex more strict.

a) Rehabilitation plan

29 An insurance business must prepare a rehabilitation plan, as a rule within two months, that will return the insurance business to the yellow zone as a rule within two years and to the green zone as a rule within three years after the notice to the FINMA.

30 The rehabilitation plan shall consist of at least the elements mentioned in para. IV.C.a) of this Annex. The projected time line for the projected income statement and the projected balance sheet must amount to at least six semesters from the completion of the rehabilitation plan. The rehabilitation plan must, in addition, show which risks the insurance business is able to immediately reduce and with which methods. The influence of various – including negative – scenarios on the effectiveness of the rehabilitation measures is to be determined.

b) Other possible interventions

31 To the extent that the above-mentioned interventions alone are not sufficient in order to correct the inadequate solvency, the FINMA shall adopt additional measures. In this regard the FINMA may, in particular:

32 • order special liquidity planning.

33 • order an approval obligation for especially risky new business and renewals.

34 • prohibit new business and renewal business.

- prohibit risky and complex transactions to the extent it is not assured that these serve the improvement of the SST quotient. 35

- require the insurance business to make organizational changes, such as more intensive controlling, monitoring, reporting and auditing by the internal audit function. 36

E. Measures in the red zone

Upon entry into the red zone, an insurance business must promptly take immediate measures for the protection of insureds. It must be apparent to the FINMA within a short time whether measures adopted by the insurance business lead to success. In particular, the following measures by an insurance business could be appropriate in the red zone: 37

- an immediate increase in the RBC or a reduction of the TC 38

- a voluntary transfer of the insurance portfolio 39

- a partial transfer of the insurance portfolio, with the result that the SST quotient after the transfer is outside of the red zone. 40

If it is not possible for the insurance business to adopt appropriate measures and the measures ordered by the FINMA also do not lead to short-term success, the FINMA shall withdraw the insurance business's license. 41

Explanation: 42

The FINMA cannot tolerate an insurance business in the red zone. This has the consequence that it can only approve or adopt measures that operate immediately for the improvement of the situation. For example, a continuation of the business with the objective of writing profitable business and thereby to improve the solvency situation incrementally through retained profits is not an acceptable alternative in the red zone.

F. Cooperation of management

If the directors and officers do not carry out the measures imposed by the FINMA in the yellow, orange or red zones in manner that avoids a further jeopardization of the interests of the insureds, the FINMA shall require the discharge of the relevant persons as contemplated under Art. 51, para. 2, provision f ISL. If the responsible directors and officers do not comply, then the FINMA shall adopt measures under Art. 51, para. 2, provision c ISL. 43